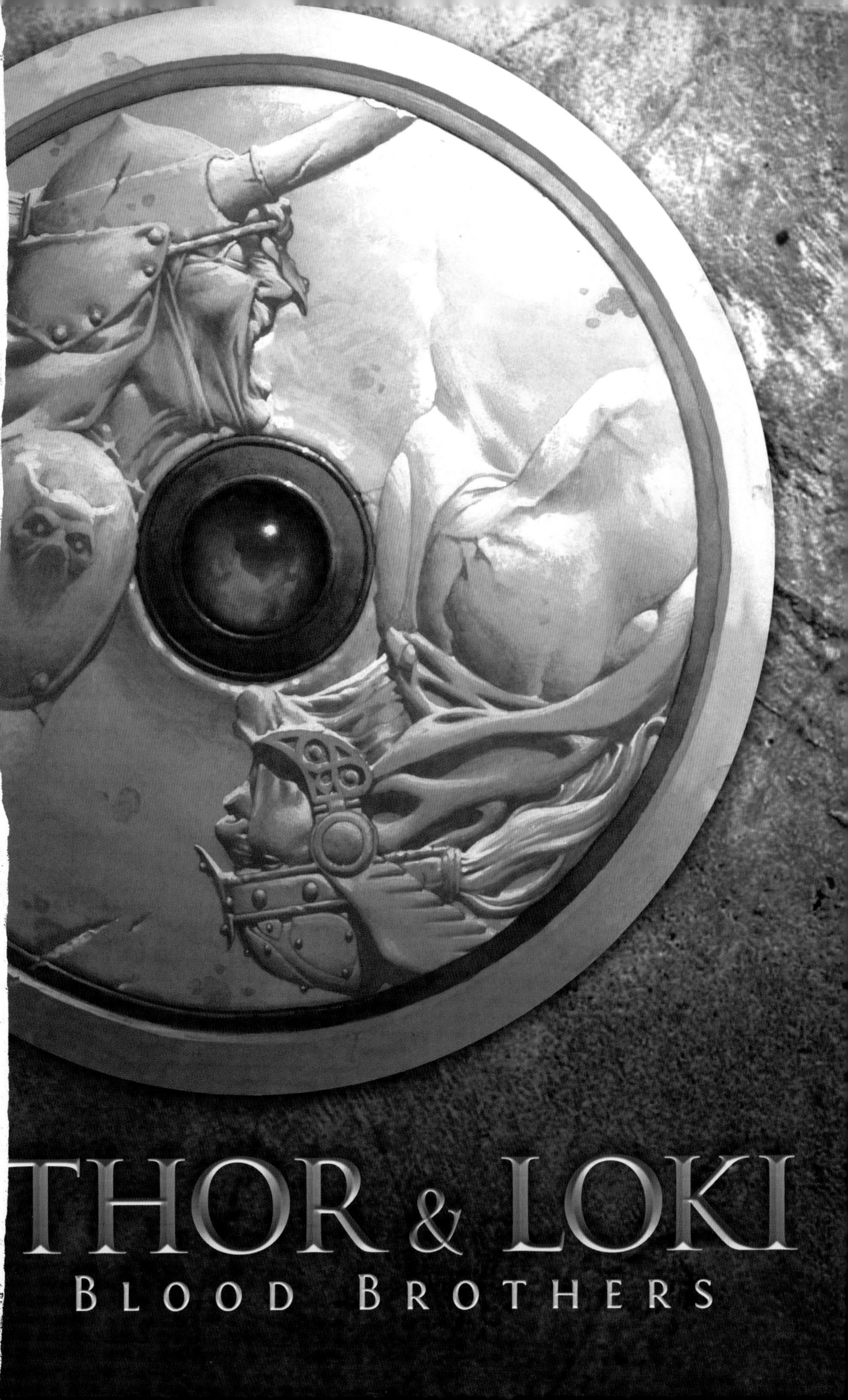

THOR & LOKI
BLOOD BROTHERS

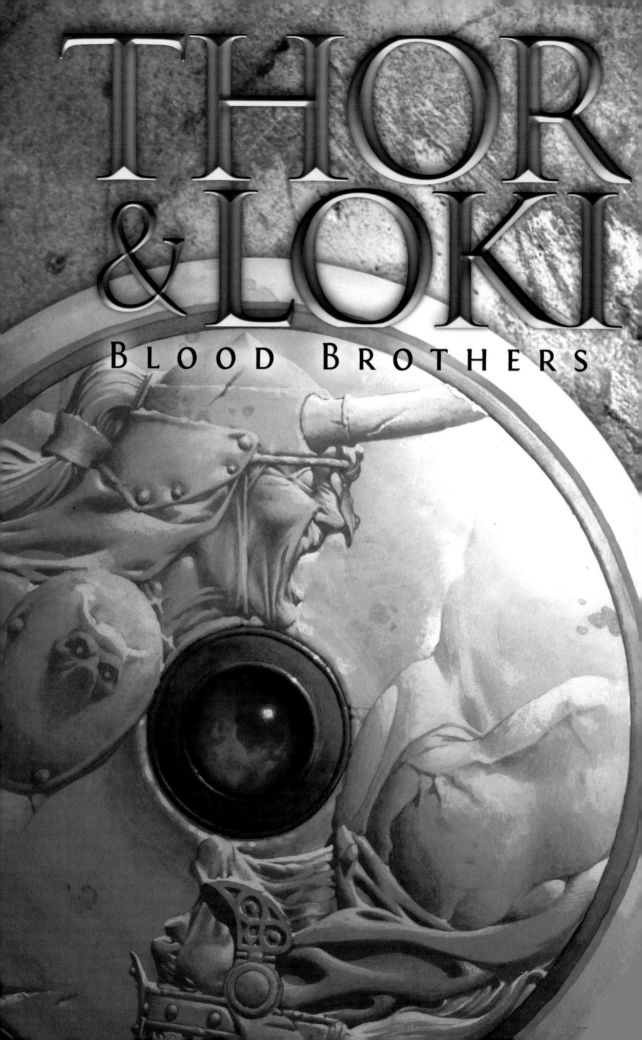

# THOR & LOKI

## BLOOD BROTHERS

Writer: ROBERT RODI • Artist: ESAD RIBIC
Letterers: VIRTUAL CALLIGRAPHY'S CORY PETIT
& RANDY GENTILE
Assistant Editors: CORY SEDLMEIER
& JOHN MIESEGAES
Editor: AXEL ALONSO
SPECIAL THANKS TO ROBERT GLAVAK

## JOURNEY INTO MYSTERY #85 & #112

Writer: STAN LEE • Penciler: JACK KIRBY
Inkers: DICK AYERS & VINCE COLLETTA
Art Reconstruction: MICHAEL KELLEHER
& PACIFIC RIM GRAPHICS
Color Reconstruction: MICHAEL KELLEHER
& KELLUSTRATION
Masterworks Editor: CORY SEDLMEIER

## THOR #12

Writer: J. MICHAEL STRACZYNSKI
Penciler: OLIVIER COIPEL
Inker: MARK MORALES
Colorist: LAURA MARTIN
Letterer: CHRIS ELIOPOULOS
Assistant Editor: ALEJANDRO ARBONA
Editor: WARREN SIMONS

Collection Editor: JENNIFER GRÜNWALD
Editorial Assistants: JAMES EMMETT & JOE HOCHSTEIN
Assistant Editors: ALEX STARBUCK & NELSON RIBEIRO
Editor, Special Projects: MARK D. BEAZLEY
Senior Editor, Special Projects: JEFF YOUNGQUIST
Senior Vice President of Sales: DAVID GABRIEL
Book Designer: RODOLFO MURAGUCHI

Editor in Chief: JOE QUESADA
Publisher: DAN BUCKLEY
Executive Producer: ALAN FINE

THOR & LOKI: BLOOD BROTHERS. Contains material originally published in magazine form as LOKI #1-4, JOURNEY INTO MYSTERY #85 and #112, and THOR (2007) #12. First printing 2010. ISBN# 978-0-7851-4968-2. Published by MARVEL WORLDWIDE, INC., a subsidiary of MARVEL ENTERTAINMENT, LLC. OFFICE OF PUBLICATION: 417 5th Avenue, New York, NY 10016. Copyright © 1962, 1965, 2004, 2009 and 2010 Marvel Characters, Inc. All rights reserved. $24.99 per copy in the U.S. and $27.99 in Canada (GST #R127032852); Canadian Agreement #40668537. All characters featured in this issue and the distinctive names and likenesses thereof, and all related indicia are trademarks of Marvel Characters, Inc. No similarity between any of the names, characters, persons, and/or institutions in this magazine with those of any living or dead person or institution is intended, and any such similarity which may exist is purely coincidental. Printed in China. ALAN FINE, EVP - Office of the President, Marvel Worldwide, Inc. and EVP & CMO Marvel Characters B.V.; DAN BUCKLEY, Chief Executive Officer and Publisher - Print, Animation & Digital Media; JIM SOKOLOWSKI, Chief Operating Officer; DAVID GABRIEL, SVP of Publishing Sales & Circulation; DAVID BOGART, SVP of Business Affairs & Talent Management; MICHAEL PASCIULLO, VP Merchandising & Communications; JIM O'KEEFE, VP of Operations & Logistics; DAN CARR, Executive Director of Publishing Technology; JUSTIN F. GABRIE, Director of Publishing & Editorial Operations; SUSAN CRESPI, Editorial Operations Manager; ALEX MORALES, Publishing Operations Manager; STAN LEE, Chairman Emeritus. For information regarding advertising in Marvel Comics or on Marvel.com, please contact Ron Stern, VP of Business Development, at rstern@marvel.com. For Marvel subscription inquiries, please call 800-217-9158. Manufactured between 11/10/10 and 12/15/10 by R.R. DONNELLEY ASIA PRINTING SOLUTIONS, DONGGUAN, GUANGDONG, CHINA.

10 9 8 7 6 5 4 3 2 1

# ONE

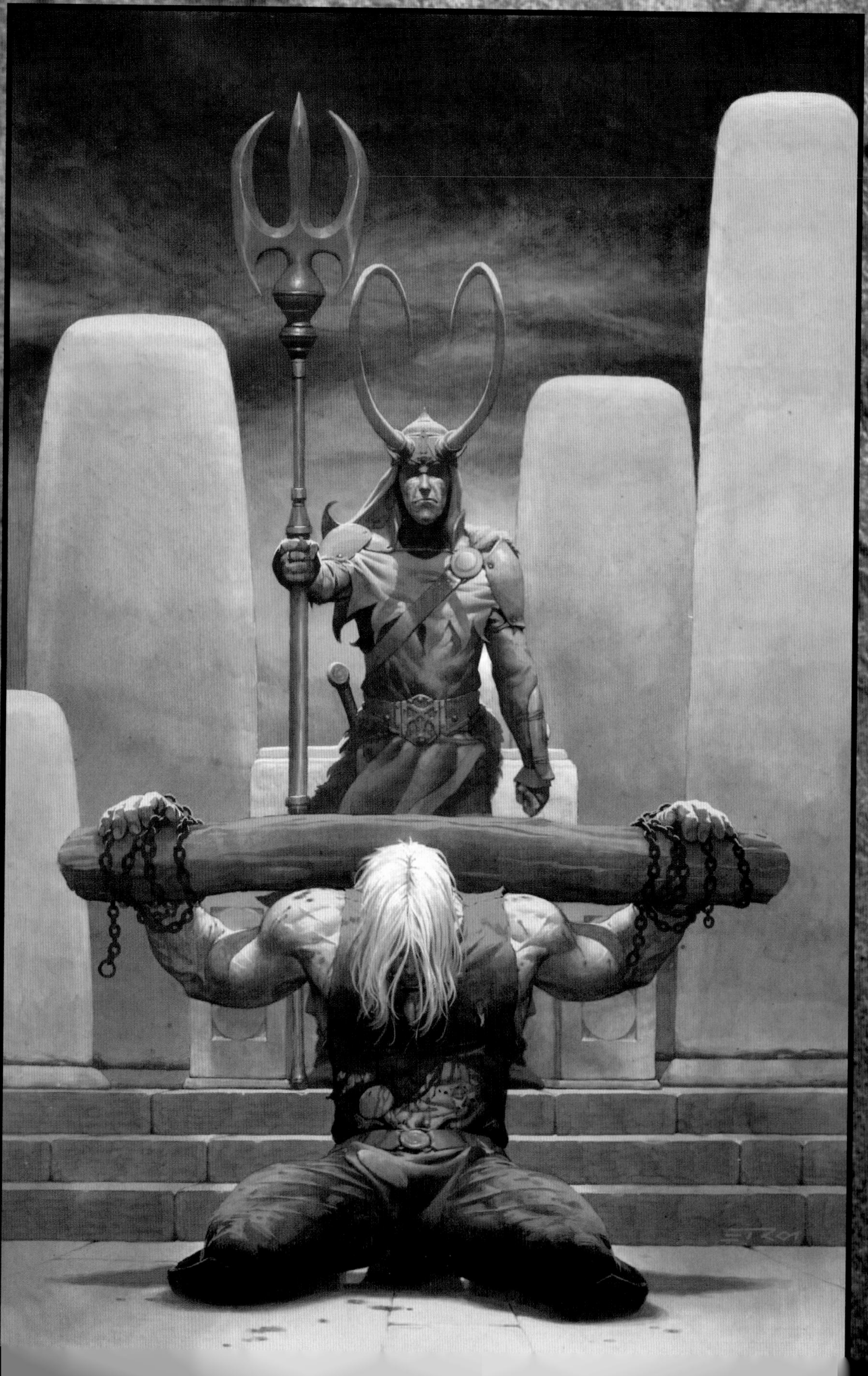

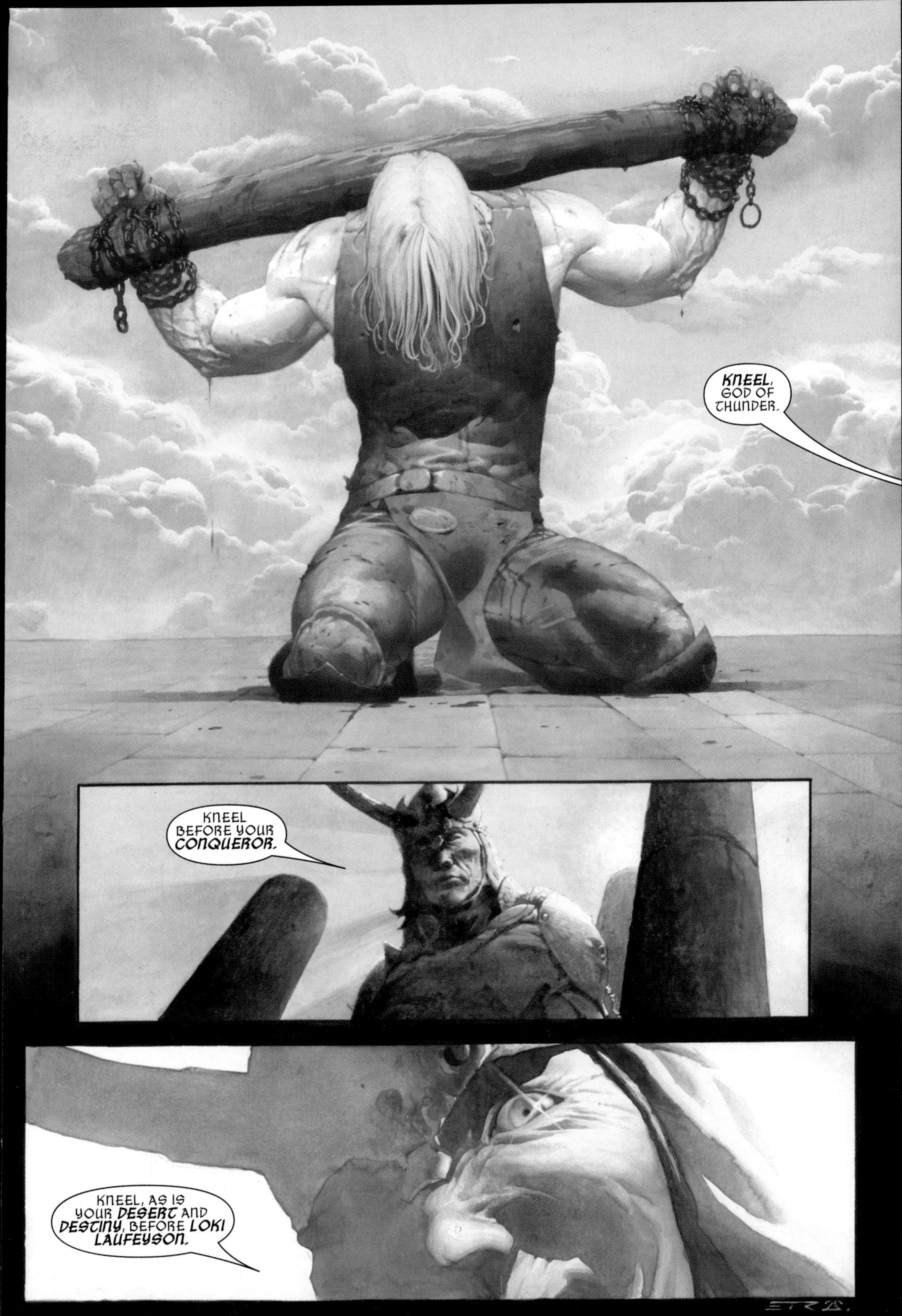
KNEEL, GOD OF THUNDER.
KNEEL BEFORE YOUR CONQUEROR.
KNEEL, AS IS YOUR DESERT AND DESTINY, BEFORE LOKI LAUFEYSON.

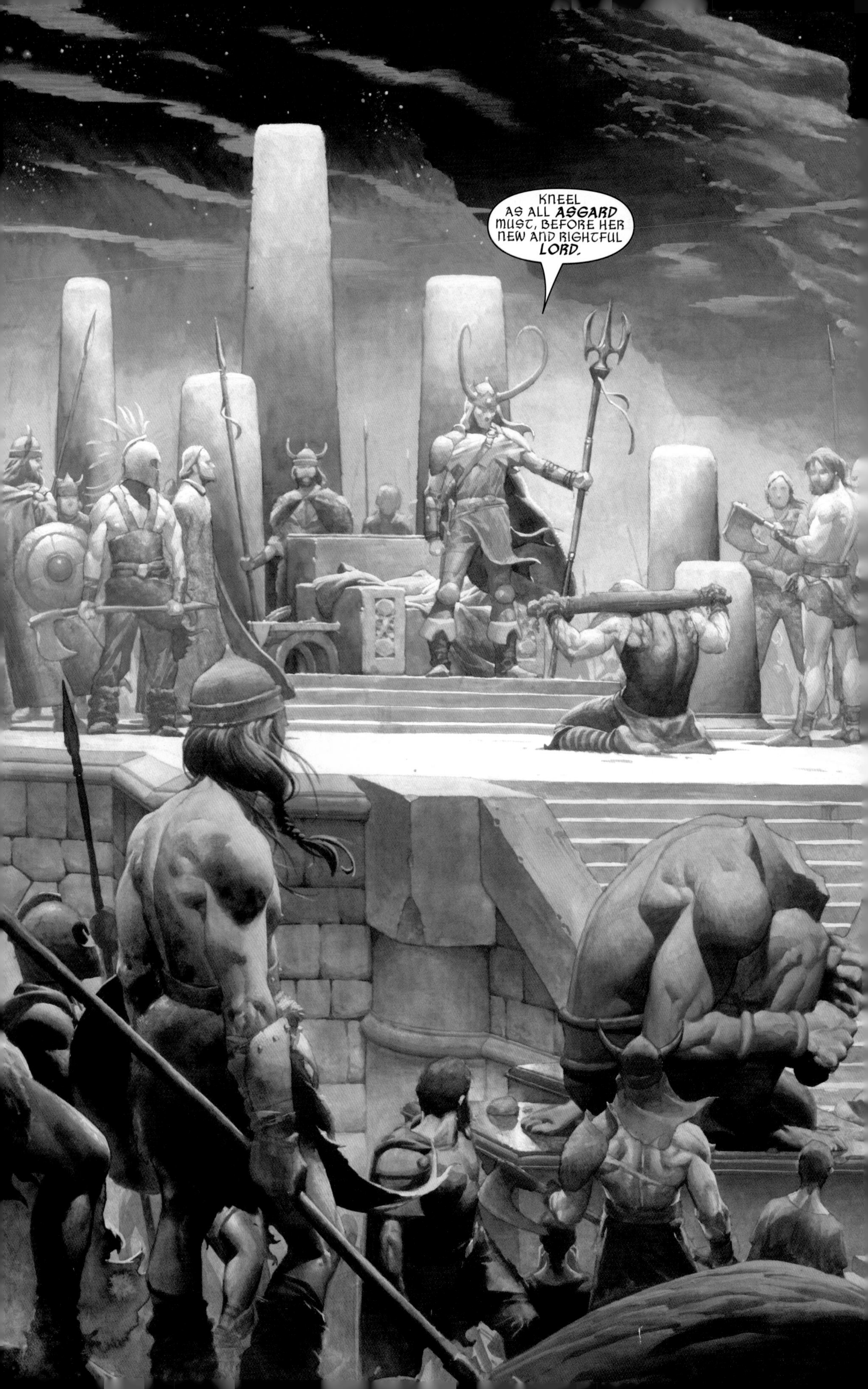
KNEEL AS ALL ASGARD MUST, BEFORE HER NEW AND RIGHTFUL LORD.

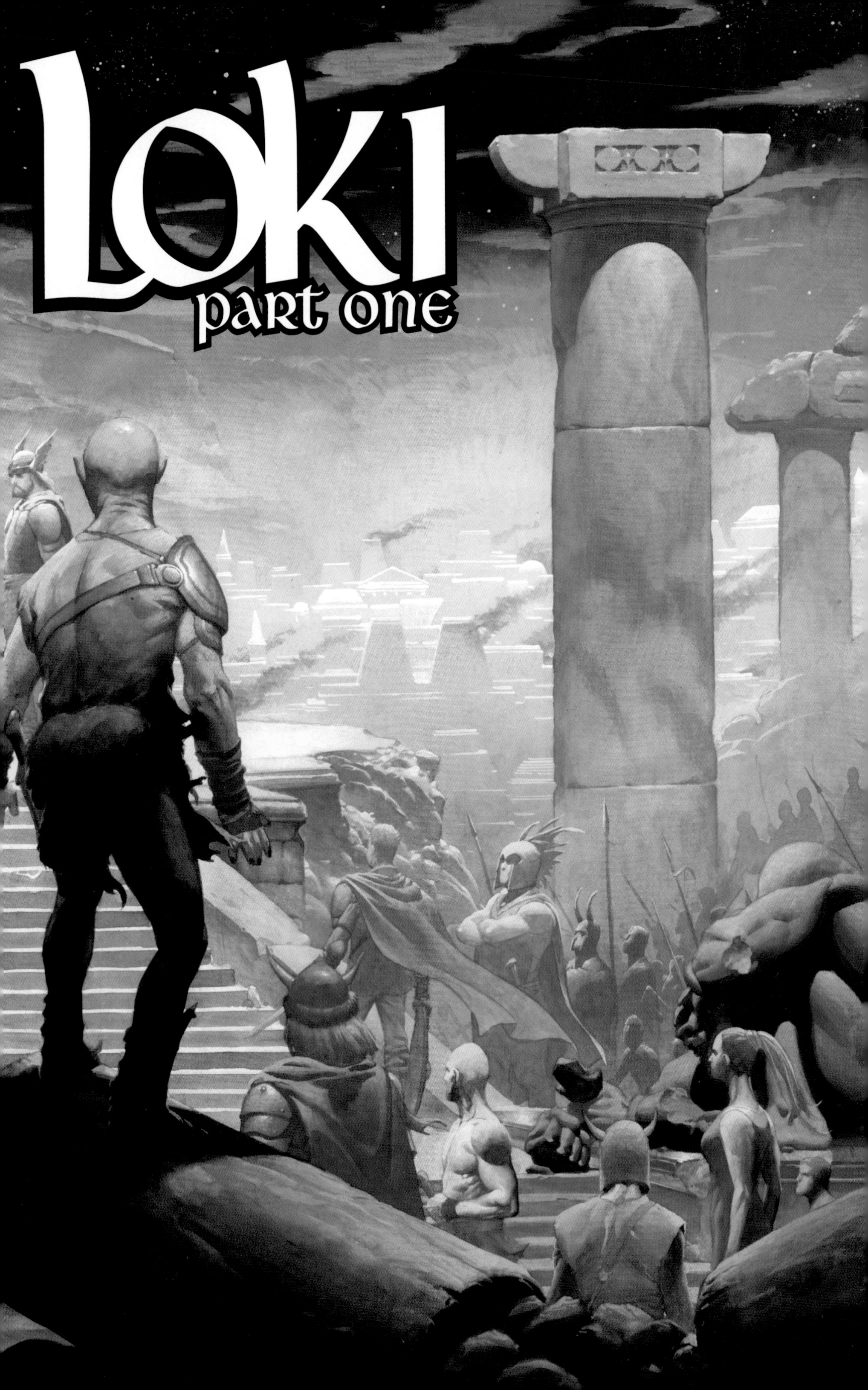
LOKI
part one

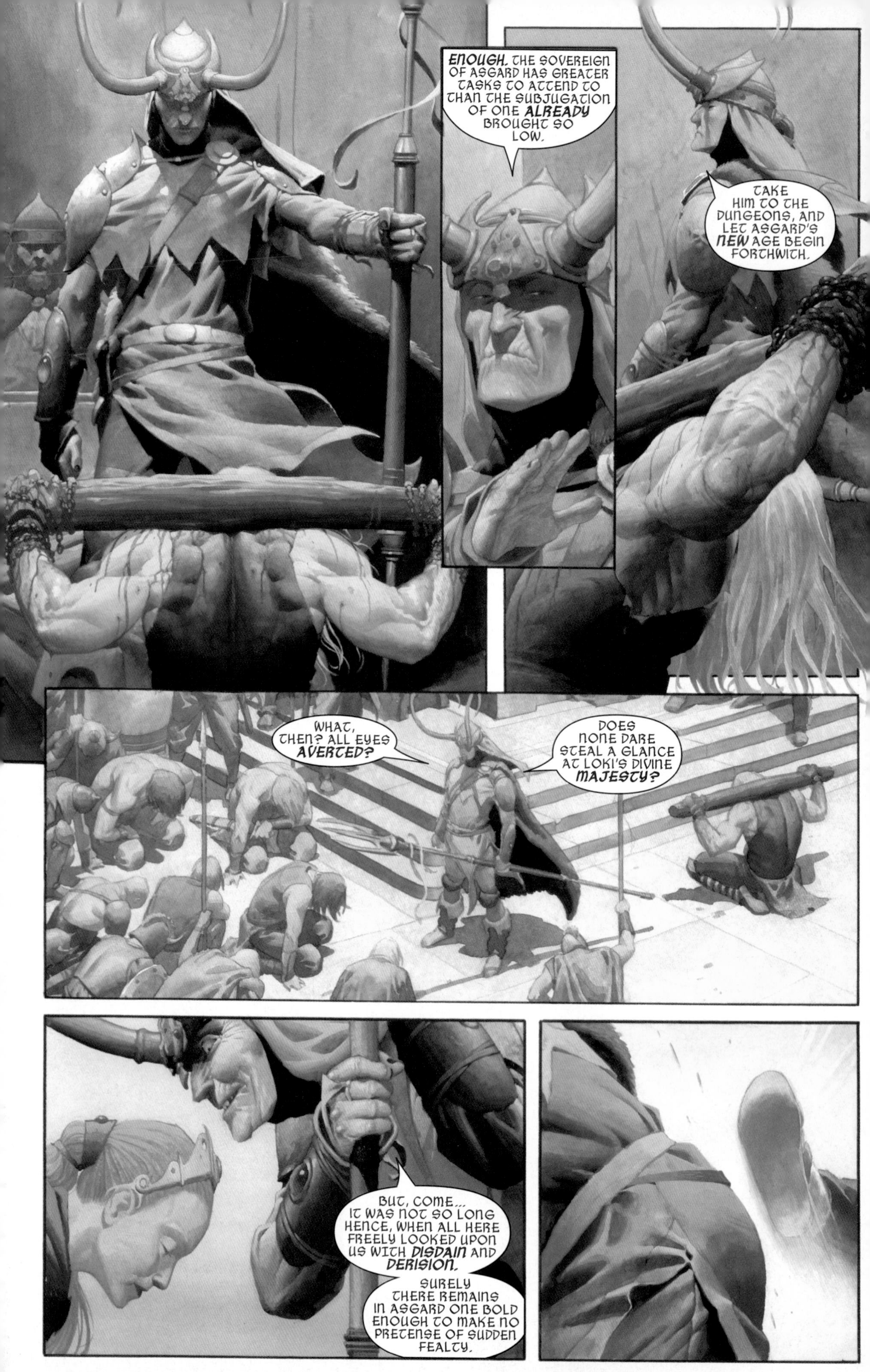

ENOUGH. THE SOVEREIGN OF ASGARD HAS GREATER TASKS TO ATTEND TO THAN THE SUBJUGATION OF ONE ALREADY BROUGHT SO LOW.
TAKE HIM TO THE DUNGEONS, AND LET ASGARD'S NEW AGE BEGIN FORTHWITH.
WHAT, THEN? ALL EYES AVERTED?
DOES NONE DARE STEAL A GLANCE AT LOKI'S DIVINE MAJESTY?
BUT, COME... IT WAS NOT SO LONG HENCE, WHEN ALL HERE FREELY LOOKED UPON US WITH DISDAIN AND DERISION.
SURELY THERE REMAINS IN ASGARD ONE BOLD ENOUGH TO MAKE NO PRETENSE OF SUDDEN FEALTY.

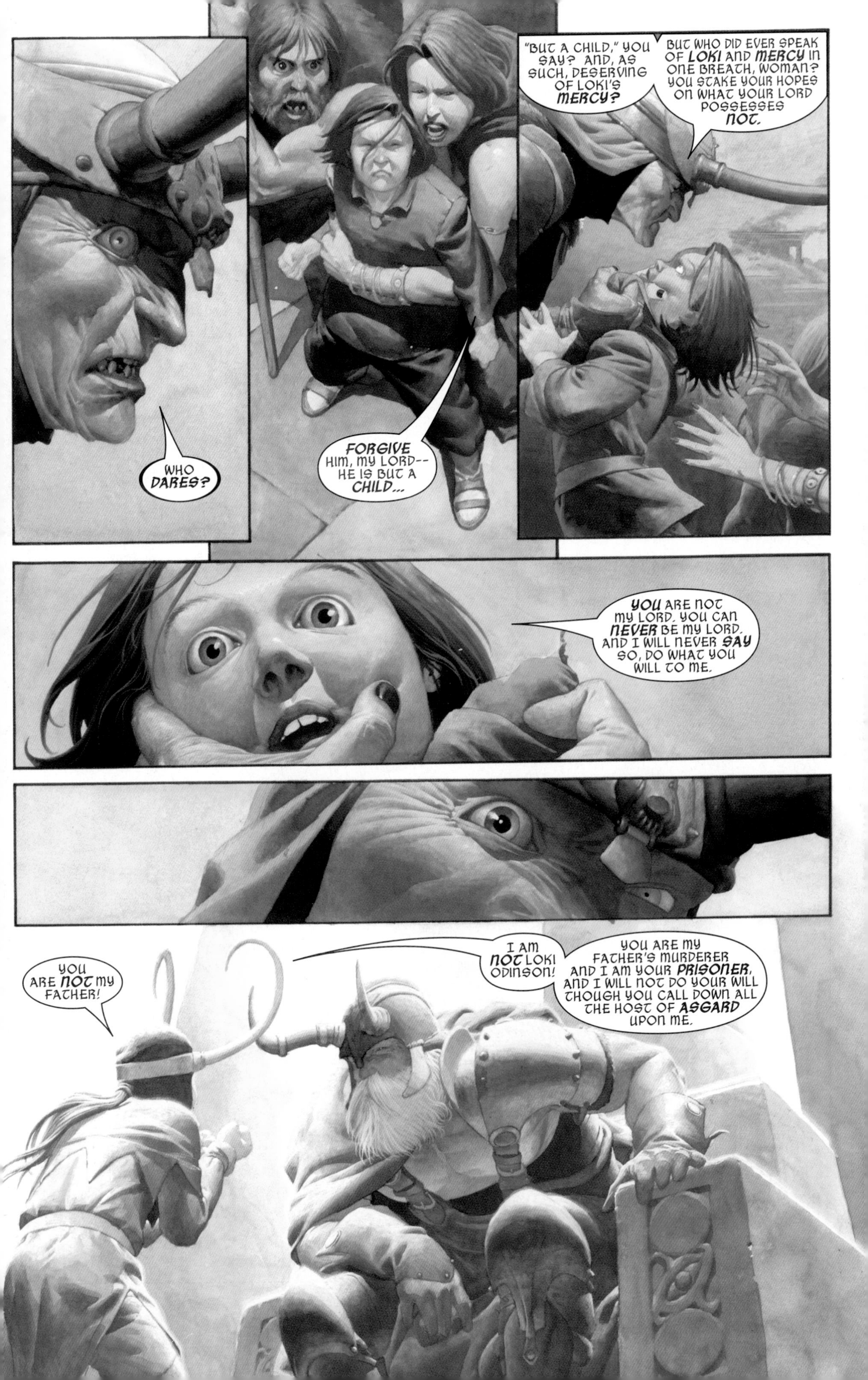
WHO DARES?
FORGIVE HIM, MY LORD-- HE IS BUT A CHILD...
"BUT A CHILD," YOU SAY? AND, AS SUCH, DESERVING OF LOKI'S MERCY?
BUT WHO DID EVER SPEAK OF LOKI AND MERCY IN ONE BREATH, WOMAN? YOU STAKE YOUR HOPES ON WHAT YOUR LORD POSSESSES NOT.
YOU ARE NOT MY LORD. YOU CAN NEVER BE MY LORD. AND I WILL NEVER SAY SO, DO WHAT YOU WILL TO ME.
YOU ARE NOT MY FATHER!
I AM NOT LOKI ODINSON!
YOU ARE MY FATHER'S MURDERER AND I AM YOUR PRISONER, AND I WILL NOT DO YOUR WILL THOUGH YOU CALL DOWN ALL THE HOST OF ASGARD UPON ME.

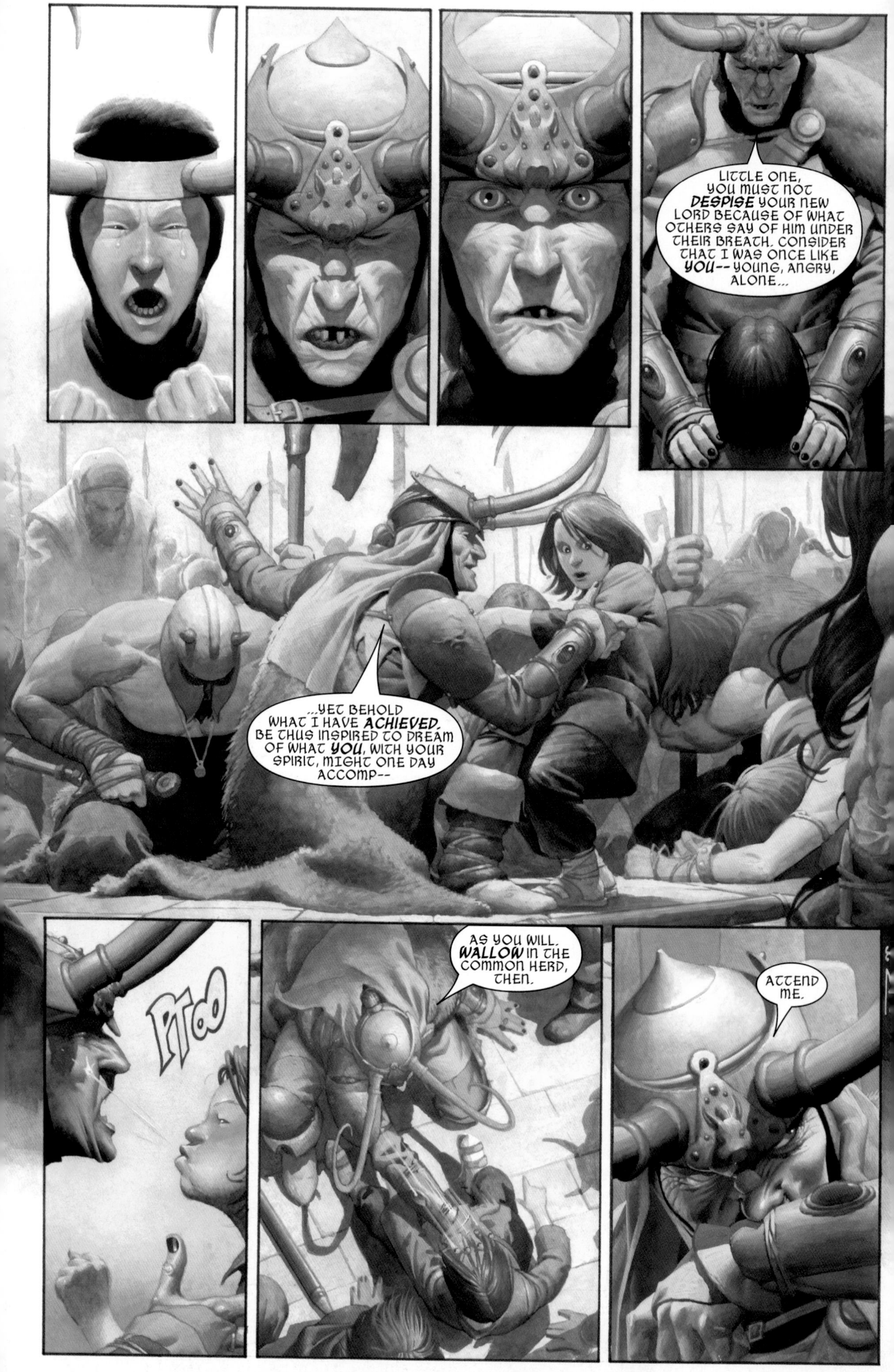
LITTLE ONE, YOU MUST NOT DESPISE YOUR NEW LORD BECAUSE OF WHAT OTHERS SAY OF HIM UNDER THEIR BREATH. CONSIDER THAT I WAS ONCE LIKE YOU-- YOUNG, ANGRY, ALONE...
...YET BEHOLD WHAT I HAVE ACHIEVED. BE THUS INSPIRED TO DREAM OF WHAT YOU, WITH YOUR SPIRIT, MIGHT ONE DAY ACCOMP--
PTOO
AS YOU WILL. WALLOW IN THE COMMON HERD, THEN.
ATTEND ME.

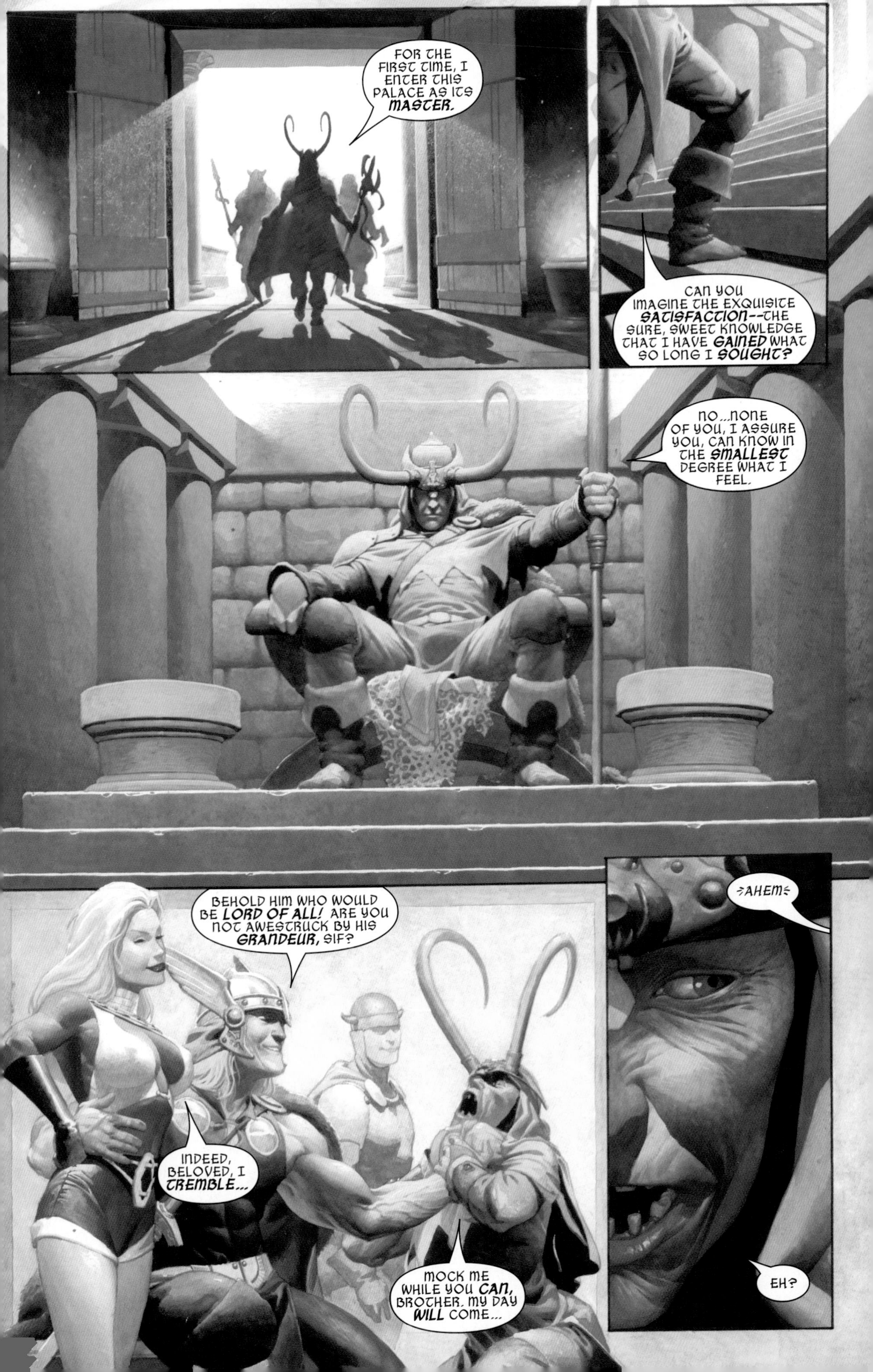

FOR THE FIRST TIME, I ENTER THIS PALACE AS ITS **MASTER.**
CAN YOU IMAGINE THE EXQUISITE **SATISFACTION**--THE SURE, SWEET KNOWLEDGE THAT I HAVE **GAINED** WHAT SO LONG I **SOUGHT?**
NO...NONE OF YOU, I ASSURE YOU, CAN KNOW IN THE **SMALLEST** DEGREE WHAT I FEEL.
BEHOLD HIM WHO WOULD BE **LORD OF ALL!** ARE YOU NOT AWESTRUCK BY HIS **GRANDEUR,** SIF?
INDEED, BELOVED, I **TREMBLE...**
MOCK ME WHILE YOU **CAN,** BROTHER. MY DAY **WILL** COME...
*AHEM*
EH?

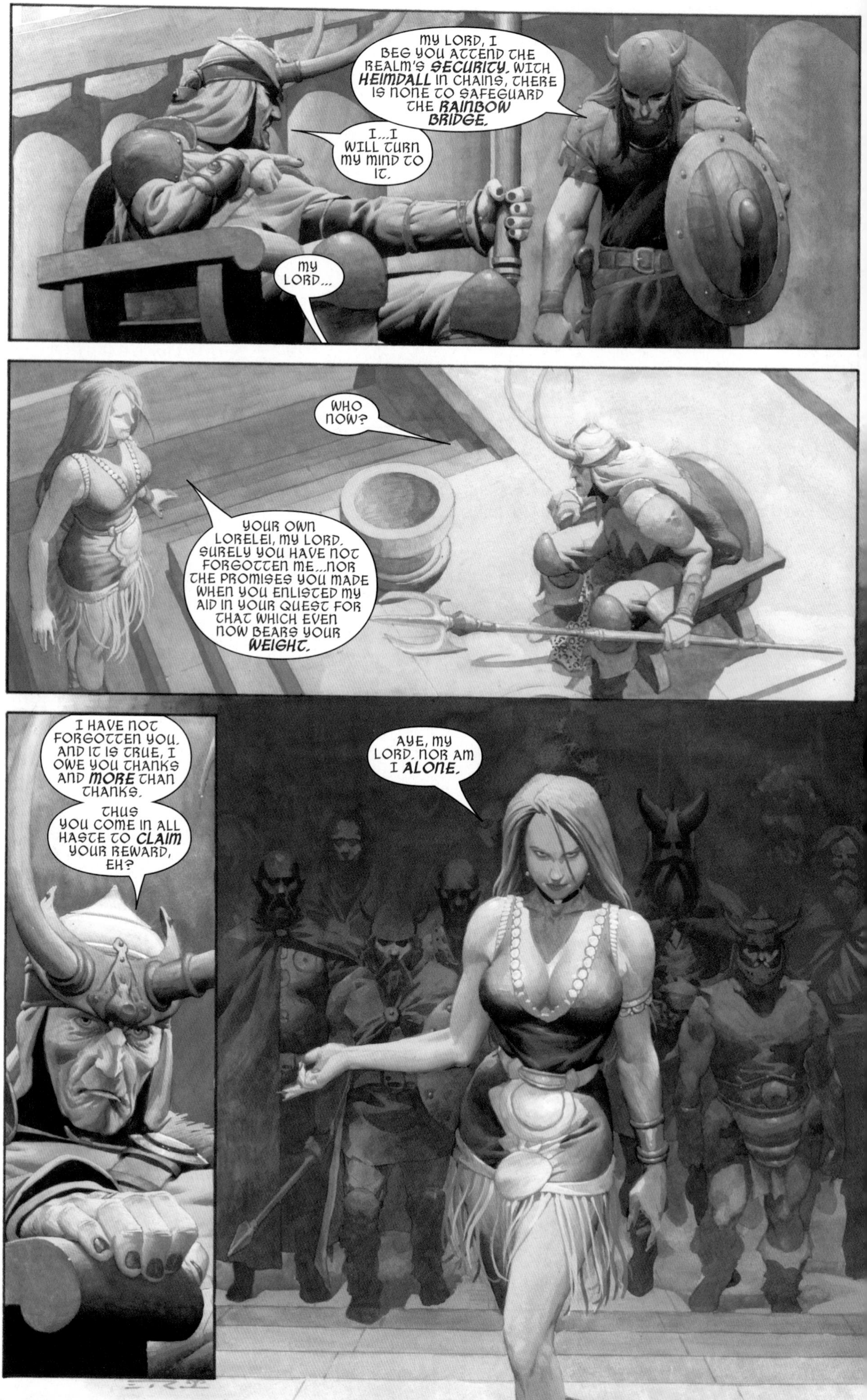
MY LORD, I BEG YOU ATTEND THE REALM'S SECURITY. WITH HEIMDALL IN CHAINS, THERE IS NONE TO SAFEGUARD THE RAINBOW BRIDGE.
I...I WILL TURN MY MIND TO IT.
MY LORD...
WHO NOW?
YOUR OWN LORELEI, MY LORD. SURELY YOU HAVE NOT FORGOTTEN ME...NOR THE PROMISES YOU MADE WHEN YOU ENLISTED MY AID IN YOUR QUEST FOR THAT WHICH EVEN NOW BEARS YOUR WEIGHT.
I HAVE NOT FORGOTTEN YOU. AND IT IS TRUE, I OWE YOU THANKS AND MORE THAN THANKS.
THUS YOU COME IN ALL HASTE TO CLAIM YOUR REWARD, EH?
AYE, MY LORD. NOR AM I ALONE.

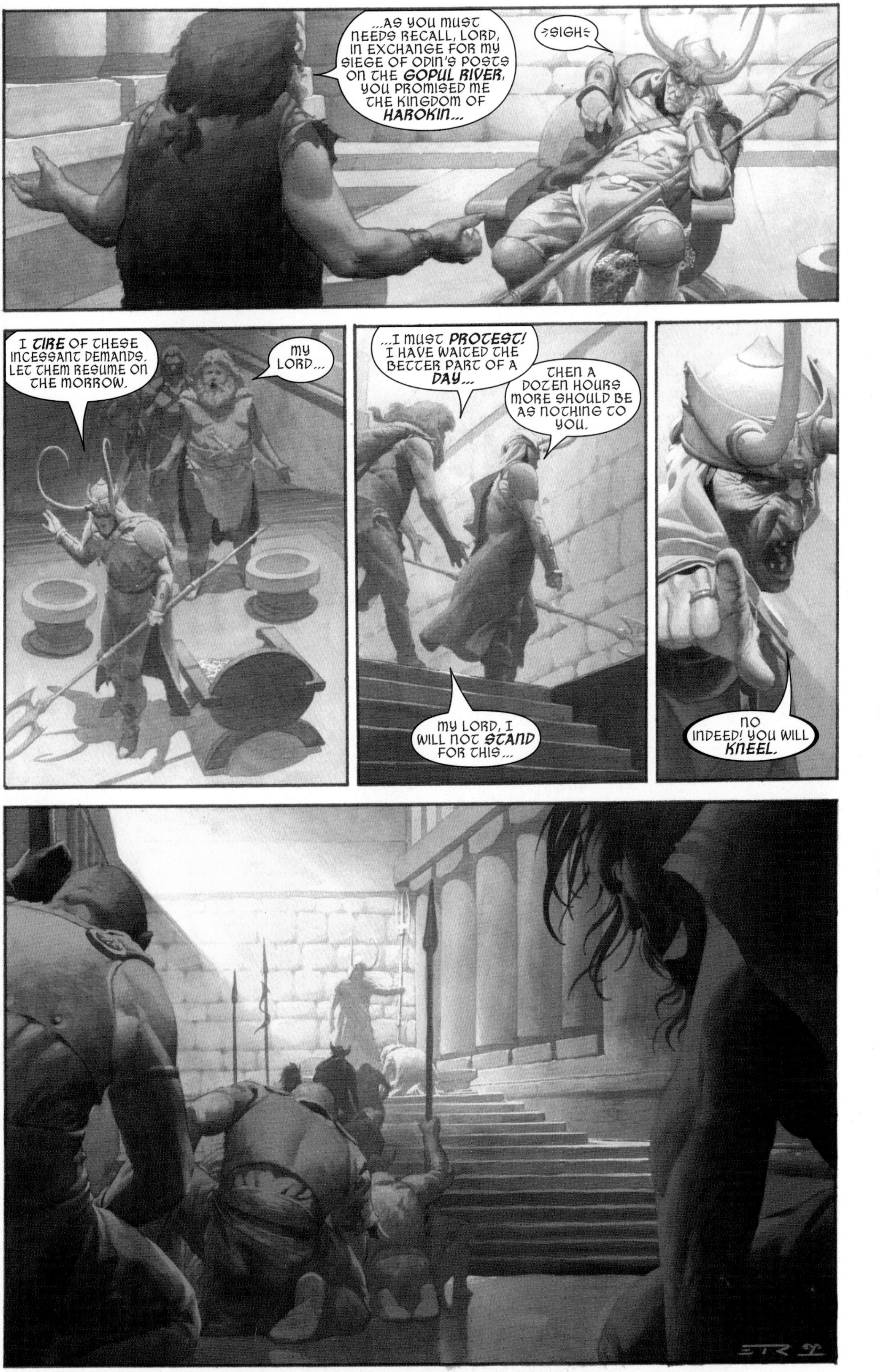
...AS YOU MUST NEEDS RECALL, LORD, IN EXCHANGE FOR MY SIEGE OF ODIN'S POSTS ON THE GOPUL RIVER, YOU PROMISED ME THE KINGDOM OF HAROKIN...
<SIGH>
I TIRE OF THESE INCESSANT DEMANDS. LET THEM RESUME ON THE MORROW.
MY LORD...
...I MUST PROTEST! I HAVE WAITED THE BETTER PART OF A DAY...
THEN A DOZEN HOURS MORE SHOULD BE AS NOTHING TO YOU.
MY LORD, I WILL NOT STAND FOR THIS...
NO INDEED! YOU WILL KNEEL.

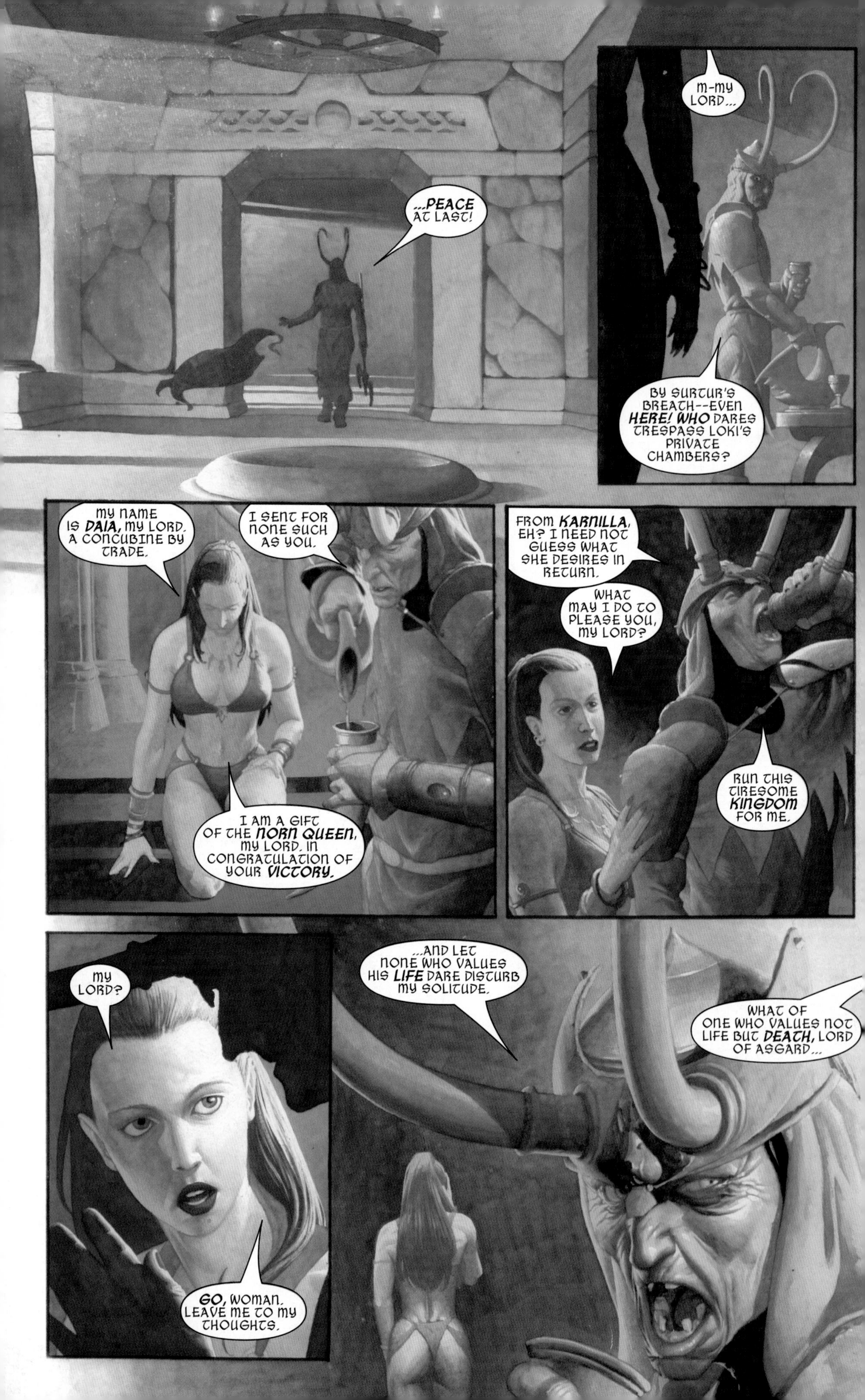
...PEACE AT LAST!
M-MY LORD...
BY SURTUR'S BREATH--EVEN HERE! WHO DARES TRESPASS LOKI'S PRIVATE CHAMBERS?
MY NAME IS DAIA, MY LORD. A CONCUBINE BY TRADE.
I SENT FOR NONE SUCH AS YOU.
I AM A GIFT OF THE NORN QUEEN, MY LORD. IN CONGRATULATION OF YOUR VICTORY.
FROM KARNILLA, EH? I NEED NOT GUESS WHAT SHE DESIRES IN RETURN.
WHAT MAY I DO TO PLEASE YOU, MY LORD?
RUN THIS TIRESOME KINGDOM FOR ME.
MY LORD?
GO, WOMAN. LEAVE ME TO MY THOUGHTS.
...AND LET NONE WHO VALUES HIS LIFE DARE DISTURB MY SOLITUDE.
WHAT OF ONE WHO VALUES NOT LIFE BUT DEATH, LORD OF ASGARD...

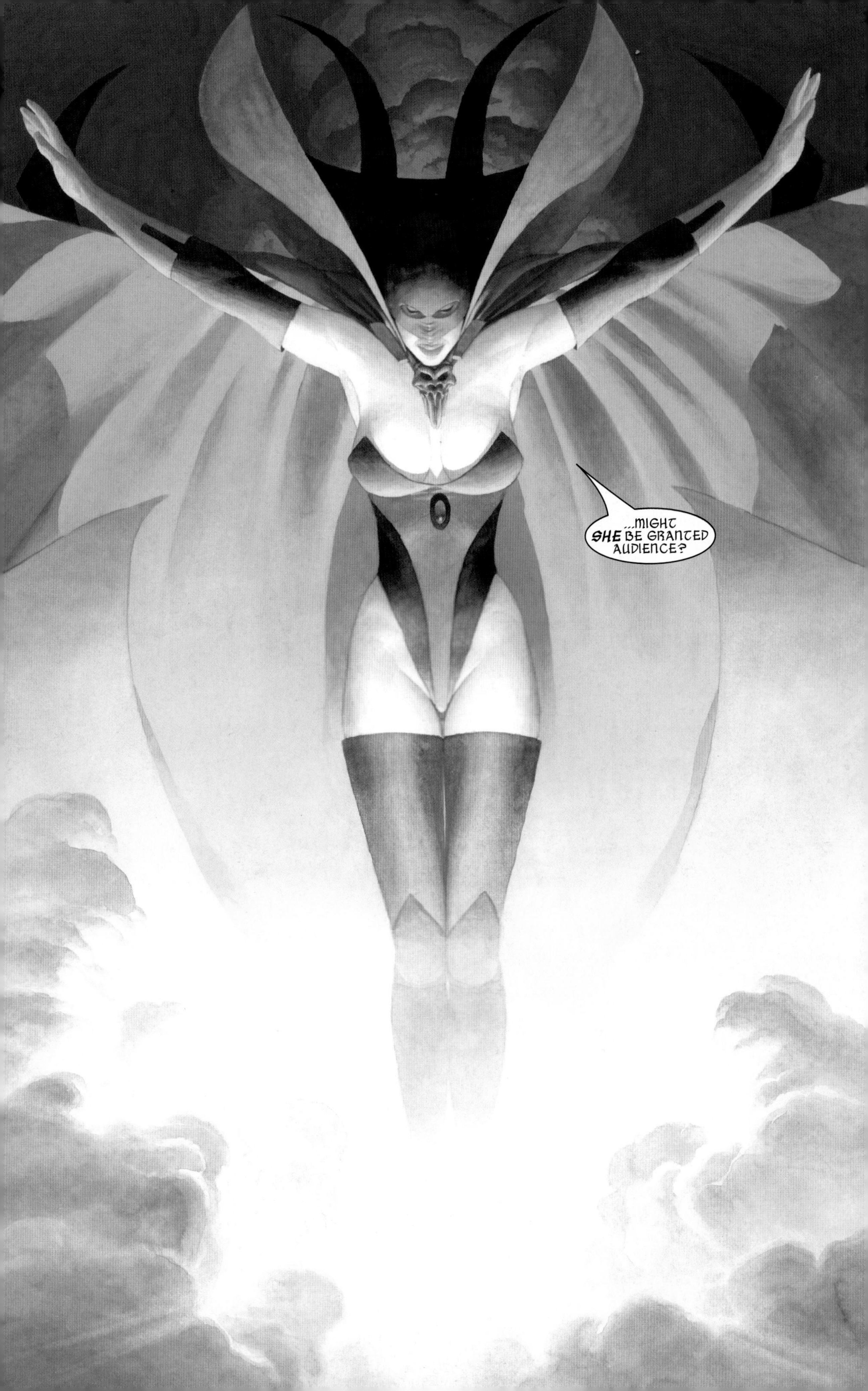
...MIGHT SHE BE GRANTED AUDIENCE?

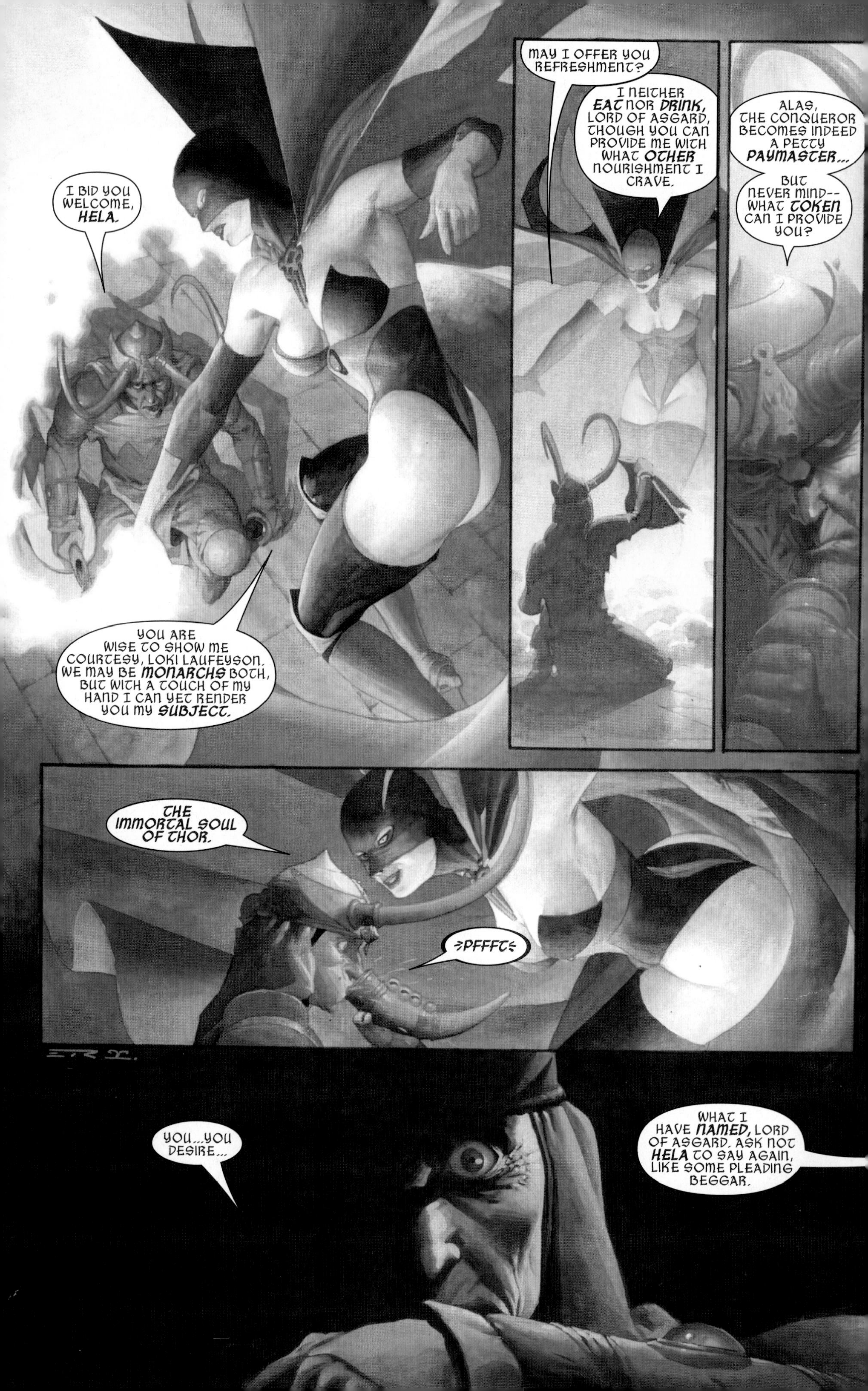
I BID YOU WELCOME, HELA.
YOU ARE WISE TO SHOW ME COURTESY, LOKI LAUFEYSON. WE MAY BE MONARCHS BOTH, BUT WITH A TOUCH OF MY HAND I CAN YET RENDER YOU MY SUBJECT.
MAY I OFFER YOU REFRESHMENT?
I NEITHER EAT NOR DRINK, LORD OF ASGARD, THOUGH YOU CAN PROVIDE ME WITH WHAT OTHER NOURISHMENT I CRAVE.
ALAS, THE CONQUEROR BECOMES INDEED A PETTY PAYMASTER...
BUT NEVER MIND-- WHAT TOKEN CAN I PROVIDE YOU?
THE IMMORTAL SOUL OF THOR.
=PFFFT=
YOU...YOU DESIRE...
WHAT I HAVE NAMED, LORD OF ASGARD. ASK NOT HELA TO SAY AGAIN, LIKE SOME PLEADING BEGGAR.

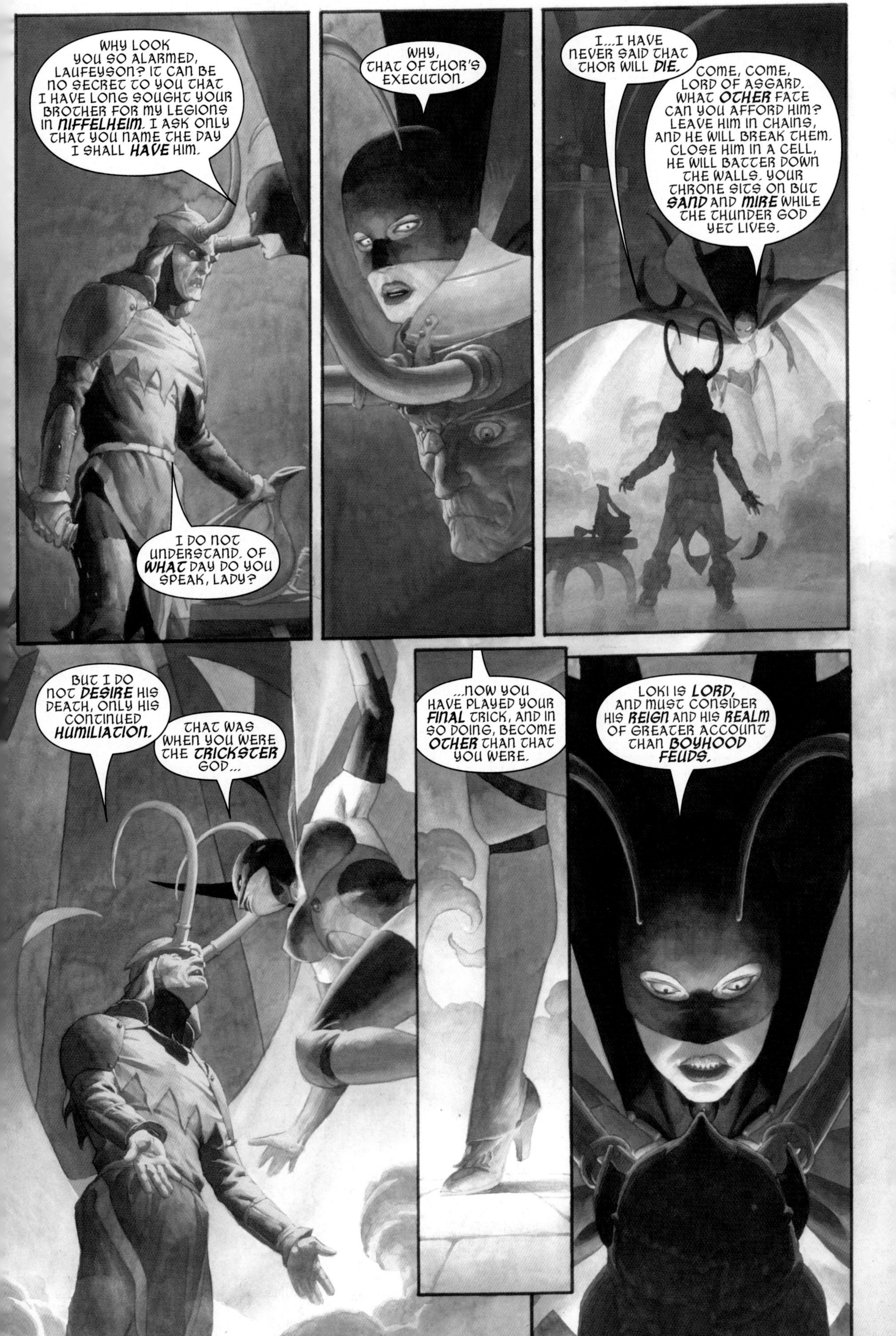

WHY LOOK YOU SO ALARMED, LAUFEYSON? IT CAN BE NO SECRET TO YOU THAT I HAVE LONG SOUGHT YOUR BROTHER FOR MY LEGIONS IN NIFFELHEIM. I ASK ONLY THAT YOU NAME THE DAY I SHALL HAVE HIM.
I DO NOT UNDERSTAND. OF WHAT DAY DO YOU SPEAK, LADY?
WHY, THAT OF THOR'S EXECUTION.
I...I HAVE NEVER SAID THAT THOR WILL DIE.
COME, COME, LORD OF ASGARD. WHAT OTHER FATE CAN YOU AFFORD HIM? LEAVE HIM IN CHAINS, AND HE WILL BREAK THEM. CLOSE HIM IN A CELL, HE WILL BATTER DOWN THE WALLS. YOUR THRONE SITS ON BUT SAND AND MIRE WHILE THE THUNDER GOD YET LIVES.
BUT I DO NOT DESIRE HIS DEATH, ONLY HIS CONTINUED HUMILIATION.
THAT WAS WHEN YOU WERE THE TRICKSTER GOD...
...NOW YOU HAVE PLAYED YOUR FINAL TRICK, AND IN SO DOING, BECOME OTHER THAN THAT YOU WERE.
LOKI IS LORD, AND MUST CONSIDER HIS REIGN AND HIS REALM OF GREATER ACCOUNT THAN BOYHOOD FEUDS.

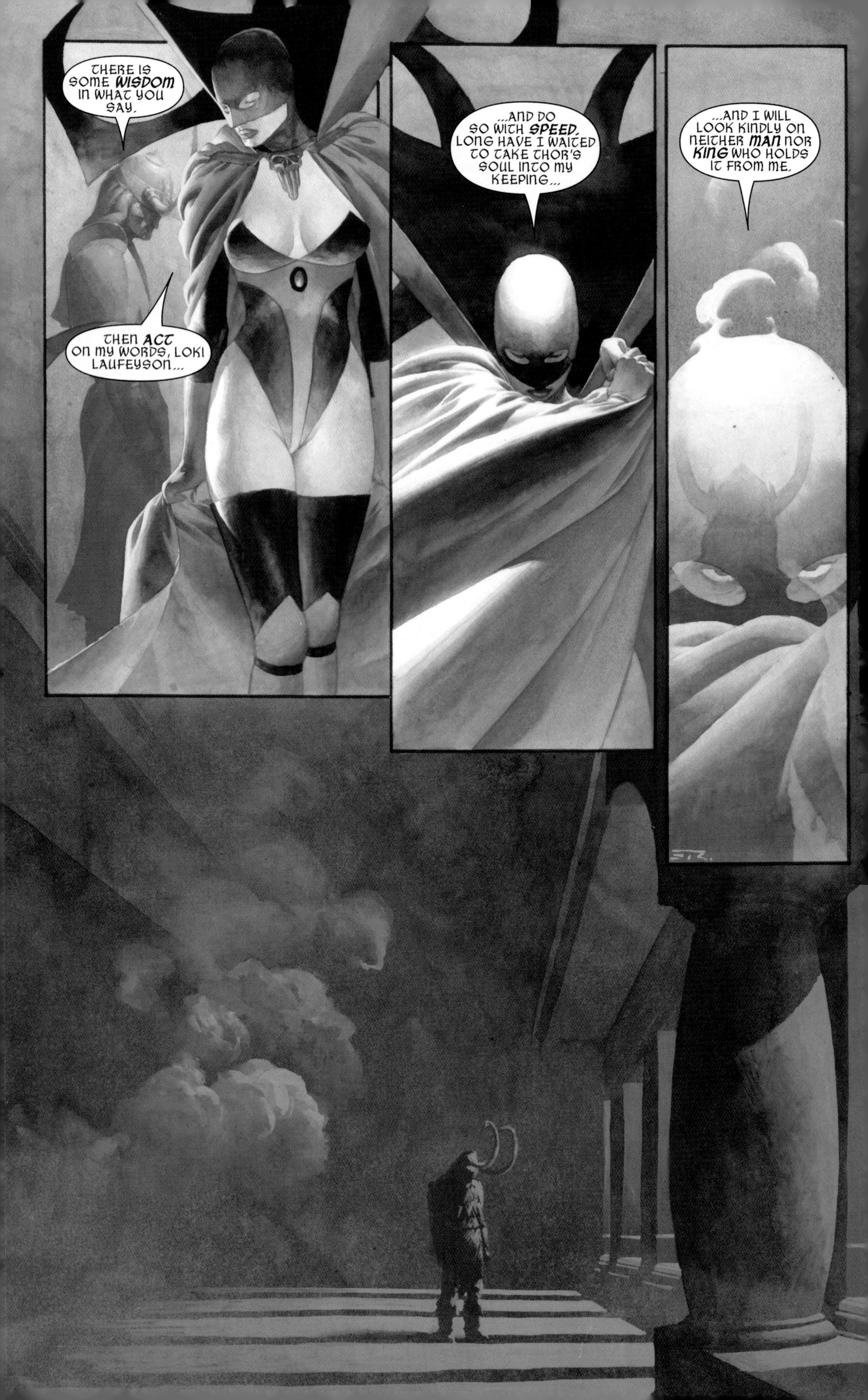
THERE IS SOME WISDOM IN WHAT YOU SAY.
THEN ACT ON MY WORDS, LOKI LAUFEYSON...
...AND DO SO WITH SPEED. LONG HAVE I WAITED TO TAKE THOR'S SOUL INTO MY KEEPING...
...AND I WILL LOOK KINDLY ON NEITHER MAN NOR KING WHO HOLDS IT FROM ME.

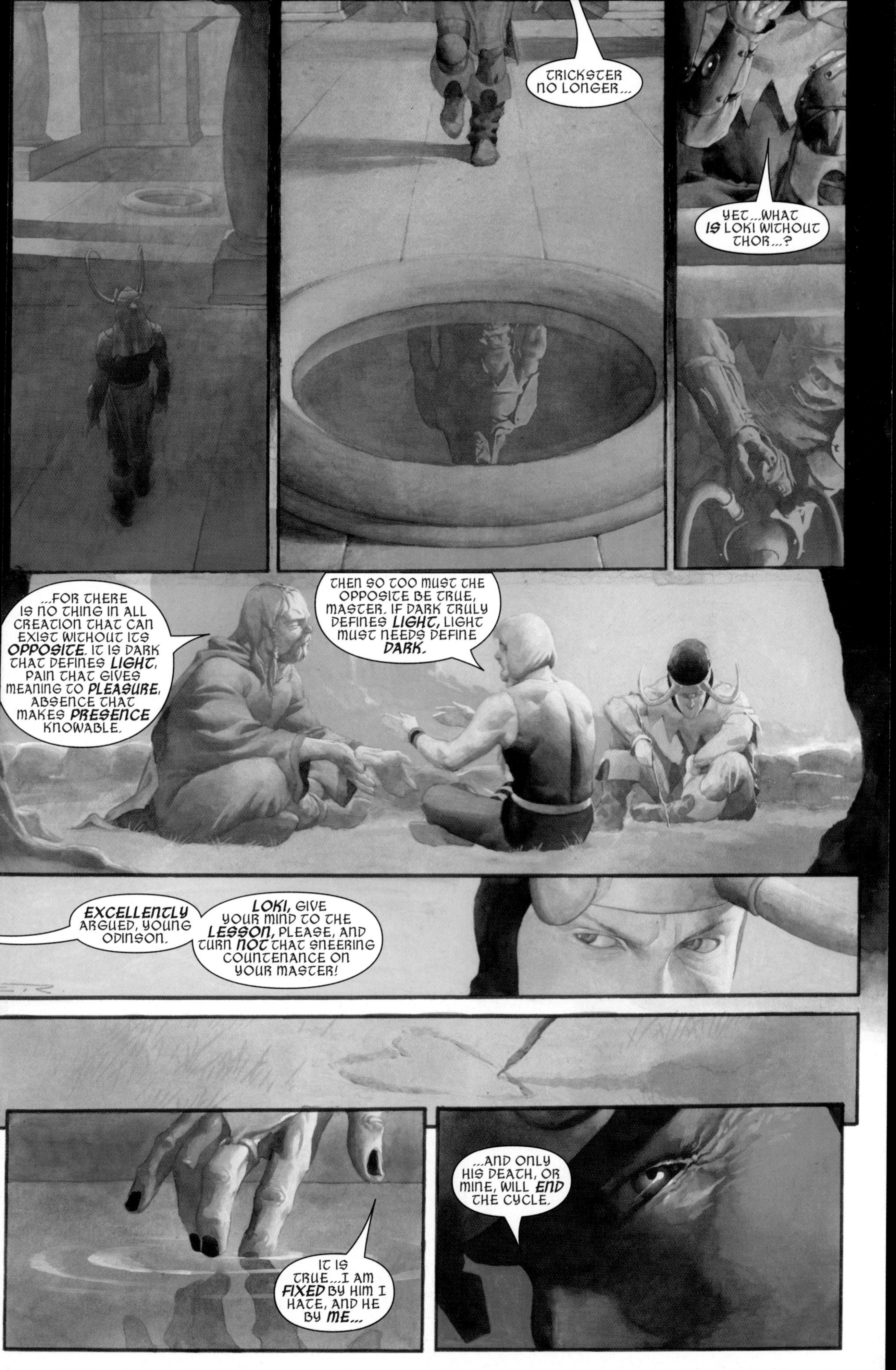
TRICKSTER NO LONGER...
YET...WHAT IS LOKI WITHOUT THOR...?
...FOR THERE IS NO THING IN ALL CREATION THAT CAN EXIST WITHOUT ITS OPPOSITE. IT IS DARK THAT DEFINES LIGHT, PAIN THAT GIVES MEANING TO PLEASURE, ABSENCE THAT MAKES PRESENCE KNOWABLE.
THEN SO TOO MUST THE OPPOSITE BE TRUE, MASTER. IF DARK TRULY DEFINES LIGHT, LIGHT MUST NEEDS DEFINE DARK.
EXCELLENTLY ARGUED, YOUNG ODINSON.
LOKI, GIVE YOUR MIND TO THE LESSON, PLEASE, AND TURN NOT THAT SNEERING COUNTENANCE ON YOUR MASTER!
IT IS TRUE...I AM FIXED BY HIM I HATE, AND HE BY ME...
...AND ONLY HIS DEATH, OR MINE, WILL END THE CYCLE.

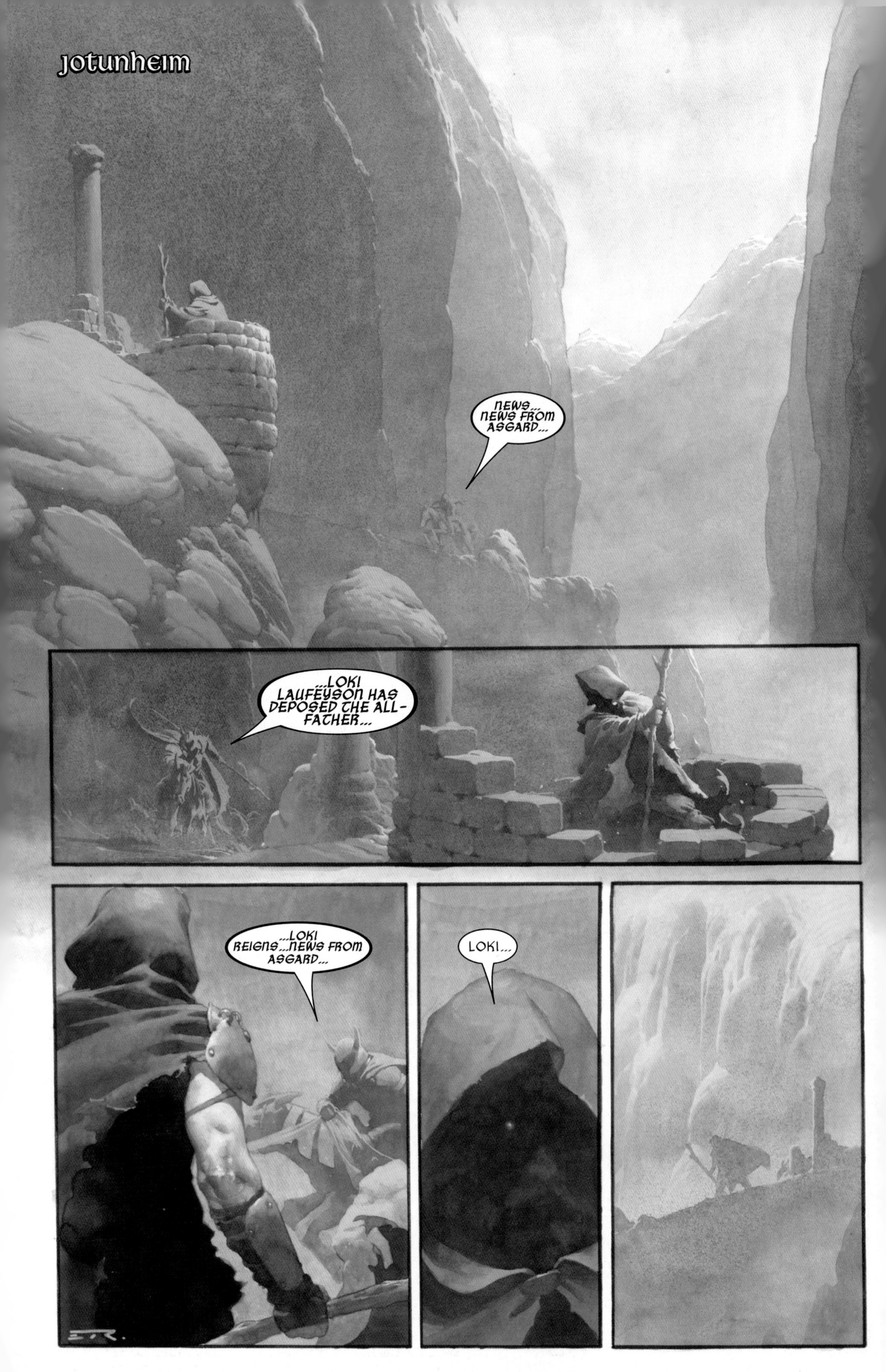
JOTUNHEIM
NEWS... NEWS FROM ASGARD...
...LOKI LAUFEYSON HAS DEPOSED THE ALL-FATHER...
...LOKI REIGNS...NEWS FROM ASGARD...
LOKI...

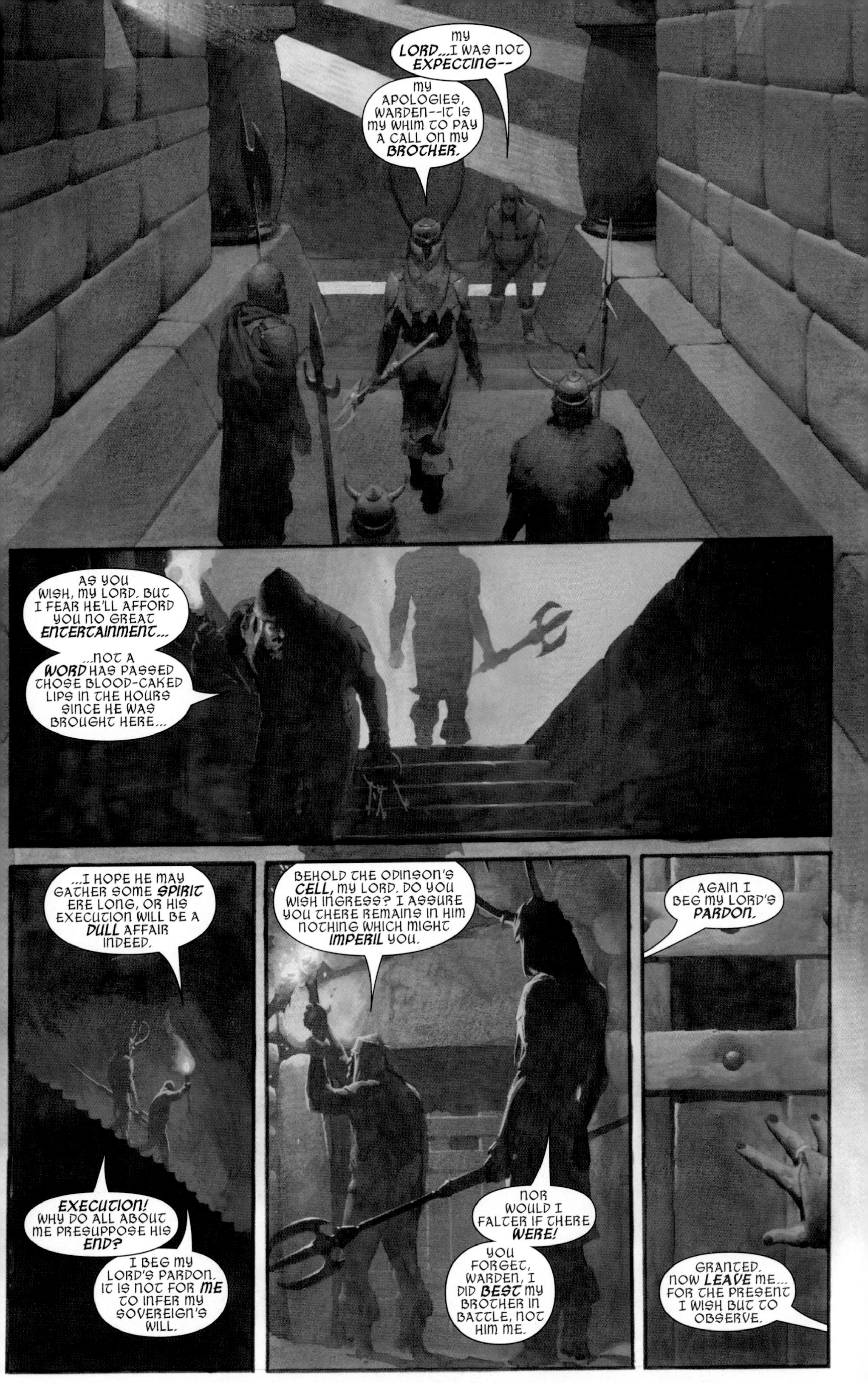

MY LORD...I WAS NOT EXPECTING--
MY APOLOGIES, WARDEN--IT IS MY WHIM TO PAY A CALL ON MY BROTHER.
AS YOU WISH, MY LORD. BUT I FEAR HE'LL AFFORD YOU NO GREAT ENTERTAINMENT...
...NOT A WORD HAS PASSED THOSE BLOOD-CAKED LIPS IN THE HOURS SINCE HE WAS BROUGHT HERE...
...I HOPE HE MAY GATHER SOME SPIRIT ERE LONG, OR HIS EXECUTION WILL BE A DULL AFFAIR INDEED.
EXECUTION! WHY DO ALL ABOUT ME PRESUPPOSE HIS END?
I BEG MY LORD'S PARDON. IT IS NOT FOR ME TO INFER MY SOVEREIGN'S WILL.
BEHOLD THE ODINSON'S CELL, MY LORD. DO YOU WISH INGRESS? I ASSURE YOU THERE REMAINS IN HIM NOTHING WHICH MIGHT IMPERIL YOU.
NOR WOULD I FALTER IF THERE WERE!
YOU FORGET, WARDEN, I DID BEST MY BROTHER IN BATTLE, NOT HIM ME.
AGAIN I BEG MY LORD'S PARDON.
GRANTED. NOW LEAVE ME... FOR THE PRESENT I WISH BUT TO OBSERVE.

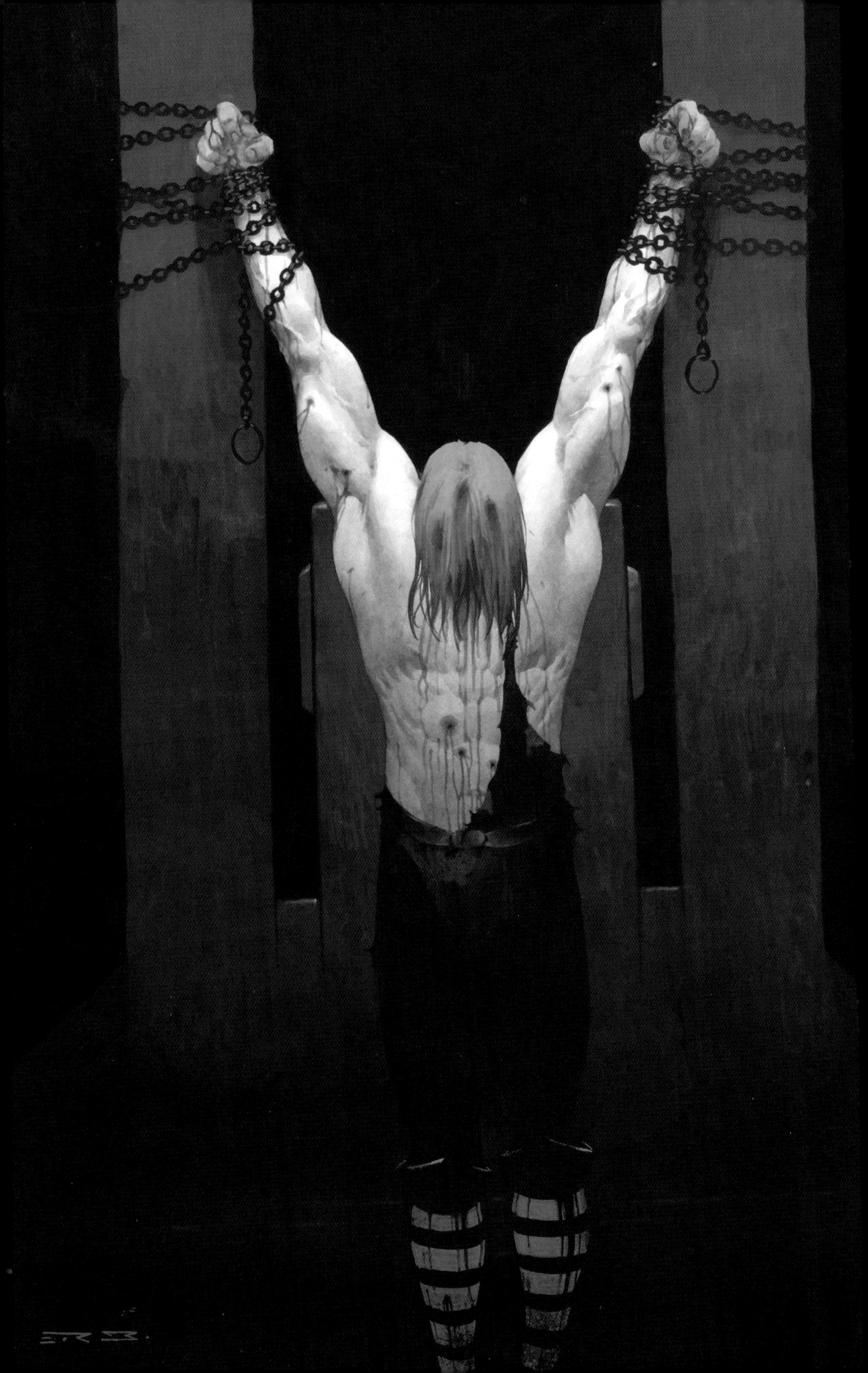

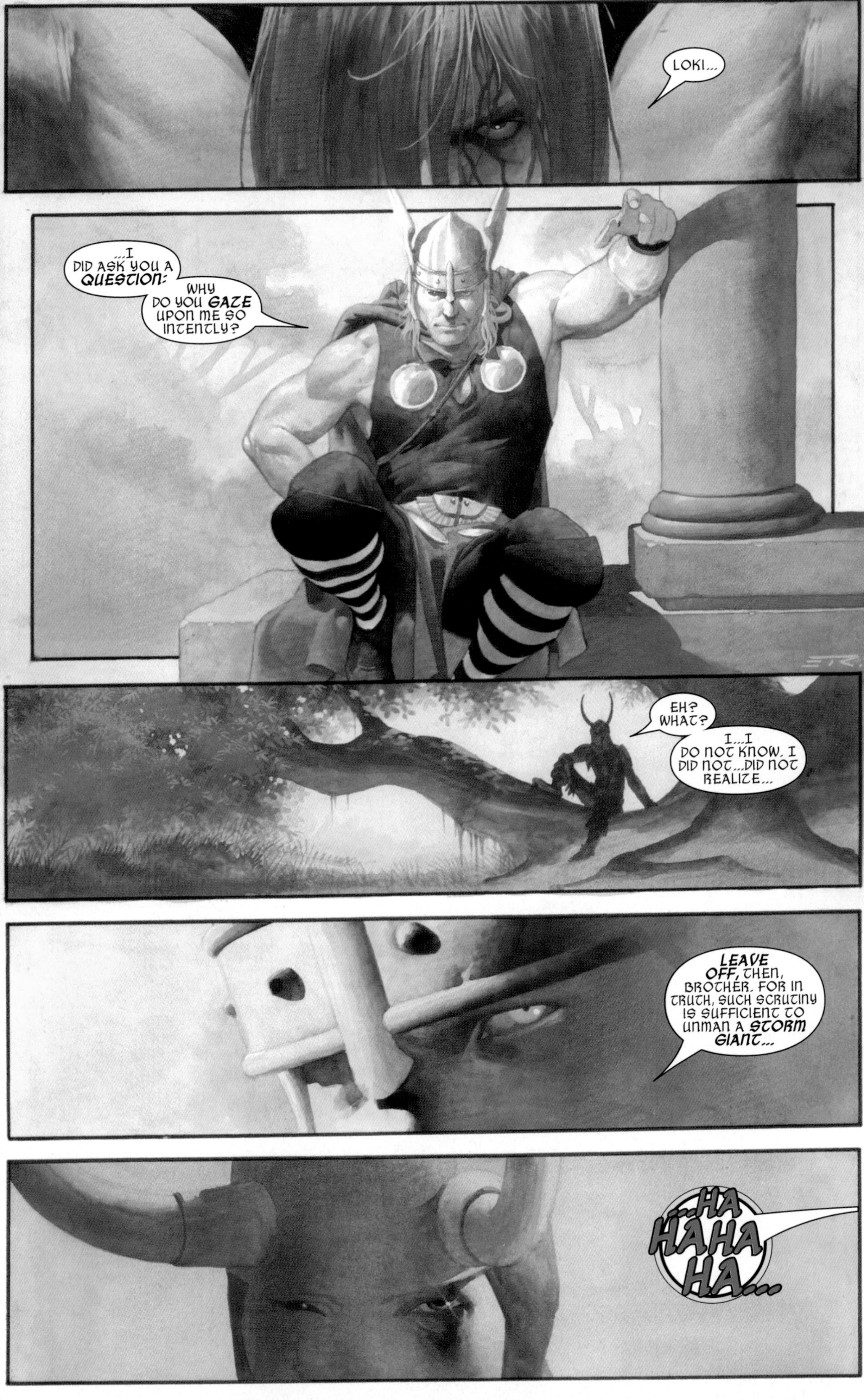
LOKI...
...I DID ASK YOU A QUESTION:
WHY DO YOU GAZE UPON ME SO INTENTLY?
EH? WHAT?
I...I DO NOT KNOW. I DID NOT...DID NOT REALIZE...
LEAVE OFF, THEN, BROTHER. FOR IN TRUTH, SUCH SCRUTINY IS SUFFICIENT TO UNMAN A STORM GIANT...
...HA HAHAHA HA...

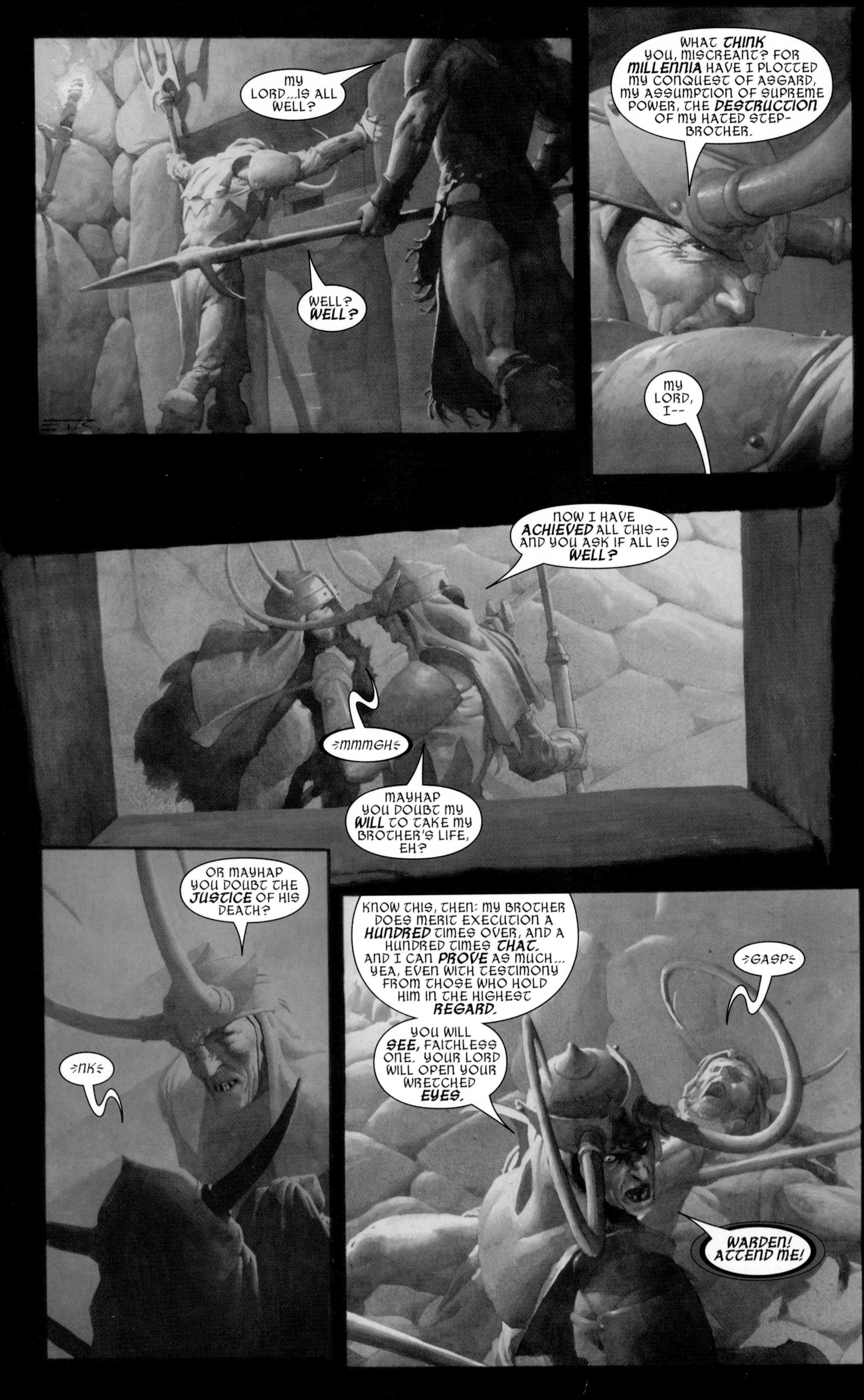

MY LORD...IS ALL WELL?
WELL? WELL?
WHAT THINK YOU, MISCREANT? FOR MILLENNIA HAVE I PLOTTED MY CONQUEST OF ASGARD, MY ASSUMPTION OF SUPREME POWER, THE DESTRUCTION OF MY HATED STEP-BROTHER.
MY LORD, I--
NOW I HAVE ACHIEVED ALL THIS-- AND YOU ASK IF ALL IS WELL?
MMMGH
MAYHAP YOU DOUBT MY WILL TO TAKE MY BROTHER'S LIFE, EH?
OR MAYHAP YOU DOUBT THE JUSTICE OF HIS DEATH?
NK
KNOW THIS, THEN: MY BROTHER DOES MERIT EXECUTION A HUNDRED TIMES OVER, AND A HUNDRED TIMES THAT. AND I CAN PROVE AS MUCH... YEA, EVEN WITH TESTIMONY FROM THOSE WHO HOLD HIM IN THE HIGHEST REGARD.
YOU WILL SEE, FAITHLESS ONE. YOUR LORD WILL OPEN YOUR WRETCHED EYES.
GASP
WARDEN! ATTEND ME!

AT YOUR **SERVICE**, MY LORD.

HAVE YOU YOUR **KEYS** ABOUT YOU, WARDEN?

YES, MY LORD...

THEN **LEAD** ME WHERE I WILL...

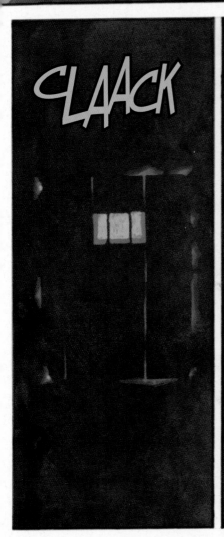

CLAACK

I SEE NO ONE.

GIVE YOUR EYES A MOMENT TO **ADJUST**, MY LORD.

AH...YES.

**BEHOLD**, SCURRILOUS ONE. KNOW YOU THE **TRAITOR** YOU SEE BEFORE YOU?

N-NO, MY LORD...

I DO NOT WONDER. WHO WOULD MISTAKE THIS PALE, WRETCHED **HUSK** FOR THE BEWITCHING CREATURE WHO STOLE THOR'S HEART...

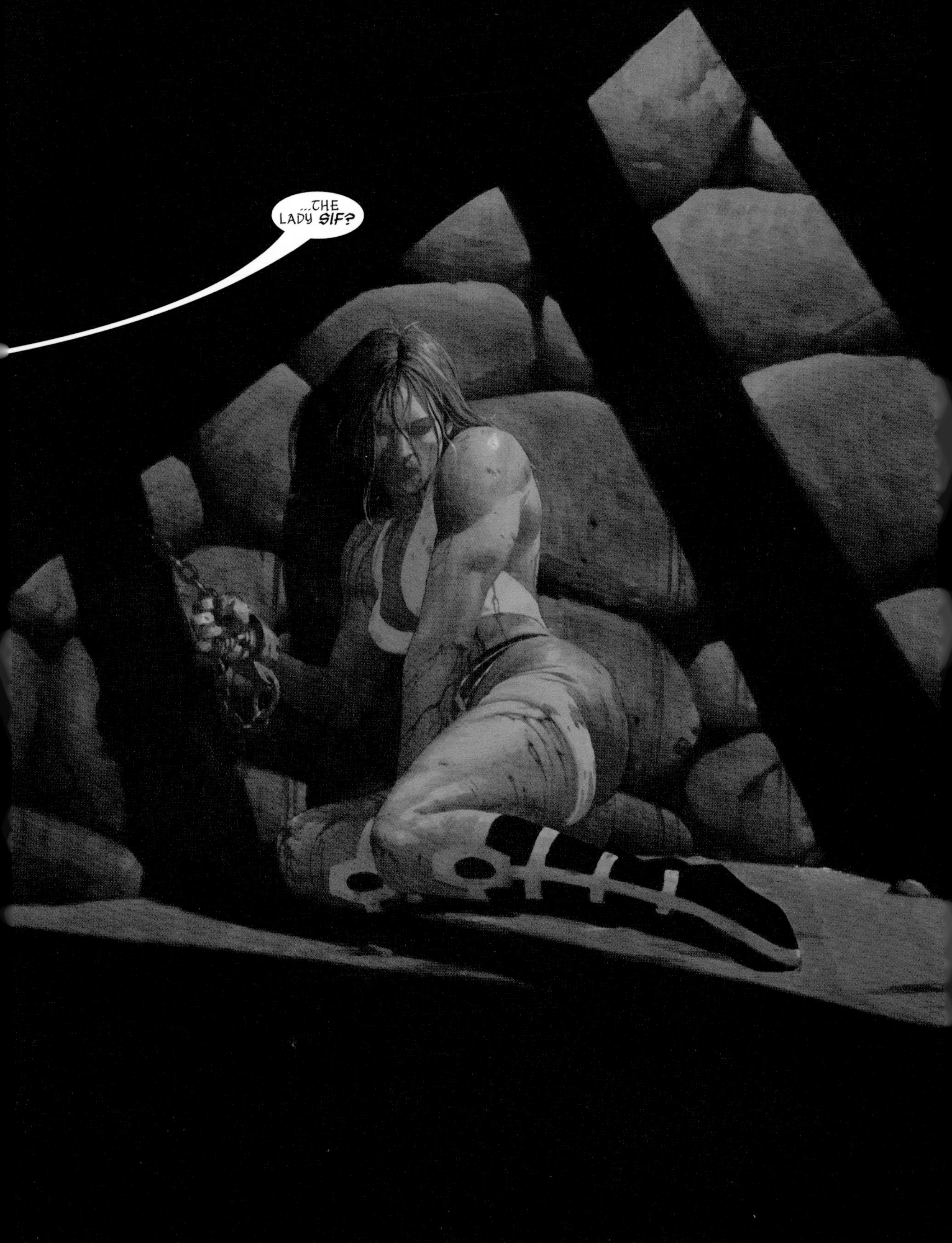
...THE LADY SIF?

# TWO

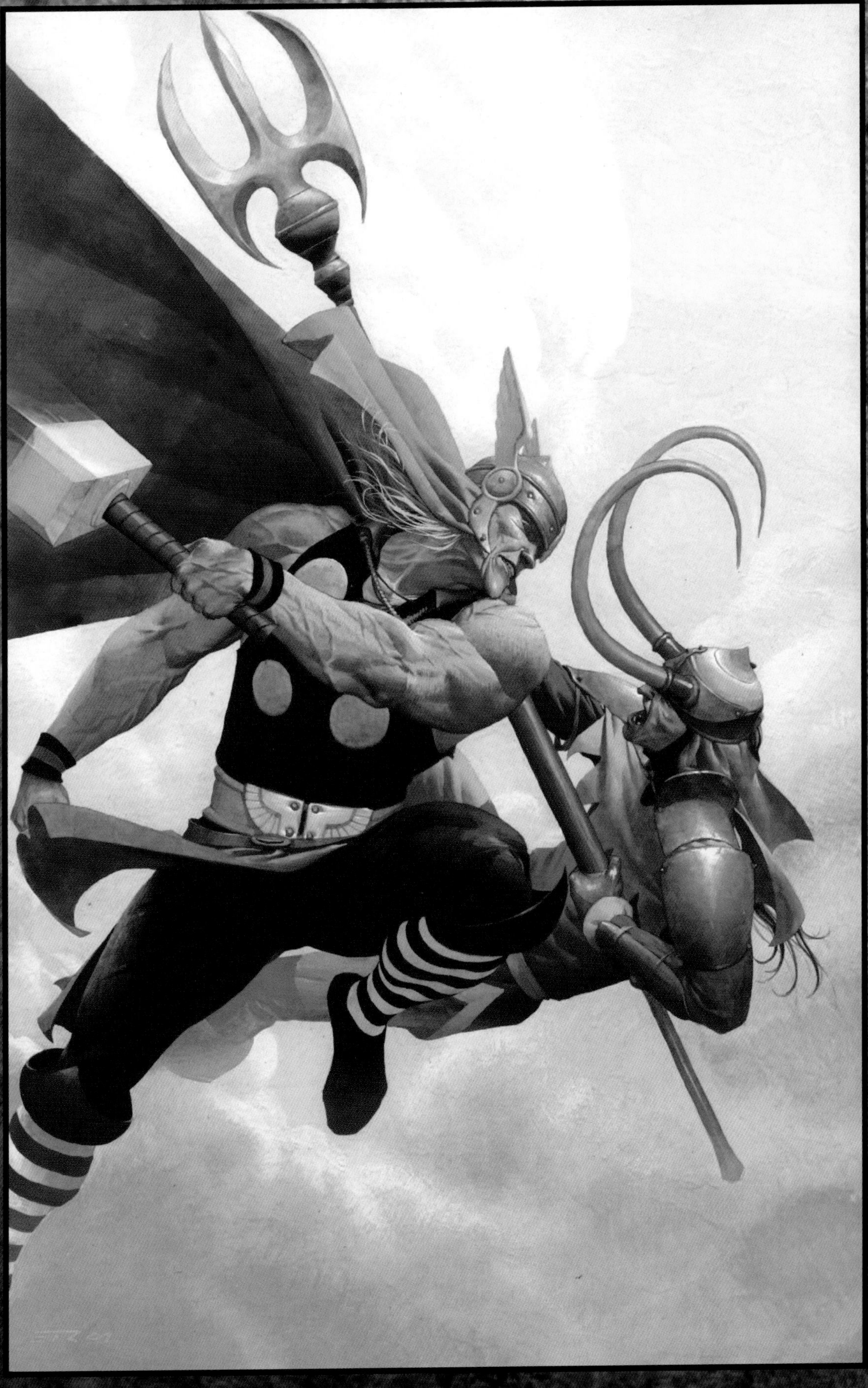

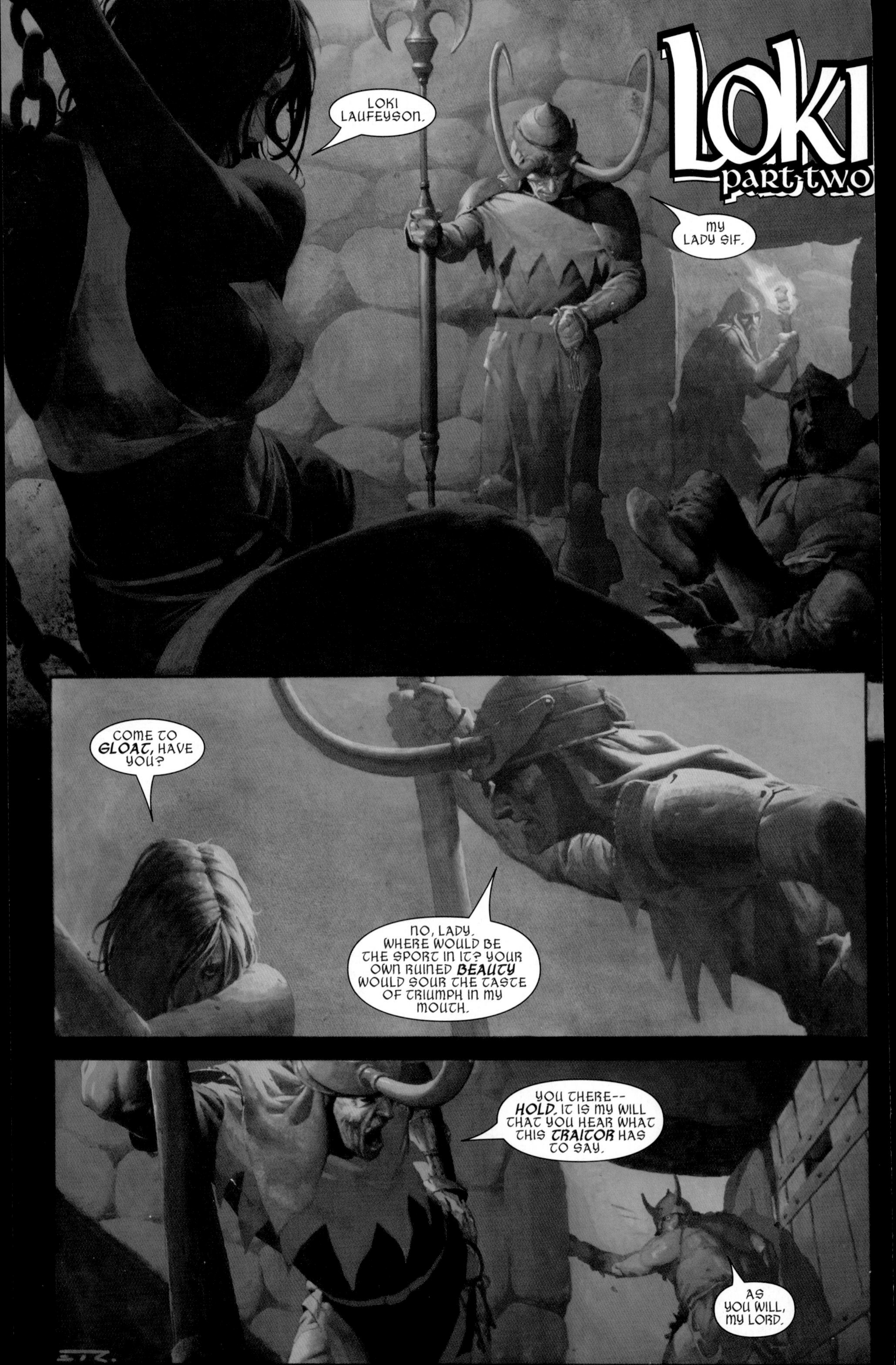
LOKI
part two
LOKI LAUFEYSON.
MY LADY SIF.
COME TO GLOAT, HAVE YOU?
NO, LADY. WHERE WOULD BE THE SPORT IN IT? YOUR OWN RUINED BEAUTY WOULD SOUR THE TASTE OF TRIUMPH IN MY MOUTH.
YOU THERE-- HOLD. IT IS MY WILL THAT YOU HEAR WHAT THIS TRAITOR HAS TO SAY.
AS YOU WILL, MY LORD.

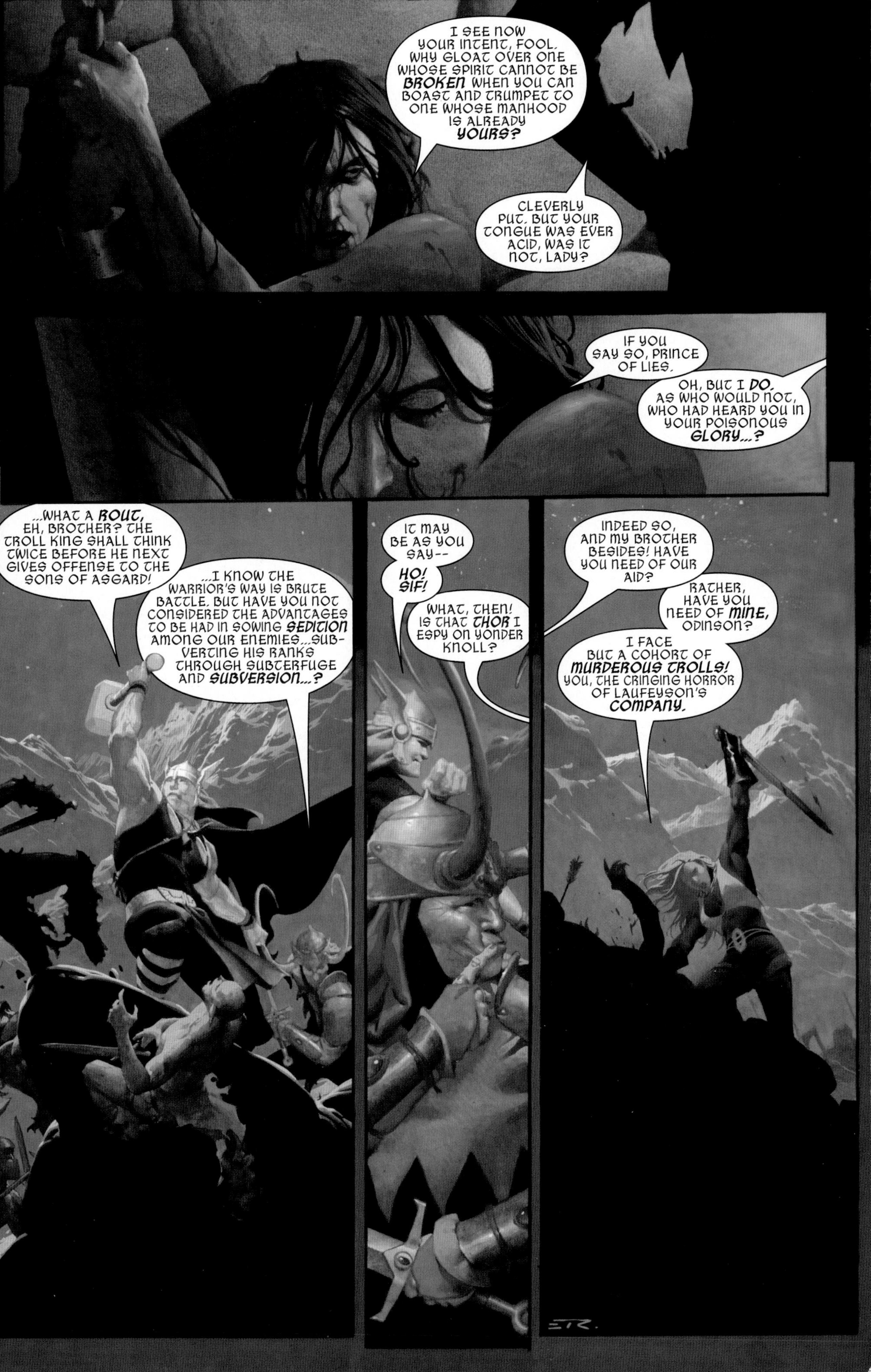
I SEE NOW YOUR INTENT, FOOL. WHY GLOAT OVER ONE WHOSE SPIRIT CANNOT BE BROKEN WHEN YOU CAN BOAST AND TRUMPET TO ONE WHOSE MANHOOD IS ALREADY YOURS?
CLEVERLY PUT. BUT YOUR TONGUE WAS EVER ACID, WAS IT NOT, LADY?
IF YOU SAY SO, PRINCE OF LIES.
OH, BUT I DO. AS WHO WOULD NOT, WHO HAD HEARD YOU IN YOUR POISONOUS GLORY...?
...WHAT A ROUT, EH, BROTHER? THE TROLL KING SHALL THINK TWICE BEFORE HE NEXT GIVES OFFENSE TO THE SONS OF ASGARD!
...I KNOW THE WARRIOR'S WAY IS BRUTE BATTLE. BUT HAVE YOU NOT CONSIDERED THE ADVANTAGES TO BE HAD IN SOWING SEDITION AMONG OUR ENEMIES...SUBVERTING HIS RANKS THROUGH SUBTERFUGE AND SUBVERSION...?
IT MAY BE AS YOU SAY--
HO! SIF!
WHAT, THEN! IS THAT THOR I ESPY ON YONDER KNOLL?
INDEED SO, AND MY BROTHER BESIDES! HAVE YOU NEED OF OUR AID?
RATHER, HAVE YOU NEED OF MINE, ODINSON?
I FACE BUT A COHORT OF MURDEROUS TROLLS! YOU, THE CRINGING HORROR OF LAUFEYSON'S COMPANY.
ETR.

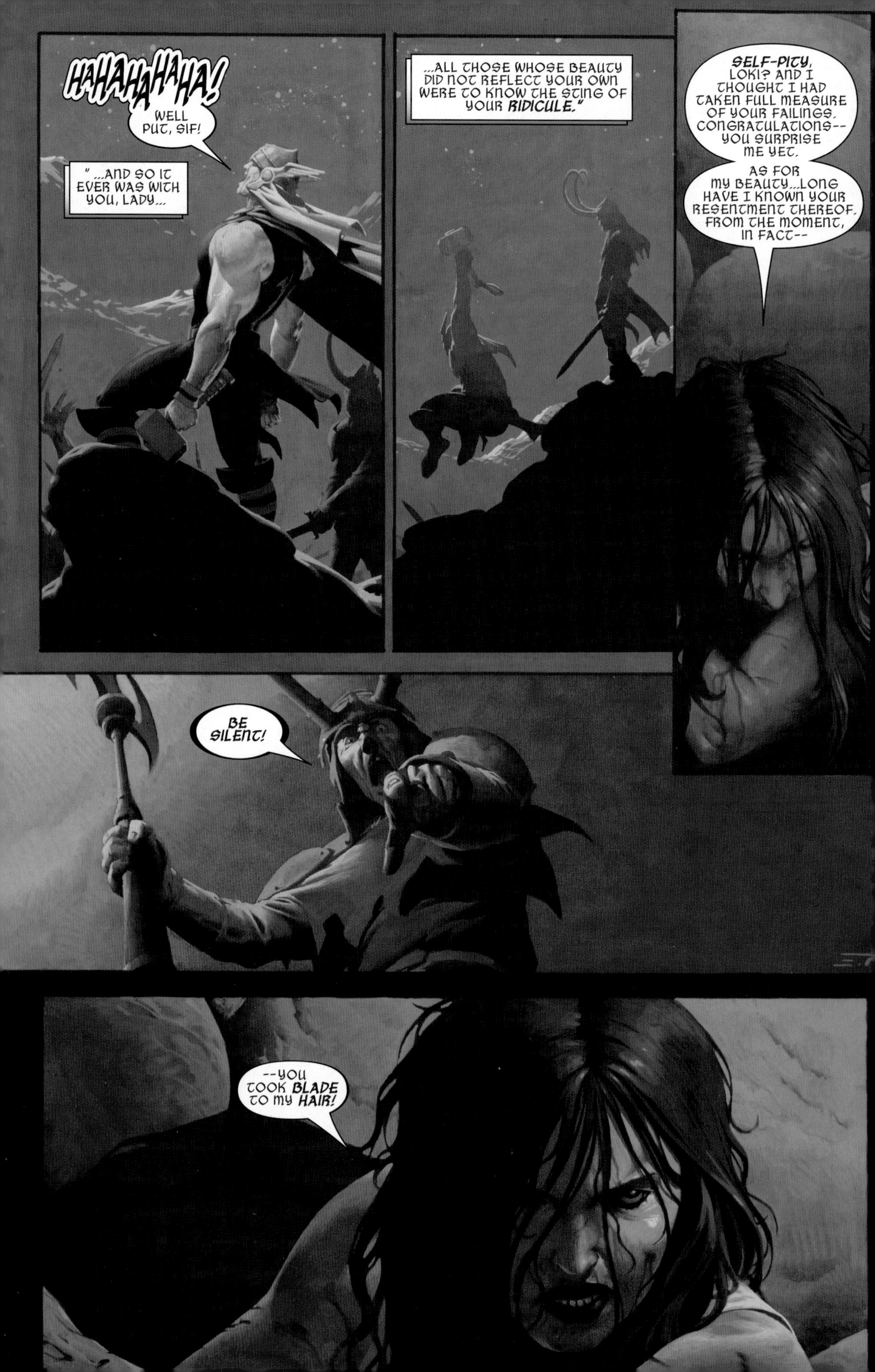
HAHAHAHAHA!
WELL PUT, SIF!
"...AND SO IT EVER WAS WITH YOU, LADY...
...ALL THOSE WHOSE BEAUTY DID NOT REFLECT YOUR OWN WERE TO KNOW THE STING OF YOUR RIDICULE."
SELF-PITY, LOKI? AND I THOUGHT I HAD TAKEN FULL MEASURE OF YOUR FAILINGS. CONGRATULATIONS-- YOU SURPRISE ME YET.
AS FOR MY BEAUTY...LONG HAVE I KNOWN YOUR RESENTMENT THEREOF. FROM THE MOMENT, IN FACT--
BE SILENT!
--YOU TOOK BLADE TO MY HAIR!

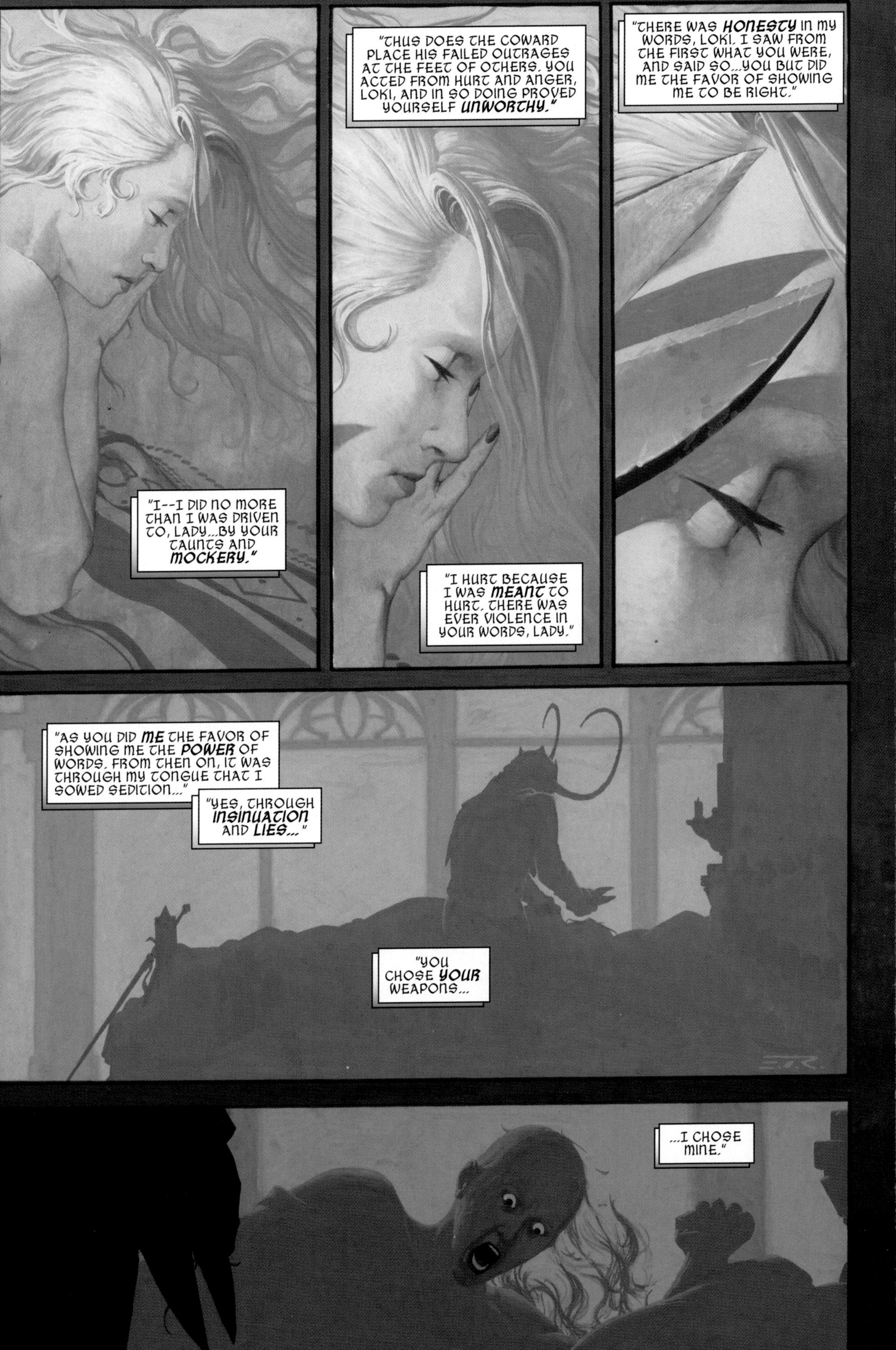
"I--I DID NO MORE THAN I WAS DRIVEN TO, LADY...BY YOUR TAUNTS AND MOCKERY."
"THUS DOES THE COWARD PLACE HIS FAILED OUTRAGES AT THE FEET OF OTHERS. YOU ACTED FROM HURT AND ANGER, LOKI, AND IN SO DOING PROVED YOURSELF UNWORTHY."
"I HURT BECAUSE I WAS MEANT TO HURT. THERE WAS EVER VIOLENCE IN YOUR WORDS, LADY."
"THERE WAS HONESTY IN MY WORDS, LOKI. I SAW FROM THE FIRST WHAT YOU WERE, AND SAID SO...YOU BUT DID ME THE FAVOR OF SHOWING ME TO BE RIGHT."
"AS YOU DID ME THE FAVOR OF SHOWING ME THE POWER OF WORDS. FROM THEN ON, IT WAS THROUGH MY TONGUE THAT I SOWED SEDITION..."
"YES, THROUGH INSINUATION AND LIES..."
"YOU CHOSE YOUR WEAPONS...
...I CHOSE MINE."

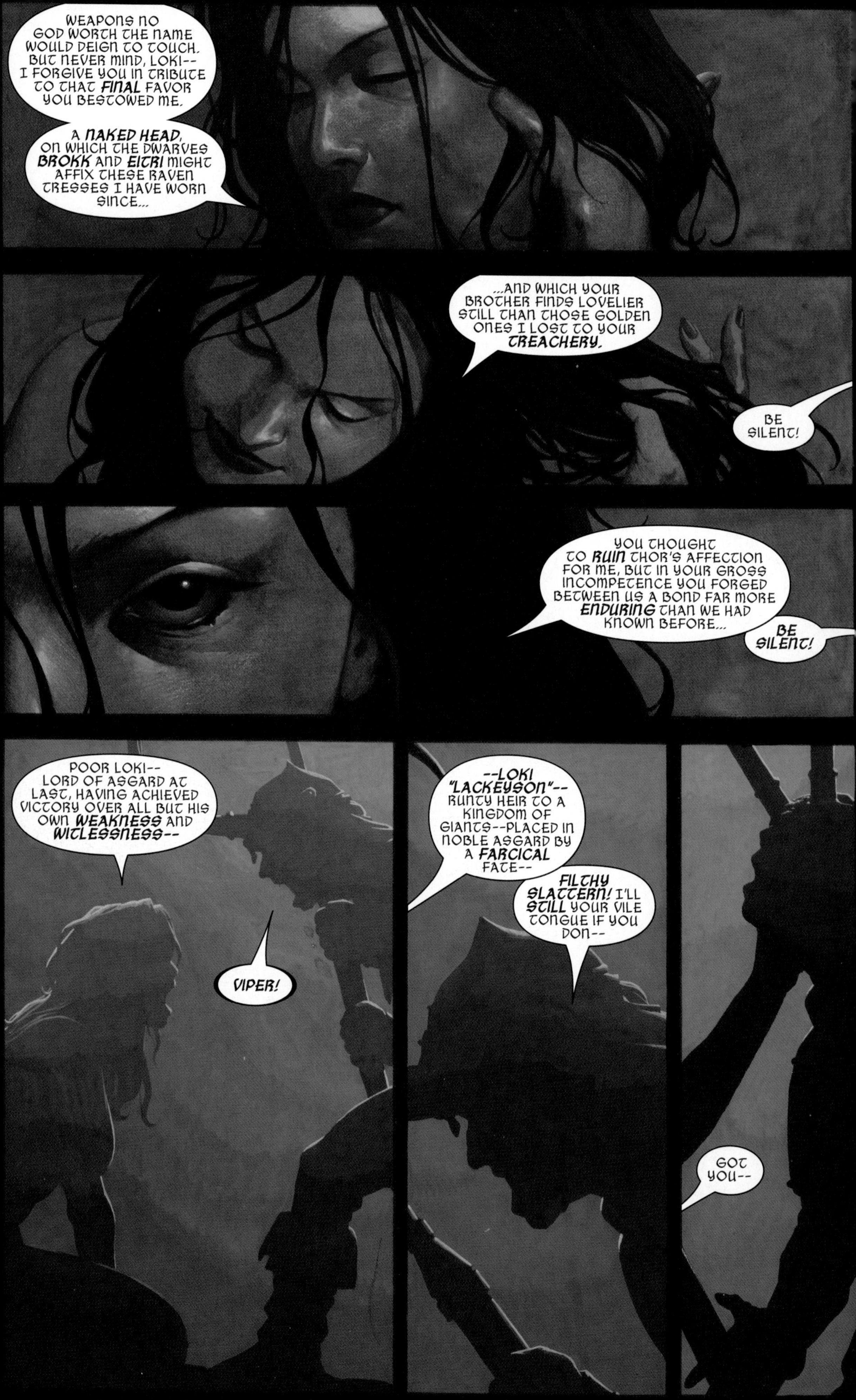
WEAPONS NO GOD WORTH THE NAME WOULD DEIGN TO TOUCH. BUT NEVER MIND, LOKI-- I FORGIVE YOU IN TRIBUTE TO THAT FINAL FAVOR YOU BESTOWED ME.
A NAKED HEAD, ON WHICH THE DWARVES BROKK AND EITRI MIGHT AFFIX THESE RAVEN TRESSES I HAVE WORN SINCE...
...AND WHICH YOUR BROTHER FINDS LOVELIER STILL THAN THOSE GOLDEN ONES I LOST TO YOUR TREACHERY.
BE SILENT!
YOU THOUGHT TO RUIN THOR'S AFFECTION FOR ME, BUT IN YOUR GROSS INCOMPETENCE YOU FORGED BETWEEN US A BOND FAR MORE ENDURING THAN WE HAD KNOWN BEFORE...
BE SILENT!
POOR LOKI-- LORD OF ASGARD AT LAST, HAVING ACHIEVED VICTORY OVER ALL BUT HIS OWN WEAKNESS AND WITLESSNESS--
VIPER!
--LOKI "LACKEYSON"-- RUNTY HEIR TO A KINGDOM OF GIANTS--PLACED IN NOBLE ASGARD BY A FARCICAL FATE--
FILTHY SLATTERN! I'LL STILL YOUR VILE TONGUE IF YOU DON--
GOT YOU--

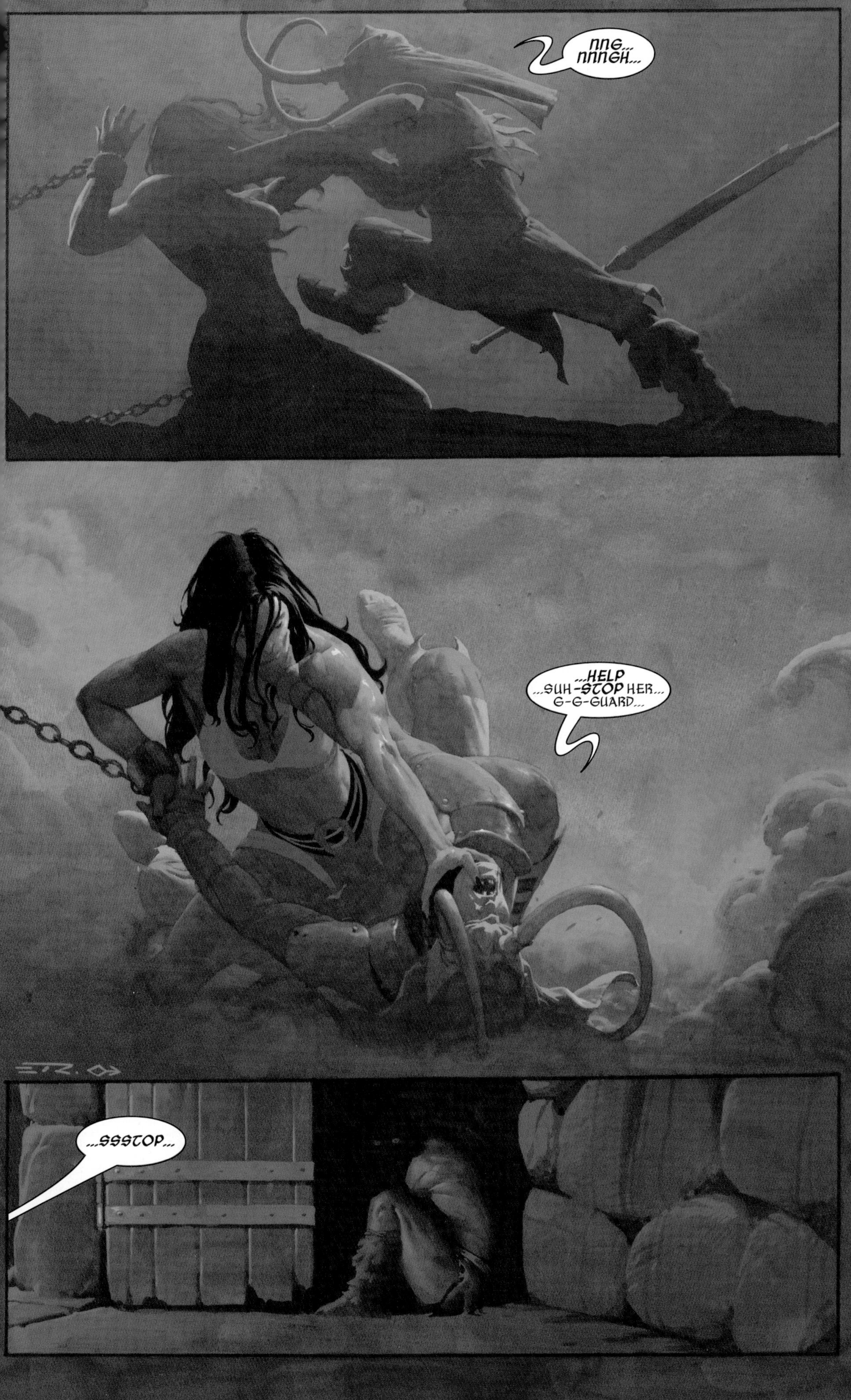
NNG... NNNGH...
...HELP ...SUH-STOP HER... G-G-GUARD...
...SSSTOP...

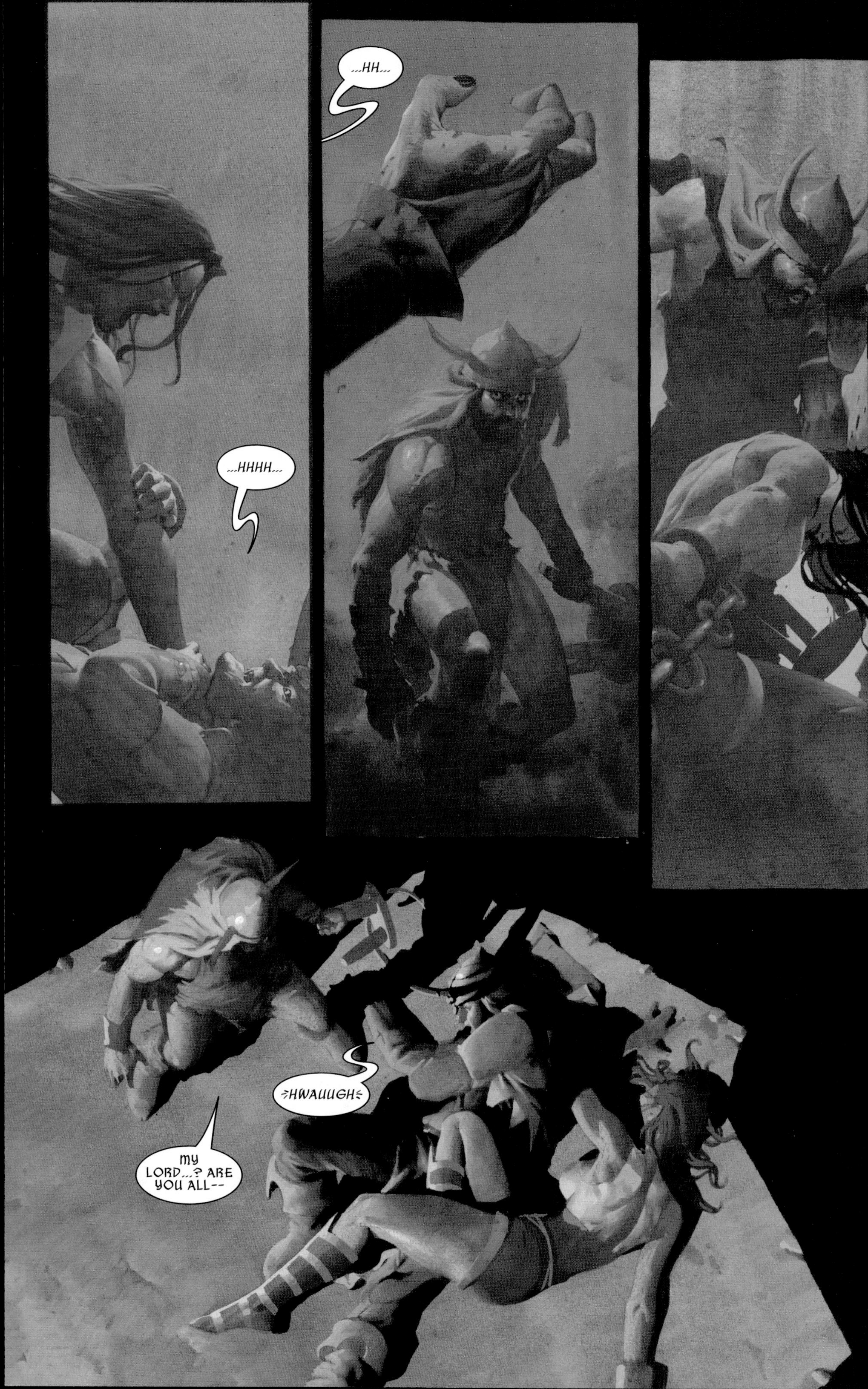
...HHHH...
...HH...
MY LORD...? ARE YOU ALL--
=HWAUUGH=

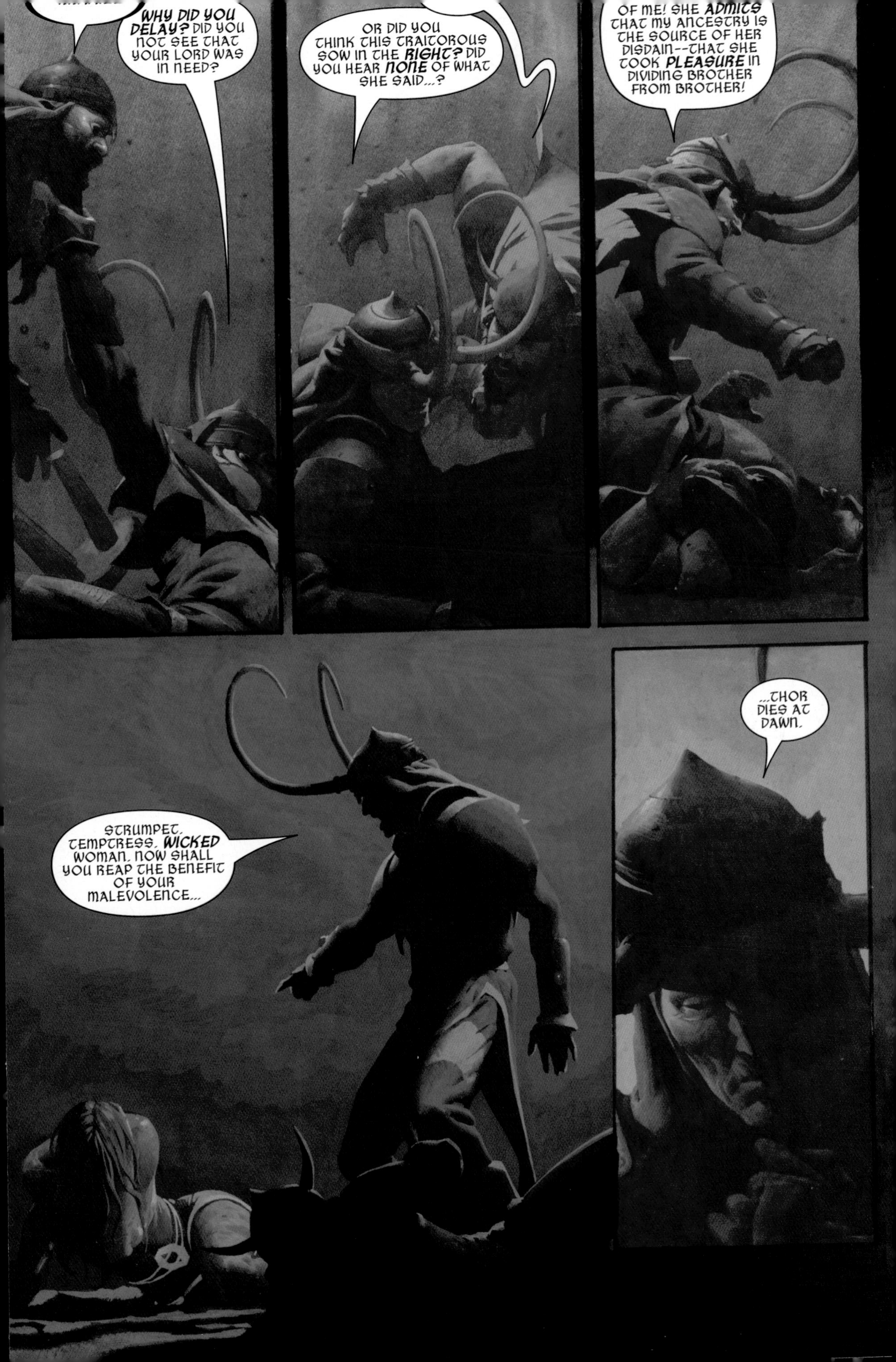
WHY DID YOU DELAY? DID YOU NOT SEE THAT YOUR LORD WAS IN NEED?
OR DID YOU THINK THIS TRAITOROUS SOW IN THE RIGHT? DID YOU HEAR NONE OF WHAT SHE SAID...?
OF ME! SHE ADMITS THAT MY ANCESTRY IS THE SOURCE OF HER DISDAIN--THAT SHE TOOK PLEASURE IN DIVIDING BROTHER FROM BROTHER!
STRUMPET. TEMPTRESS. WICKED WOMAN. NOW SHALL YOU REAP THE BENEFIT OF YOUR MALEVOLENCE...
...THOR DIES AT DAWN.

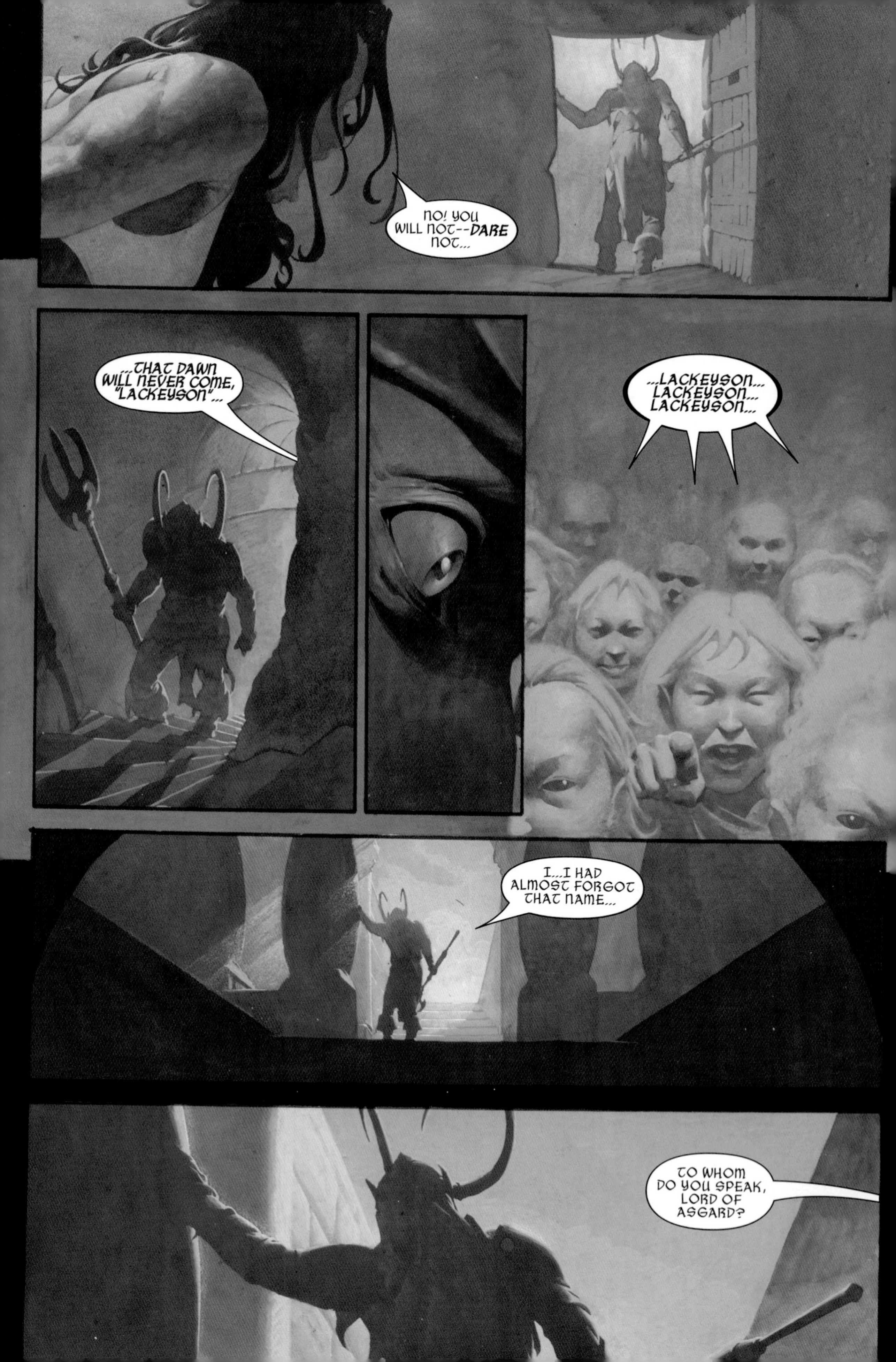
NO! YOU WILL NOT--DARE NOT...
...THAT DAWN WILL NEVER COME, "LACKEYSON"...
...LACKEYSON... LACKEYSON... LACKEYSON...
I...I HAD ALMOST FORGOT THAT NAME...
TO WHOM DO YOU SPEAK, LORD OF ASGARD?

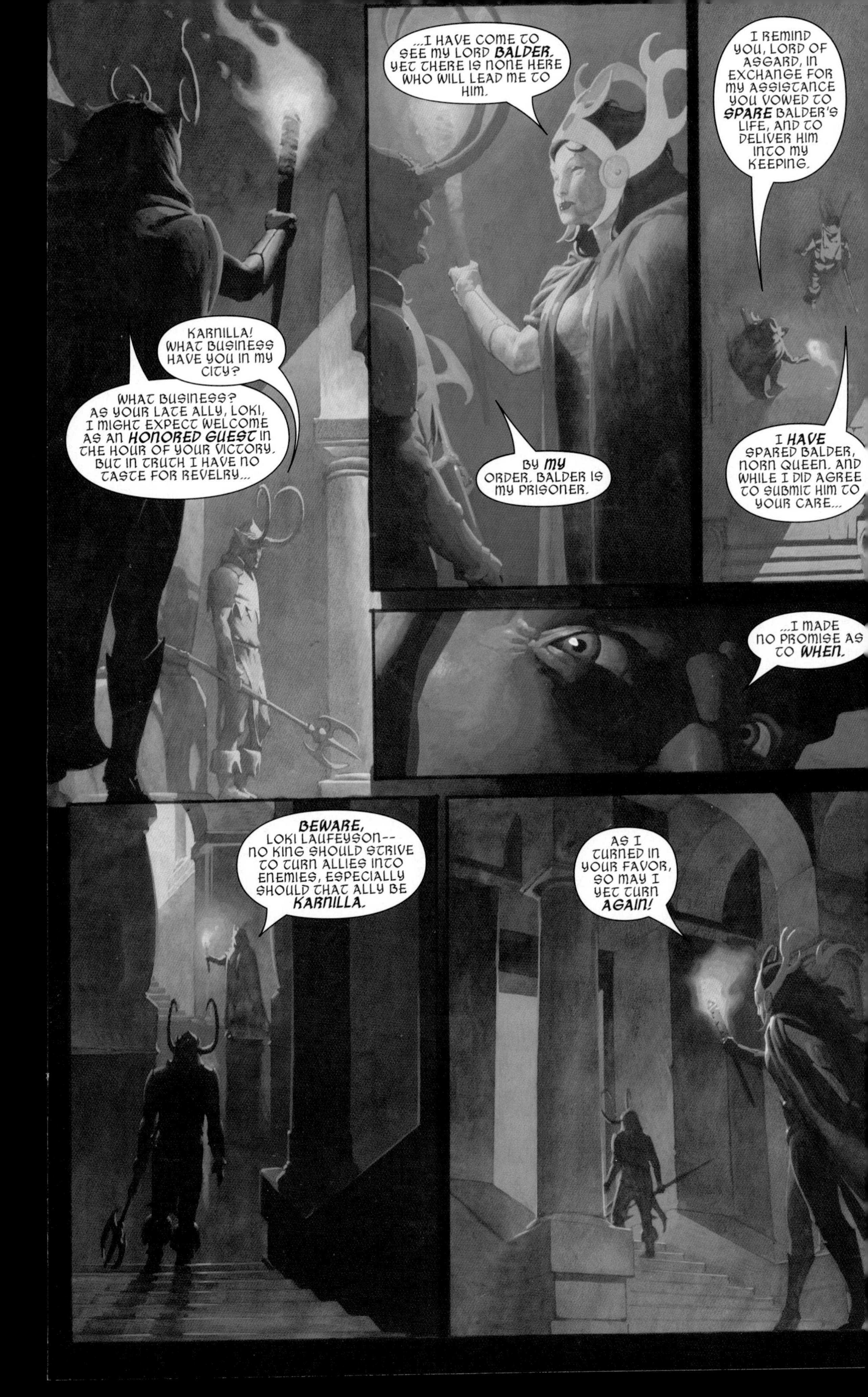
KARNILLA! WHAT BUSINESS HAVE YOU IN MY CITY?
WHAT BUSINESS? AS YOUR LATE ALLY, LOKI, I MIGHT EXPECT WELCOME AS AN HONORED GUEST IN THE HOUR OF YOUR VICTORY. BUT IN TRUTH I HAVE NO TASTE FOR REVELRY...
...I HAVE COME TO SEE MY LORD BALDER. YET THERE IS NONE HERE WHO WILL LEAD ME TO HIM.
BY MY ORDER. BALDER IS MY PRISONER.
I REMIND YOU, LORD OF ASGARD, IN EXCHANGE FOR MY ASSISTANCE YOU VOWED TO SPARE BALDER'S LIFE, AND TO DELIVER HIM INTO MY KEEPING.
I HAVE SPARED BALDER, NORN QUEEN. AND WHILE I DID AGREE TO SUBMIT HIM TO YOUR CARE...
...I MADE NO PROMISE AS TO WHEN.
BEWARE, LOKI LAUFEYSON-- NO KING SHOULD STRIVE TO TURN ALLIES INTO ENEMIES, ESPECIALLY SHOULD THAT ALLY BE KARNILLA.
AS I TURNED IN YOUR FAVOR, SO MAY I YET TURN AGAIN!

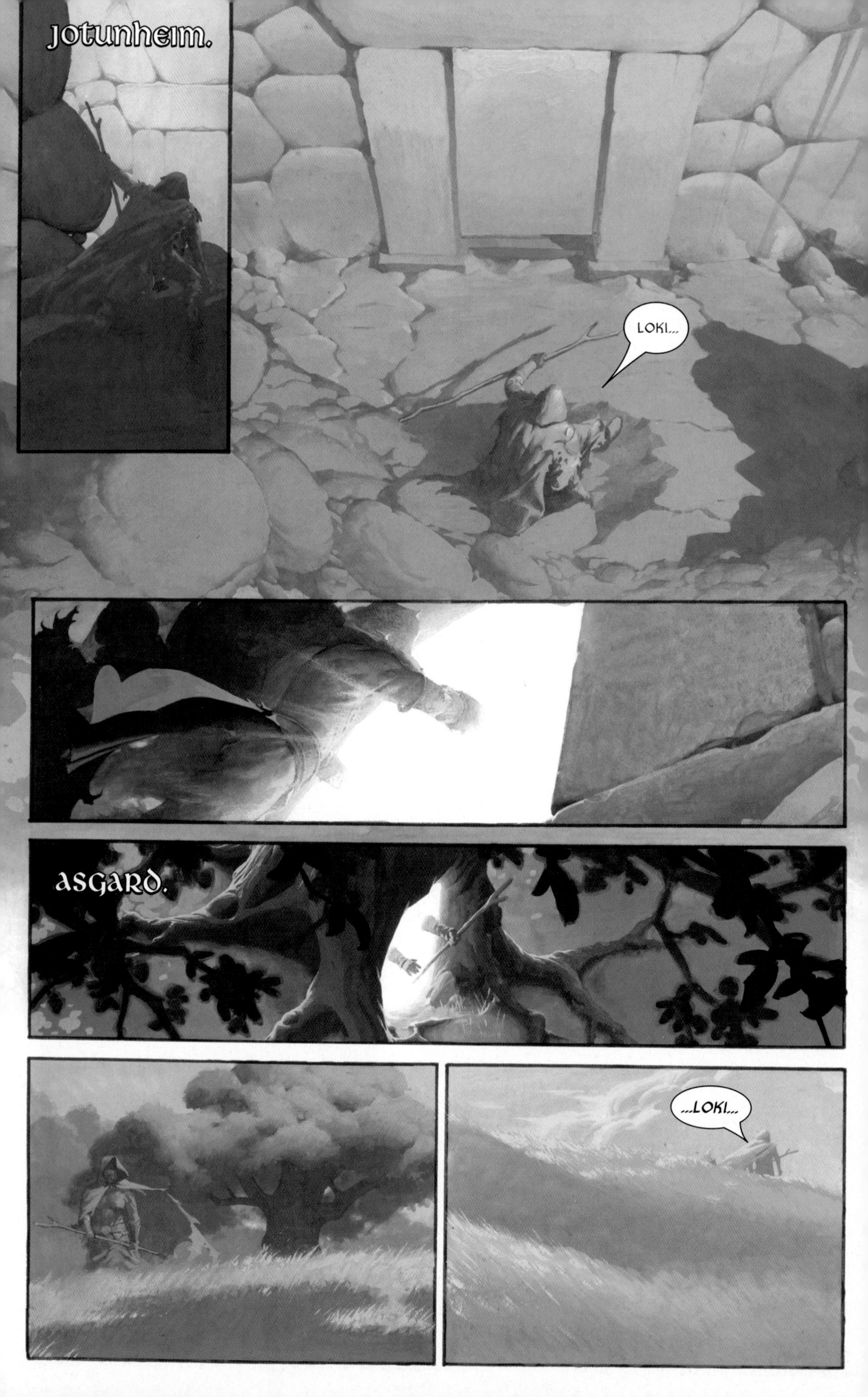
JOTUNHEIM.
LOKI...
ASGARD.
...LOKI...

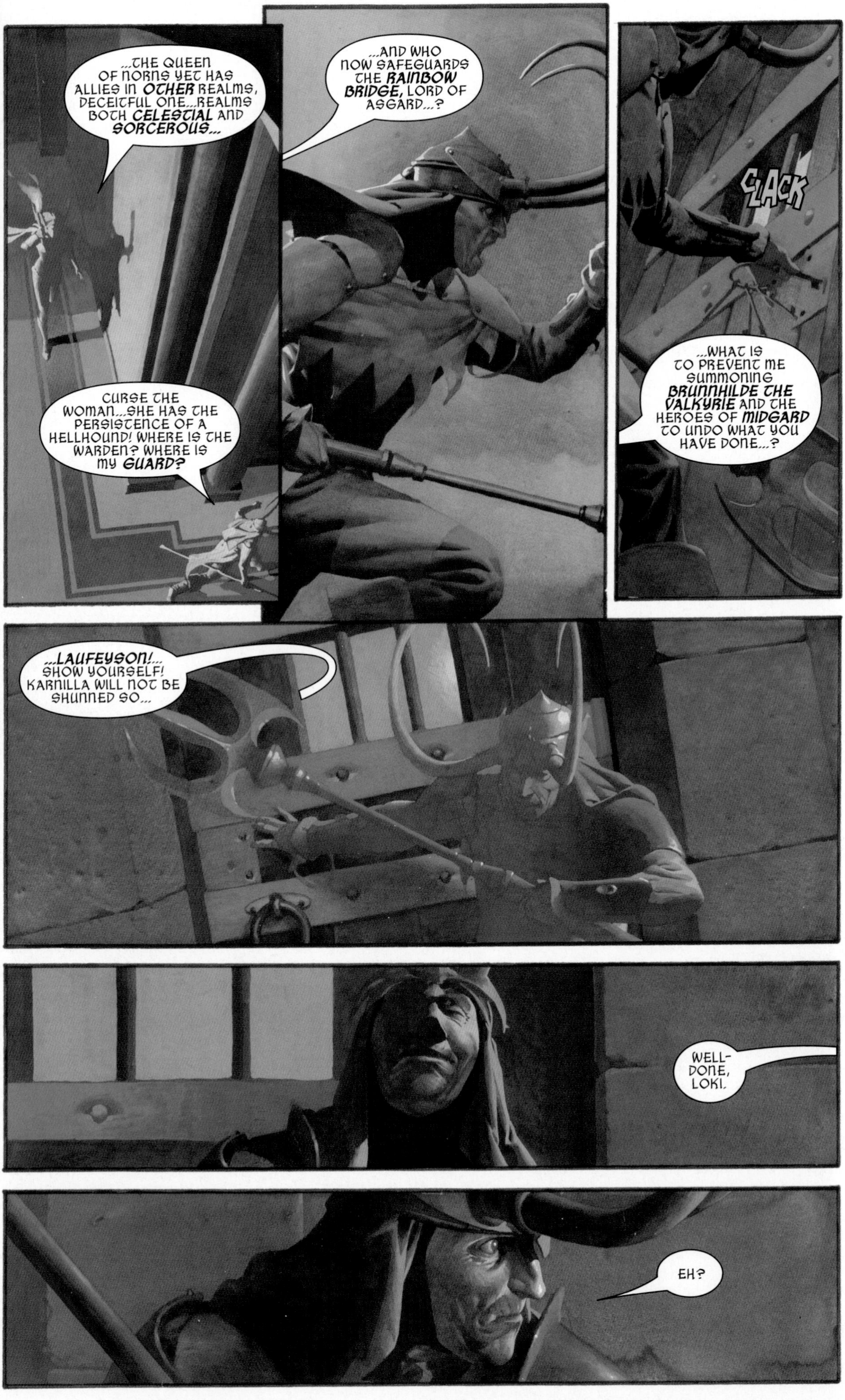
...THE QUEEN OF NORNS YET HAS ALLIES IN OTHER REALMS, DECEITFUL ONE...REALMS BOTH CELESTIAL AND SORCEROUS...
CURSE THE WOMAN...SHE HAS THE PERSISTENCE OF A HELLHOUND! WHERE IS THE WARDEN? WHERE IS MY GUARD?
...AND WHO NOW SAFEGUARDS THE RAINBOW BRIDGE, LORD OF ASGARD...?
CLACK
...WHAT IS TO PREVENT ME SUMMONING BRUNNHILDE THE VALKYRIE AND THE HEROES OF MIDGARD TO UNDO WHAT YOU HAVE DONE...?
...LAUFEYSON!... SHOW YOURSELF! KARNILLA WILL NOT BE SHUNNED SO...
WELL-DONE, LOKI.
EH?

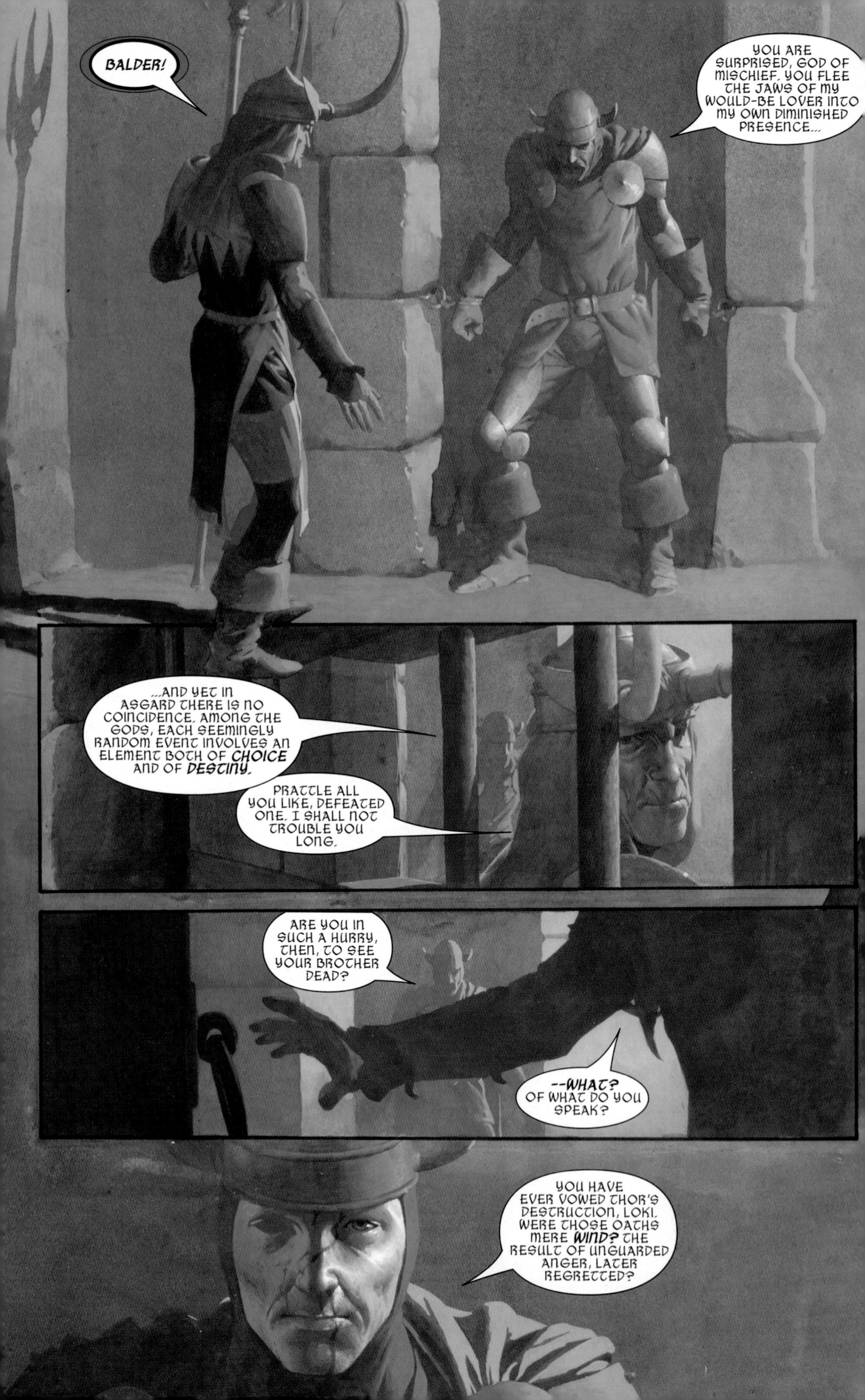
BALDER!
YOU ARE SURPRISED, GOD OF MISCHIEF. YOU FLEE THE JAWS OF MY WOULD-BE LOVER INTO MY OWN DIMINISHED PRESENCE...
...AND YET IN ASGARD THERE IS NO COINCIDENCE. AMONG THE GODS, EACH SEEMINGLY RANDOM EVENT INVOLVES AN ELEMENT BOTH OF CHOICE AND OF DESTINY.
PRATTLE ALL YOU LIKE, DEFEATED ONE. I SHALL NOT TROUBLE YOU LONG.
ARE YOU IN SUCH A HURRY, THEN, TO SEE YOUR BROTHER DEAD?
--WHAT? OF WHAT DO YOU SPEAK?
YOU HAVE EVER VOWED THOR'S DESTRUCTION, LOKI. WERE THOSE OATHS MERE WIND? THE RESULT OF UNGUARDED ANGER, LATER REGRETTED?

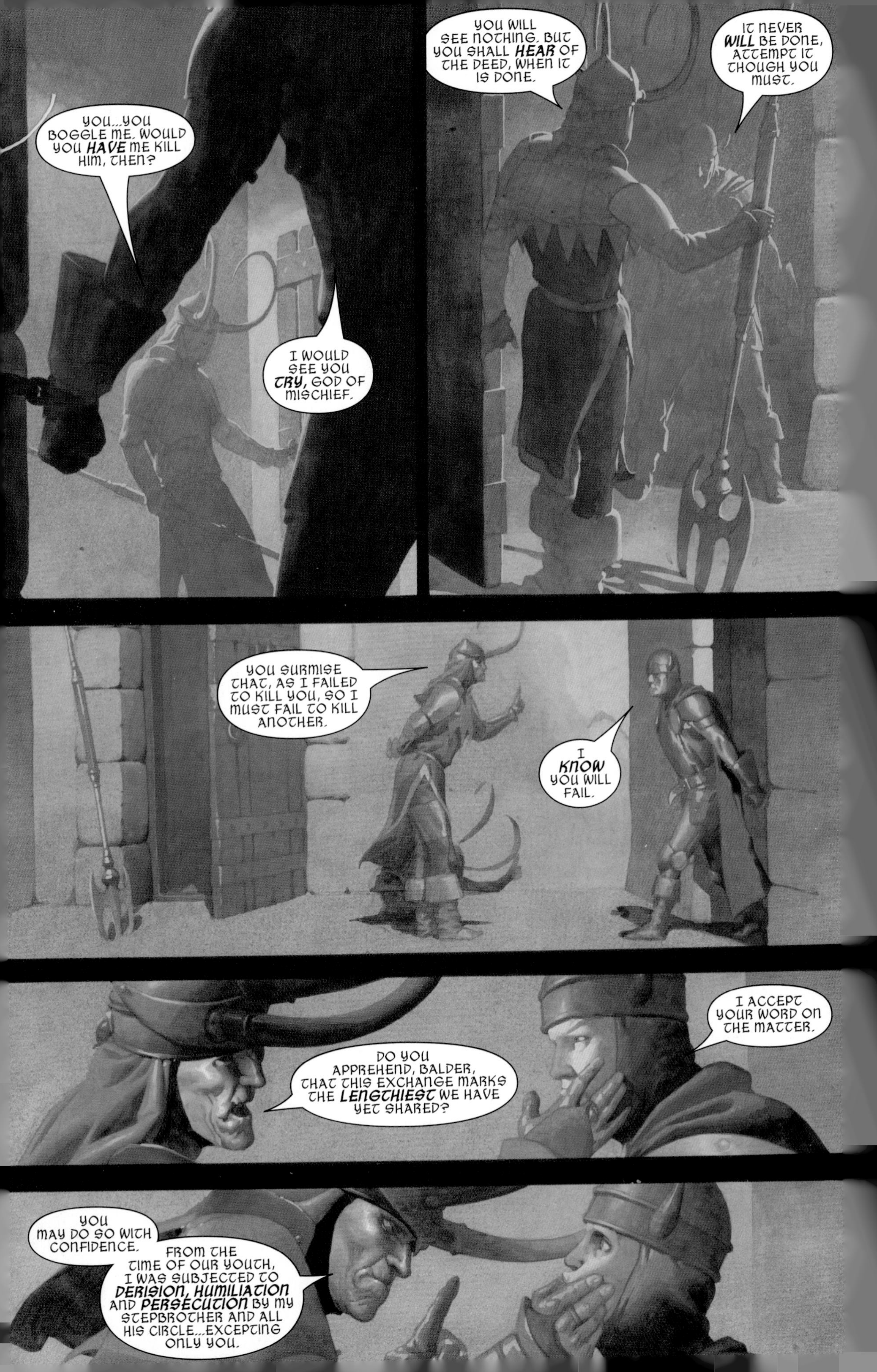
YOU...YOU BOGGLE ME. WOULD YOU HAVE ME KILL HIM, THEN?
I WOULD SEE YOU TRY, GOD OF MISCHIEF.
YOU WILL SEE NOTHING. BUT YOU SHALL HEAR OF THE DEED, WHEN IT IS DONE.
IT NEVER WILL BE DONE, ATTEMPT IT THOUGH YOU MUST.
YOU SURMISE THAT, AS I FAILED TO KILL YOU, SO I MUST FAIL TO KILL ANOTHER.
I KNOW YOU WILL FAIL.
DO YOU APPREHEND, BALDER, THAT THIS EXCHANGE MARKS THE LENGTHIEST WE HAVE YET SHARED?
I ACCEPT YOUR WORD ON THE MATTER.
YOU MAY DO SO WITH CONFIDENCE.
FROM THE TIME OF OUR YOUTH, I WAS SUBJECTED TO DERISION, HUMILIATION AND PERSECUTION BY MY STEPBROTHER AND ALL HIS CIRCLE...EXCEPTING ONLY YOU.

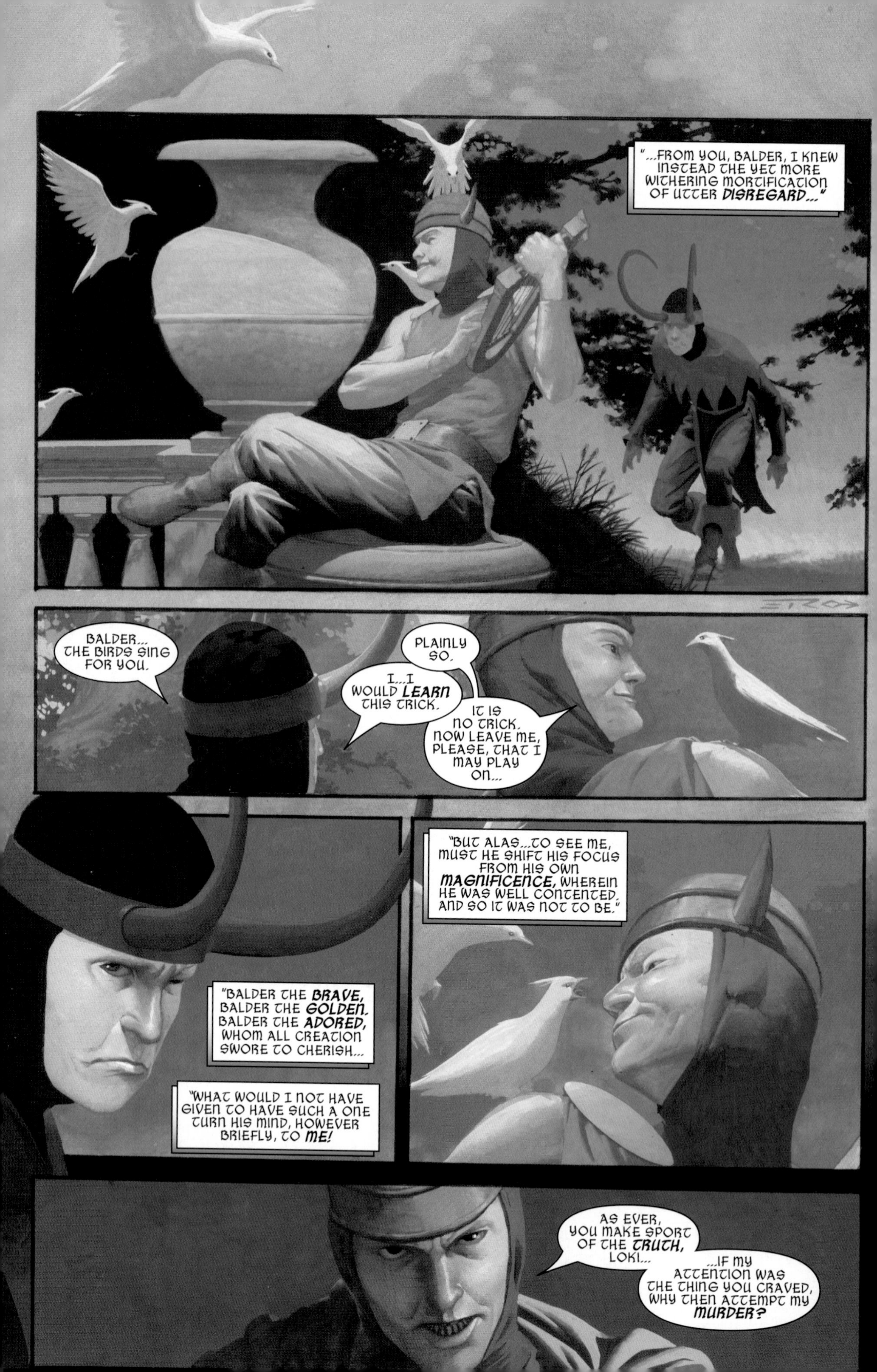
"...FROM YOU, BALDER, I KNEW INSTEAD THE YET MORE WITHERING MORTIFICATION OF UTTER DISREGARD..."
BALDER... THE BIRDS SING FOR YOU.
PLAINLY SO.
I...I WOULD LEARN THIS TRICK.
IT IS NO TRICK. NOW LEAVE ME, PLEASE, THAT I MAY PLAY ON...
"BALDER THE BRAVE, BALDER THE GOLDEN, BALDER THE ADORED, WHOM ALL CREATION SWORE TO CHERISH...
"WHAT WOULD I NOT HAVE GIVEN TO HAVE SUCH A ONE TURN HIS MIND, HOWEVER BRIEFLY, TO ME!
"BUT ALAS...TO SEE ME, MUST HE SHIFT HIS FOCUS FROM HIS OWN MAGNIFICENCE, WHEREIN HE WAS WELL CONTENTED. AND SO IT WAS NOT TO BE."
AS EVER, YOU MAKE SPORT OF THE TRUTH, LOKI...
...IF MY ATTENTION WAS THE THING YOU CRAVED, WHY THEN ATTEMPT MY MURDER?

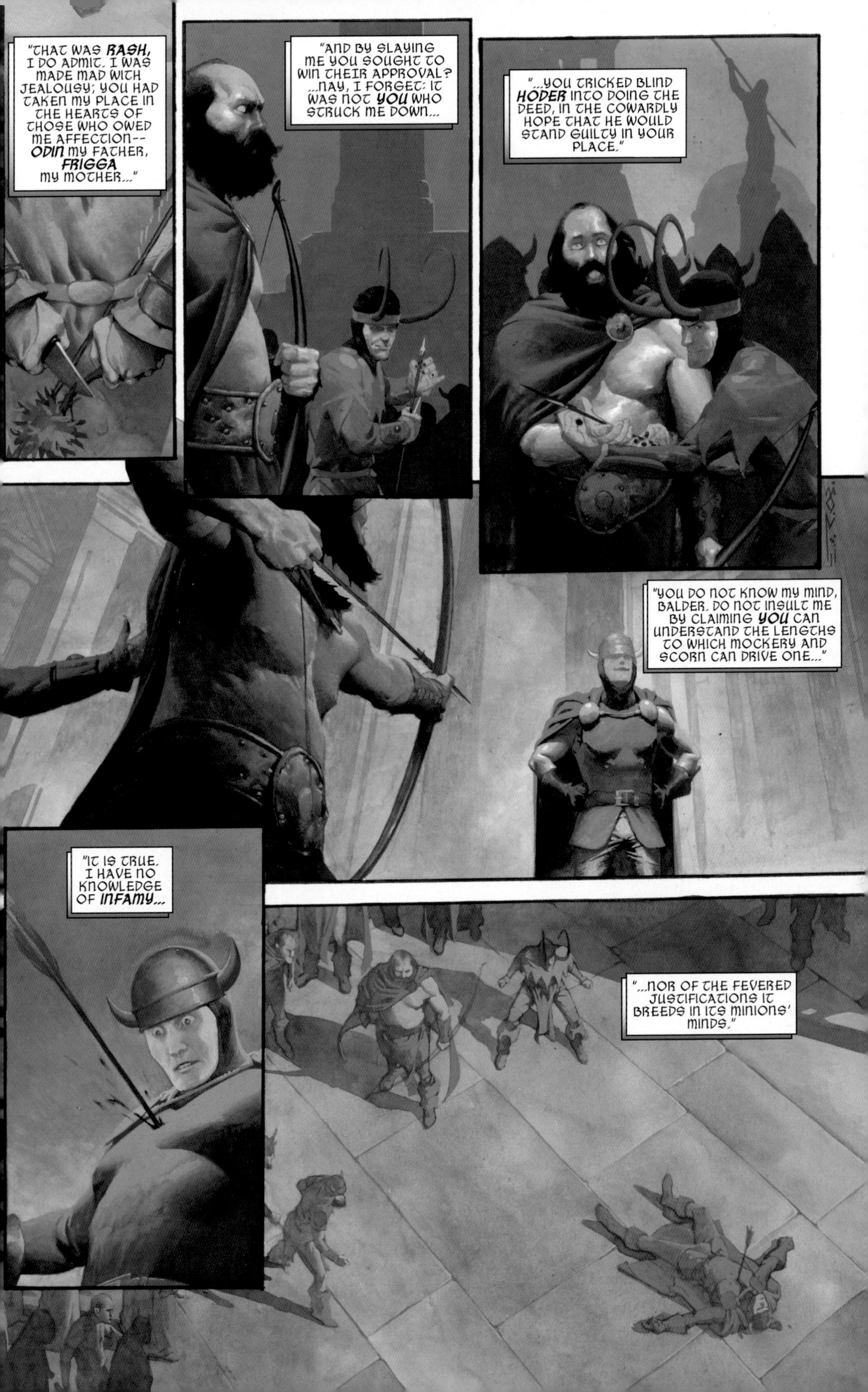

"THAT WAS RASH, I DO ADMIT. I WAS MADE MAD WITH JEALOUSY; YOU HAD TAKEN MY PLACE IN THE HEARTS OF THOSE WHO OWED ME AFFECTION-- ODIN MY FATHER, FRIGGA MY MOTHER..."
"AND BY SLAYING ME YOU SOUGHT TO WIN THEIR APPROVAL? ...NAY, I FORGET: IT WAS NOT YOU WHO STRUCK ME DOWN...
"...YOU TRICKED BLIND HODER INTO DOING THE DEED, IN THE COWARDLY HOPE THAT HE WOULD STAND GUILTY IN YOUR PLACE."
"YOU DO NOT KNOW MY MIND, BALDER. DO NOT INSULT ME BY CLAIMING YOU CAN UNDERSTAND THE LENGTHS TO WHICH MOCKERY AND SCORN CAN DRIVE ONE..."
"IT IS TRUE. I HAVE NO KNOWLEDGE OF INFAMY...
"...NOR OF THE FEVERED JUSTIFICATIONS IT BREEDS IN ITS MINIONS' MINDS."

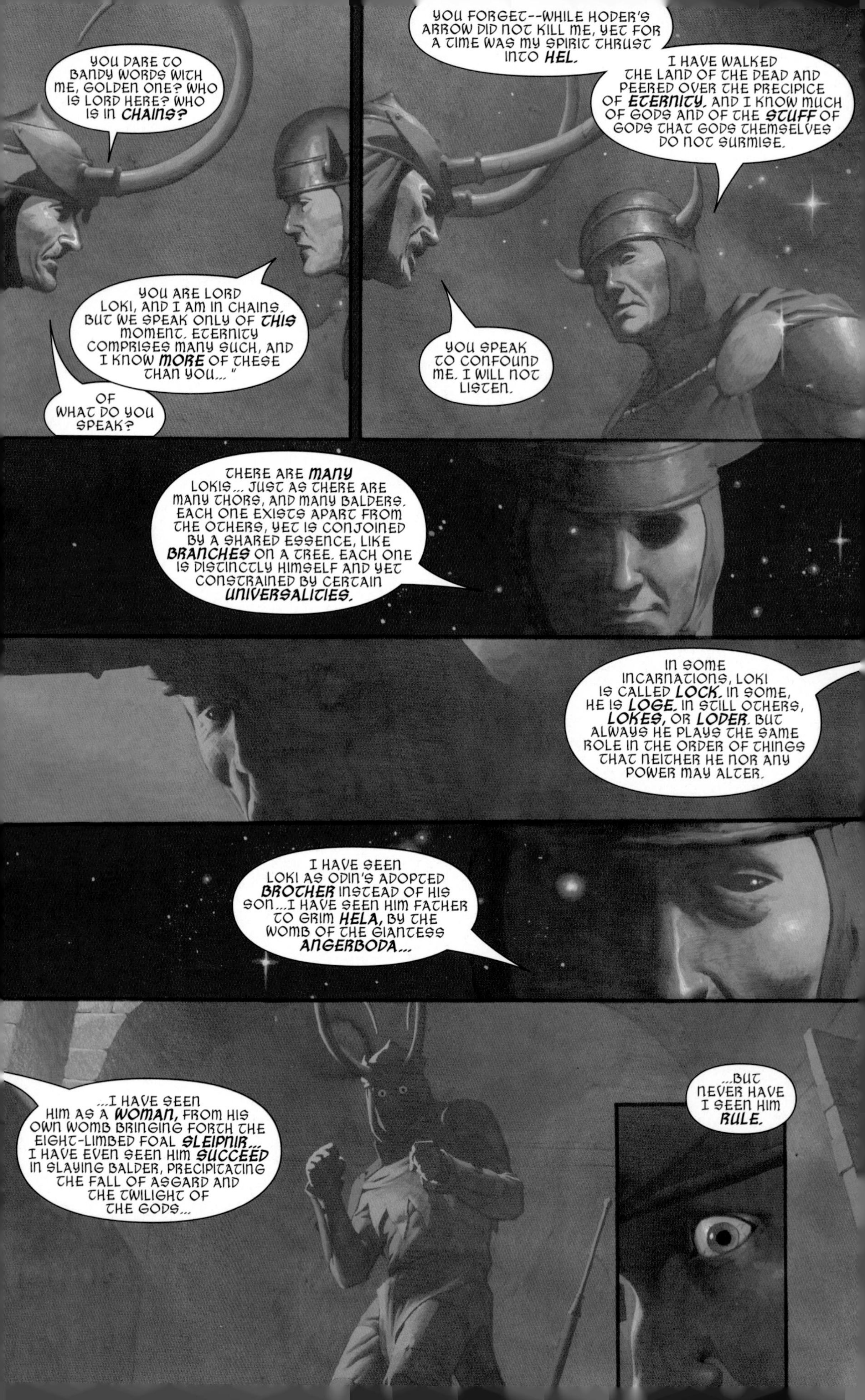
YOU DARE TO BANDY WORDS WITH ME, GOLDEN ONE? WHO IS LORD HERE? WHO IS IN CHAINS?
YOU ARE LORD LOKI, AND I AM IN CHAINS. BUT WE SPEAK ONLY OF THIS MOMENT. ETERNITY COMPRISES MANY SUCH, AND I KNOW MORE OF THESE THAN YOU... "
OF WHAT DO YOU SPEAK?
YOU FORGET--WHILE HODER'S ARROW DID NOT KILL ME, YET FOR A TIME WAS MY SPIRIT THRUST INTO HEL.
I HAVE WALKED THE LAND OF THE DEAD AND PEERED OVER THE PRECIPICE OF ETERNITY. AND I KNOW MUCH OF GODS AND OF THE STUFF OF GODS THAT GODS THEMSELVES DO NOT SURMISE.
YOU SPEAK TO CONFOUND ME. I WILL NOT LISTEN.
THERE ARE MANY LOKIS... JUST AS THERE ARE MANY THORS, AND MANY BALDERS. EACH ONE EXISTS APART FROM THE OTHERS, YET IS CONJOINED BY A SHARED ESSENCE, LIKE BRANCHES ON A TREE. EACH ONE IS DISTINCTLY HIMSELF AND YET CONSTRAINED BY CERTAIN UNIVERSALITIES.
IN SOME INCARNATIONS, LOKI IS CALLED LOCK. IN SOME, HE IS LOGE. IN STILL OTHERS, LOKES, OR LODER. BUT ALWAYS HE PLAYS THE SAME ROLE IN THE ORDER OF THINGS THAT NEITHER HE NOR ANY POWER MAY ALTER.
I HAVE SEEN LOKI AS ODIN'S ADOPTED BROTHER INSTEAD OF HIS SON...I HAVE SEEN HIM FATHER TO GRIM HELA, BY THE WOMB OF THE GIANTESS ANGERBODA...
...I HAVE SEEN HIM AS A WOMAN, FROM HIS OWN WOMB BRINGING FORTH THE EIGHT-LIMBED FOAL SLEIPNIR... I HAVE EVEN SEEN HIM SUCCEED IN SLAYING BALDER, PRECIPITATING THE FALL OF ASGARD AND THE TWILIGHT OF THE GODS...
...BUT NEVER HAVE I SEEN HIM RULE.

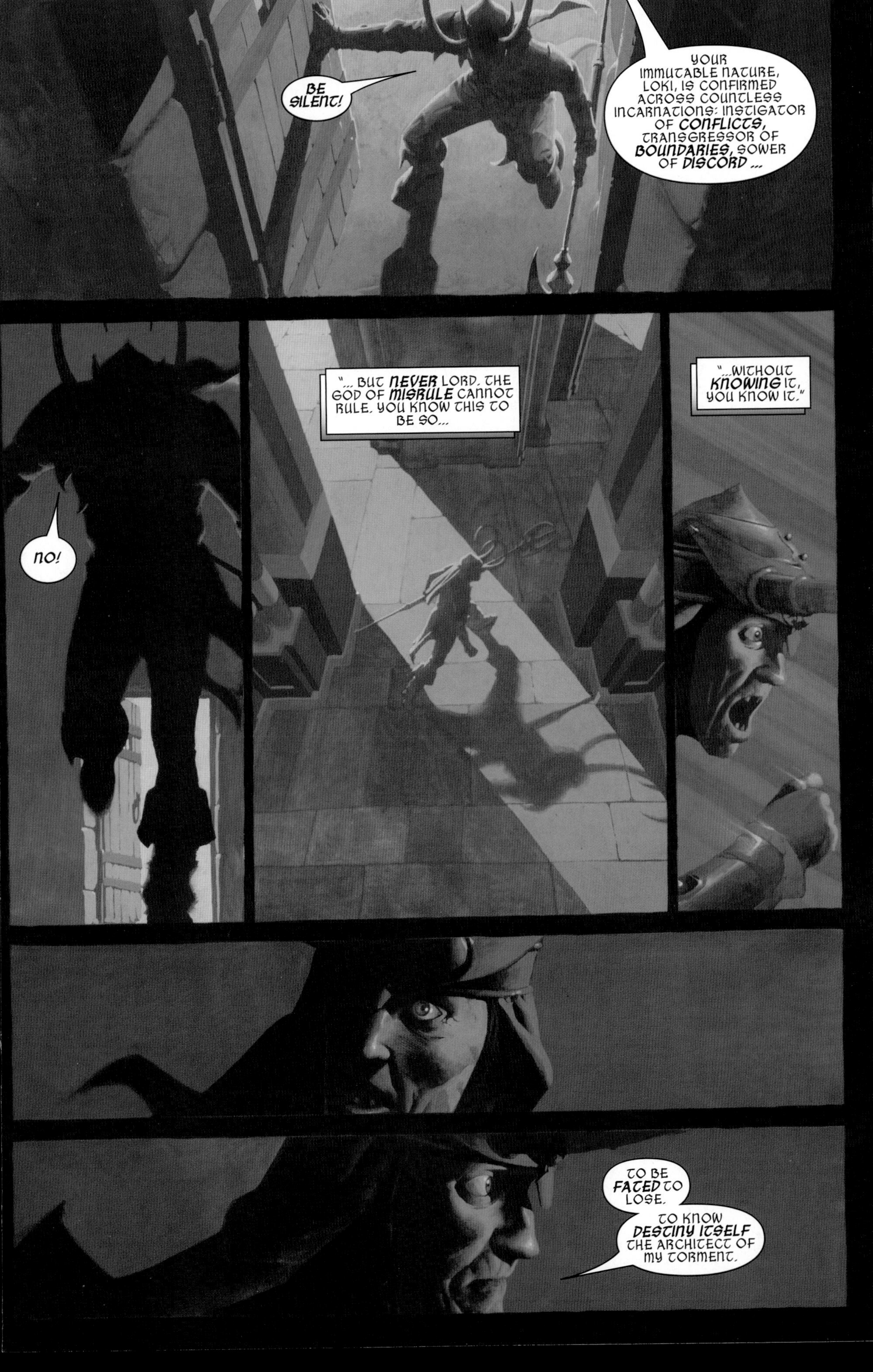
BE SILENT!
YOUR IMMUTABLE NATURE, LOKI, IS CONFIRMED ACROSS COUNTLESS INCARNATIONS: INSTIGATOR OF CONFLICTS, TRANSGRESSOR OF BOUNDARIES, SOWER OF DISCORD ...
NO!
"... BUT NEVER LORD. THE GOD OF MISRULE CANNOT RULE. YOU KNOW THIS TO BE SO...
"...WITHOUT KNOWING IT, YOU KNOW IT."
TO BE FATED TO LOSE.
TO KNOW DESTINY ITSELF THE ARCHITECT OF MY TORMENT.

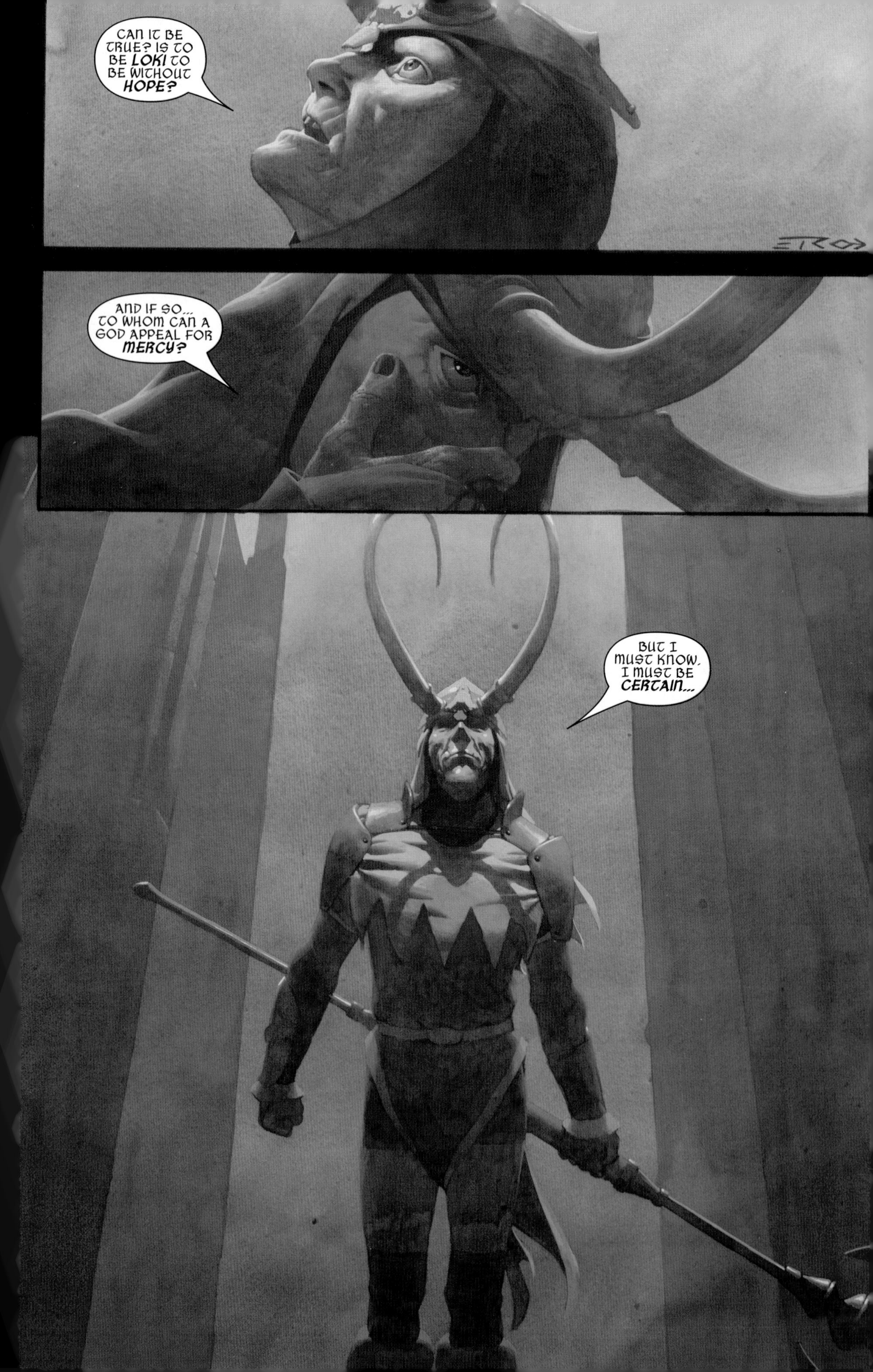
CAN IT BE TRUE? IS TO BE LOKI TO BE WITHOUT HOPE?
AND IF SO... TO WHOM CAN A GOD APPEAL FOR MERCY?
BUT I MUST KNOW. I MUST BE CERTAIN...

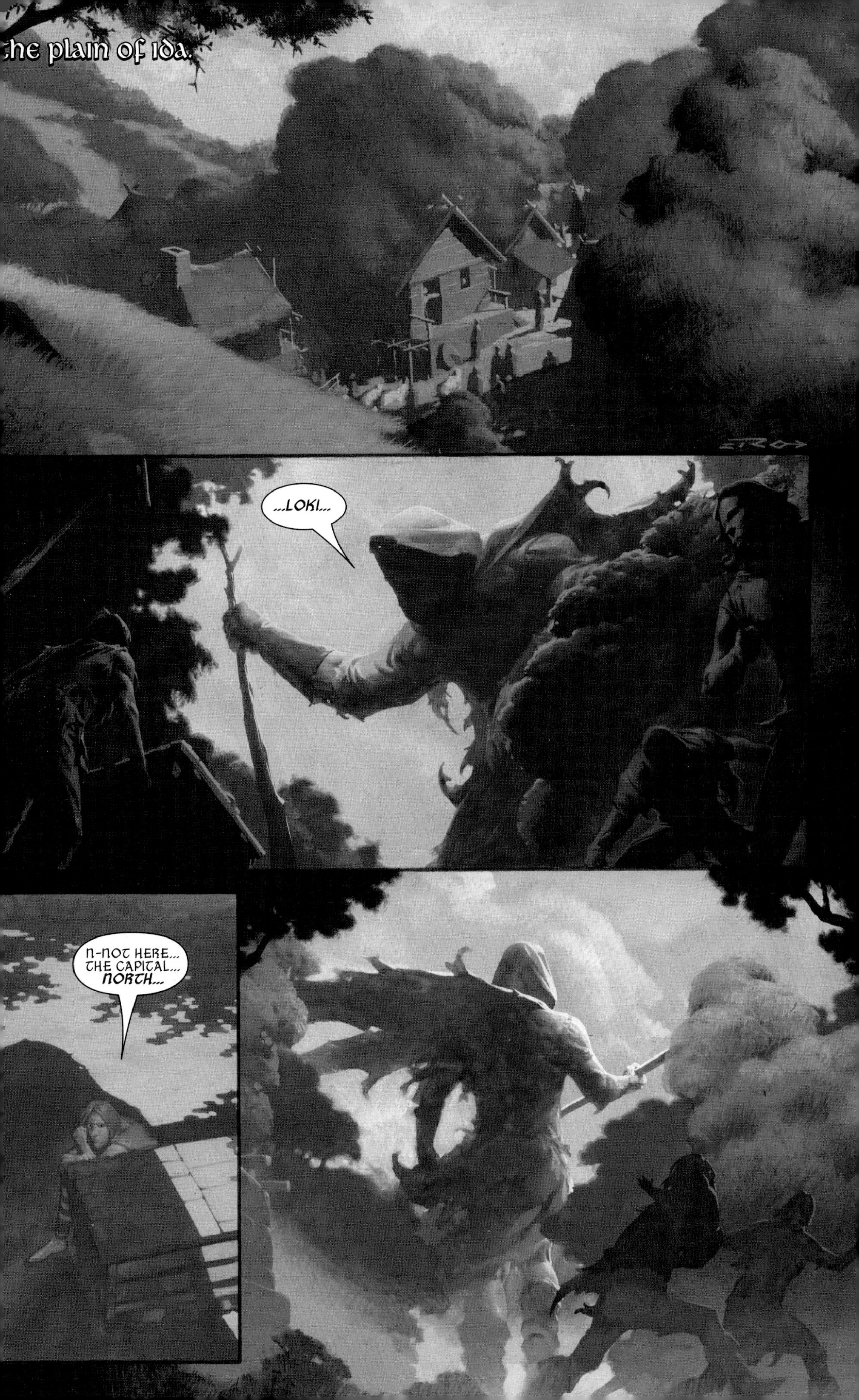
the plain of ida.
...LOKI...
N-NOT HERE...
THE CAPITAL...
NORTH...

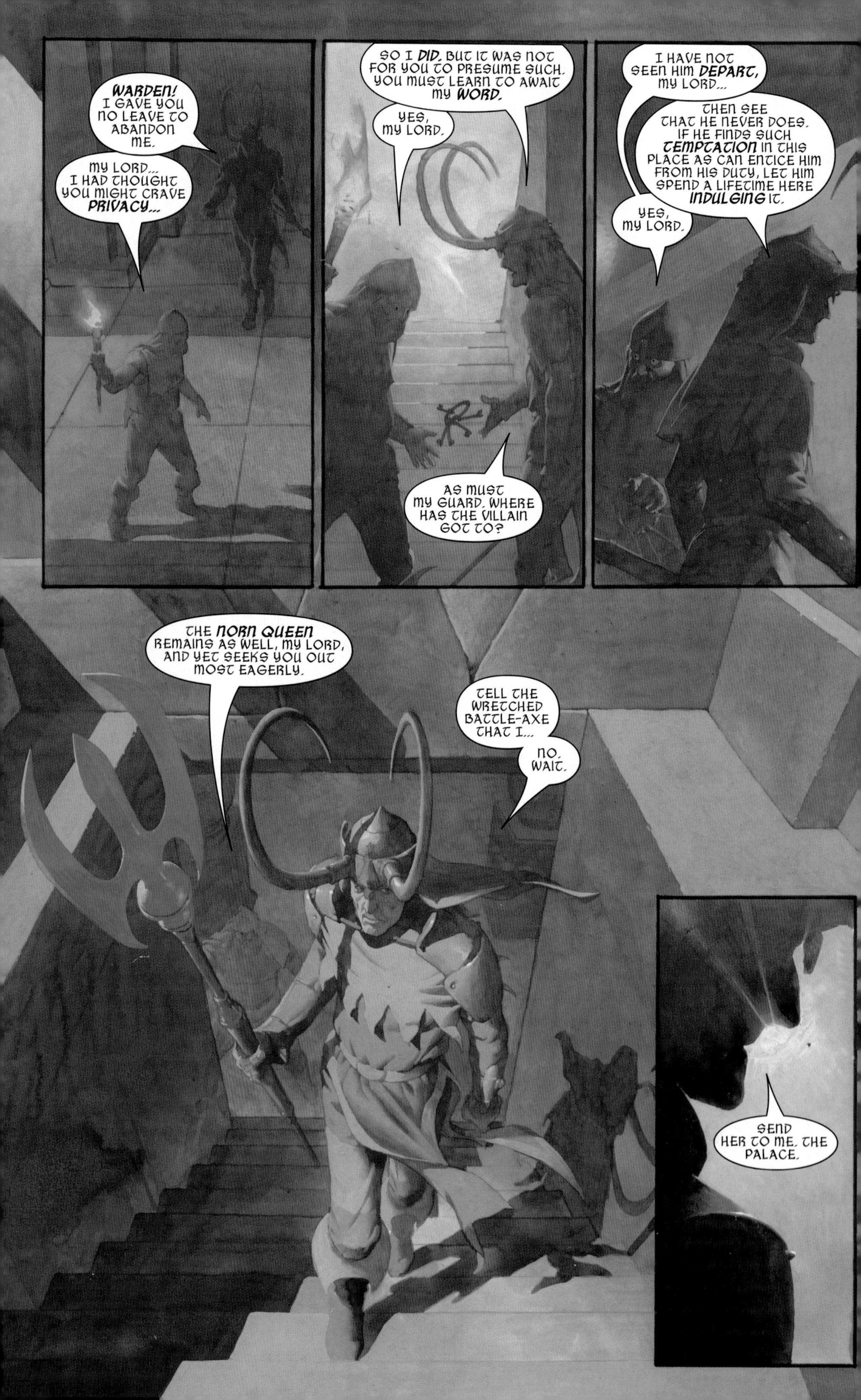
WARDEN! I GAVE YOU NO LEAVE TO ABANDON ME.
MY LORD... I HAD THOUGHT YOU MIGHT CRAVE PRIVACY...
SO I DID. BUT IT WAS NOT FOR YOU TO PRESUME SUCH. YOU MUST LEARN TO AWAIT MY WORD.
YES, MY LORD.
AS MUST MY GUARD. WHERE HAS THE VILLAIN GOT TO?
I HAVE NOT SEEN HIM DEPART, MY LORD...
THEN SEE THAT HE NEVER DOES. IF HE FINDS SUCH TEMPTATION IN THIS PLACE AS CAN ENTICE HIM FROM HIS DUTY, LET HIM SPEND A LIFETIME HERE INDULGING IT.
YES, MY LORD.
THE NORN QUEEN REMAINS AS WELL, MY LORD, AND YET SEEKS YOU OUT MOST EAGERLY.
TELL THE WRETCHED BATTLE-AXE THAT I...
NO. WAIT.
SEND HER TO ME. THE PALACE.

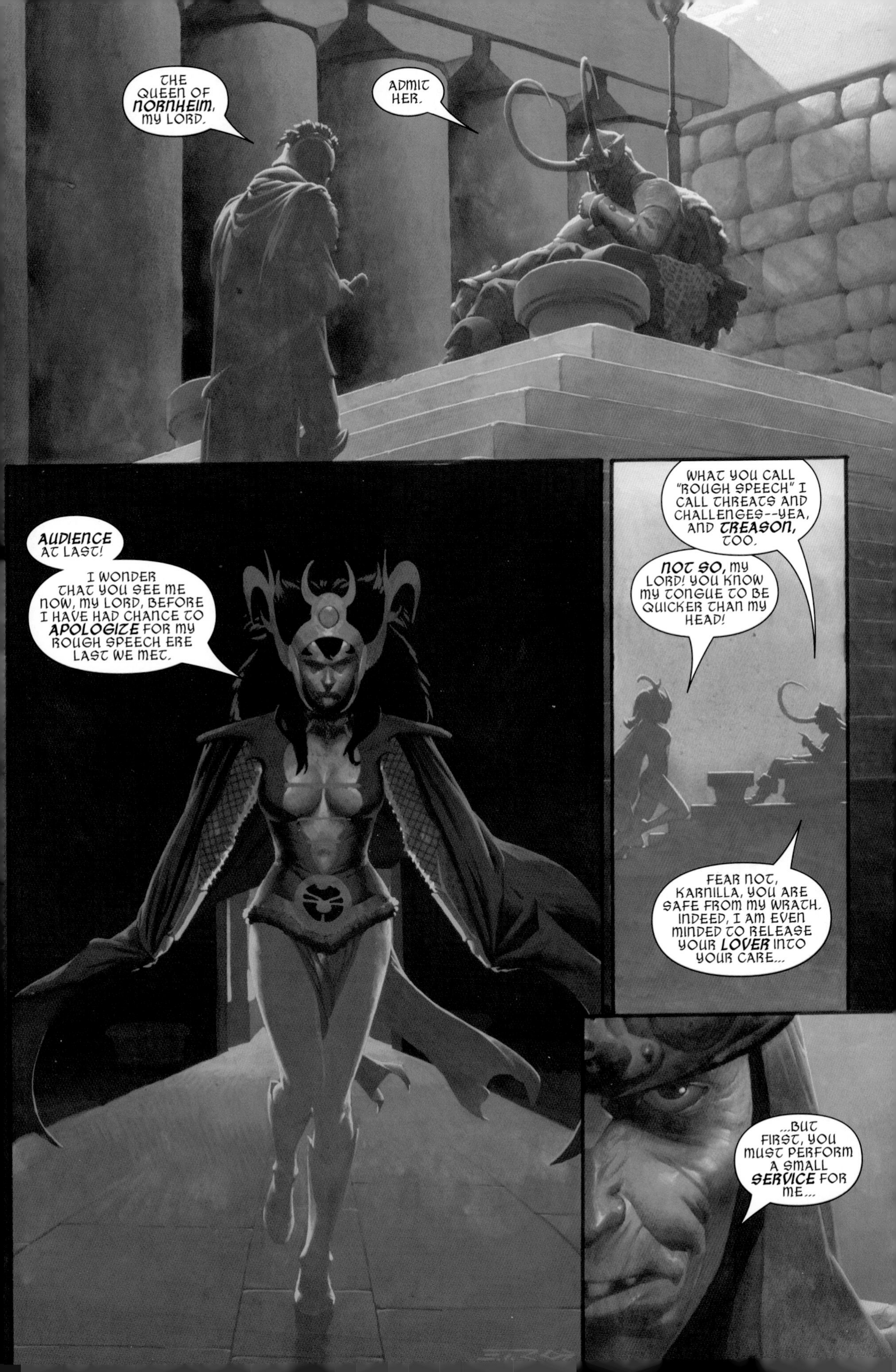
THE QUEEN OF NORNHEIM, MY LORD.
ADMIT HER.
AUDIENCE AT LAST!
I WONDER THAT YOU SEE ME NOW, MY LORD, BEFORE I HAVE HAD CHANCE TO APOLOGIZE FOR MY ROUGH SPEECH ERE LAST WE MET.
WHAT YOU CALL "ROUGH SPEECH" I CALL THREATS AND CHALLENGES--YEA, AND TREASON, TOO.
NOT SO, MY LORD! YOU KNOW MY TONGUE TO BE QUICKER THAN MY HEAD!
FEAR NOT, KARNILLA, YOU ARE SAFE FROM MY WRATH. INDEED, I AM EVEN MINDED TO RELEASE YOUR LOVER INTO YOUR CARE...
...BUT FIRST, YOU MUST PERFORM A SMALL SERVICE FOR ME...

# THREE

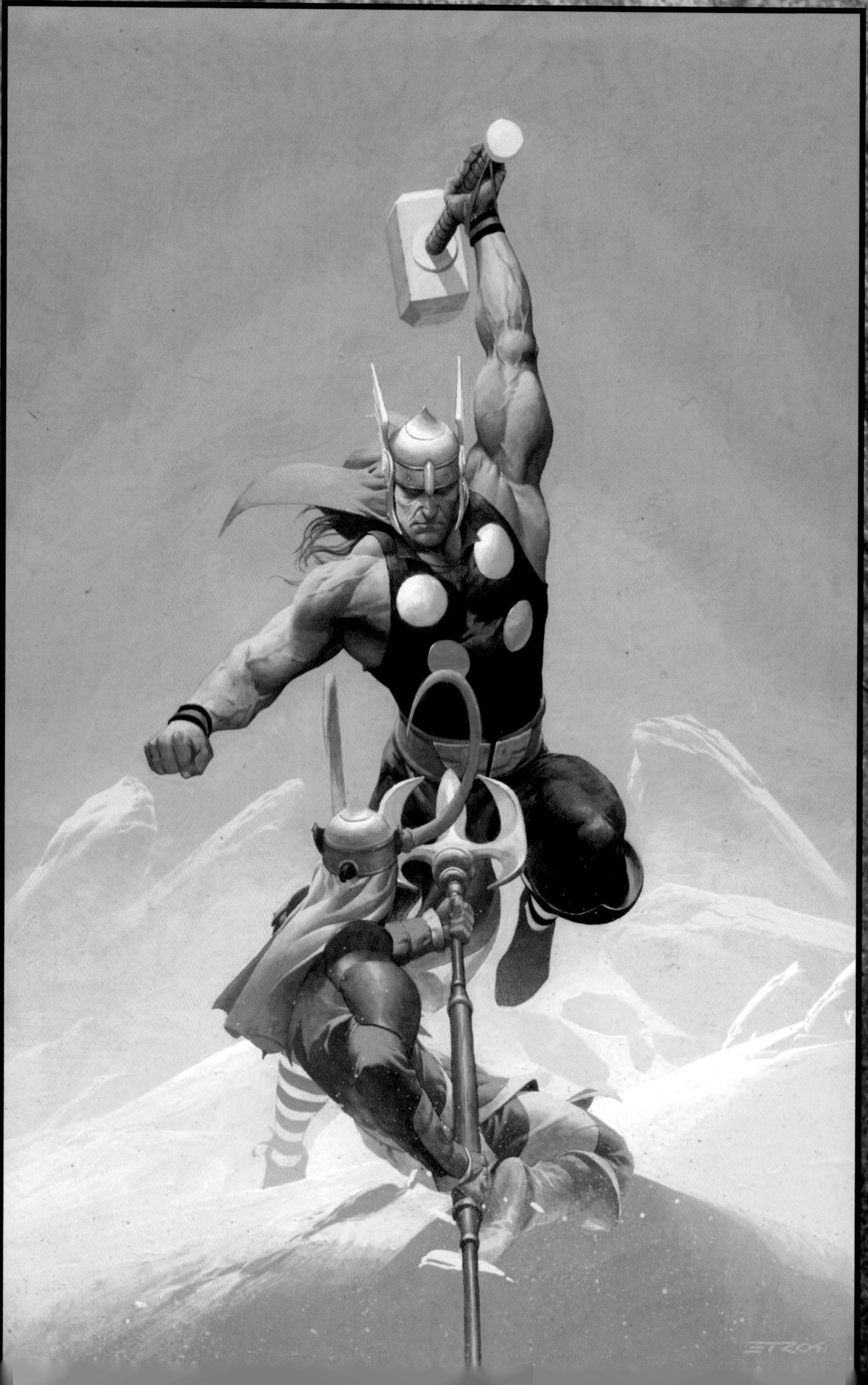

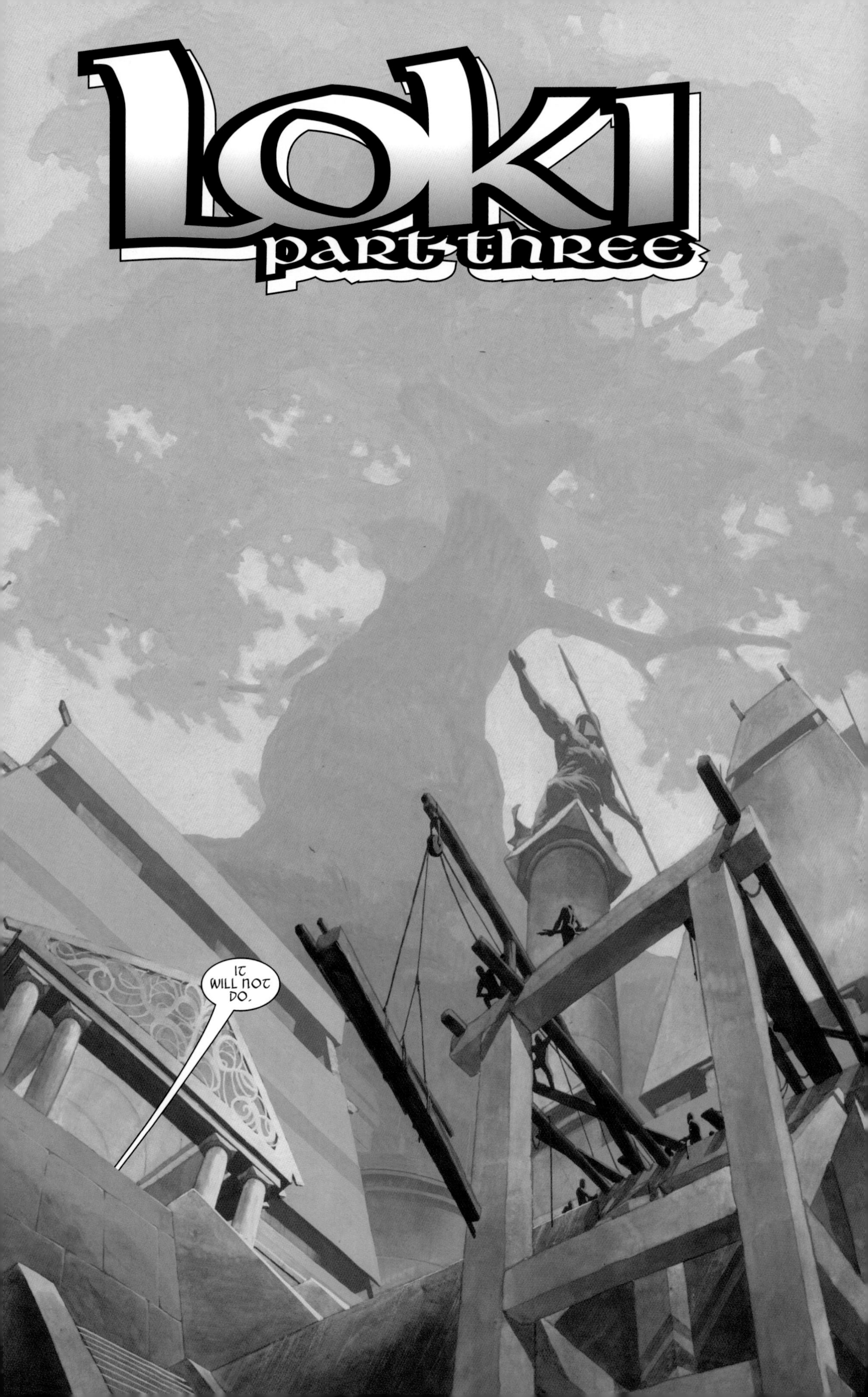
LOKI
PART THREE
IT WILL NOT DO.

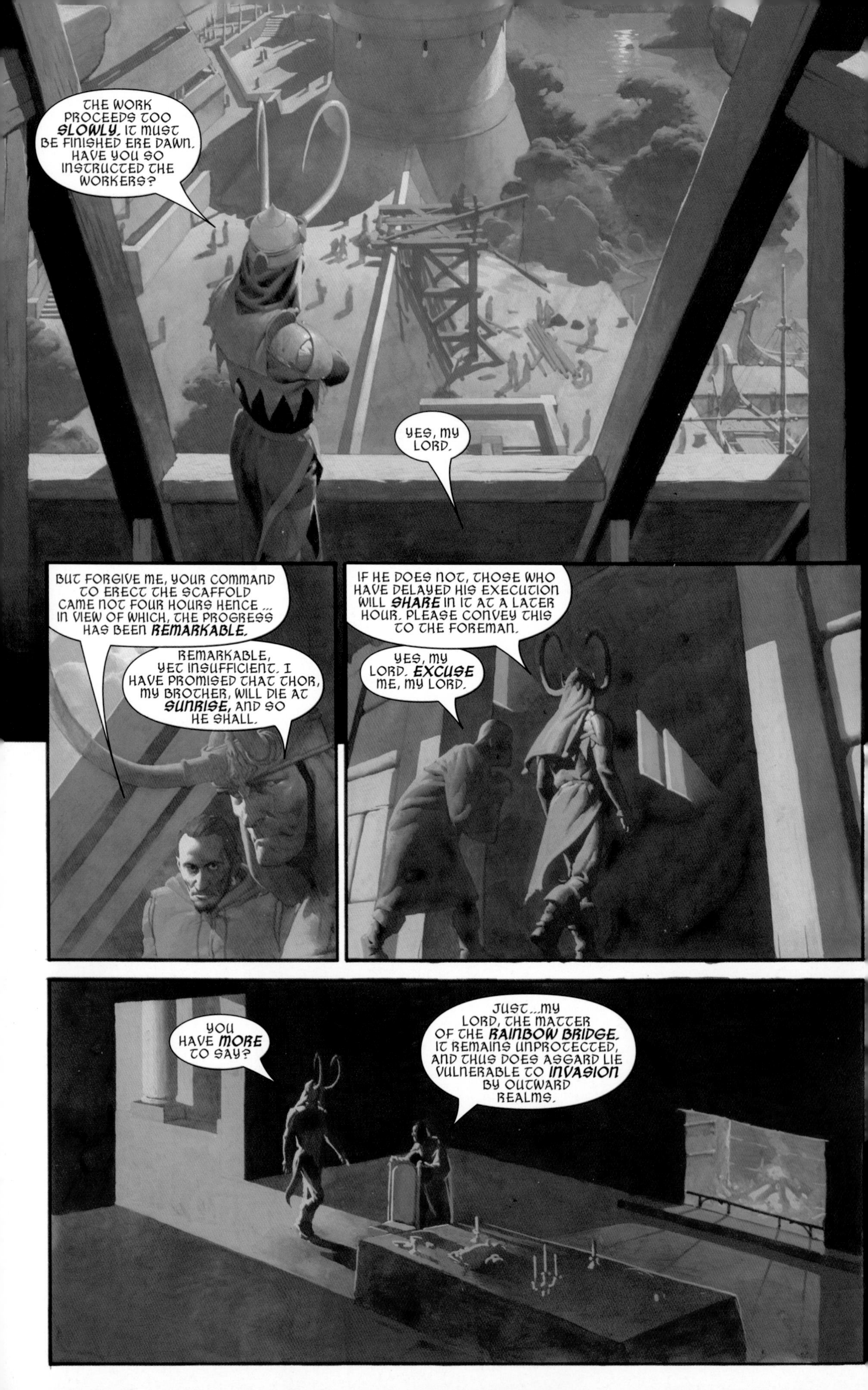
THE WORK PROCEEDS TOO SLOWLY. IT MUST BE FINISHED ERE DAWN. HAVE YOU SO INSTRUCTED THE WORKERS?
YES, MY LORD.
BUT FORGIVE ME, YOUR COMMAND TO ERECT THE SCAFFOLD CAME NOT FOUR HOURS HENCE ... IN VIEW OF WHICH, THE PROGRESS HAS BEEN REMARKABLE.
REMARKABLE, YET INSUFFICIENT. I HAVE PROMISED THAT THOR, MY BROTHER, WILL DIE AT SUNRISE, AND SO HE SHALL.
IF HE DOES NOT, THOSE WHO HAVE DELAYED HIS EXECUTION WILL SHARE IN IT AT A LATER HOUR. PLEASE CONVEY THIS TO THE FOREMAN.
YES, MY LORD. EXCUSE ME, MY LORD.
YOU HAVE MORE TO SAY?
JUST...MY LORD, THE MATTER OF THE RAINBOW BRIDGE. IT REMAINS UNPROTECTED, AND THUS DOES ASGARD LIE VULNERABLE TO INVASION BY OUTWARD REALMS.

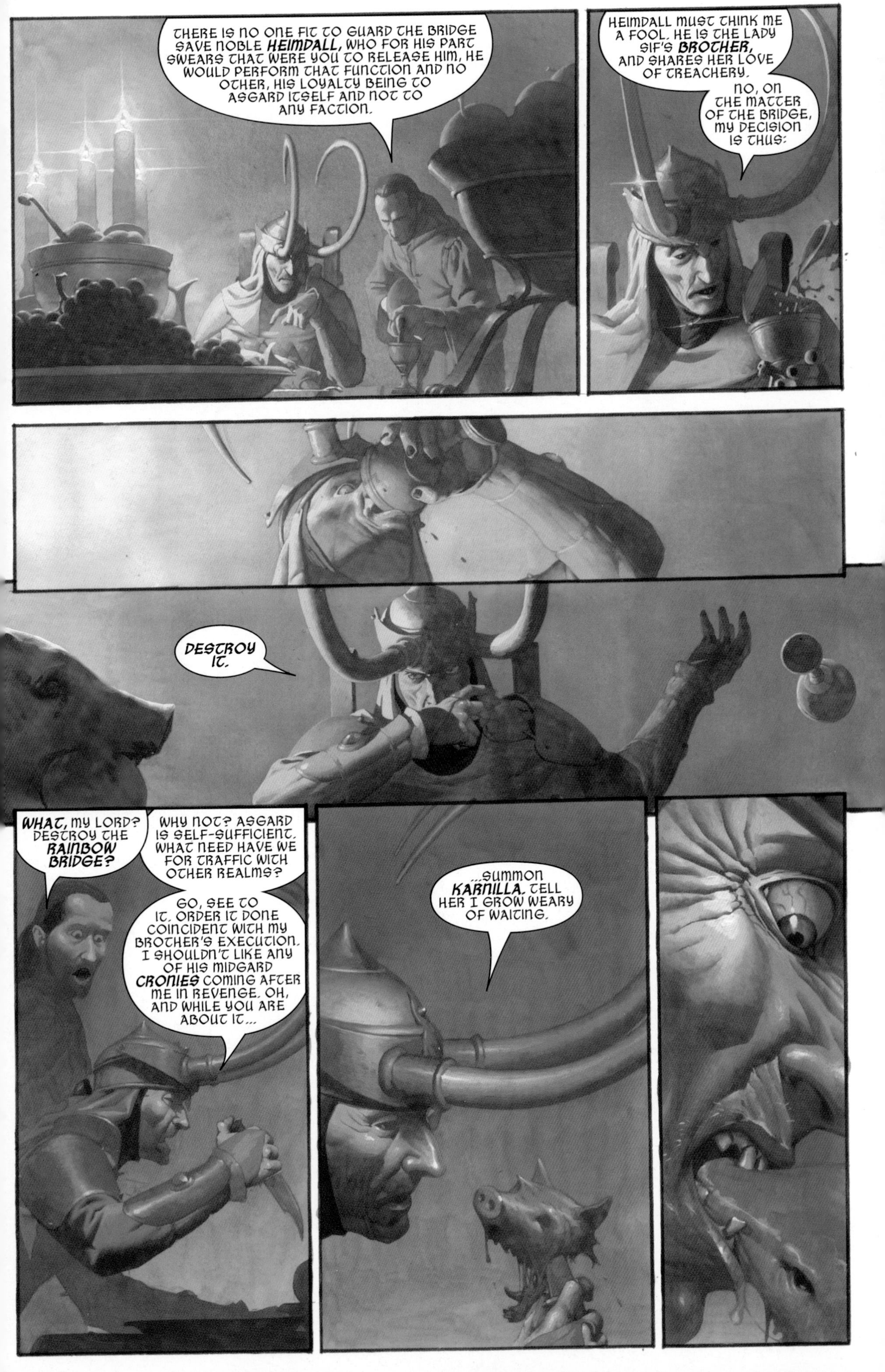
THERE IS NO ONE FIT TO GUARD THE BRIDGE SAVE NOBLE HEIMDALL, WHO FOR HIS PART SWEARS THAT WERE YOU TO RELEASE HIM, HE WOULD PERFORM THAT FUNCTION AND NO OTHER, HIS LOYALTY BEING TO ASGARD ITSELF AND NOT TO ANY FACTION.
HEIMDALL MUST THINK ME A FOOL. HE IS THE LADY SIF'S BROTHER, AND SHARES HER LOVE OF TREACHERY.
NO, ON THE MATTER OF THE BRIDGE, MY DECISION IS THUS:
DESTROY IT.
WHAT, MY LORD? DESTROY THE RAINBOW BRIDGE?
WHY NOT? ASGARD IS SELF-SUFFICIENT. WHAT NEED HAVE WE FOR TRAFFIC WITH OTHER REALMS?
GO, SEE TO IT. ORDER IT DONE COINCIDENT WITH MY BROTHER'S EXECUTION. I SHOULDN'T LIKE ANY OF HIS MIDGARD CRONIES COMING AFTER ME IN REVENGE. OH, AND WHILE YOU ARE ABOUT IT...
...SUMMON KARNILLA. TELL HER I GROW WEARY OF WAITING.

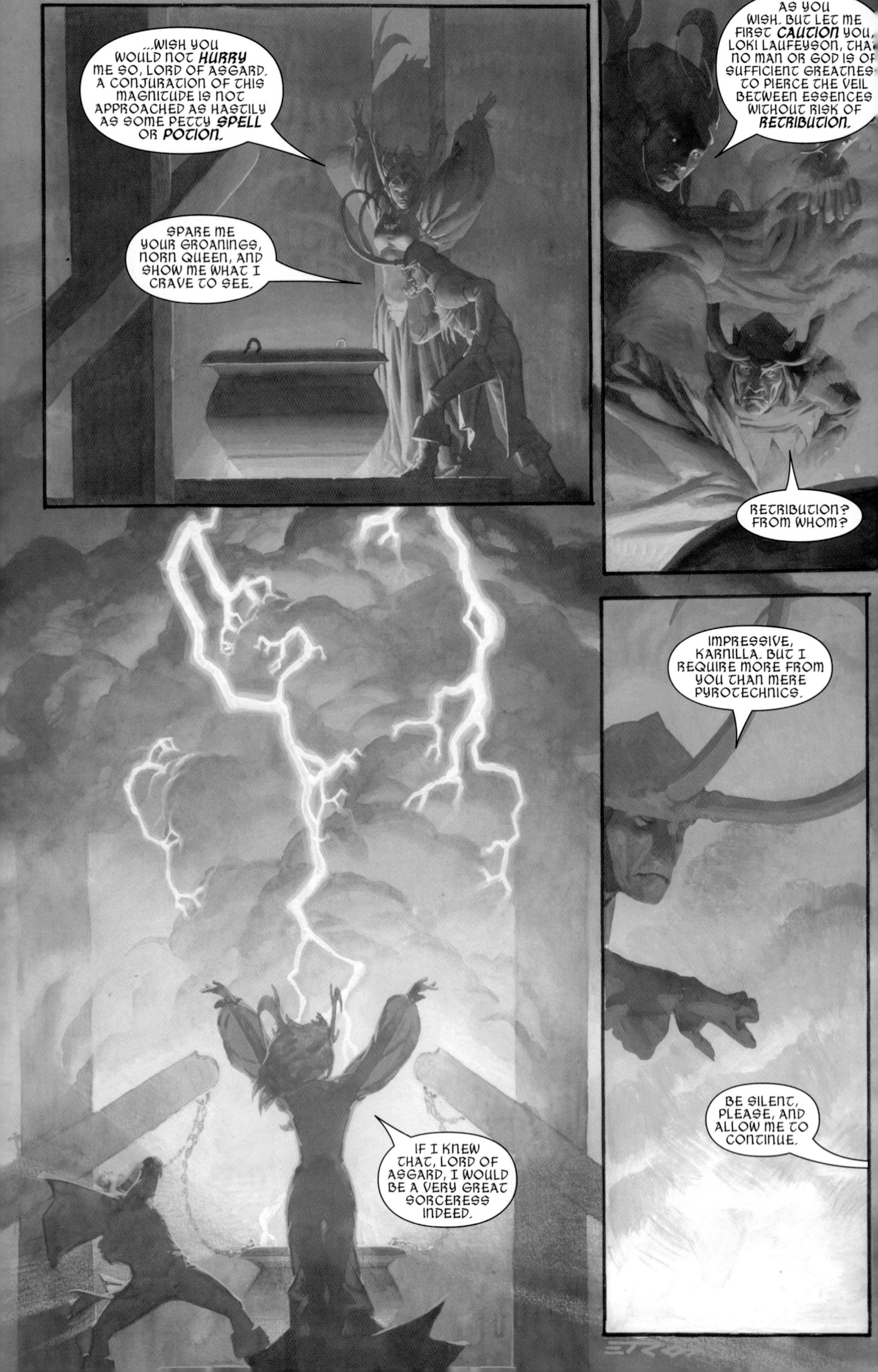
...WISH YOU WOULD NOT HURRY ME SO, LORD OF ASGARD. A CONJURATION OF THIS MAGNITUDE IS NOT APPROACHED AS HASTILY AS SOME PETTY SPELL OR POTION.
SPARE ME YOUR GROANINGS, NORN QUEEN, AND SHOW ME WHAT I CRAVE TO SEE.
AS YOU WISH. BUT LET ME FIRST CAUTION YOU, LOKI LAUFEYSON, THA NO MAN OR GOD IS OF SUFFICIENT GREATNES TO PIERCE THE VEIL BETWEEN ESSENCES WITHOUT RISK OF RETRIBUTION.
RETRIBUTION? FROM WHOM?
IF I KNEW THAT, LORD OF ASGARD, I WOULD BE A VERY GREAT SORCERESS INDEED.
IMPRESSIVE, KARNILLA. BUT I REQUIRE MORE FROM YOU THAN MERE PYROTECHNICS.
BE SILENT, PLEASE, AND ALLOW ME TO CONTINUE.

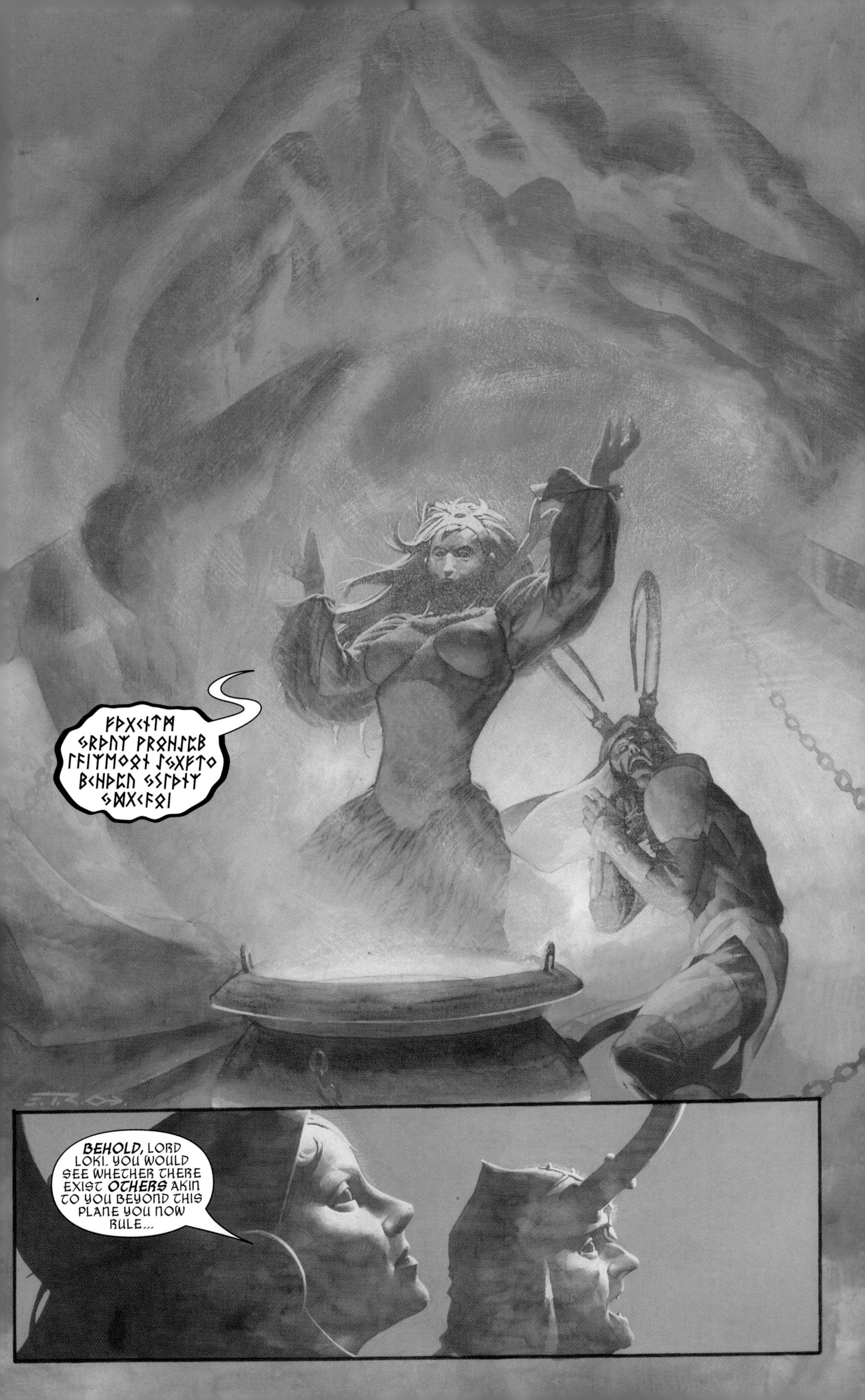

***BEHOLD,*** LORD LOKI. YOU WOULD SEE WHETHER THERE EXIST ***OTHERS*** AKIN TO YOU BEYOND THIS PLANE YOU NOW RULE...

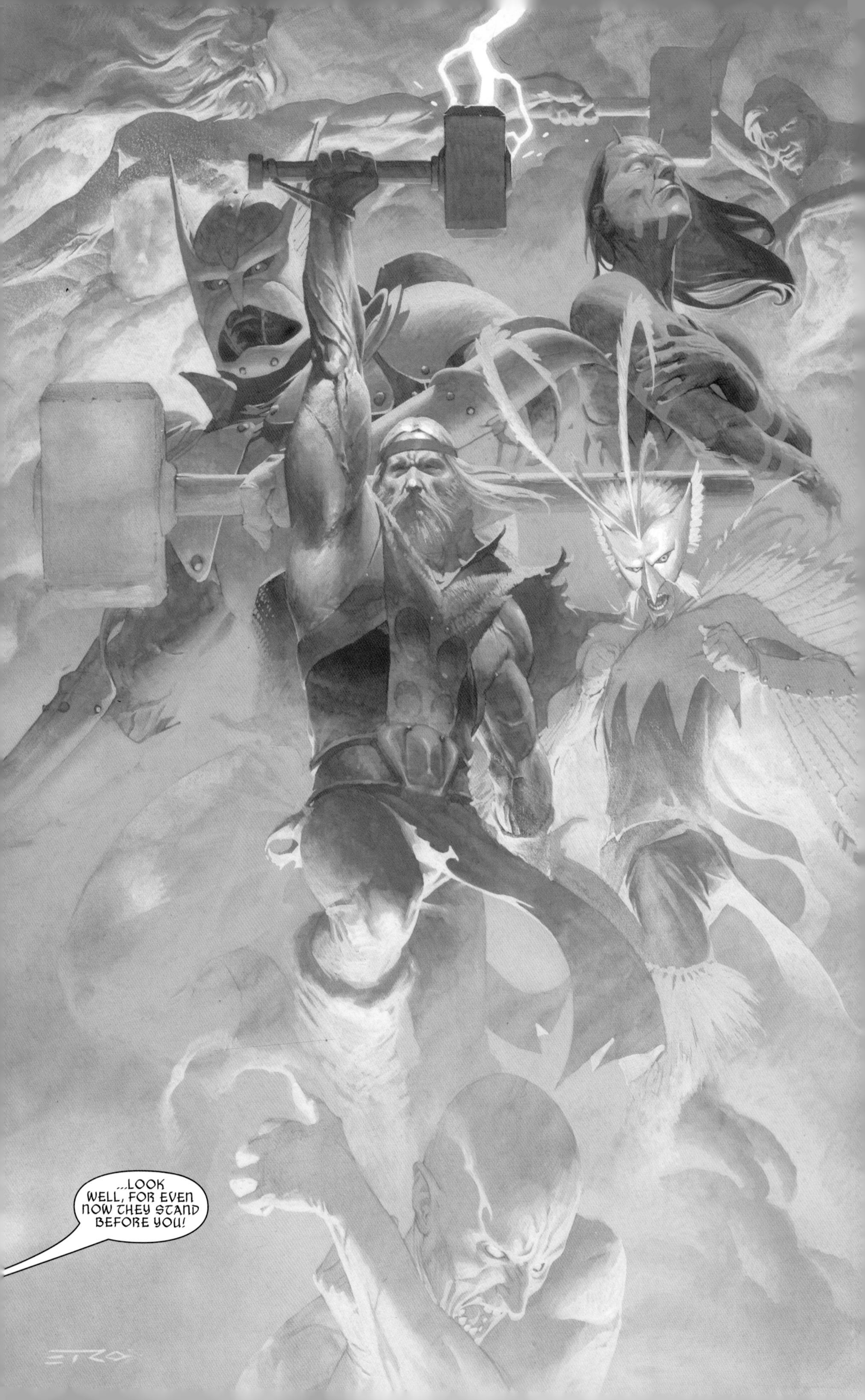
...LOOK WELL, FOR EVEN NOW THEY STAND BEFORE YOU!

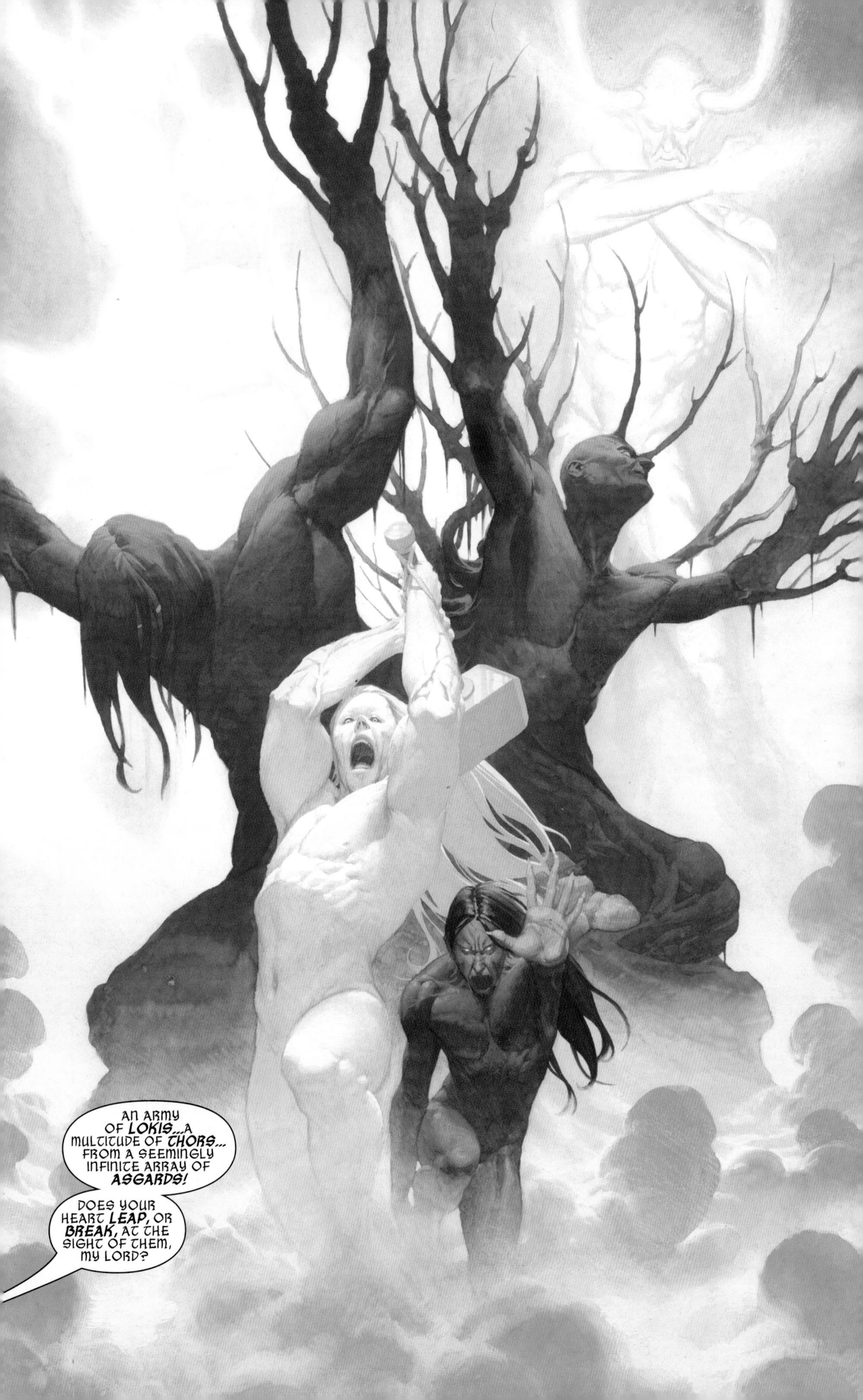
AN ARMY OF **LOKIS**...A MULTITUDE OF **THORS**... FROM A SEEMINGLY INFINITE ARRAY OF **ASGARDS!**
DOES YOUR HEART **LEAP,** OR **BREAK,** AT THE SIGHT OF THEM, MY LORD?

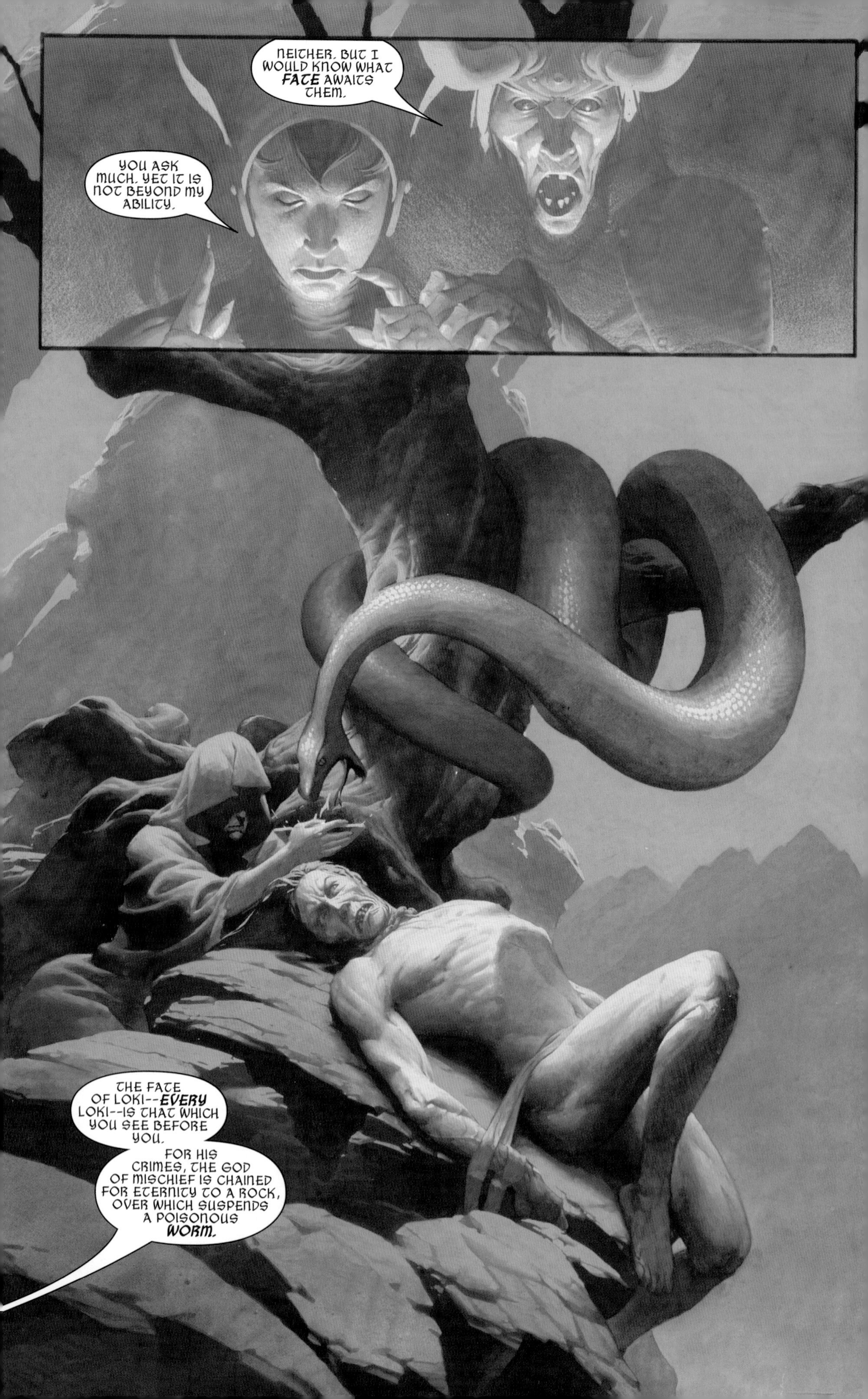
NEITHER. BUT I WOULD KNOW WHAT **FATE** AWAITS THEM.
YOU ASK MUCH. YET IT IS NOT BEYOND MY ABILITY.
THE FATE OF LOKI--**EVERY** LOKI--IS THAT WHICH YOU SEE BEFORE YOU.
FOR HIS CRIMES, THE GOD OF MISCHIEF IS CHAINED FOR ETERNITY TO A ROCK, OVER WHICH SUSPENDS A POISONOUS **WORM.**

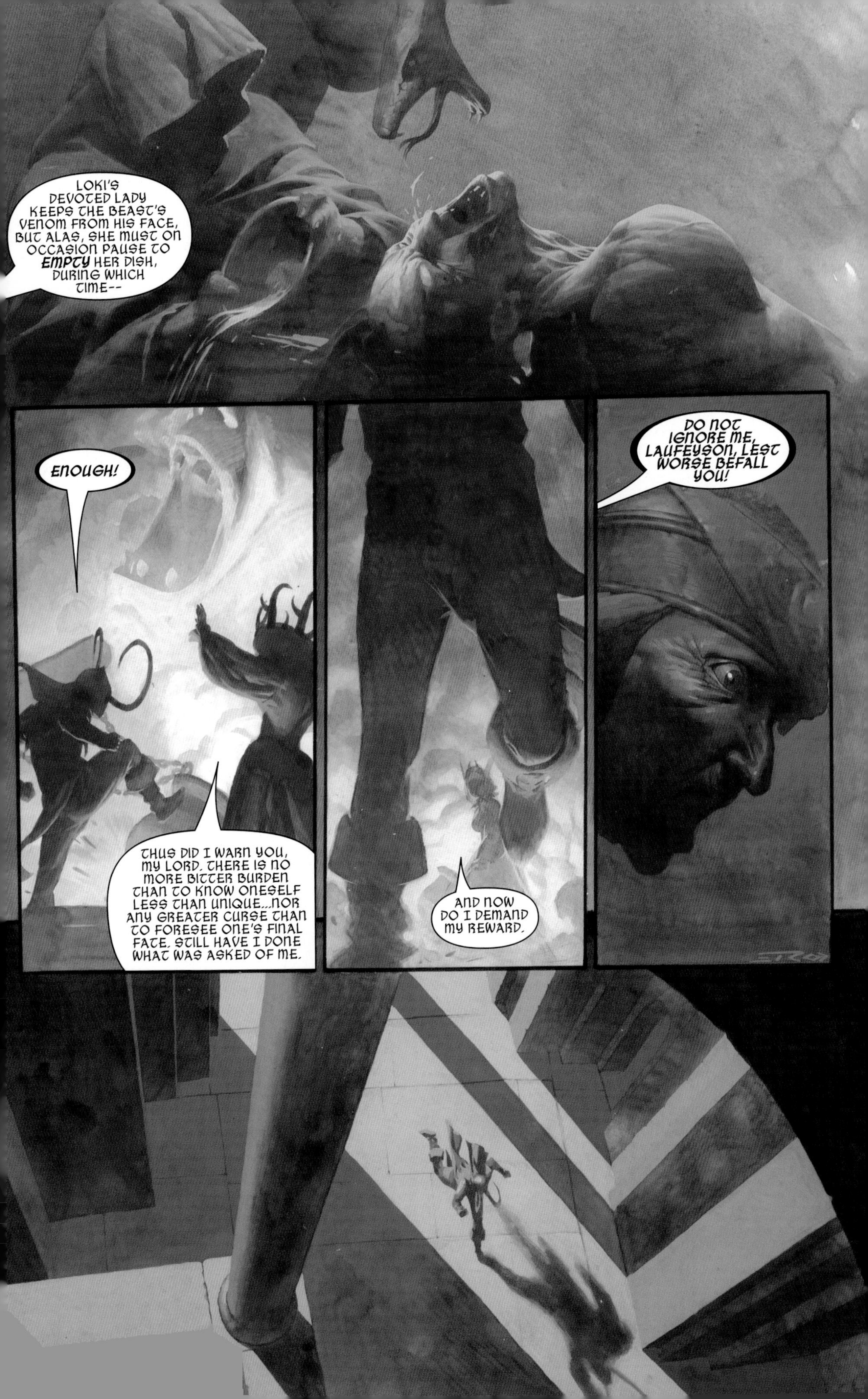

LOKI'S DEVOTED LADY KEEPS THE BEAST'S VENOM FROM HIS FACE, BUT ALAS, SHE MUST ON OCCASION PAUSE TO EMPTY HER DISH, DURING WHICH TIME--
ENOUGH!
THUS DID I WARN YOU, MY LORD. THERE IS NO MORE BITTER BURDEN THAN TO KNOW ONESELF LESS THAN UNIQUE...NOR ANY GREATER CURSE THAN TO FORESEE ONE'S FINAL FATE. STILL HAVE I DONE WHAT WAS ASKED OF ME.
AND NOW DO I DEMAND MY REWARD.
DO NOT IGNORE ME, LAUFEYSON, LEST WORSE BEFALL YOU!

the outskirts of asgard city.

...LOKI...

Y-YOU SEEK THE CONQUEROR?

YOU MUST HIE YOURSELF TO THAT PLACE... THEREIN HE RESIDES...

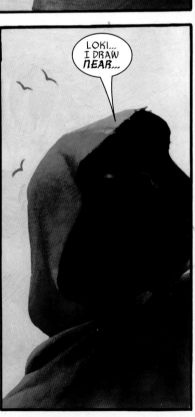

LOKI... I DRAW NEAR...

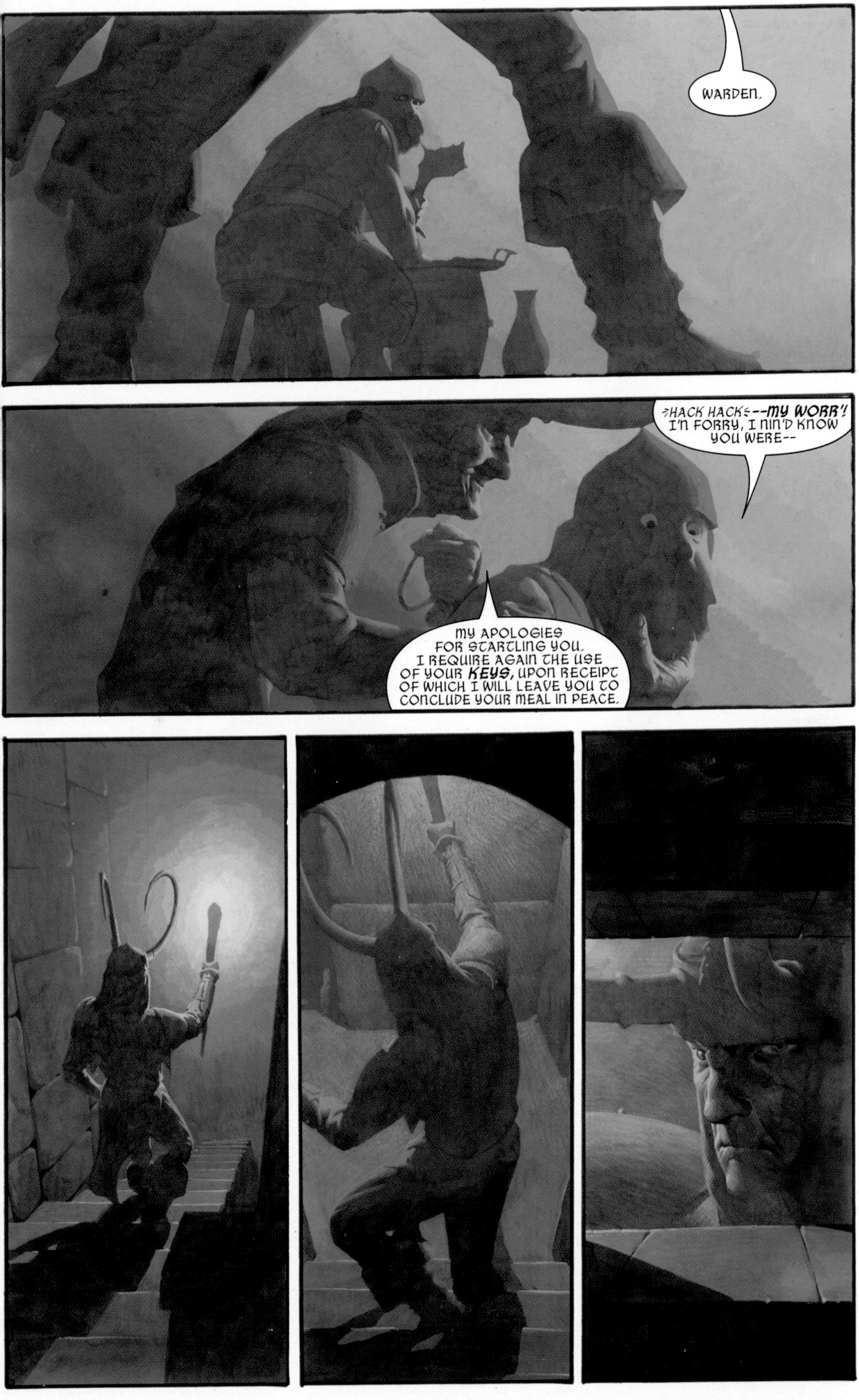
WARDEN.
=HACK HACK=--MY WORR'! I'N FORRY, I NIN'D KNOW YOU WERE--
MY APOLOGIES FOR STARTLING YOU. I REQUIRE AGAIN THE USE OF YOUR KEYS, UPON RECEIPT OF WHICH I WILL LEAVE YOU TO CONCLUDE YOUR MEAL IN PEACE.

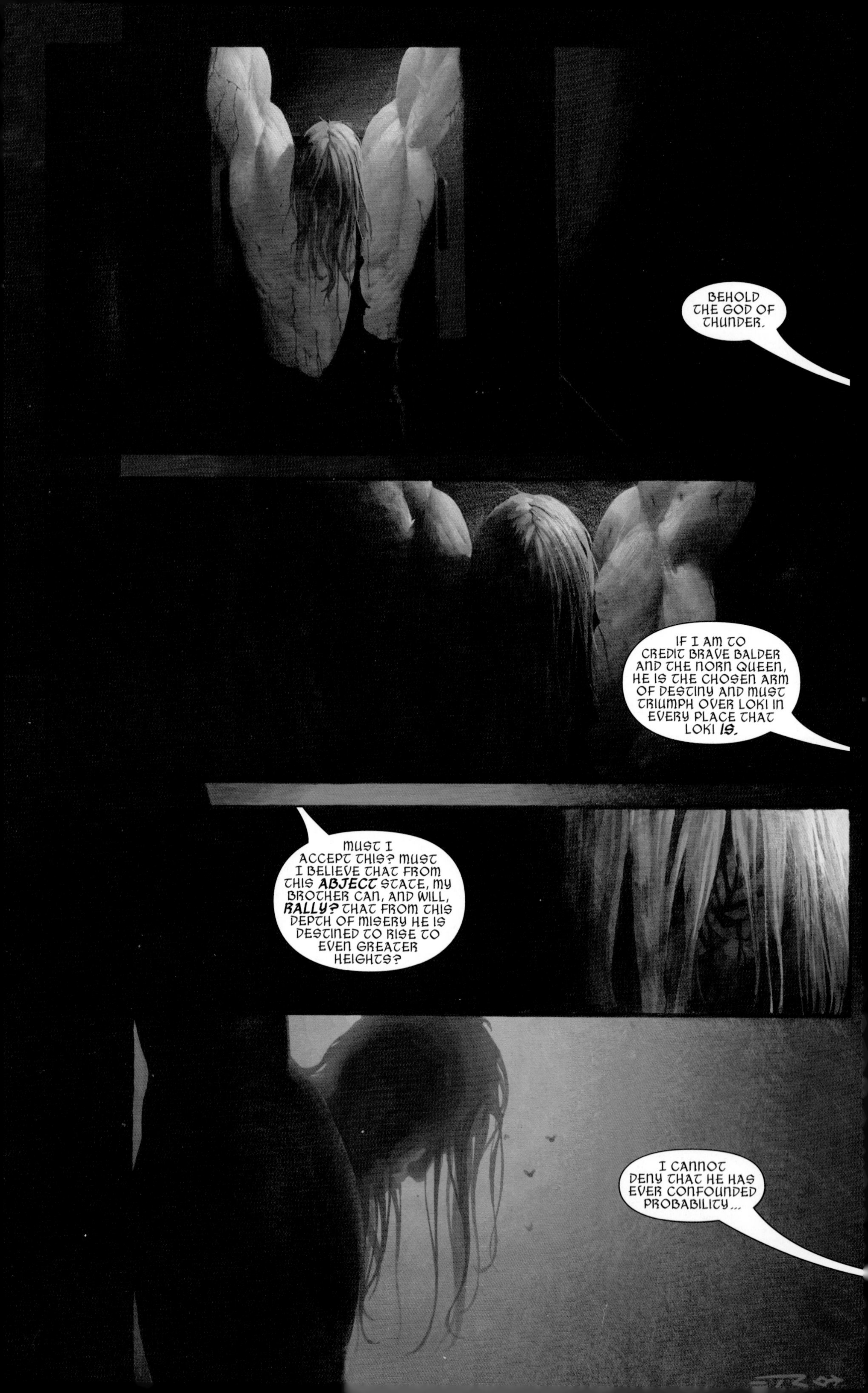
BEHOLD THE GOD OF THUNDER.
IF I AM TO CREDIT BRAVE BALDER AND THE NORN QUEEN, HE IS THE CHOSEN ARM OF DESTINY AND MUST TRIUMPH OVER LOKI IN EVERY PLACE THAT LOKI IS.
MUST I ACCEPT THIS? MUST I BELIEVE THAT FROM THIS ABJECT STATE, MY BROTHER CAN, AND WILL, RALLY? THAT FROM THIS DEPTH OF MISERY HE IS DESTINED TO RISE TO EVEN GREATER HEIGHTS?
I CANNOT DENY THAT HE HAS EVER CONFOUNDED PROBABILITY...

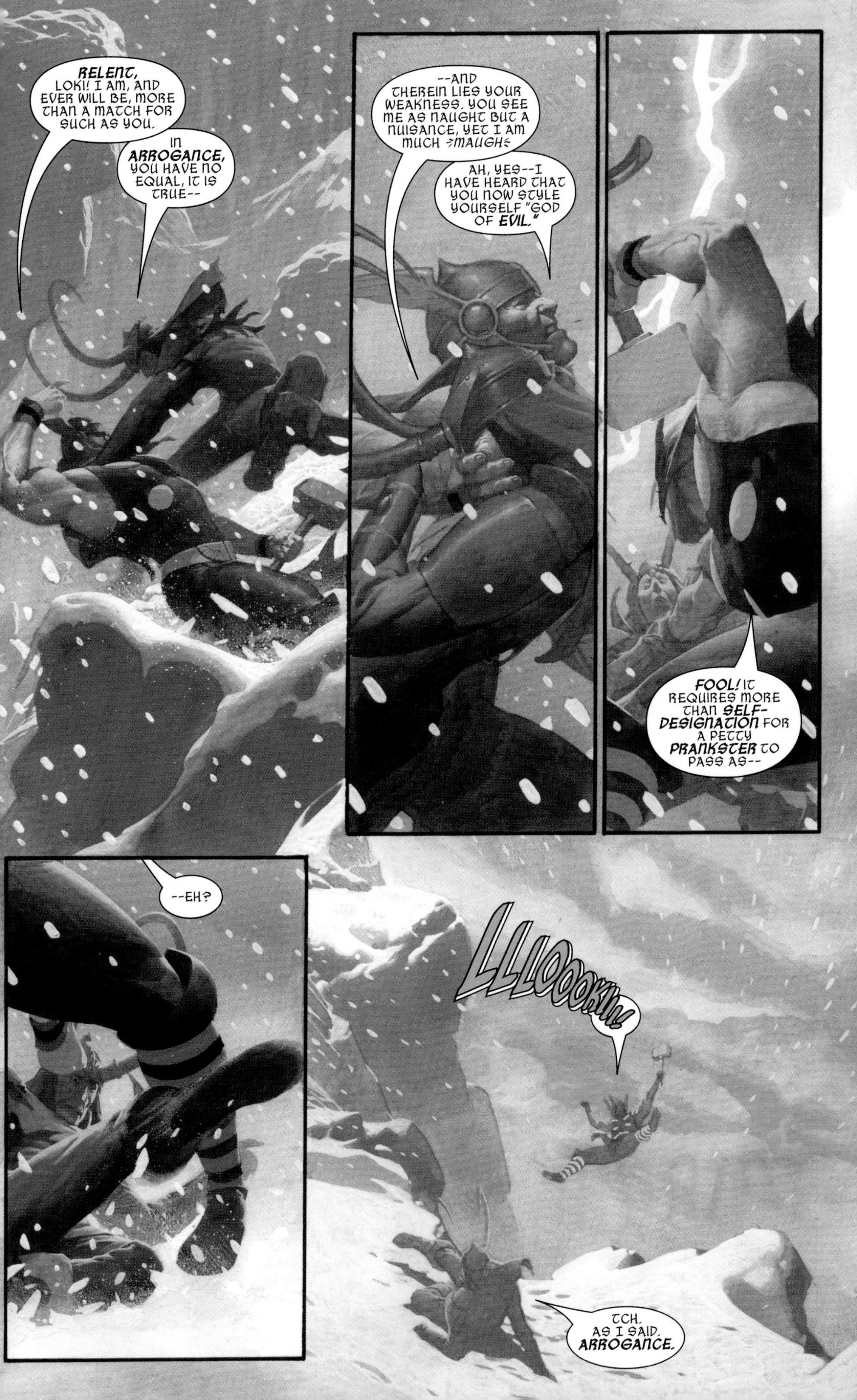

RELENT, LOKI! I AM, AND EVER WILL BE, MORE THAN A MATCH FOR SUCH AS YOU.
IN ARROGANCE, YOU HAVE NO EQUAL, IT IS TRUE--
--AND THEREIN LIES YOUR WEAKNESS. YOU SEE ME AS NAUGHT BUT A NUISANCE, YET I AM MUCH =MAUGH=
AH, YES--I HAVE HEARD THAT YOU NOW STYLE YOURSELF "GOD OF EVIL."
FOOL! IT REQUIRES MORE THAN SELF-DESIGNATION FOR A PETTY PRANKSTER TO PASS AS--
--EH?
LLLOOOOKIII!
TCH. AS I SAID. ARROGANCE.

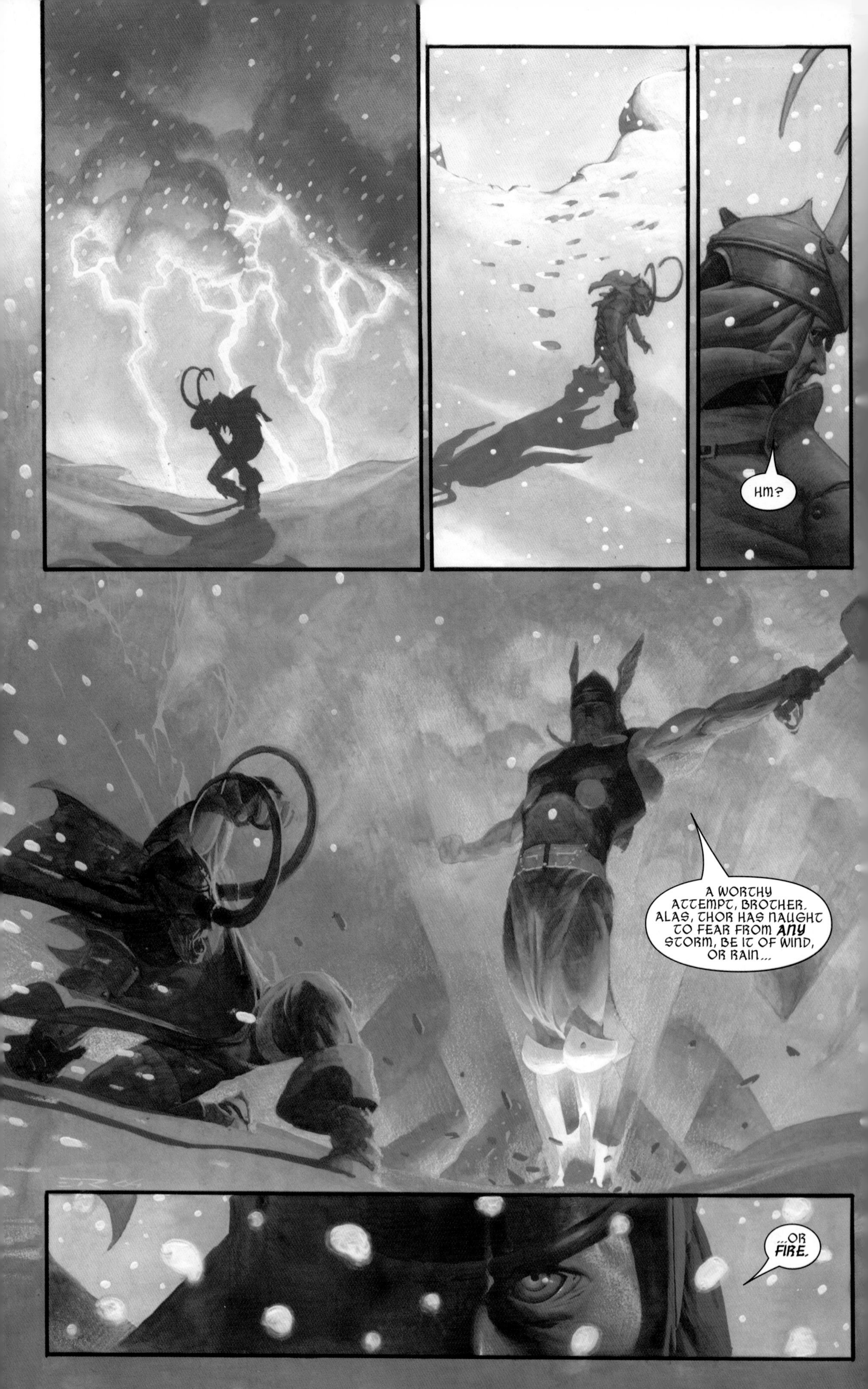
HM?
A WORTHY ATTEMPT, BROTHER. ALAS, THOR HAS NAUGHT TO FEAR FROM *ANY* STORM, BE IT OF WIND, OR RAIN...
...OR *FIRE.*

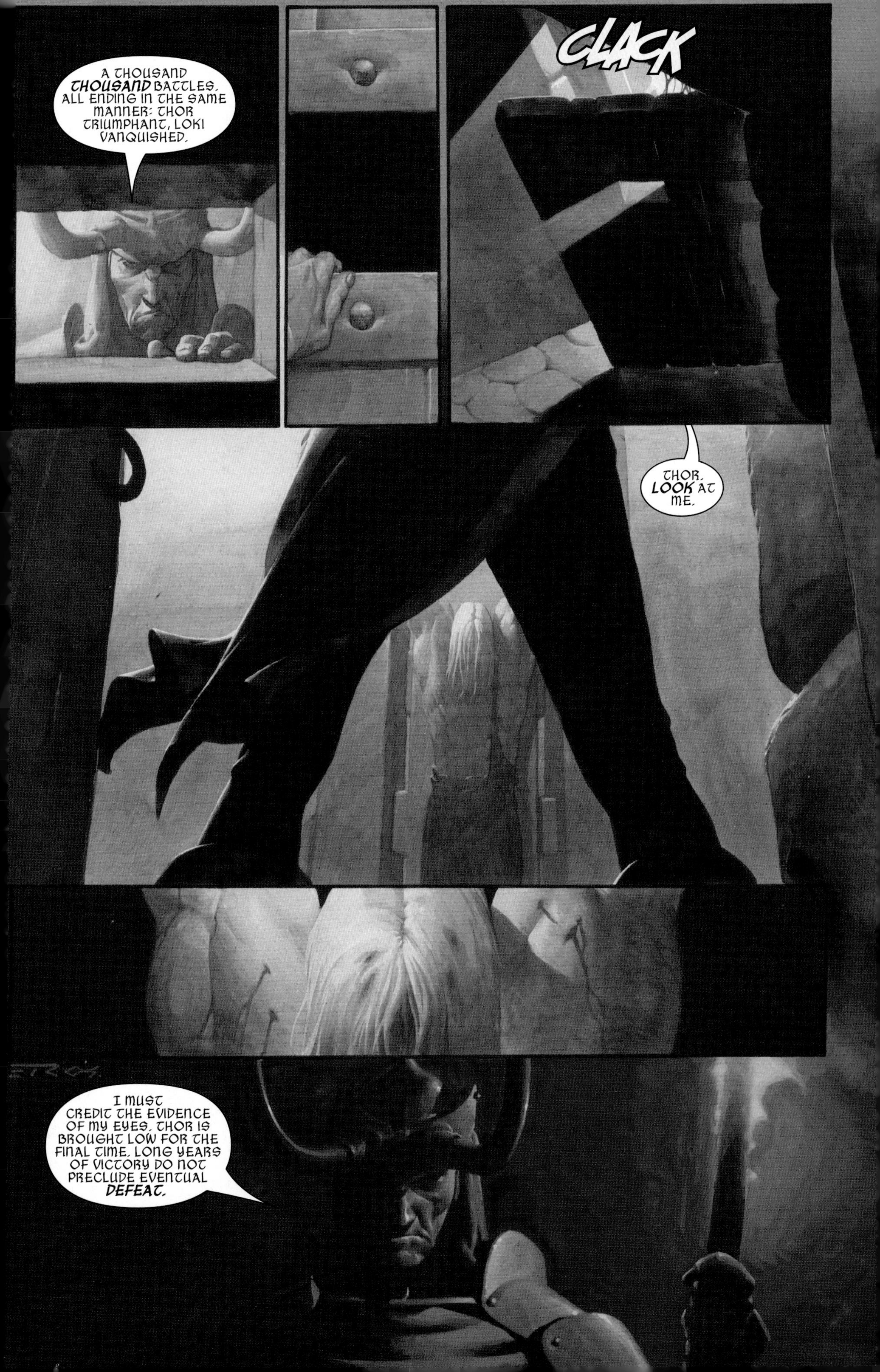
A THOUSAND THOUSAND BATTLES. ALL ENDING IN THE SAME MANNER: THOR TRIUMPHANT, LOKI VANQUISHED.
CLACK
THOR. LOOK AT ME.
I MUST CREDIT THE EVIDENCE OF MY EYES. THOR IS BROUGHT LOW FOR THE FINAL TIME. LONG YEARS OF VICTORY DO NOT PRECLUDE EVENTUAL DEFEAT.

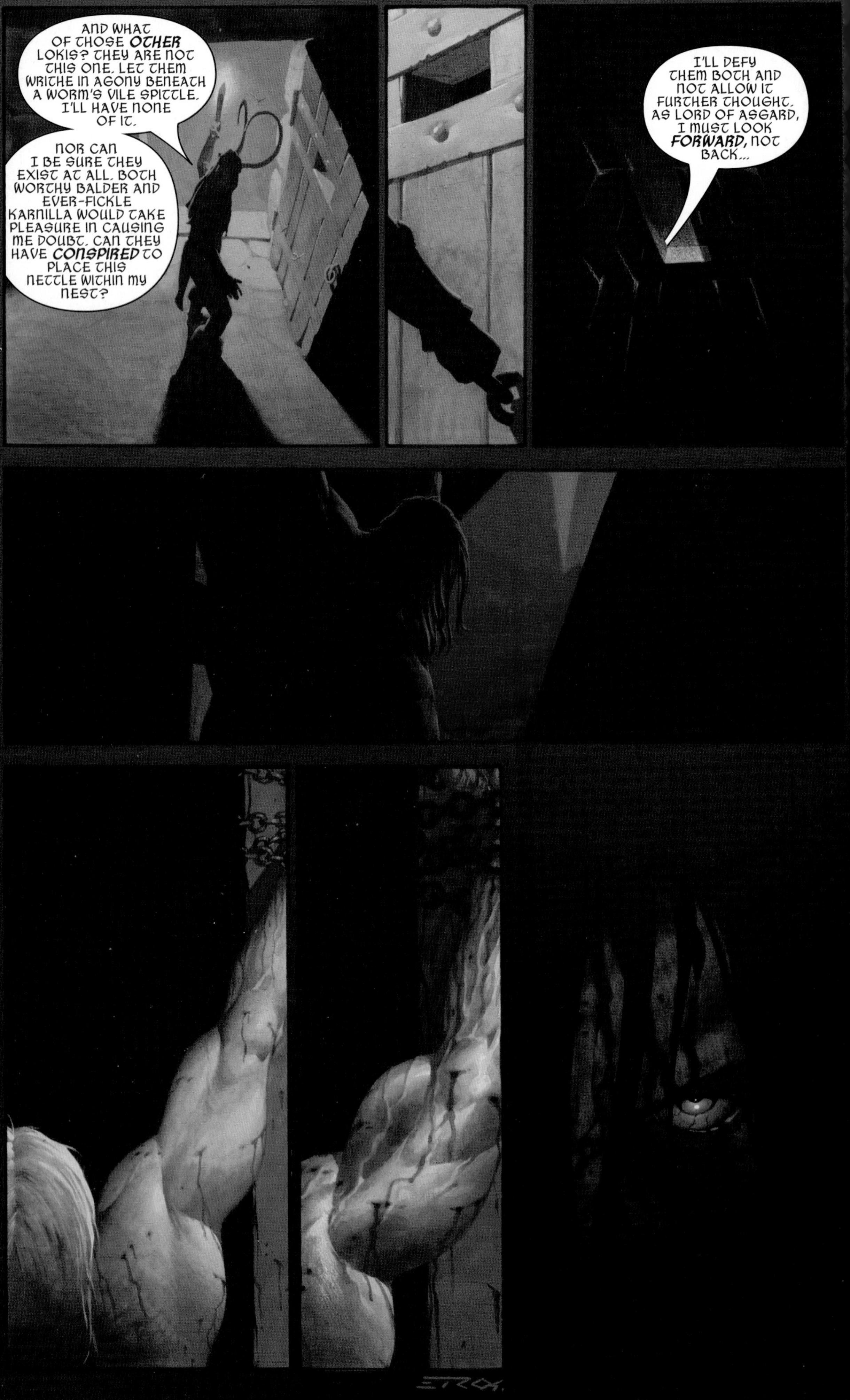

AND WHAT OF THOSE OTHER LOKIS? THEY ARE NOT THIS ONE. LET THEM WRITHE IN AGONY BENEATH A WORM'S VILE SPITTLE. I'LL HAVE NONE OF IT.
NOR CAN I BE SURE THEY EXIST AT ALL. BOTH WORTHY BALDER AND EVER-FICKLE KARNILLA WOULD TAKE PLEASURE IN CAUSING ME DOUBT. CAN THEY HAVE CONSPIRED TO PLACE THIS NETTLE WITHIN MY NEST?
I'LL DEFY THEM BOTH AND NOT ALLOW IT FURTHER THOUGHT. AS LORD OF ASGARD, I MUST LOOK FORWARD, NOT BACK...

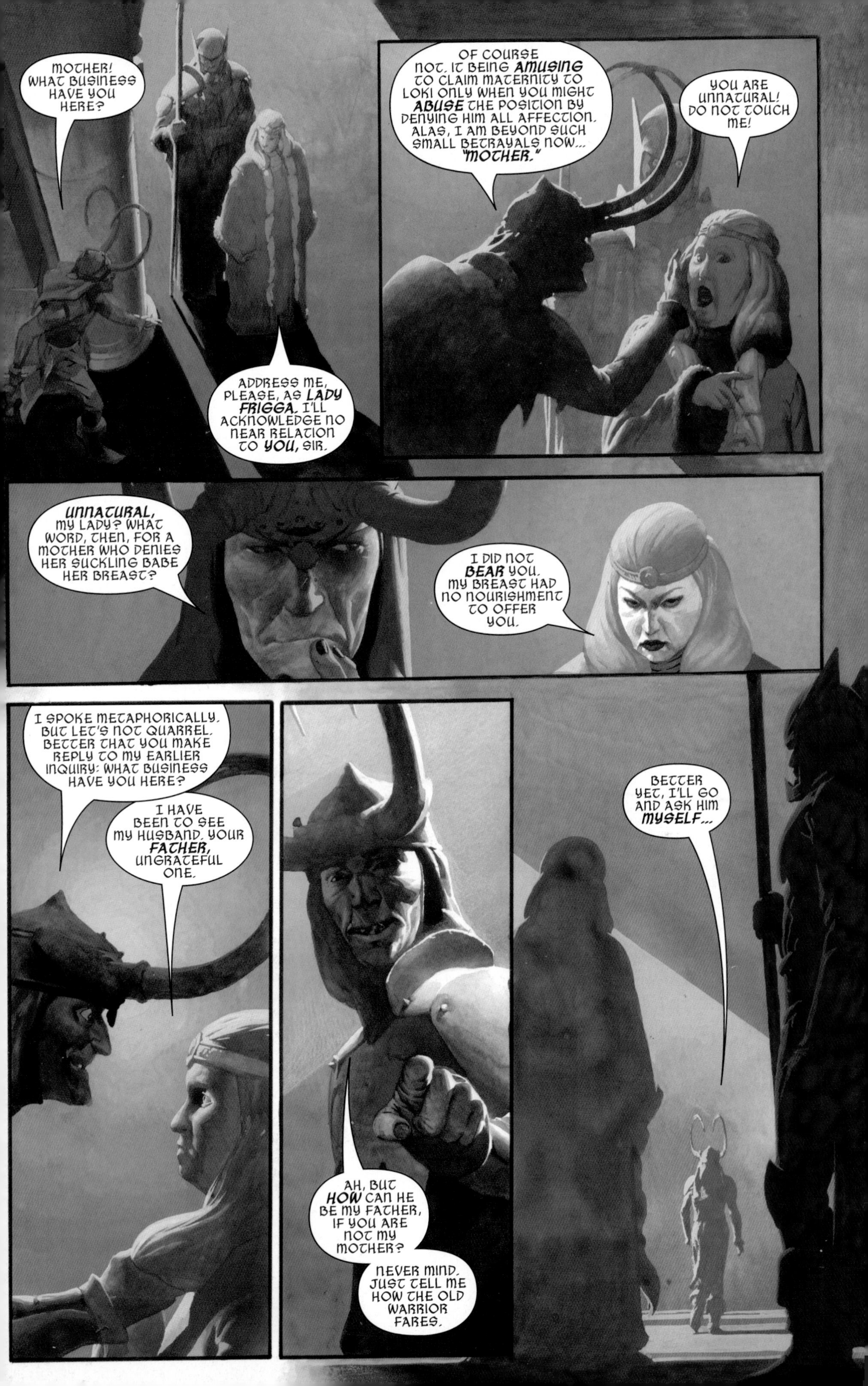
MOTHER! WHAT BUSINESS HAVE YOU HERE?
ADDRESS ME, PLEASE, AS LADY FRIGGA. I'LL ACKNOWLEDGE NO NEAR RELATION TO YOU, SIR.
OF COURSE NOT. IT BEING AMUSING TO CLAIM MATERNITY TO LOKI ONLY WHEN YOU MIGHT ABUSE THE POSITION BY DENYING HIM ALL AFFECTION. ALAS, I AM BEYOND SUCH SMALL BETRAYALS NOW... "MOTHER."
YOU ARE UNNATURAL! DO NOT TOUCH ME!
UNNATURAL, MY LADY? WHAT WORD, THEN, FOR A MOTHER WHO DENIES HER SUCKLING BABE HER BREAST?
I DID NOT BEAR YOU. MY BREAST HAD NO NOURISHMENT TO OFFER YOU.
I SPOKE METAPHORICALLY. BUT LET'S NOT QUARREL. BETTER THAT YOU MAKE REPLY TO MY EARLIER INQUIRY: WHAT BUSINESS HAVE YOU HERE?
I HAVE BEEN TO SEE MY HUSBAND. YOUR FATHER, UNGRATEFUL ONE.
AH, BUT HOW CAN HE BE MY FATHER, IF YOU ARE NOT MY MOTHER?
NEVER MIND. JUST TELL ME HOW THE OLD WARRIOR FARES.
BETTER YET, I'LL GO AND ASK HIM MYSELF...

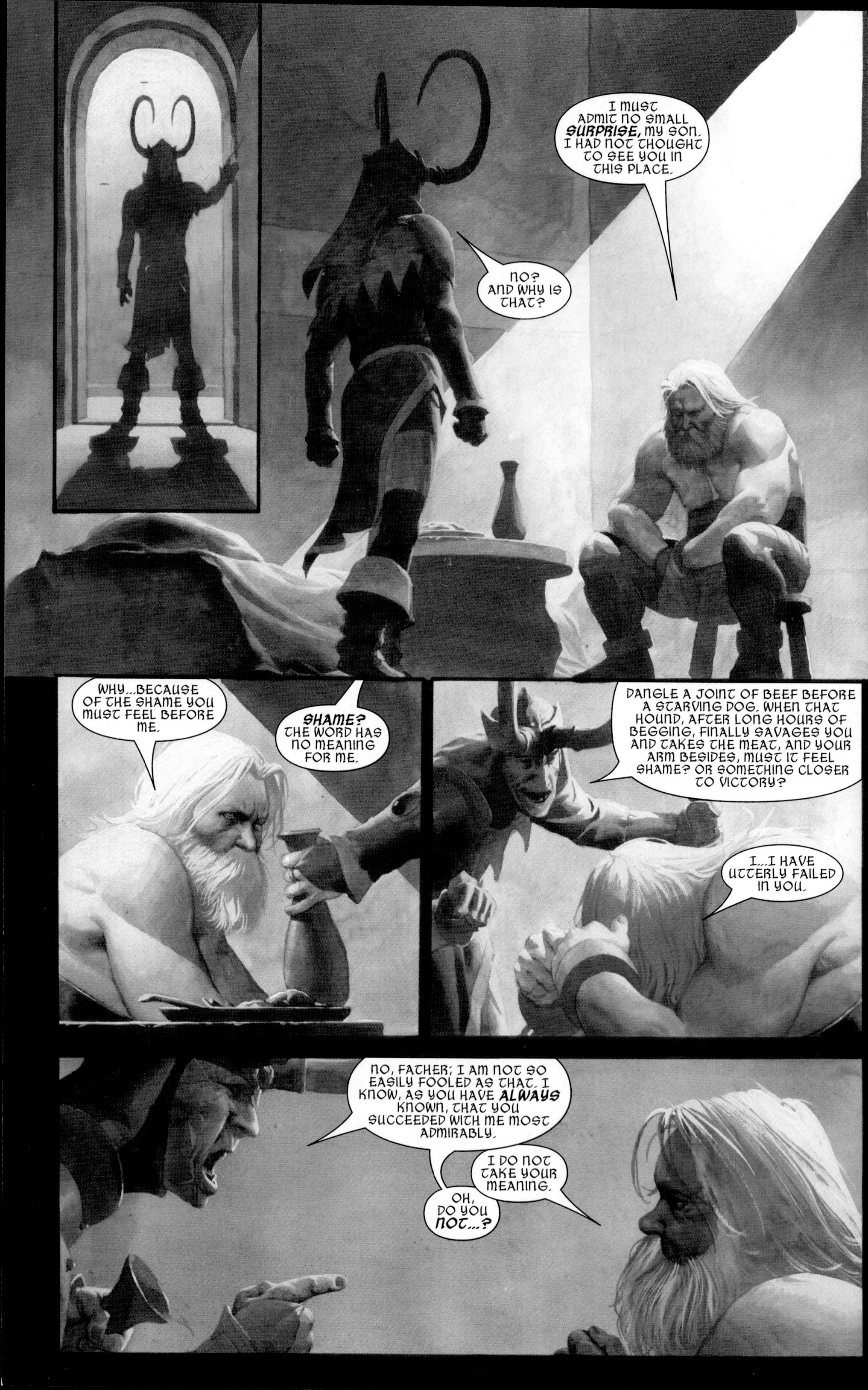
I MUST ADMIT NO SMALL SURPRISE, MY SON. I HAD NOT THOUGHT TO SEE YOU IN THIS PLACE.
NO? AND WHY IS THAT?
WHY...BECAUSE OF THE SHAME YOU MUST FEEL BEFORE ME.
SHAME? THE WORD HAS NO MEANING FOR ME.
DANGLE A JOINT OF BEEF BEFORE A STARVING DOG. WHEN THAT HOUND, AFTER LONG HOURS OF BEGGING, FINALLY SAVAGES YOU AND TAKES THE MEAT, AND YOUR ARM BESIDES, MUST IT FEEL SHAME? OR SOMETHING CLOSER TO VICTORY?
I...I HAVE UTTERLY FAILED IN YOU.
NO, FATHER; I AM NOT SO EASILY FOOLED AS THAT. I KNOW, AS YOU HAVE ALWAYS KNOWN, THAT YOU SUCCEEDED WITH ME MOST ADMIRABLY.
I DO NOT TAKE YOUR MEANING.
OH, DO YOU NOT...?

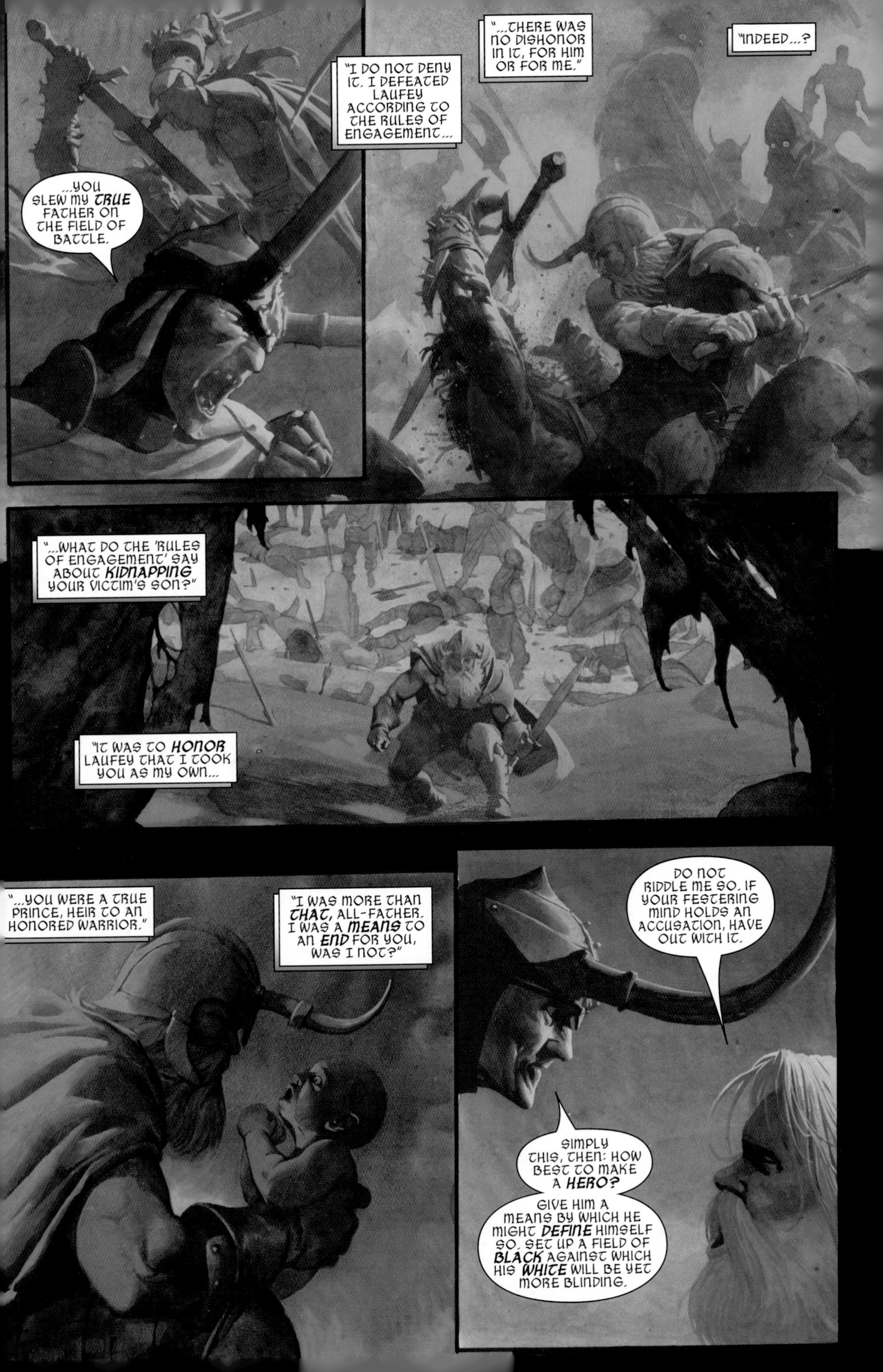
...YOU SLEW MY TRUE FATHER ON THE FIELD OF BATTLE.
"I DO NOT DENY IT. I DEFEATED LAUFEY ACCORDING TO THE RULES OF ENGAGEMENT...
"...THERE WAS NO DISHONOR IN IT, FOR HIM OR FOR ME."
"INDEED...?
"...WHAT DO THE 'RULES OF ENGAGEMENT' SAY ABOUT KIDNAPPING YOUR VICTIM'S SON?"
"IT WAS TO HONOR LAUFEY THAT I TOOK YOU AS MY OWN...
"...YOU WERE A TRUE PRINCE, HEIR TO AN HONORED WARRIOR."
"I WAS MORE THAN THAT, ALL-FATHER. I WAS A MEANS TO AN END FOR YOU, WAS I NOT?"
DO NOT RIDDLE ME SO. IF YOUR FESTERING MIND HOLDS AN ACCUSATION, HAVE OUT WITH IT.
SIMPLY THIS, THEN: HOW BEST TO MAKE A HERO?
GIVE HIM A MEANS BY WHICH HE MIGHT DEFINE HIMSELF SO. SET UP A FIELD OF BLACK AGAINST WHICH HIS WHITE WILL BE YET MORE BLINDING.

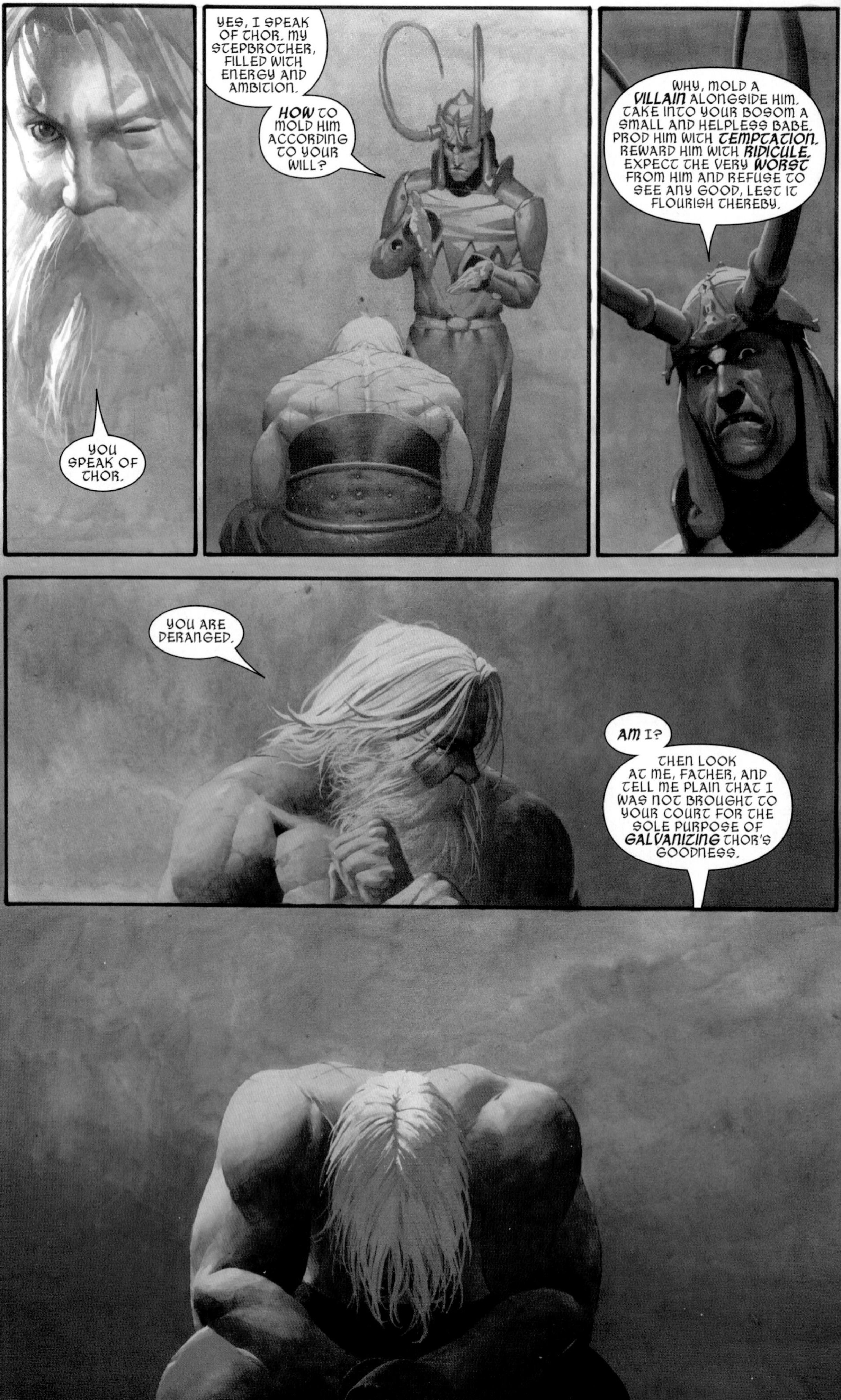
YOU SPEAK OF THOR.
YES, I SPEAK OF THOR. MY STEPBROTHER, FILLED WITH ENERGY AND AMBITION.
HOW TO MOLD HIM ACCORDING TO YOUR WILL?
WHY, MOLD A VILLAIN ALONGSIDE HIM. TAKE INTO YOUR BOSOM A SMALL AND HELPLESS BABE. PROD HIM WITH TEMPTATION. REWARD HIM WITH RIDICULE. EXPECT THE VERY WORST FROM HIM AND REFUSE TO SEE ANY GOOD, LEST IT FLOURISH THEREBY.
YOU ARE DERANGED.
AM I?
THEN LOOK AT ME, FATHER, AND TELL ME PLAIN THAT I WAS NOT BROUGHT TO YOUR COURT FOR THE SOLE PURPOSE OF GALVANIZING THOR'S GOODNESS.

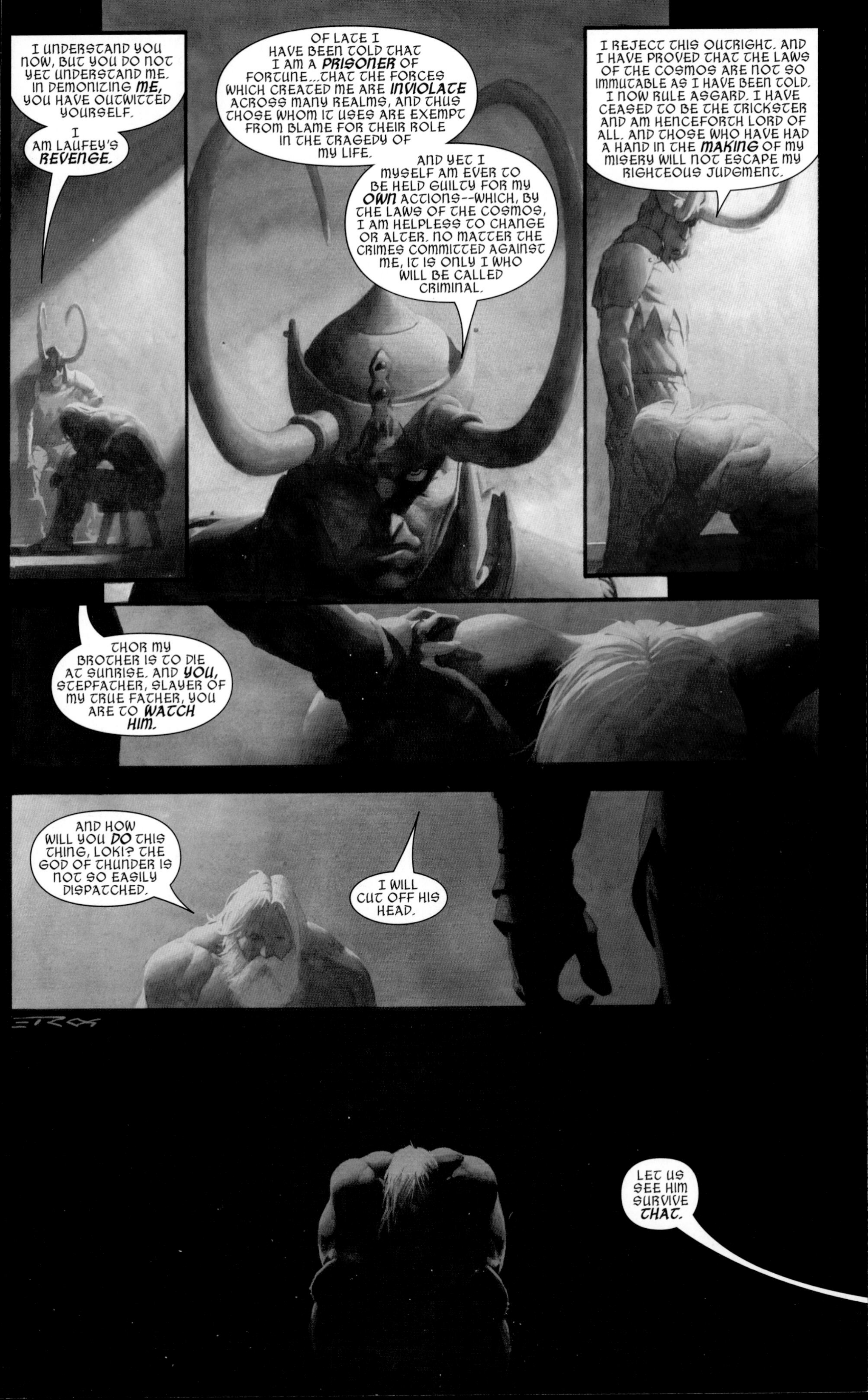

I UNDERSTAND YOU NOW, BUT YOU DO NOT YET UNDERSTAND ME. IN DEMONIZING ME, YOU HAVE OUTWITTED YOURSELF.
I AM LAUFEY'S REVENGE.
OF LATE I HAVE BEEN TOLD THAT I AM A PRISONER OF FORTUNE...THAT THE FORCES WHICH CREATED ME ARE INVIOLATE ACROSS MANY REALMS, AND THUS THOSE WHOM IT USES ARE EXEMPT FROM BLAME FOR THEIR ROLE IN THE TRAGEDY OF MY LIFE.
AND YET I MYSELF AM EVER TO BE HELD GUILTY FOR MY OWN ACTIONS--WHICH, BY THE LAWS OF THE COSMOS, I AM HELPLESS TO CHANGE OR ALTER. NO MATTER THE CRIMES COMMITTED AGAINST ME, IT IS ONLY I WHO WILL BE CALLED CRIMINAL.
I REJECT THIS OUTRIGHT, AND I HAVE PROVED THAT THE LAWS OF THE COSMOS ARE NOT SO IMMUTABLE AS I HAVE BEEN TOLD. I NOW RULE ASGARD. I HAVE CEASED TO BE THE TRICKSTER AND AM HENCEFORTH LORD OF ALL. AND THOSE WHO HAVE HAD A HAND IN THE MAKING OF MY MISERY WILL NOT ESCAPE MY RIGHTEOUS JUDGMENT.
THOR MY BROTHER IS TO DIE AT SUNRISE. AND YOU, STEPFATHER, SLAYER OF MY TRUE FATHER, YOU ARE TO WATCH HIM.
AND HOW WILL YOU DO THIS THING, LOKI? THE GOD OF THUNDER IS NOT SO EASILY DISPATCHED.
I WILL CUT OFF HIS HEAD.
LET US SEE HIM SURVIVE THAT.

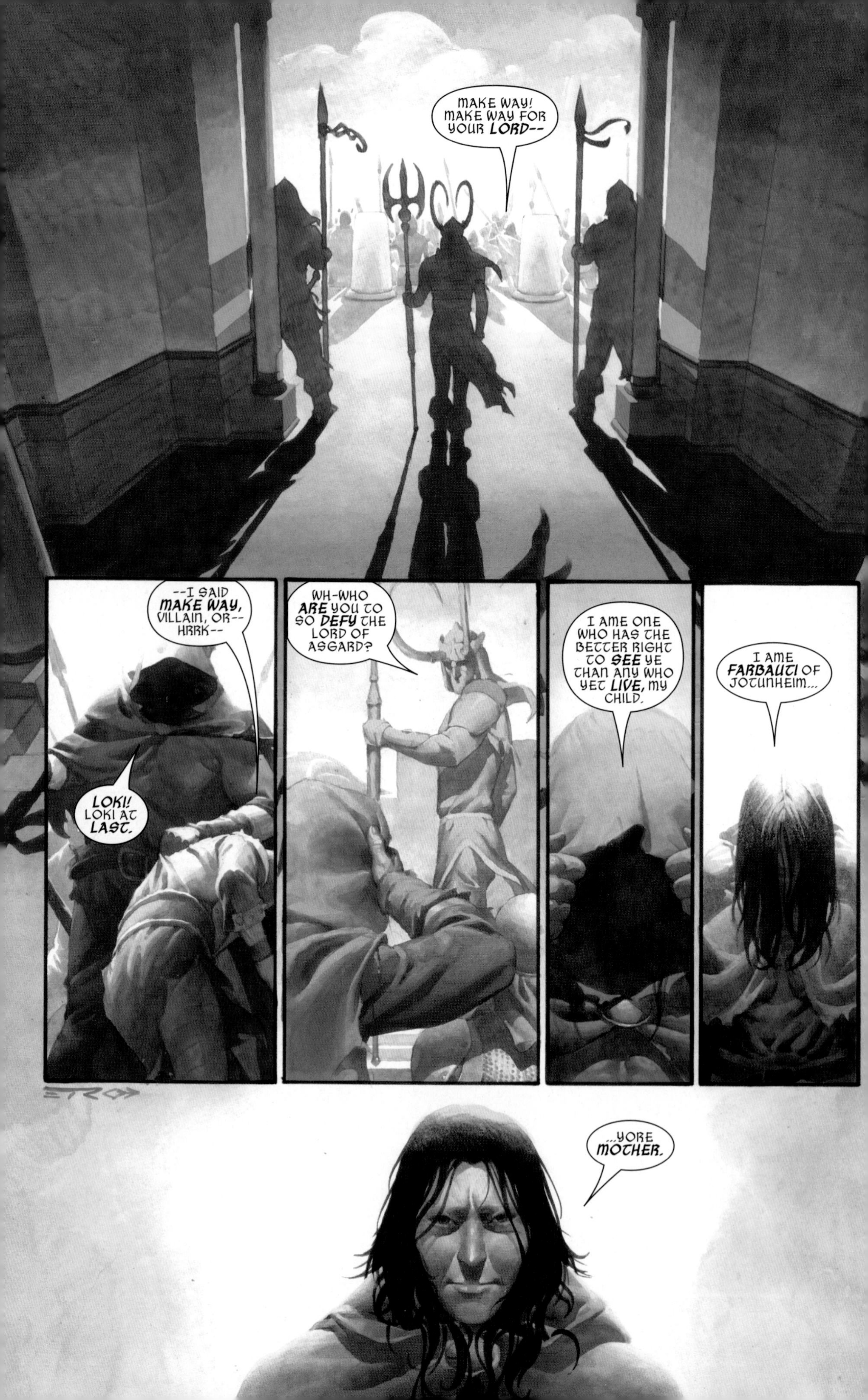
MAKE WAY! MAKE WAY FOR YOUR LORD--
--I SAID MAKE WAY, VILLAIN, OR-- HRRK--
LOKI! LOKI AT LAST.
WH-WHO ARE YOU TO SO DEFY THE LORD OF ASGARD?
I AME ONE WHO HAS THE BETTER RIGHT TO SEE YE THAN ANY WHO YET LIVE, MY CHILD.
I AME FARBAUTI OF JOTUNHEIM...
...YORE MOTHER.

# FOUR

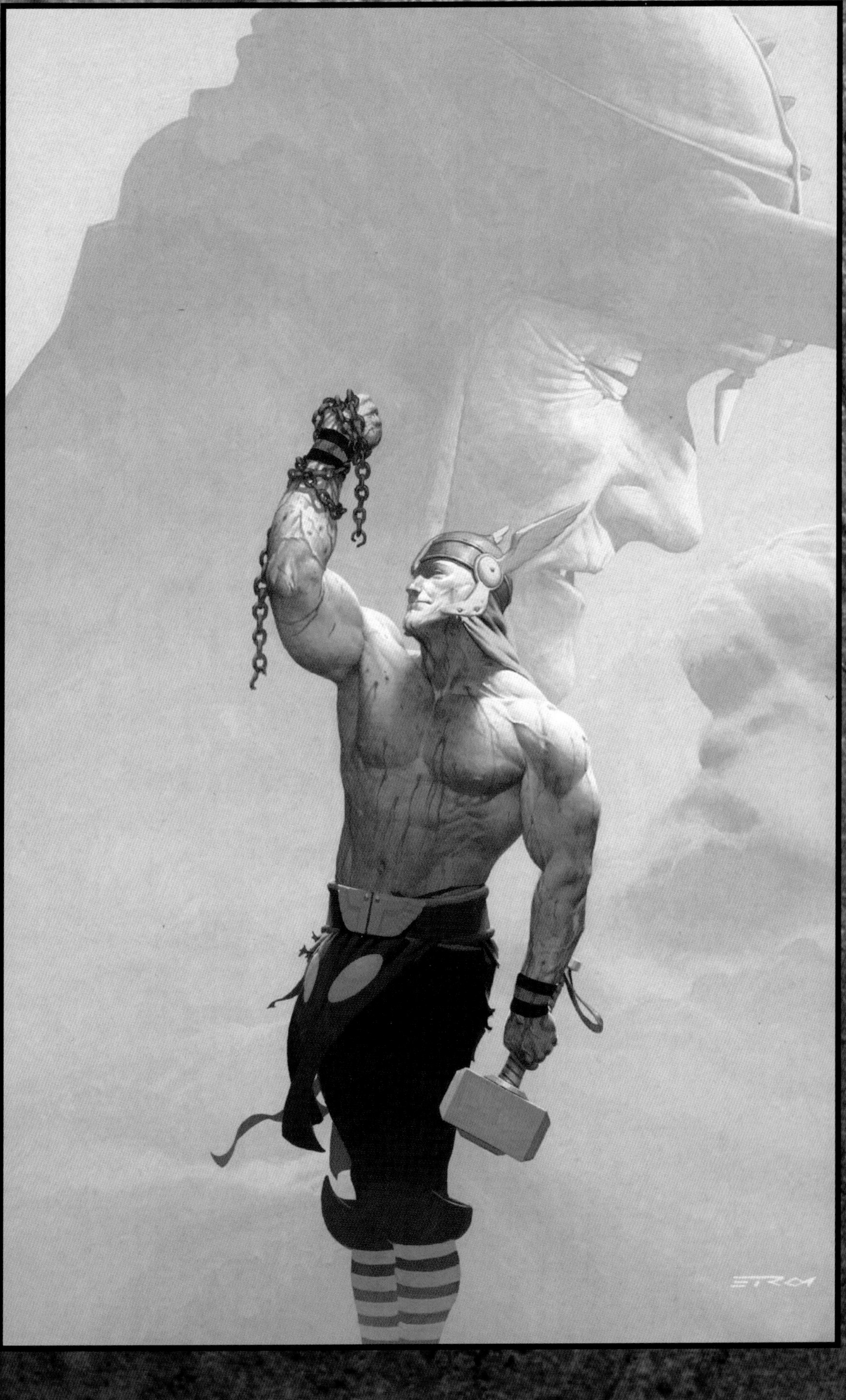

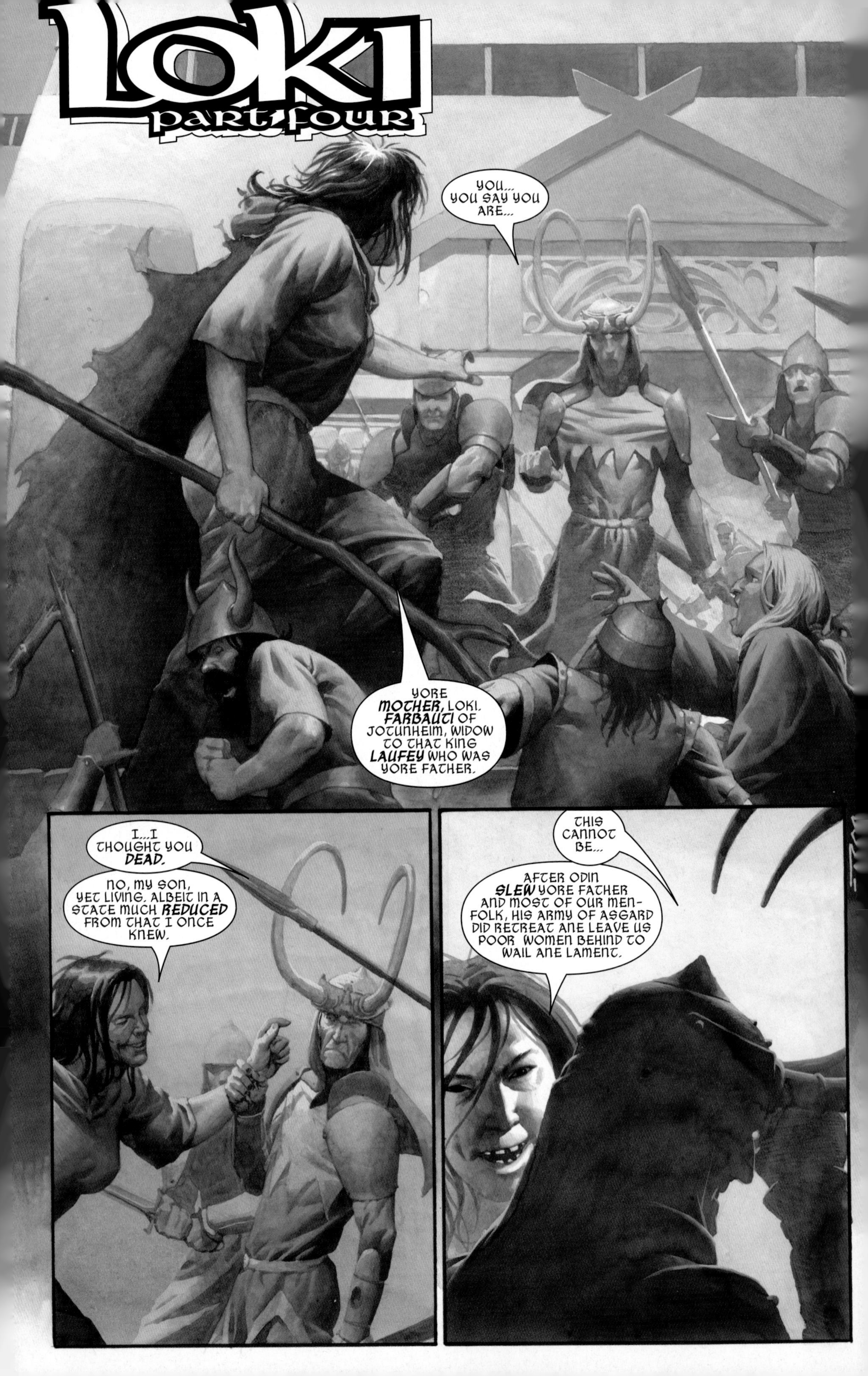
LOKI
PART FOUR
YOU... YOU SAY YOU ARE...
YORE MOTHER, LOKI. FARBAUTI OF JOTUNHEIM, WIDOW TO THAT KING LAUFEY WHO WAS YORE FATHER.
I...I THOUGHT YOU DEAD.
NO, MY SON, YET LIVING. ALBEIT IN A STATE MUCH REDUCED FROM THAT I ONCE KNEW.
THIS CANNOT BE...
AFTER ODIN SLEW YORE FATHER AND MOST OF OUR MEN-FOLK, HIS ARMY OF ASGARD DID RETREAT ANE LEAVE US POOR WOMEN BEHIND TO WAIL ANE LAMENT.

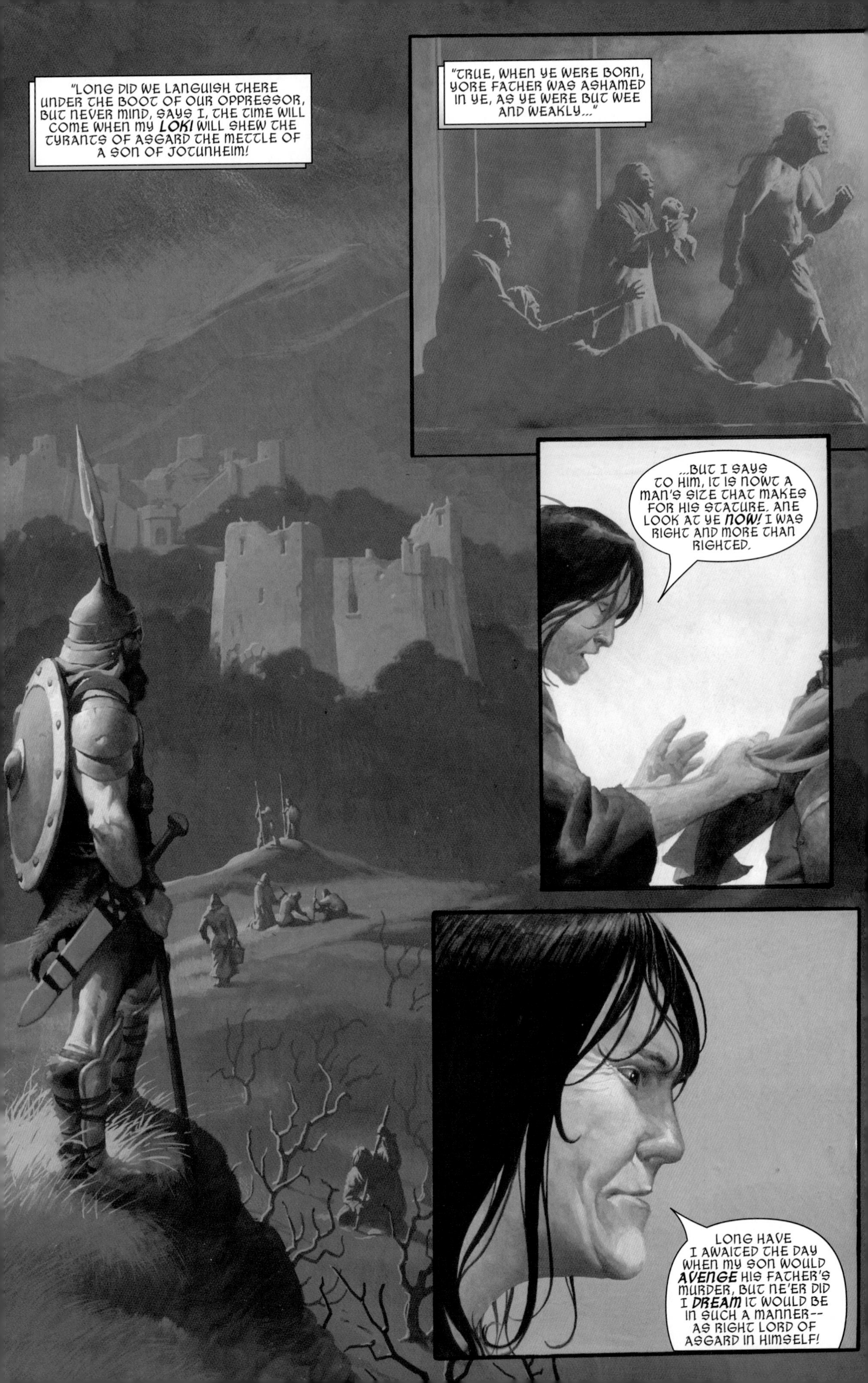
"LONG DID WE LANGUISH THERE UNDER THE BOOT OF OUR OPPRESSOR, BUT NEVER MIND, SAYS I, THE TIME WILL COME WHEN MY LOKI WILL SHEW THE TYRANTS OF ASGARD THE METTLE OF A SON OF JOTUNHEIM!
"TRUE, WHEN YE WERE BORN, YORE FATHER WAS ASHAMED IN YE, AS YE WERE BUT WEE AND WEAKLY..."
...BUT I SAYS TO HIM, IT IS NOWT A MAN'S SIZE THAT MAKES FOR HIS STATURE. ANE LOOK AT YE NOW! I WAS RIGHT AND MORE THAN RIGHTED.
LONG HAVE I AWAITED THE DAY WHEN MY SON WOULD AVENGE HIS FATHER'S MURDER, BUT NE'ER DID I DREAM IT WOULD BE IN SUCH A MANNER-- AS RIGHT LORD OF ASGARD IN HIMSELF!

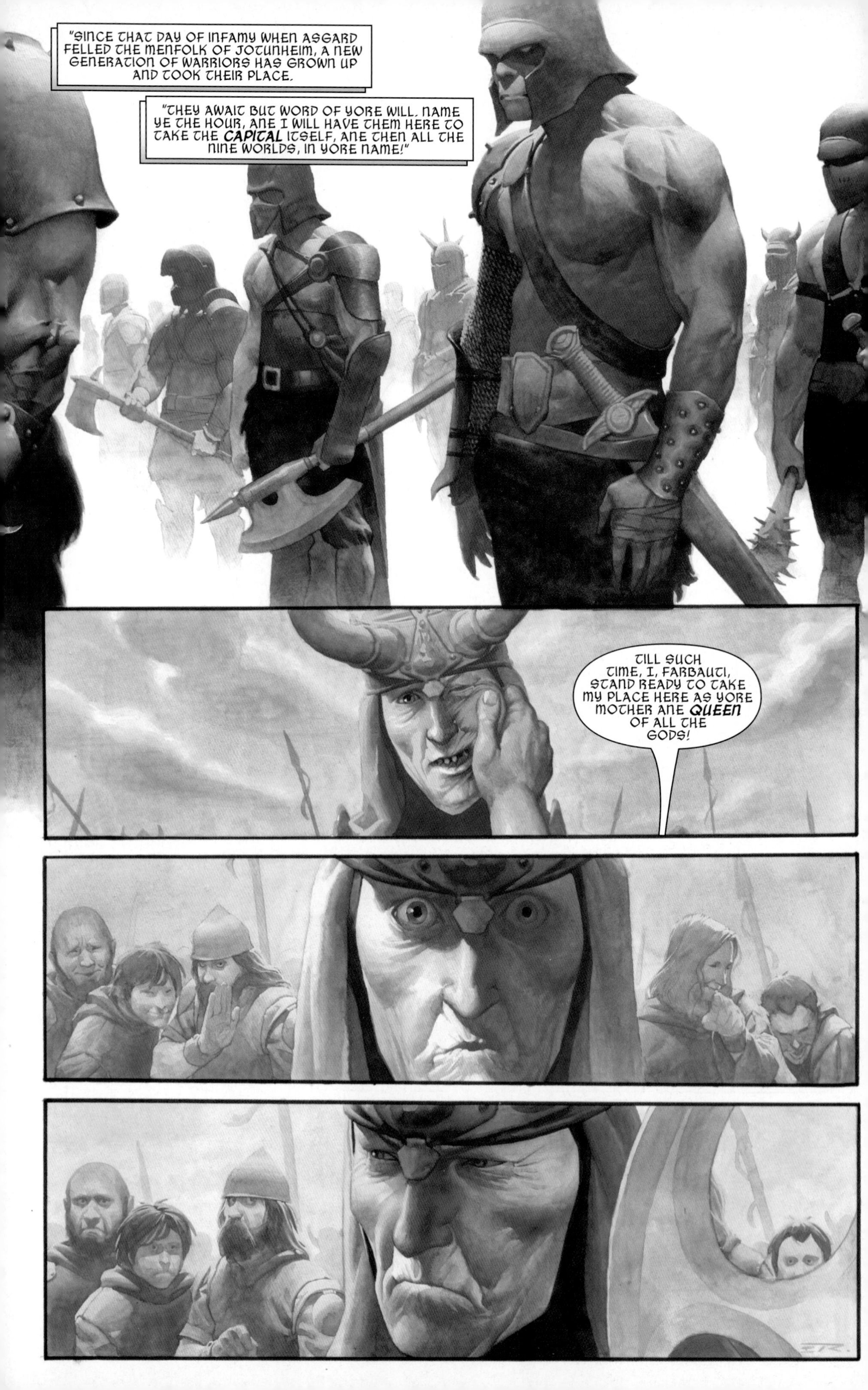
"SINCE THAT DAY OF INFAMY WHEN ASGARD FELLED THE MENFOLK OF JOTUNHEIM, A NEW GENERATION OF WARRIORS HAS GROWN UP AND TOOK THEIR PLACE.
"THEY AWAIT BUT WORD OF YORE WILL. NAME YE THE HOUR, ANE I WILL HAVE THEM HERE TO TAKE THE CAPITAL ITSELF, ANE THEN ALL THE NINE WORLDS, IN YORE NAME!"
TILL SUCH TIME, I, FARBAUTI, STAND READY TO TAKE MY PLACE HERE AS YORE MOTHER ANE QUEEN OF ALL THE GODS!

IT SHALL, OF COURSE, BE AS YOU *SAY*, MOTHER. BUT LET ME FIRST HAVE YOU INSTALLED IN ACCOMMODATIONS SUITABLE TO YOUR *RANK*, WHERE YOU MAY REST AND REFRESH YOURSELF AFTER YOUR LONG JOURNEY.

TAKE HER TO SOME SUITE OF ROOMS *FAR*, *FAR* FROM THE COURT. SEE THAT SHE WANTS FOR NOTHING, BUT SEE TO IT AS WELL THAT SHE GOES *NOWHERE*. HOUSE ARREST IN ALL BUT NAME. IS THIS CLEAR TO YOU?

YES, MY LORD.

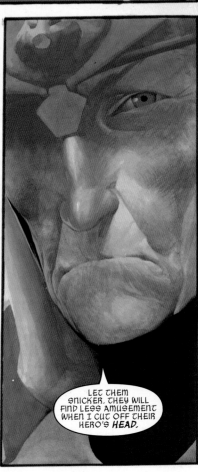

LET THEM SNICKER. THEY WILL FIND LESS AMUSEMENT WHEN I CUT OFF THEIR HERO'S *HEAD*.

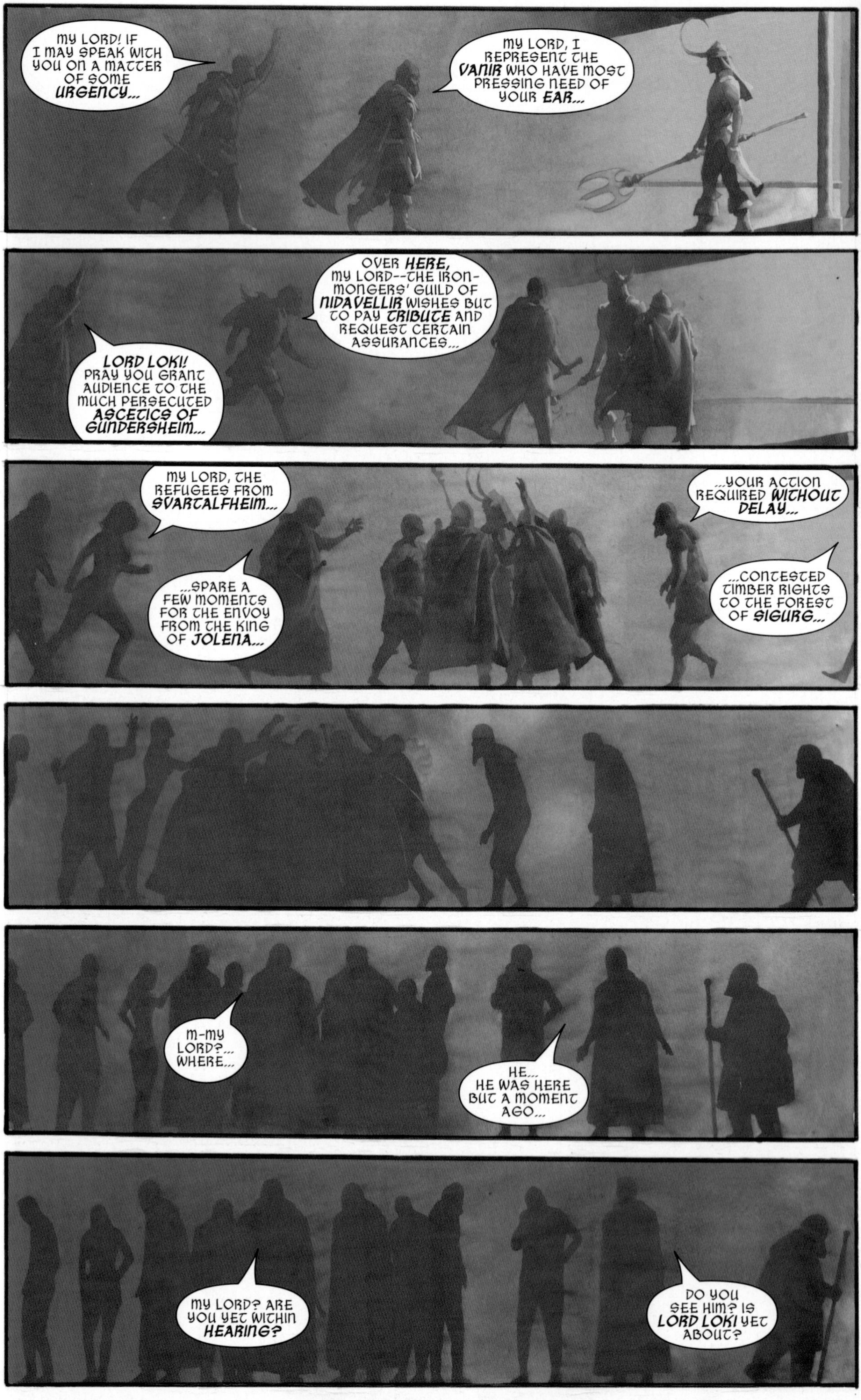
MY LORD! IF I MAY SPEAK WITH YOU ON A MATTER OF SOME URGENCY...
MY LORD, I REPRESENT THE VANIR WHO HAVE MOST PRESSING NEED OF YOUR EAR...
OVER HERE, MY LORD--THE IRON-MONGERS' GUILD OF NIDAVELLIR WISHES BUT TO PAY TRIBUTE AND REQUEST CERTAIN ASSURANCES...
LORD LOKI! PRAY YOU GRANT AUDIENCE TO THE MUCH PERSECUTED ASCETICS OF GUNDERSHEIM...
MY LORD, THE REFUGEES FROM SVARTALFHEIM...
...SPARE A FEW MOMENTS FOR THE ENVOY FROM THE KING OF JOLENA...
...YOUR ACTION REQUIRED WITHOUT DELAY...
...CONTESTED TIMBER RIGHTS TO THE FOREST OF SIGURG...
M-MY LORD?... WHERE...
HE... HE WAS HERE BUT A MOMENT AGO...
MY LORD? ARE YOU YET WITHIN HEARING?
DO YOU SEE HIM? IS LORD LOKI YET ABOUT?

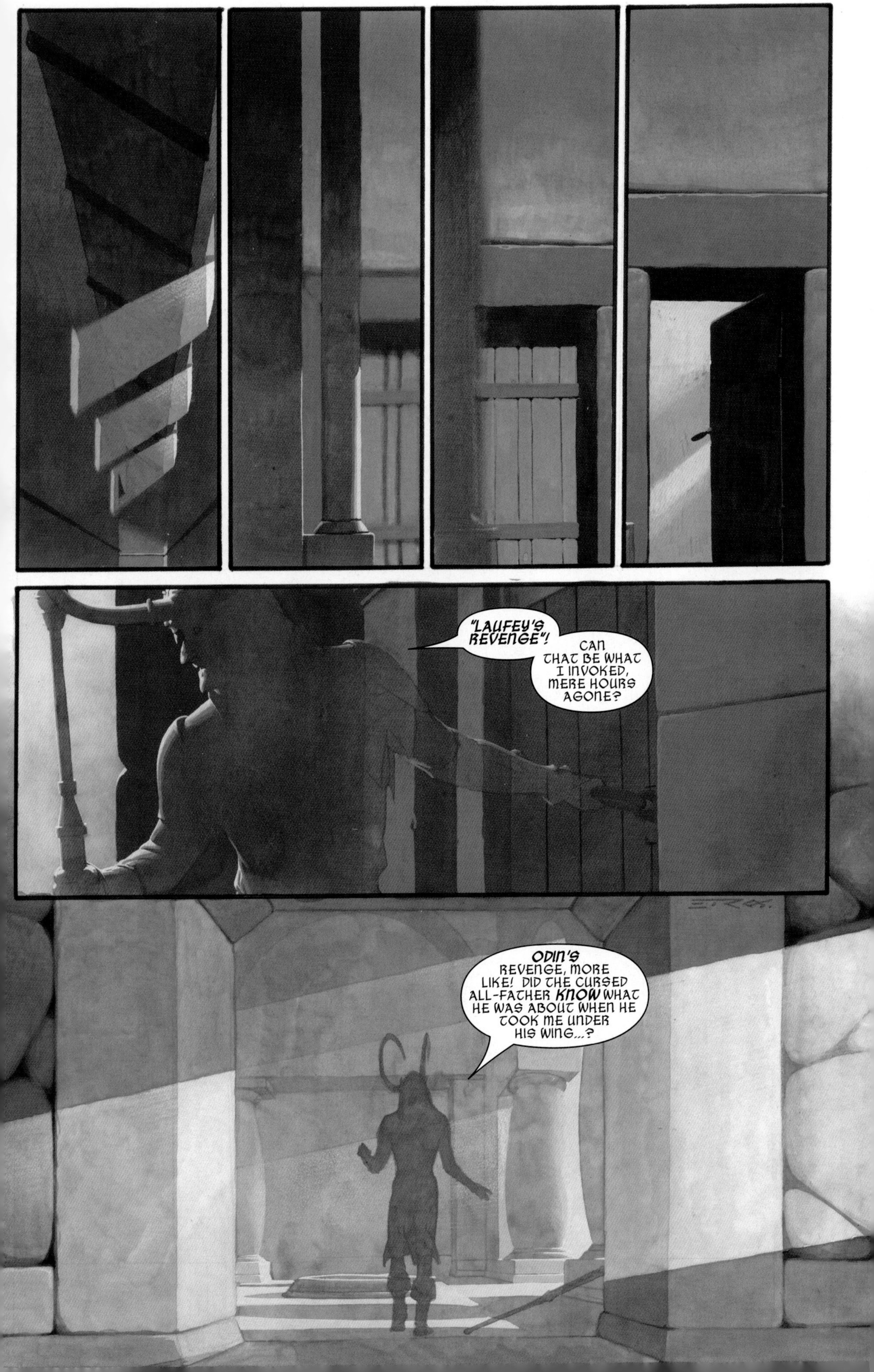
"LAUFEY'S REVENGE"! CAN THAT BE WHAT I INVOKED, MERE HOURS AGONE?
ODIN'S REVENGE, MORE LIKE! DID THE CURSED ALL-FATHER KNOW WHAT HE WAS ABOUT WHEN HE TOOK ME UNDER HIS WING...?

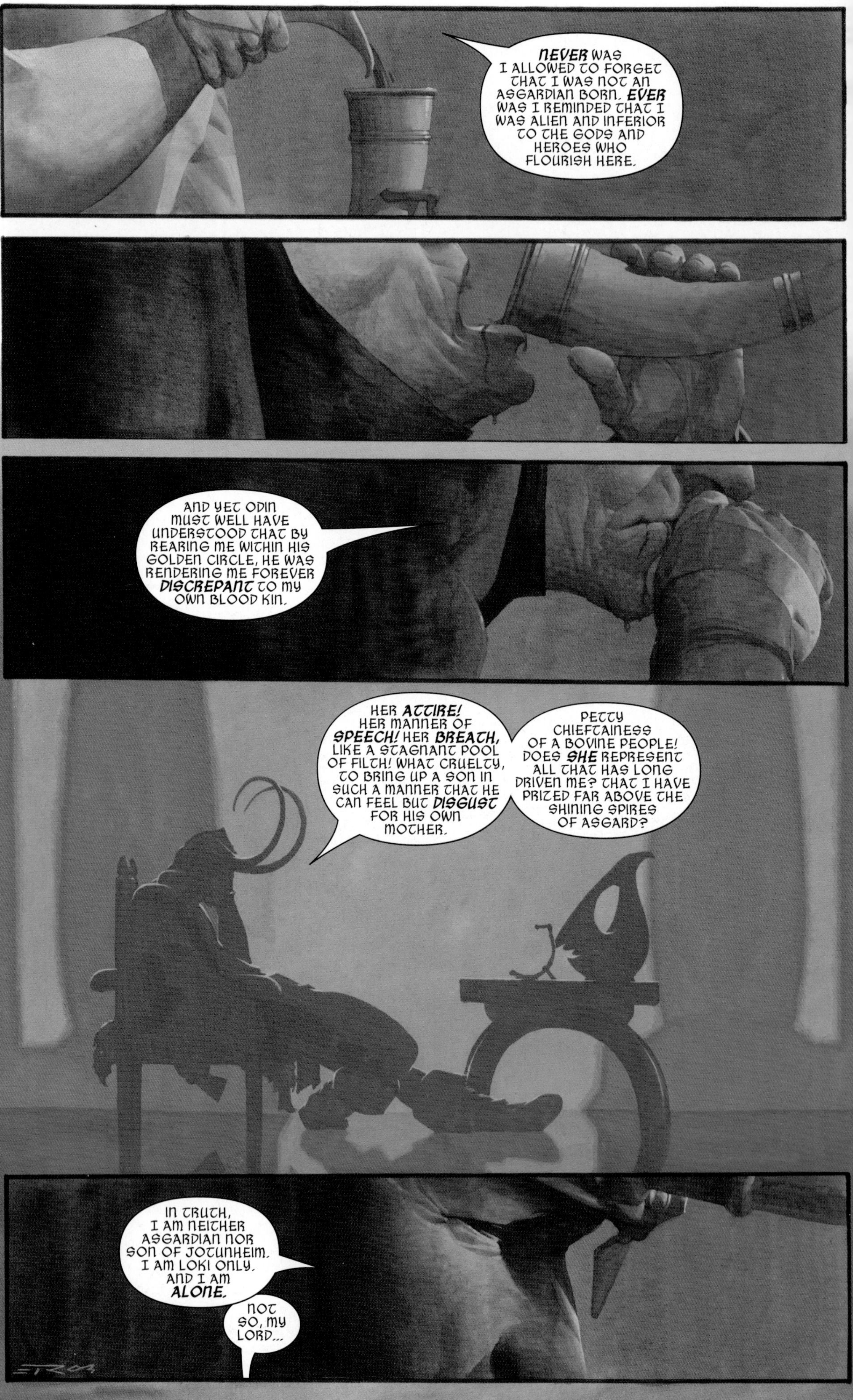
NEVER WAS I ALLOWED TO FORGET THAT I WAS NOT AN ASGARDIAN BORN. EVER WAS I REMINDED THAT I WAS ALIEN AND INFERIOR TO THE GODS AND HEROES WHO FLOURISH HERE.
AND YET ODIN MUST WELL HAVE UNDERSTOOD THAT BY REARING ME WITHIN HIS GOLDEN CIRCLE, HE WAS RENDERING ME FOREVER DISCREPANT TO MY OWN BLOOD KIN.
HER ATTIRE! HER MANNER OF SPEECH! HER BREATH, LIKE A STAGNANT POOL OF FILTH! WHAT CRUELTY, TO BRING UP A SON IN SUCH A MANNER THAT HE CAN FEEL BUT DISGUST FOR HIS OWN MOTHER.
PETTY CHIEFTAINESS OF A BOVINE PEOPLE! DOES SHE REPRESENT ALL THAT HAS LONG DRIVEN ME? THAT I HAVE PRIZED FAR ABOVE THE SHINING SPIRES OF ASGARD?
IN TRUTH, I AM NEITHER ASGARDIAN NOR SON OF JOTUNHEIM. I AM LOKI ONLY. AND I AM ALONE.
NOT SO, MY LORD...

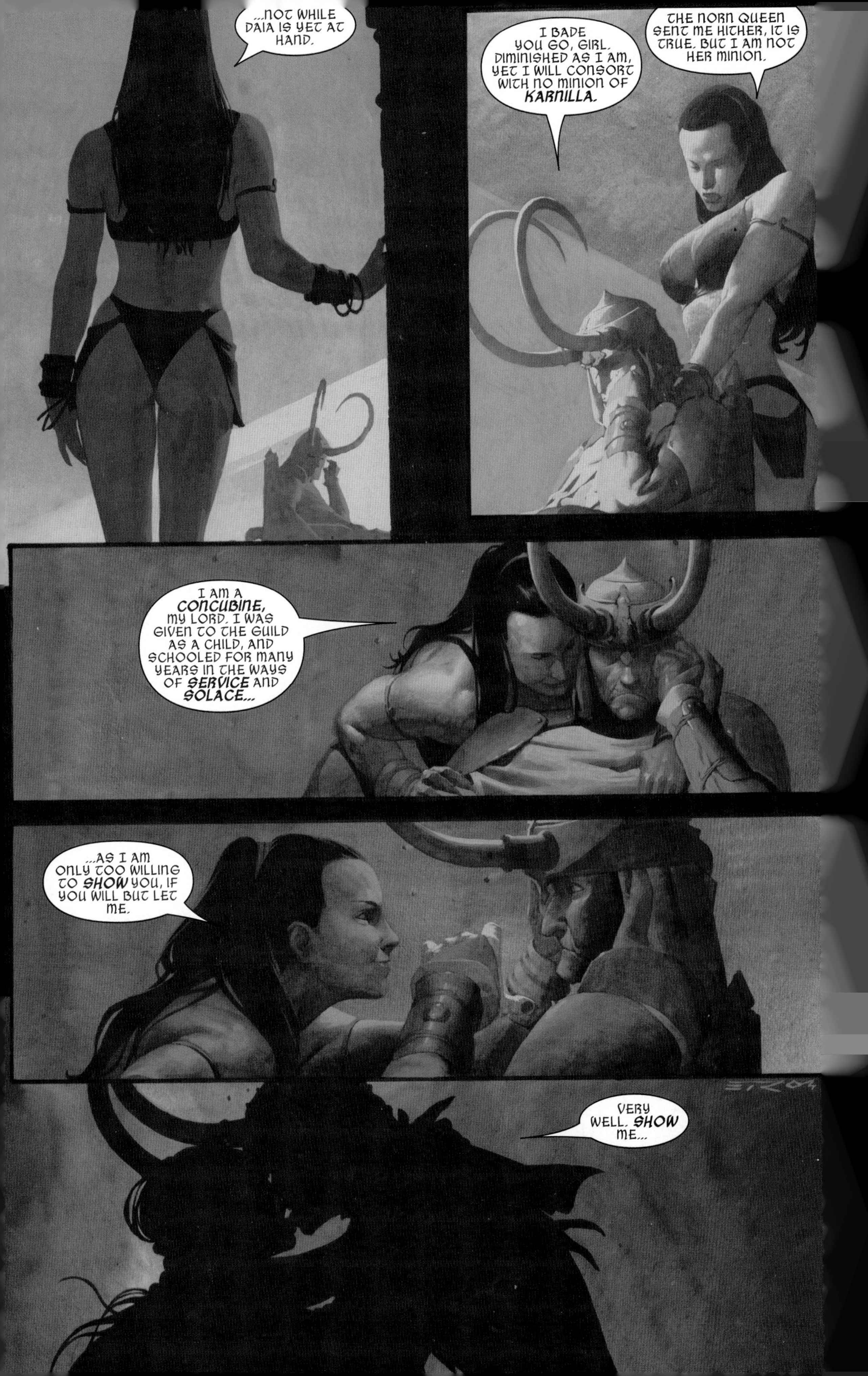
...NOT WHILE DAIA IS YET AT HAND.
I BADE YOU GO, GIRL. DIMINISHED AS I AM, YET I WILL CONSORT WITH NO MINION OF KARNILLA.
THE NORN QUEEN SENT ME HITHER, IT IS TRUE. BUT I AM NOT HER MINION.
I AM A CONCUBINE, MY LORD. I WAS GIVEN TO THE GUILD AS A CHILD, AND SCHOOLED FOR MANY YEARS IN THE WAYS OF SERVICE AND SOLACE...
...AS I AM ONLY TOO WILLING TO SHOW YOU, IF YOU WILL BUT LET ME.
VERY WELL. SHOW ME...

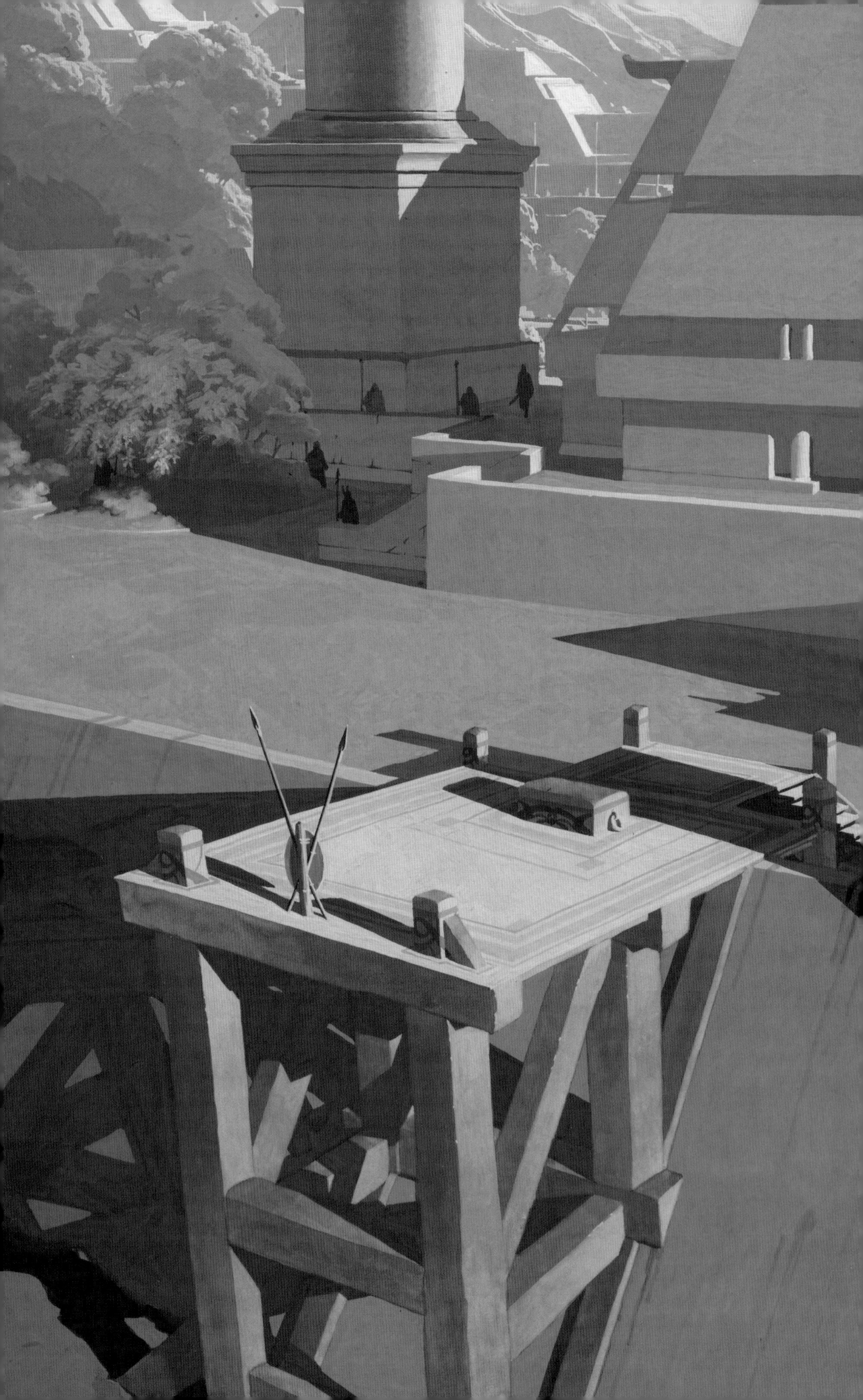

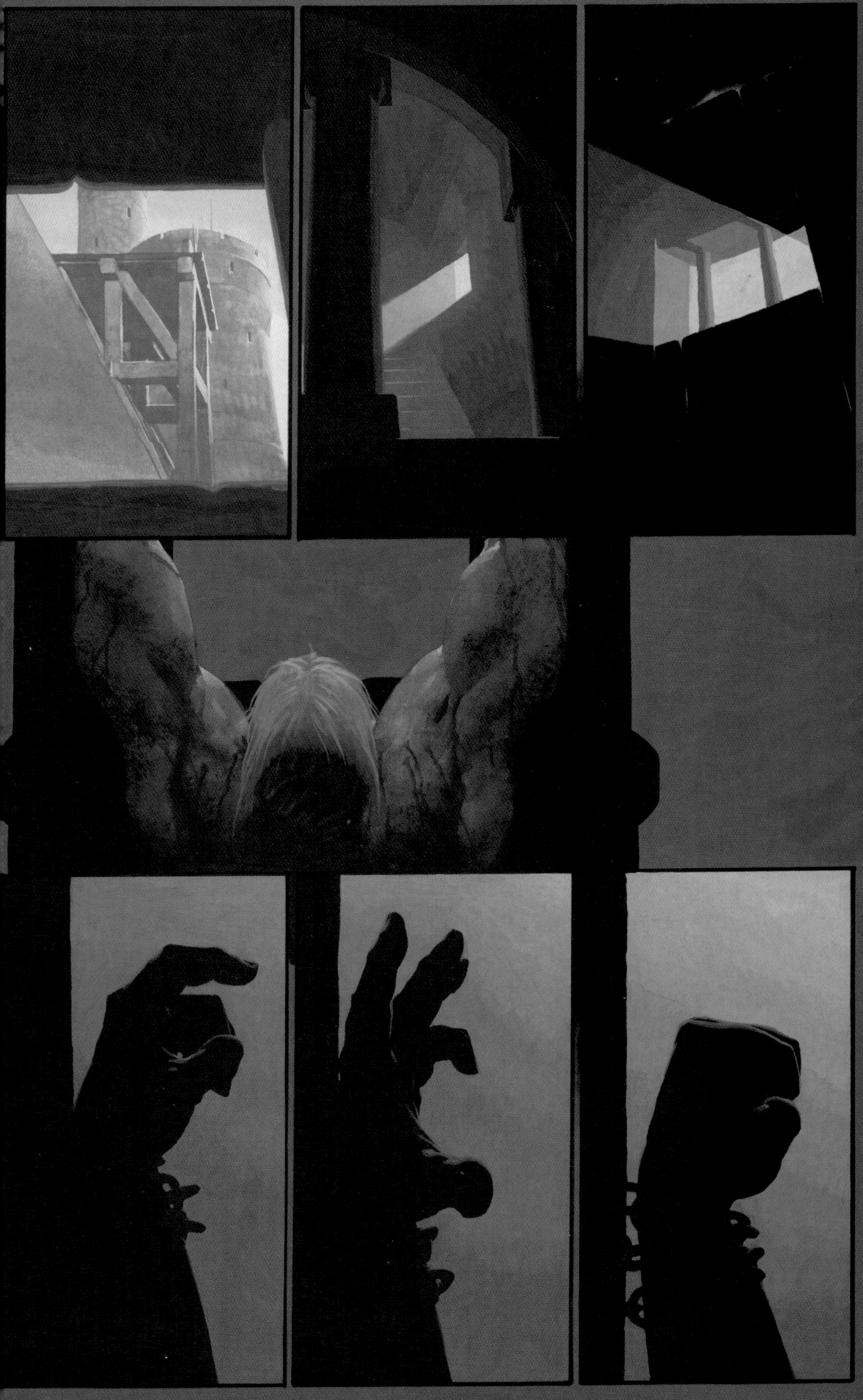

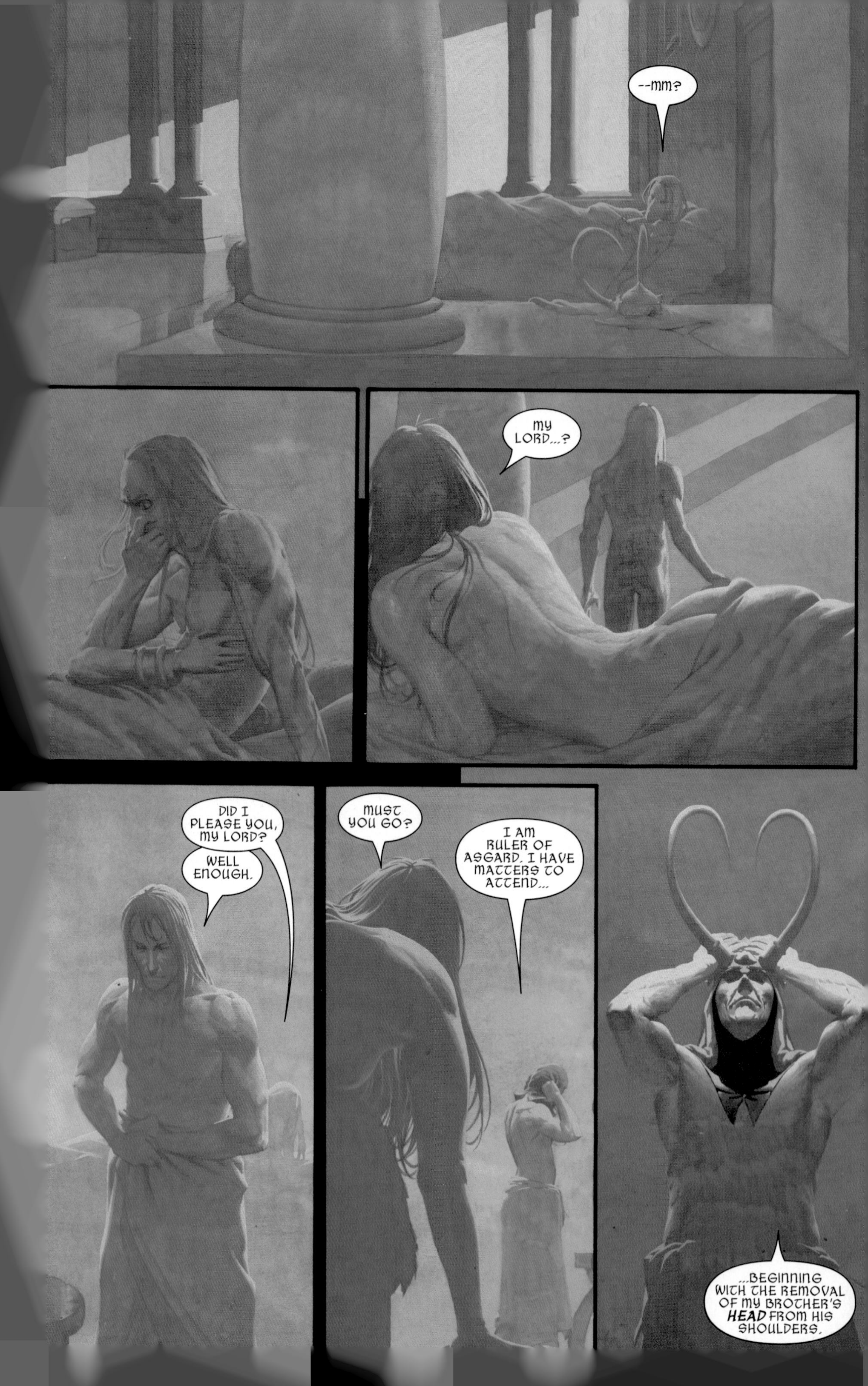
--mm?
MY LORD...?
DID I PLEASE YOU, MY LORD?
WELL ENOUGH.
MUST YOU GO?
I AM RULER OF ASGARD. I HAVE MATTERS TO ATTEND...
...BEGINNING WITH THE REMOVAL OF MY BROTHER'S **HEAD** FROM HIS SHOULDERS.

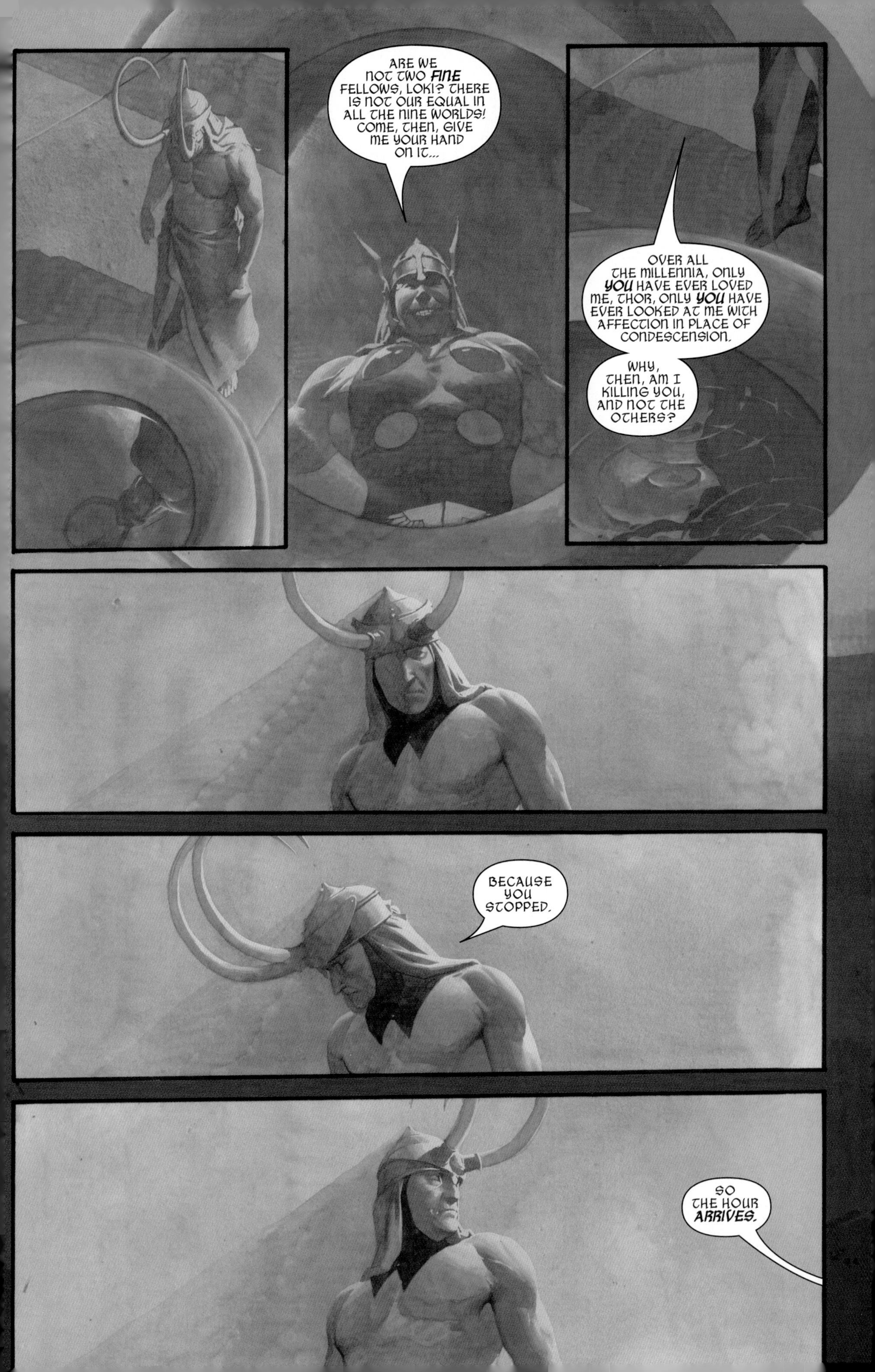
ARE WE NOT TWO FINE FELLOWS, LOKI? THERE IS NOT OUR EQUAL IN ALL THE NINE WORLDS! COME, THEN, GIVE ME YOUR HAND ON IT...
OVER ALL THE MILLENNIA, ONLY YOU HAVE EVER LOVED ME, THOR, ONLY YOU HAVE EVER LOOKED AT ME WITH AFFECTION IN PLACE OF CONDESCENSION.
WHY, THEN, AM I KILLING YOU, AND NOT THE OTHERS?
BECAUSE YOU STOPPED.
SO THE HOUR ARRIVES.

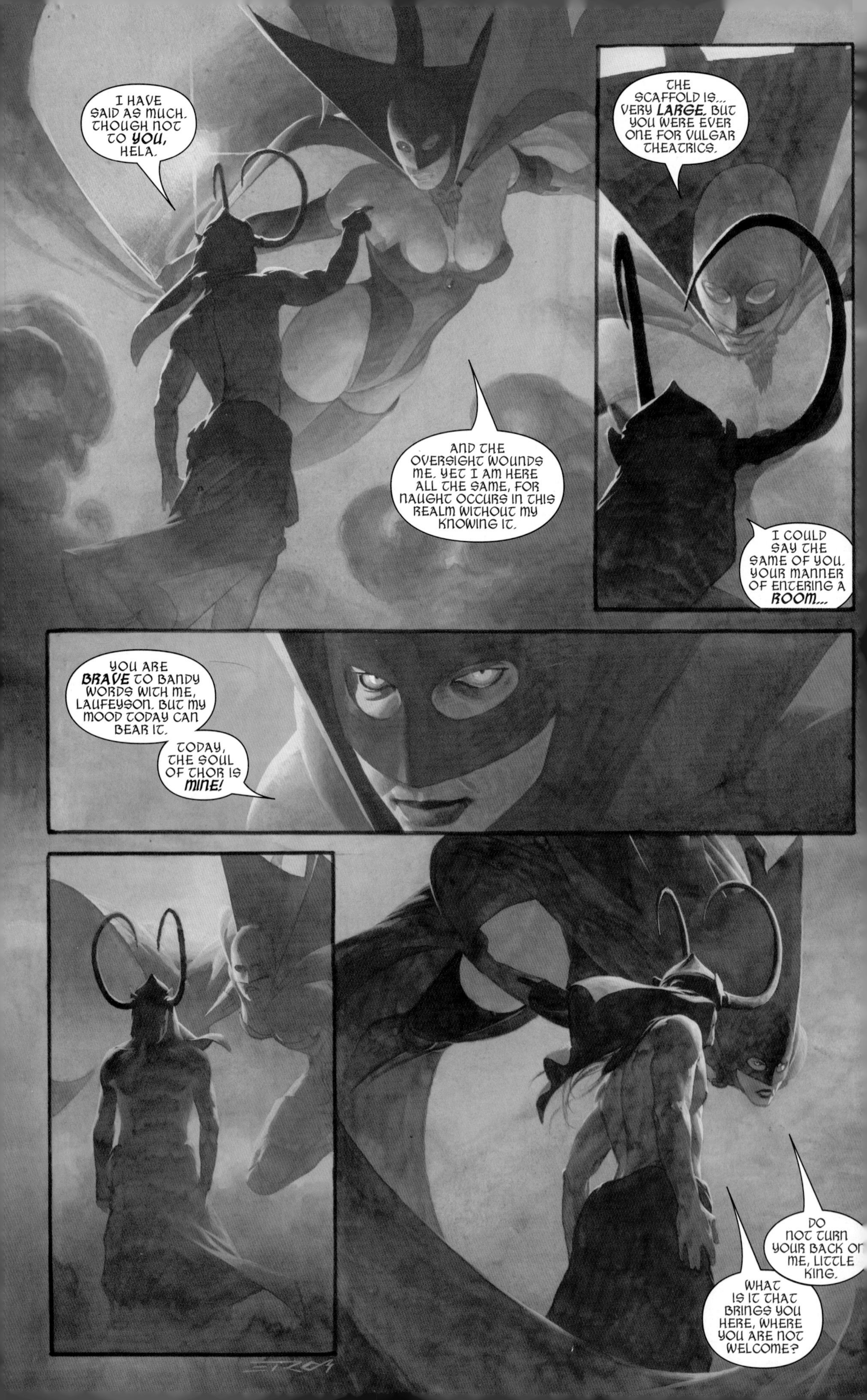
I HAVE SAID AS MUCH. THOUGH NOT TO YOU, HELA.
AND THE OVERSIGHT WOUNDS ME. YET I AM HERE ALL THE SAME, FOR NAUGHT OCCURS IN THIS REALM WITHOUT MY KNOWING IT.
THE SCAFFOLD IS... VERY LARGE. BUT YOU WERE EVER ONE FOR VULGAR THEATRICS.
I COULD SAY THE SAME OF YOU. YOUR MANNER OF ENTERING A ROOM...
YOU ARE BRAVE TO BANDY WORDS WITH ME, LAUFEYSON. BUT MY MOOD TODAY CAN BEAR IT.
TODAY, THE SOUL OF THOR IS MINE!
DO NOT TURN YOUR BACK ON ME, LITTLE KING.
WHAT IS IT THAT BRINGS YOU HERE, WHERE YOU ARE NOT WELCOME?

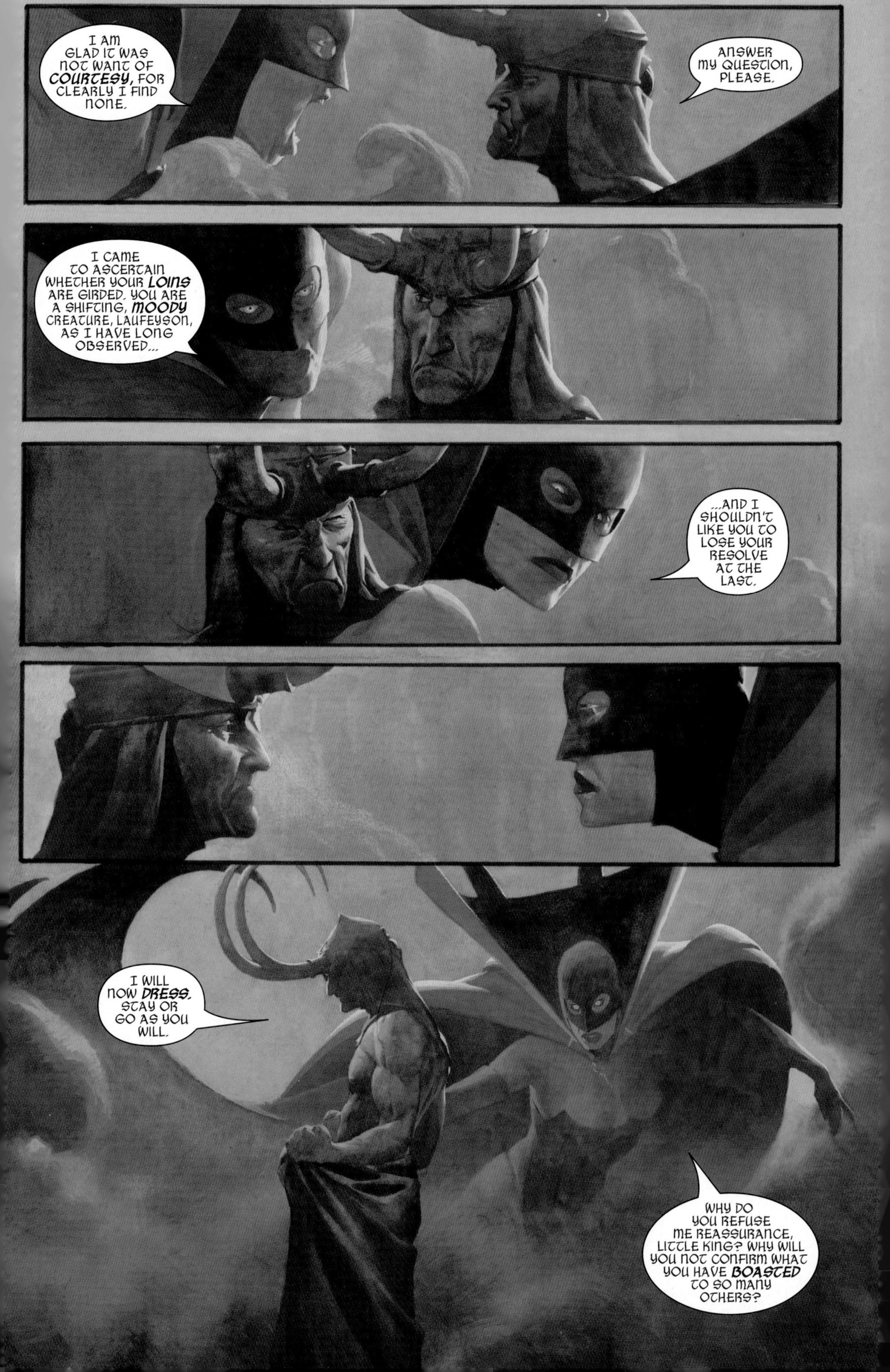
I AM GLAD IT WAS NOT WANT OF COURTESY, FOR CLEARLY I FIND NONE.
ANSWER MY QUESTION, PLEASE.
I CAME TO ASCERTAIN WHETHER YOUR LOINS ARE GIRDED. YOU ARE A SHIFTING, MOODY CREATURE, LAUFEYSON, AS I HAVE LONG OBSERVED...
...AND I SHOULDN'T LIKE YOU TO LOSE YOUR RESOLVE AT THE LAST.
I WILL NOW DRESS. STAY OR GO AS YOU WILL.
WHY DO YOU REFUSE ME REASSURANCE, LITTLE KING? WHY WILL YOU NOT CONFIRM WHAT YOU HAVE BOASTED TO SO MANY OTHERS?

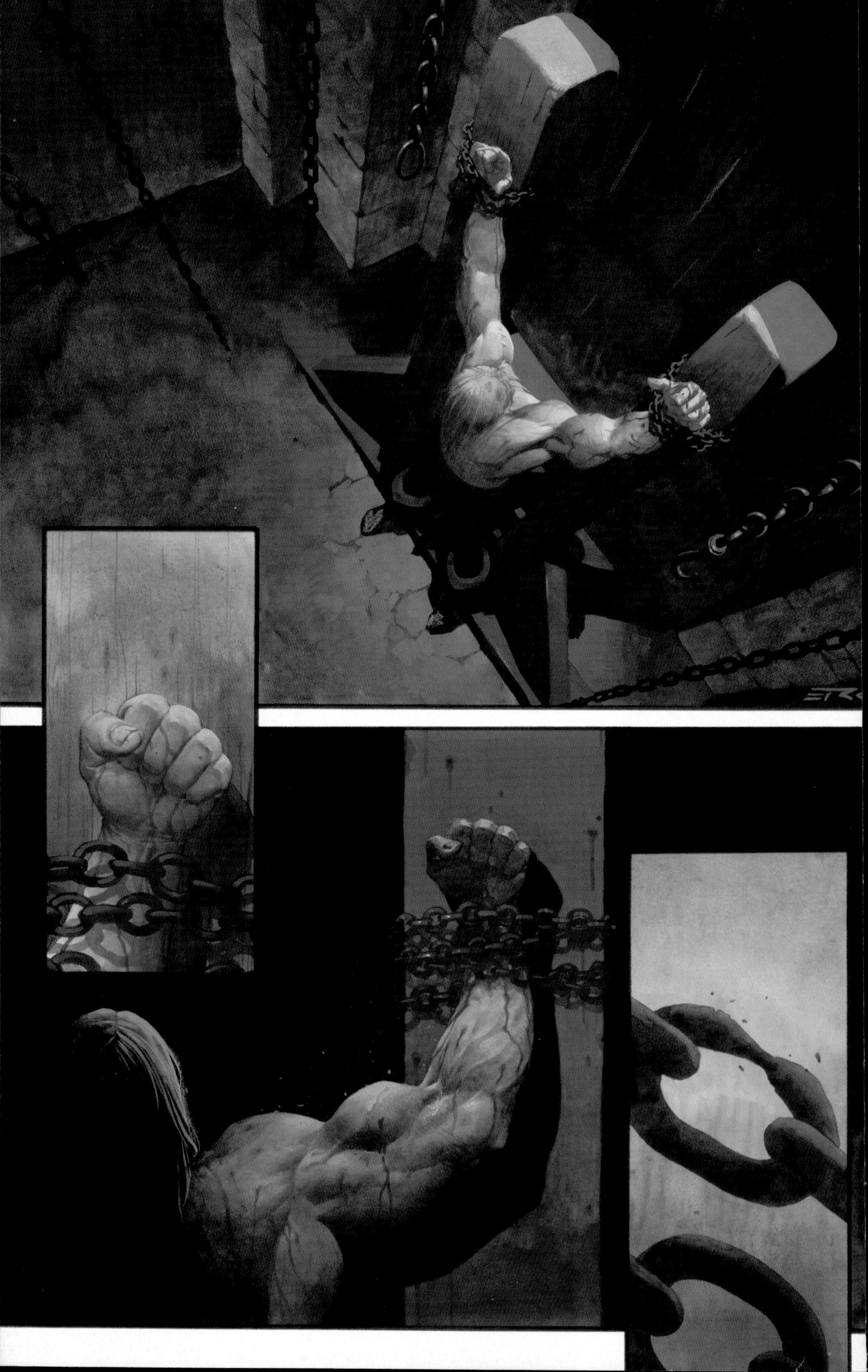

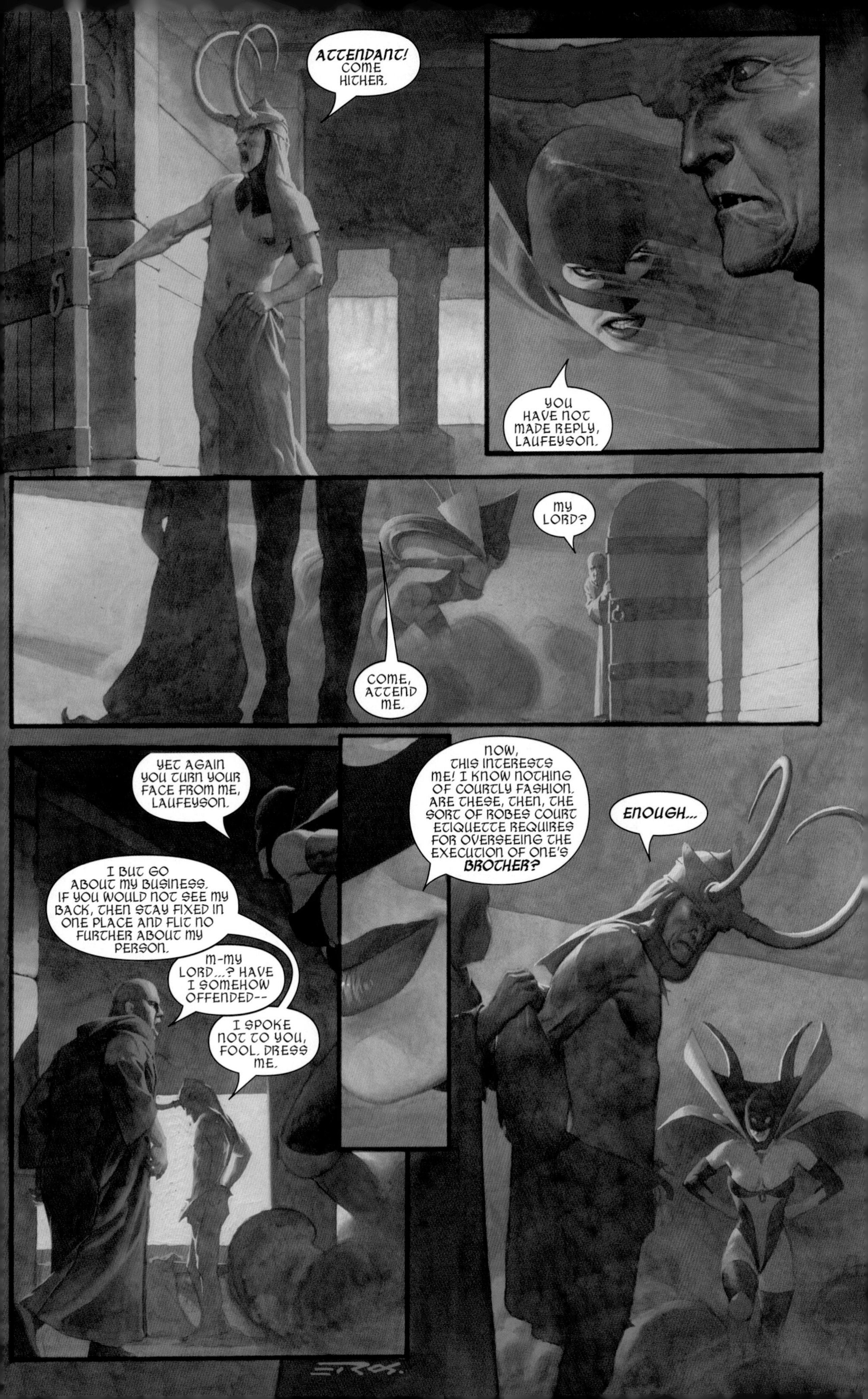
ATTENDANT! COME HITHER.
YOU HAVE NOT MADE REPLY, LAUFEYSON.
MY LORD?
COME, ATTEND ME.
YET AGAIN YOU TURN YOUR FACE FROM ME, LAUFEYSON.
I BUT GO ABOUT MY BUSINESS. IF YOU WOULD NOT SEE MY BACK, THEN STAY FIXED IN ONE PLACE AND FLIT NO FURTHER ABOUT MY PERSON.
M-MY LORD...? HAVE I SOMEHOW OFFENDED--
I SPOKE NOT TO YOU, FOOL. DRESS ME.
NOW, THIS INTERESTS ME! I KNOW NOTHING OF COURTLY FASHION. ARE THESE, THEN, THE SORT OF ROBES COURT ETIQUETTE REQUIRES FOR OVERSEEING THE EXECUTION OF ONE'S BROTHER?
ENOUGH...

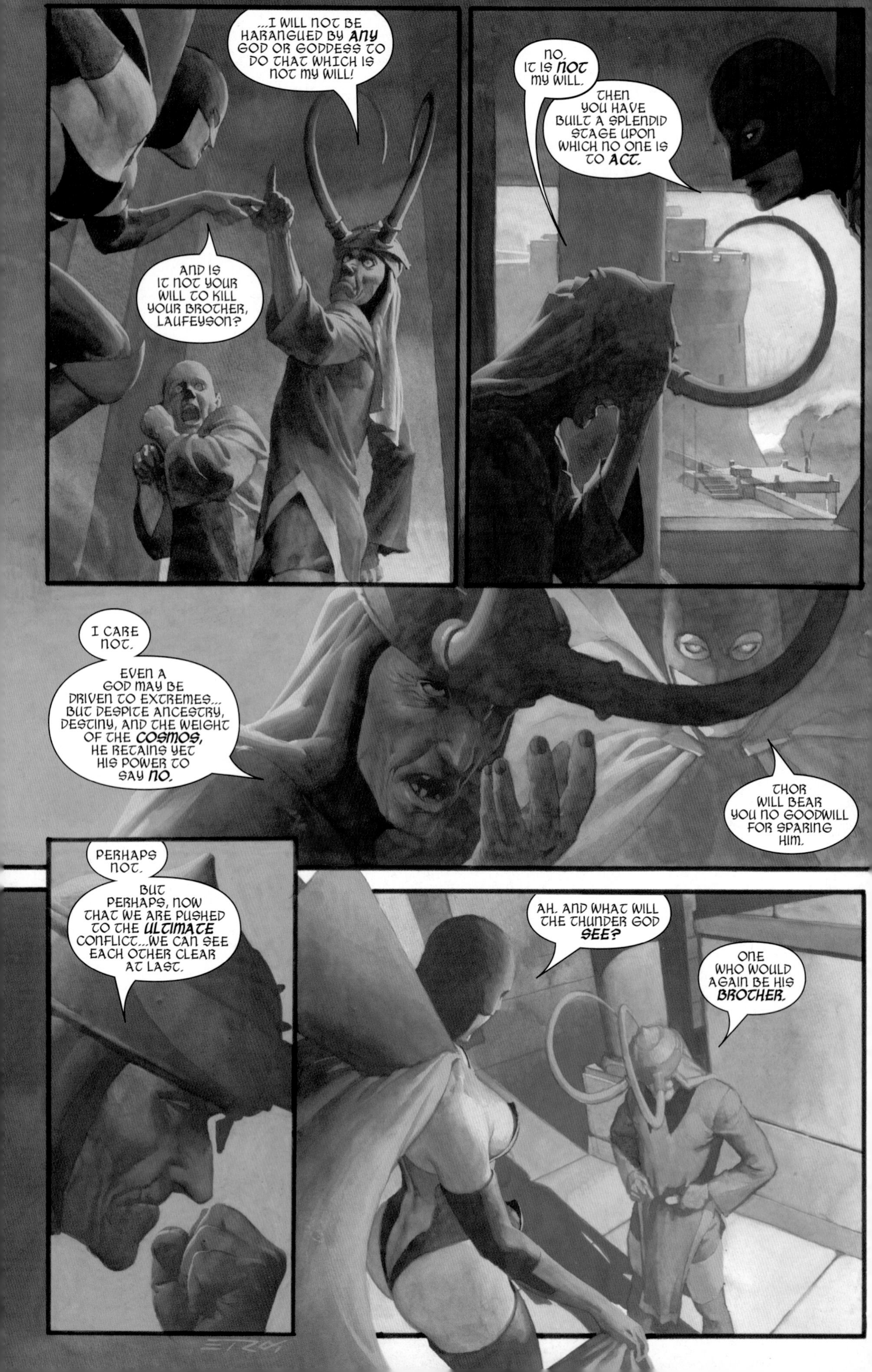
...I WILL NOT BE HARANGUED BY ANY GOD OR GODDESS TO DO THAT WHICH IS NOT MY WILL!
AND IS IT NOT YOUR WILL TO KILL YOUR BROTHER, LAUFEYSON?
NO. IT IS NOT MY WILL.
THEN YOU HAVE BUILT A SPLENDID STAGE UPON WHICH NO ONE IS TO ACT.
I CARE NOT.
EVEN A GOD MAY BE DRIVEN TO EXTREMES... BUT DESPITE ANCESTRY, DESTINY, AND THE WEIGHT OF THE COSMOS, HE RETAINS YET HIS POWER TO SAY NO.
THOR WILL BEAR YOU NO GOODWILL FOR SPARING HIM.
PERHAPS NOT.
BUT PERHAPS, NOW THAT WE ARE PUSHED TO THE ULTIMATE CONFLICT...WE CAN SEE EACH OTHER CLEAR AT LAST.
AH. AND WHAT WILL THE THUNDER GOD SEE?
ONE WHO WOULD AGAIN BE HIS BROTHER.

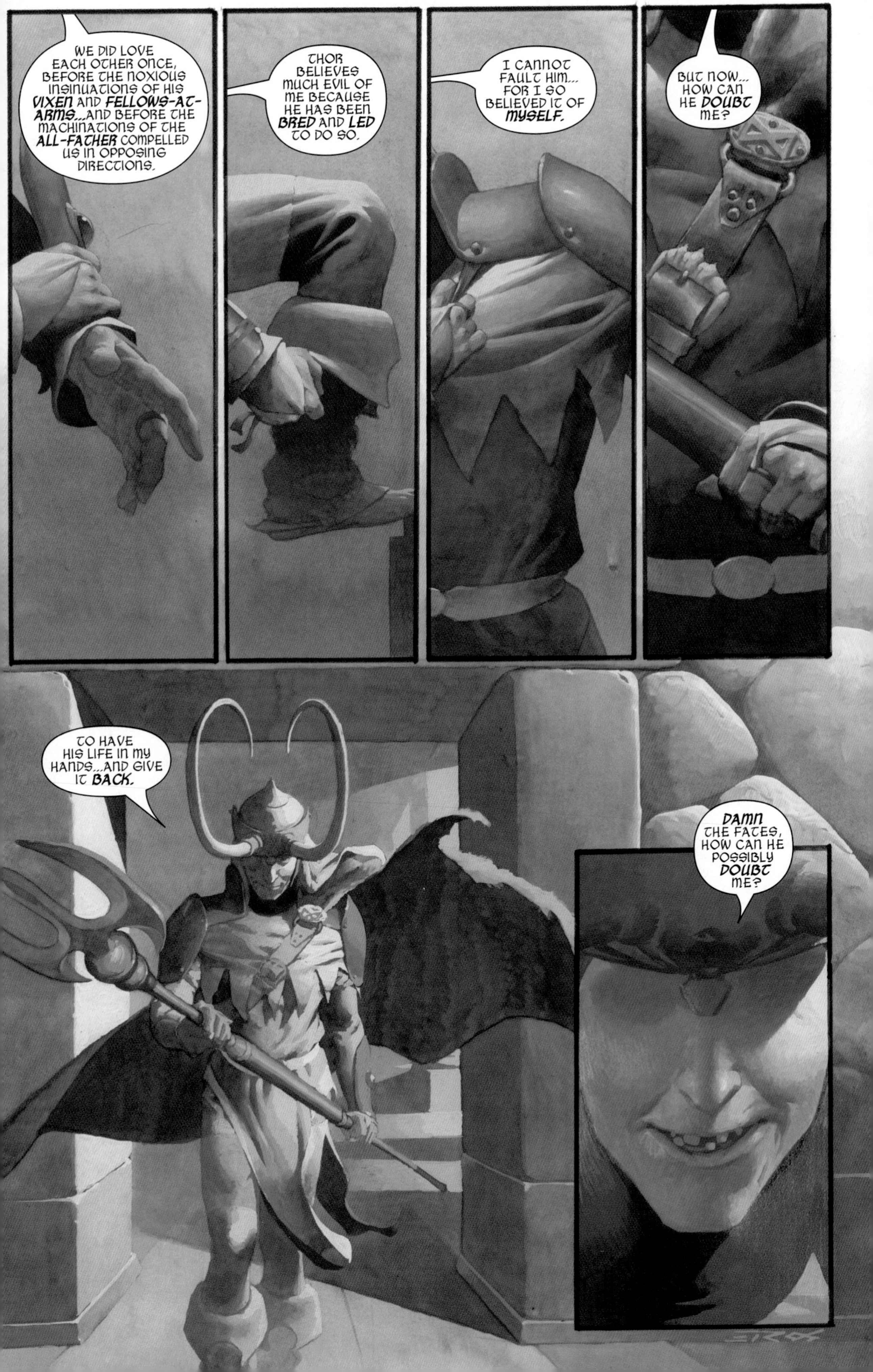
WE DID LOVE EACH OTHER ONCE, BEFORE THE NOXIOUS INSINUATIONS OF HIS VIXEN AND FELLOWS-AT-ARMS...AND BEFORE THE MACHINATIONS OF THE ALL-FATHER COMPELLED US IN OPPOSING DIRECTIONS.
THOR BELIEVES MUCH EVIL OF ME BECAUSE HE HAS BEEN BRED AND LED TO DO SO.
I CANNOT FAULT HIM... FOR I SO BELIEVED IT OF MYSELF.
BUT NOW... HOW CAN HE DOUBT ME?
TO HAVE HIS LIFE IN MY HANDS...AND GIVE IT BACK.
DAMN THE FATES, HOW CAN HE POSSIBLY DOUBT ME?

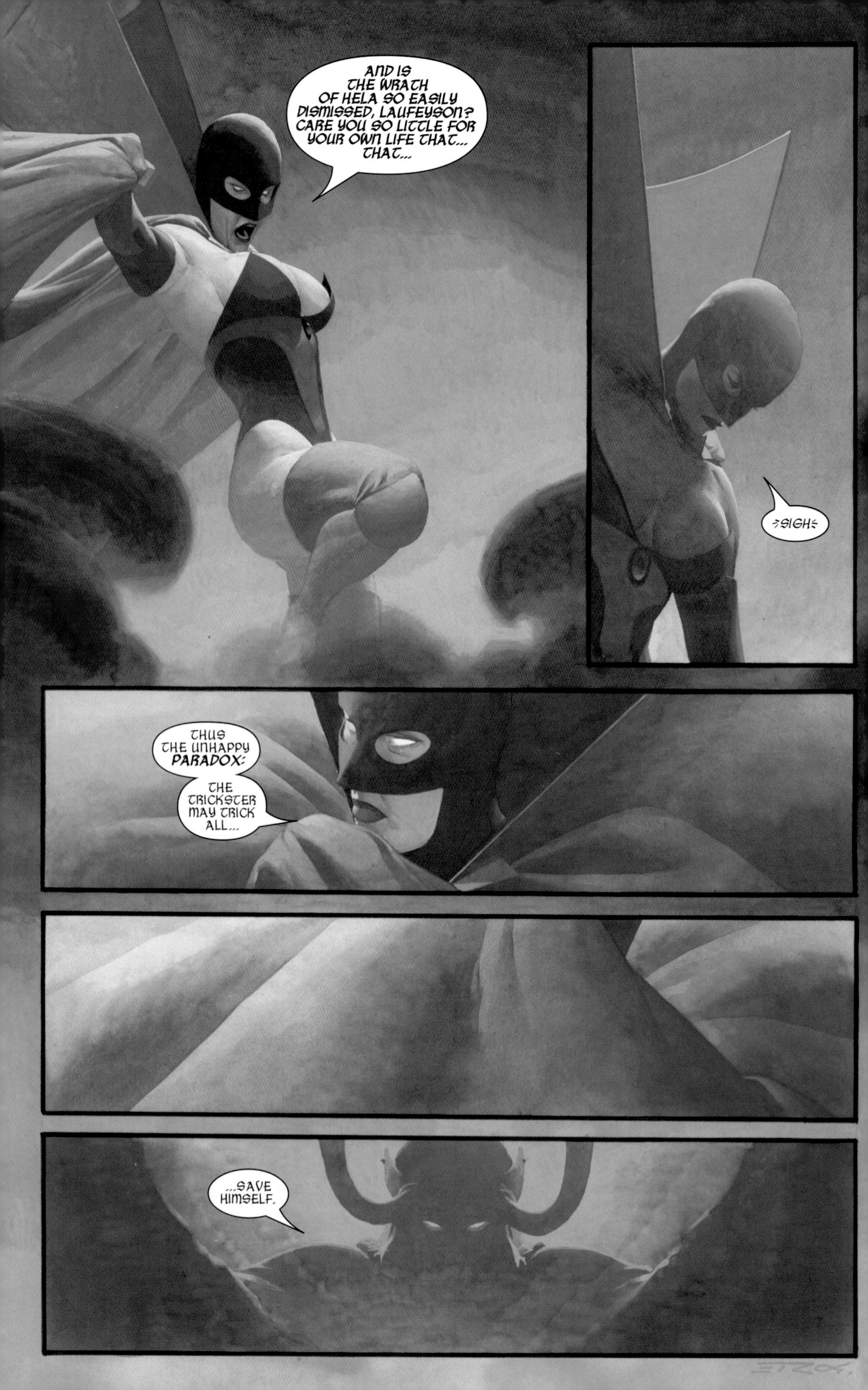
AND IS THE WRATH OF HELA SO EASILY DISMISSED, LAUFEYSON? CARE YOU SO LITTLE FOR YOUR OWN LIFE THAT... THAT...
SIGH
THUS THE UNHAPPY PARADOX:
THE TRICKSTER MAY TRICK ALL...
...SAVE HIMSELF.

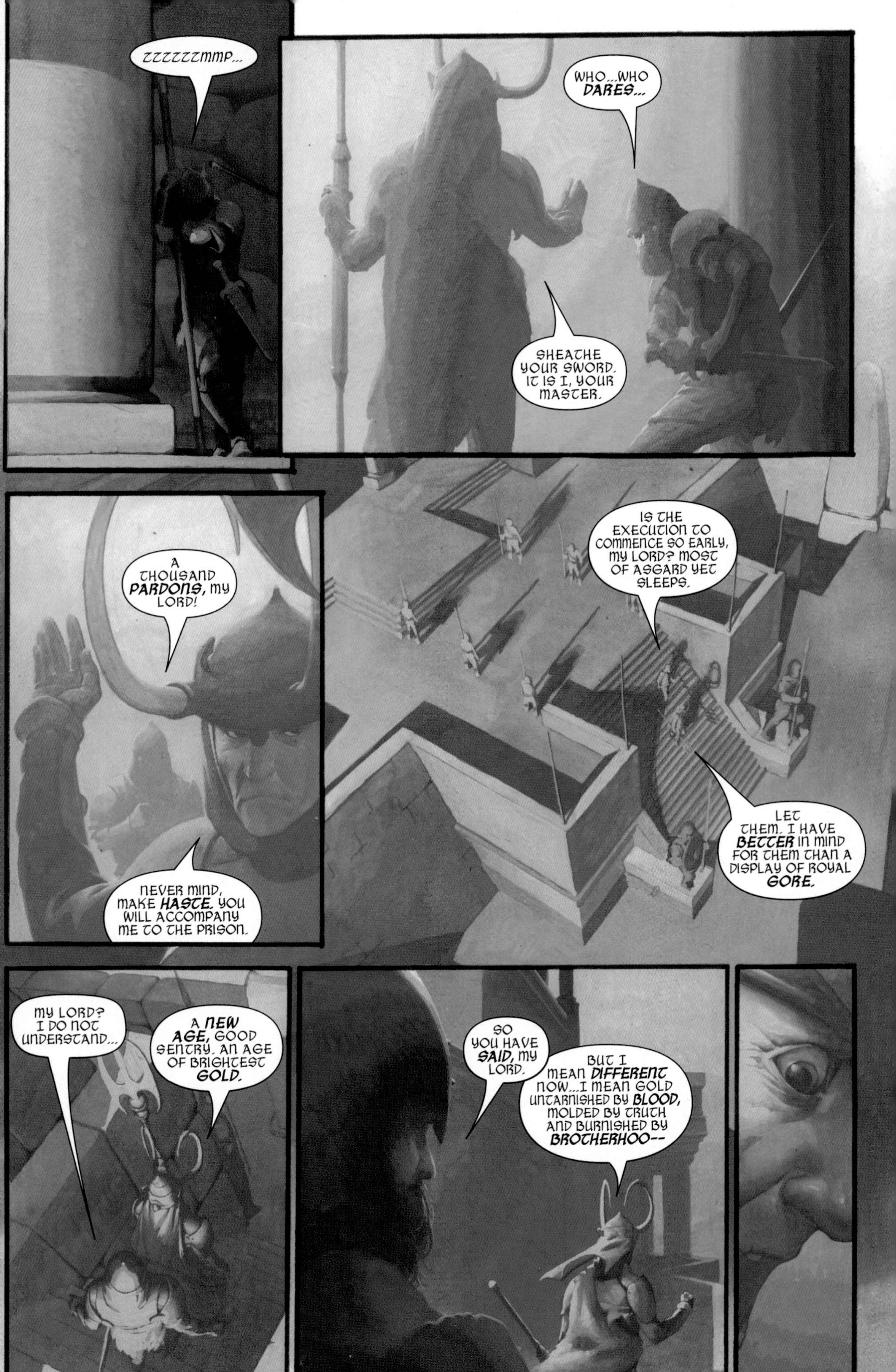
ZZZZZZMMP...
WHO...WHO DARES...
SHEATHE YOUR SWORD. IT IS I, YOUR MASTER.
A THOUSAND PARDONS, MY LORD!
NEVER MIND, MAKE HASTE. YOU WILL ACCOMPANY ME TO THE PRISON.
IS THE EXECUTION TO COMMENCE SO EARLY, MY LORD? MOST OF ASGARD YET SLEEPS.
LET THEM. I HAVE BETTER IN MIND FOR THEM THAN A DISPLAY OF ROYAL GORE.
MY LORD? I DO NOT UNDERSTAND...
A NEW AGE, GOOD SENTRY. AN AGE OF BRIGHTEST GOLD.
SO YOU HAVE SAID, MY LORD.
BUT I MEAN DIFFERENT NOW...I MEAN GOLD UNTARNISHED BY BLOOD, MOLDED BY TRUTH AND BURNISHED BY BROTHERHOO--

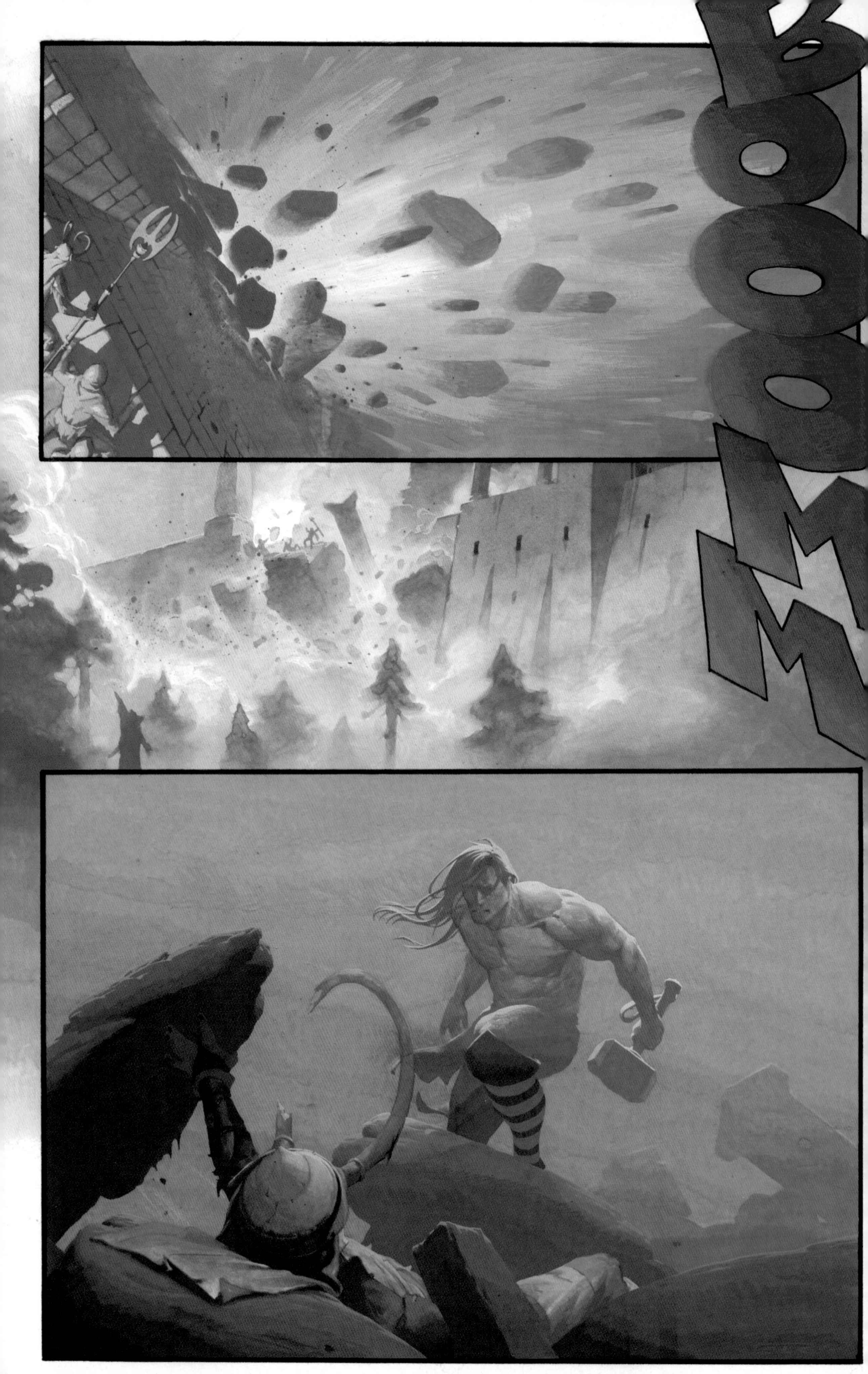
BOOOMM

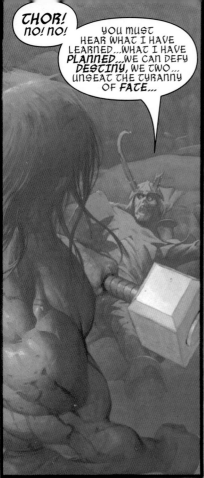

THOR! NO! NO!

YOU MUST HEAR WHAT I HAVE LEARNED...WHAT I HAVE **PLANNED**...WE CAN DEFY **DESTINY**, WE TWO... UNSEAT THE TYRANNY OF **FATE**...

DO NOT, I BEG YOU, CONSIGN ME TO ITS **POWER** AGAIN... DO NOT MAKE OF ME WHAT I **WAS**...

...MY FUTURE LOT, AND **YOURS**, HINGE ON YOUR NEXT ACTION. IF THERE IS YET MERCY IN YOU...

...IF THERE EVER **WAS** MERCY IN YOU...

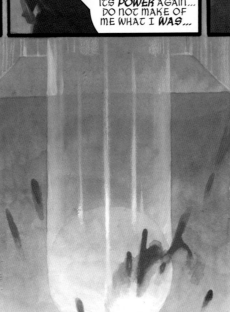

FIN.

# LOKI

## PROPOSAL FOR A
## 4-ISSUE MINI-SERIES

---

Written by Robert Rodi • Painted by Esad Ribic

---

*L*OKI will take a long, hard look at one of Marvel's most complex villains. For two decades readers have heard Thor's side of the story. Now it's time to hear Loki's.

This 4-issue miniseries will prove that there are always two sides to every story. Just as John Gardner's landmark novella *Grendel* deconstructed the Beowulf myth, allowing readers to see the legend from the monster's point of view, LOKI will reveal the dark nooks and crannies of Asgardian legend from the perspective of Odin's least favorite son. In this story Loki's insatiable lust for power, his conflicted sentiments toward Sif, his antipathy toward Balder, and the deep-seated feelings of longing and resentment toward his older brother, Thor, and uncaring father, Odin, will take on new meaning.

### STORY

We open with **LOKI** in charge of Asgard. He's somehow managed to topple the Allfather **ODIN** from power, has had the whole court — **BALDER, SIF, WARRIORS THREE** — imprisoned, and he's parading his older brother **THOR** through the streets in triumph. Most of Asgard is, of course, horrified by the sight of Thor's humiliation, but that only delights Loki all the more. He really rubs their noses in it.

The parade over, Thor is returned to prison — or better yet, put on public display. Loki returns to his quarters, where he finds **HELA, GODDESS OF DEATH,** waiting for him.

He asks what she wants.

Thor, she tells him. It's no secret that she's long desired the Thunder God's soul, but never been able to win it on her own. Now that Loki has defeated him, she's come to claim it.

Loki protests; he has no intention of killing Thor. Hela scoffs; he must kill Thor. After all, if he doesn't, Thor will soon escape and take Asgard back, just as he's defeated Loki time and time again.

Loki is shocked by this. He's never considered killing Thor. All he's ever wanted was Thor's humiliation. But Hela has a point. Loki was the Trickster God; now that he's played his ultimate trick, he must become something else — as Lord of Asgard, he must change. Alter. And this transformation must begin with Thor's execution.

If he can bring himself to do it.

Loki goes off by himself, and tries to convince himself that Thor deserves to die. He recalls his boyhood, when he was brought into the Asgardian royal family — as Loki sees it, to function as a counterpoint to Thor's perfection. He's convinced that all Odin ever wanted from him was that he make Thor look good in comparison. And Thor, too, gloried in his superiority, taking every opportunity to show Loki up, make him look bad.

Even so, Loki felt no rancor at this point in his life — his stepbrother WAS perfect: beautiful, powerful, golden. He adored him. And if Thor repaid that adoration with little slights and humiliations, it was a price Loki was only too willing to pay for his company.

But then, while they were still youths, along came SIF, BALDER and the rest — and Loki was able to witness his adored brother in the company of others whom he openly loved.

And Loki realized how much he was disdained. His love turned to anger, and his anger to hatred. He took his revenge on Sif, cutting her hair — he tried to kill Balder. But his real fury was reserved for Thor, who had shown him he was not loved. So he began a long life devoted to revenge on Thor and all whom the Thunder God cared for.

While Loki is recalling all of this, we take an occasional look in on Thor, who's struggling to escape from his confinement. (Don't know exactly how Loki's holding him; we'll work that out later.)

Loki still hasn't talked himself into killing Thor. To embolden himself, he goes to see Odin, Sif and Balder, one after the other, and tells them he's going to execute the Thunder God. Each argues with Loki, and we see how Loki's version of events differs from theirs. We also begin to realize that Loki is right — these noble Asgardians have from the start looked down their noses at him, disdained him, scorned him. It was they — and Thor especially — who created the evil in him. Realizing this, Loki's pride and anger grow strong again; unwittingly, they convince him he would be right to kill his brother.

But as Loki leaves his prisoners, his will weakens again. The idea of a world without Thor is bleak to him. What would he live for? He has no real desire to rule Asgard. The hard work of sovereignty doesn't appeal to him. He's the Trickster God ... and gods can't simply change. They're elemental principles; cosmic constants.

When he's again confronted by Hela, she urges him to carry out the execution, and he refuses.

Hela taunts him: "You've defeated your enemy, you've shackled him, you've humiliated him — now you MUST kill him! If not, what would you do?"

Loki thinks for a moment, then sadly says, "I would do it all over again."

He's made up his mind: he's going to free Thor. As he says this, Hela nods her head and says, "So it shall be. There is, I fear, only one whom

the great Trickster cannot trick ... himself." As she says this, she changes into Loki.

For a moment, there are two Lokis staring at each other across the panel. Then, the original one disappears, leaving only the Loki-Who-Was-Hela.

We realize that Hela was never there: the whole *You-Must-Kill-Thor* scenario was shape-shifter Loki's way of trying to trick himself into murdering his brother. (How he appears in two places at once remains a mystery; I'd like to inject a little of that old sense-of-wonder into the book. These are gods, after all.)

Having failed to trick himself, he goes off to free Thor.

As he goes, he wonders whether this act of mercy will win for him one moment of gratitude from Thor. He realizes that Thor's good opinion — his friendship, his love — is that which he has always desired, and, starved of them, have made him what he is today. He loathes Thor for his treatment of him, but he loathes himself even more for still loving his tormentor.

But he's delayed too long.

Arriving at Thor's cell, he finds that Thor has escaped, and is barreling right for Loki.

Seeing this, Loki is horrified — he protests; he was going to free Thor! Really he was! Honest!

But Thor has a major mad on; he beats the crap out of Loki.

We end with Thor standing over the defeated Loki. He says something along the lines of, Well, what have you got to say for yourself, my brother?

Loki looks up at him, at Thor, at all that beauty and perfection, those golden shoulders, and says, I would do it again ... I would do it all again ... I WILL do it all again.

THE END?

Character Studies

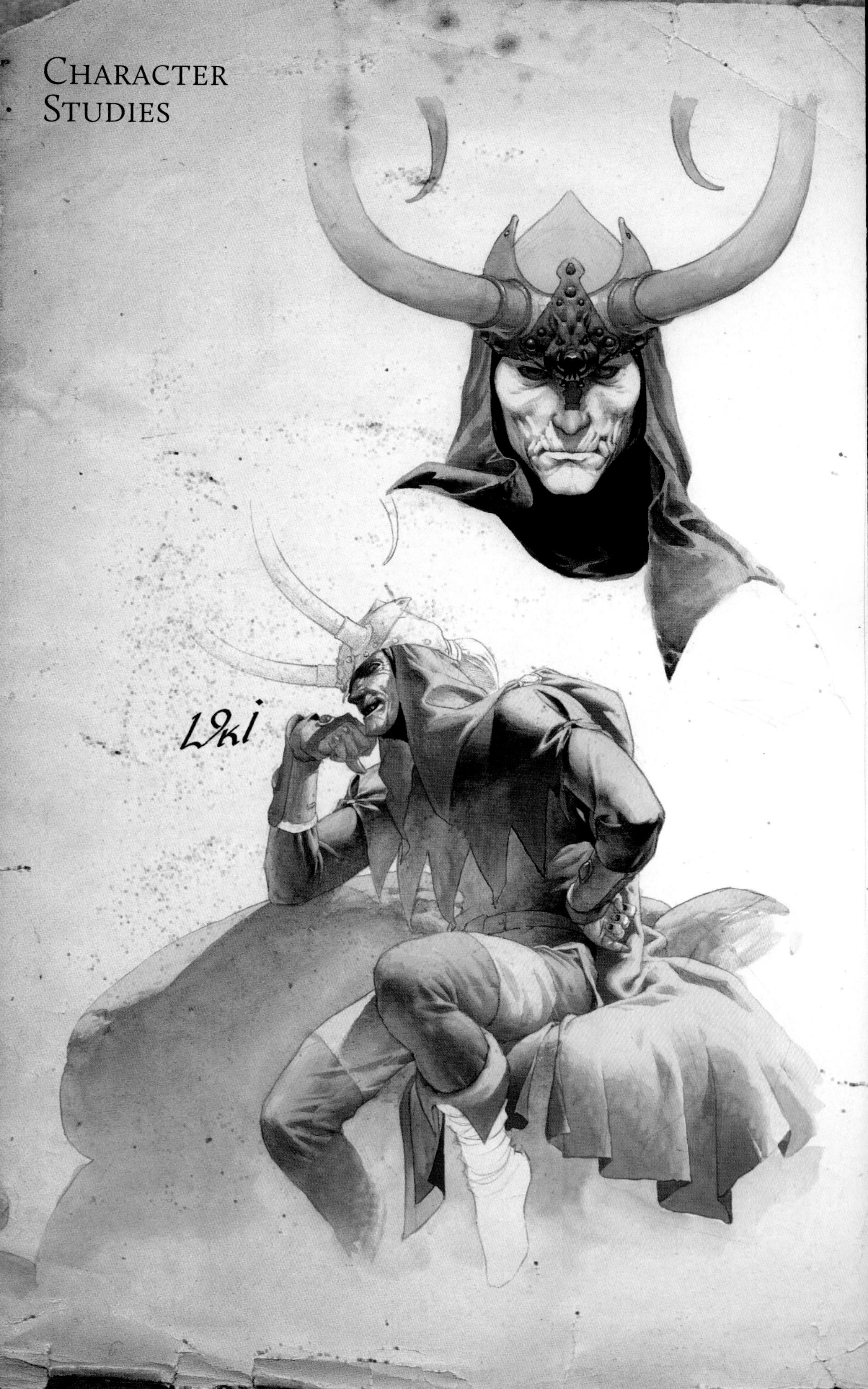
Loki

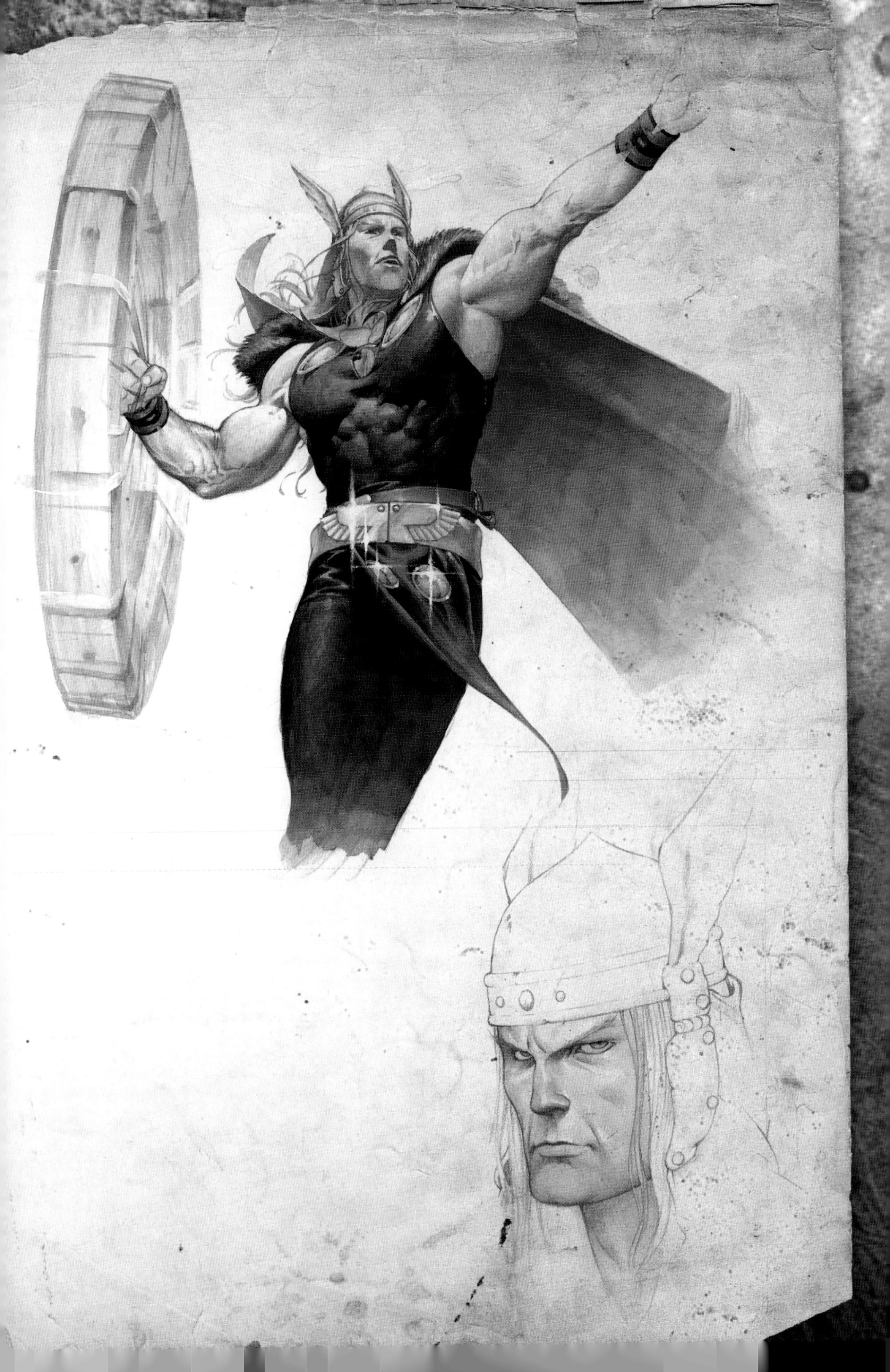

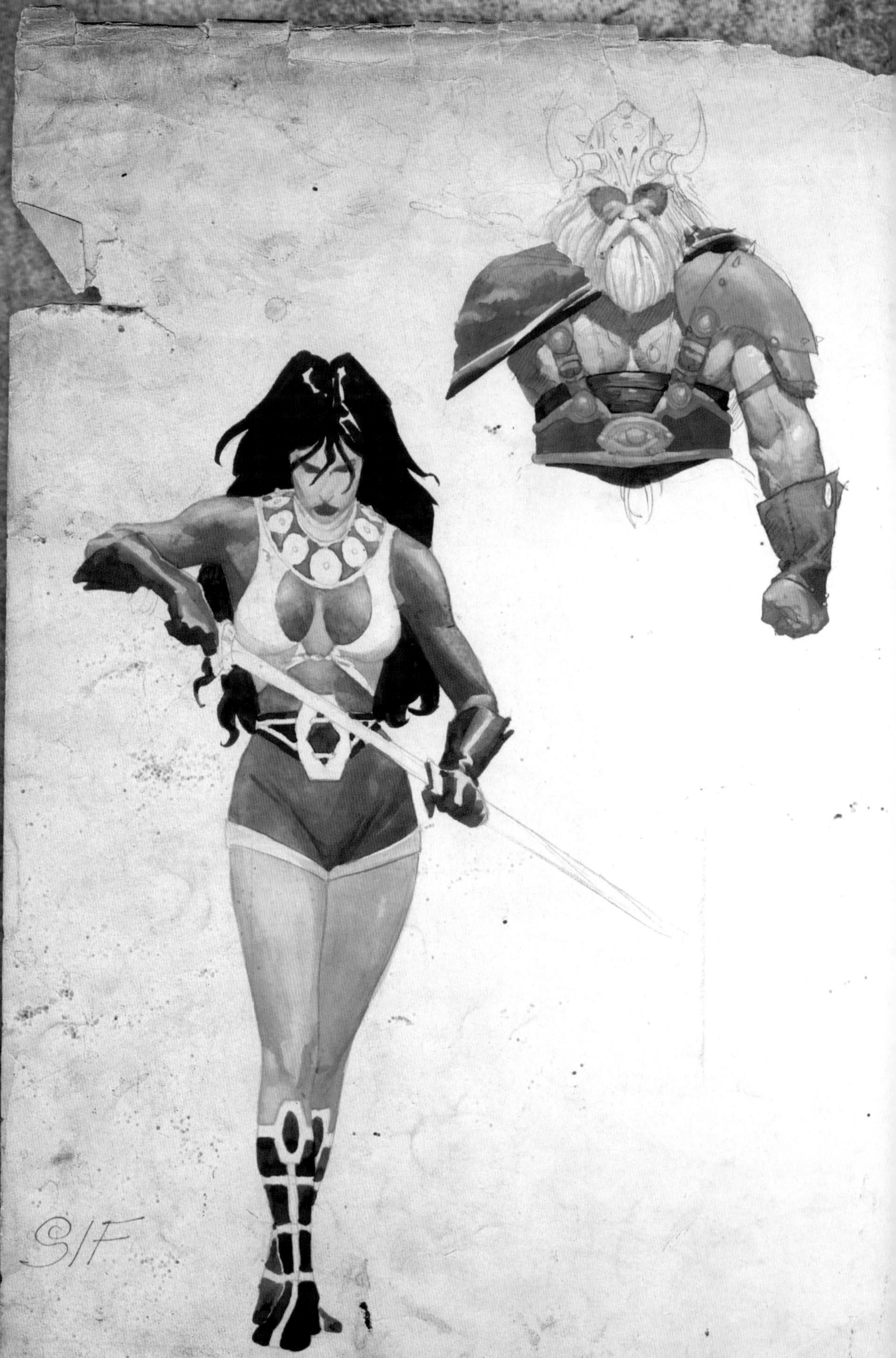
SIF

BLUE GREEN (EYES)

LORELEI
LoReLei

ODLELO

PLAST IVAHI

hela

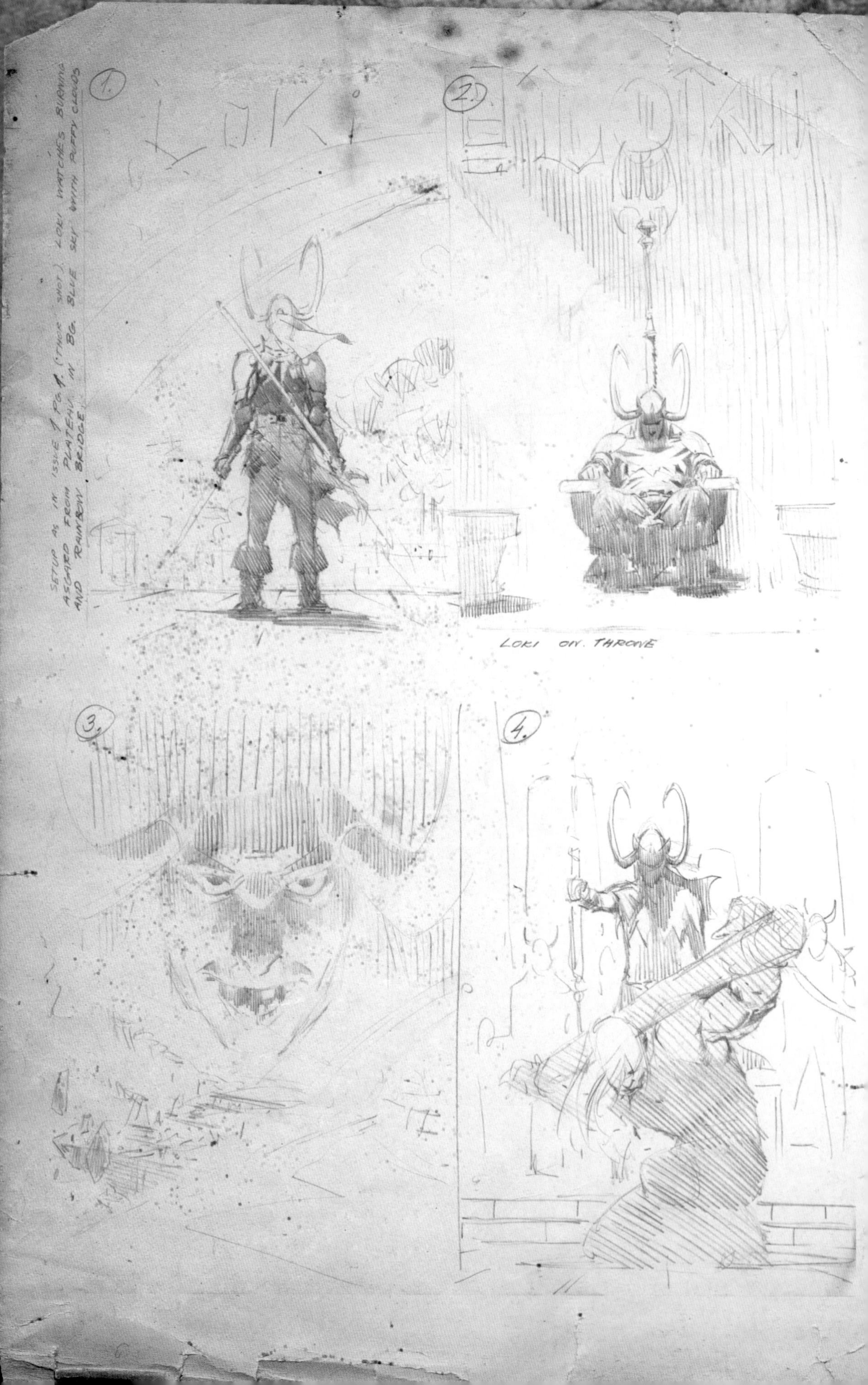
1.
SETUP AS IN ISSUE 1 PG. 1. (THOR SHOT). LOKI WATCHES BURNING ASGARD FROM PLATEAU IN BG. BLUE SKY WITH PUFFY CLOUDS AND RAINBOW BRIDGE.
2.
LOKI ON THRONE
3.
4.

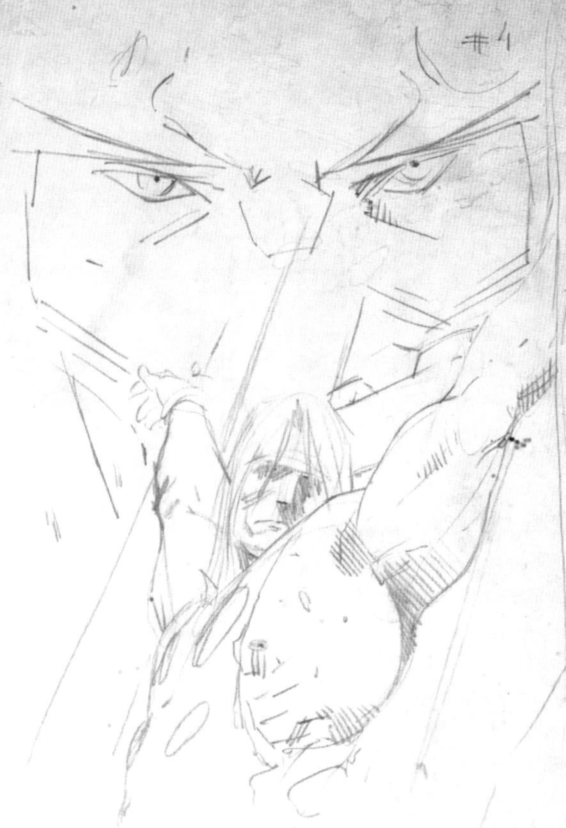
#4

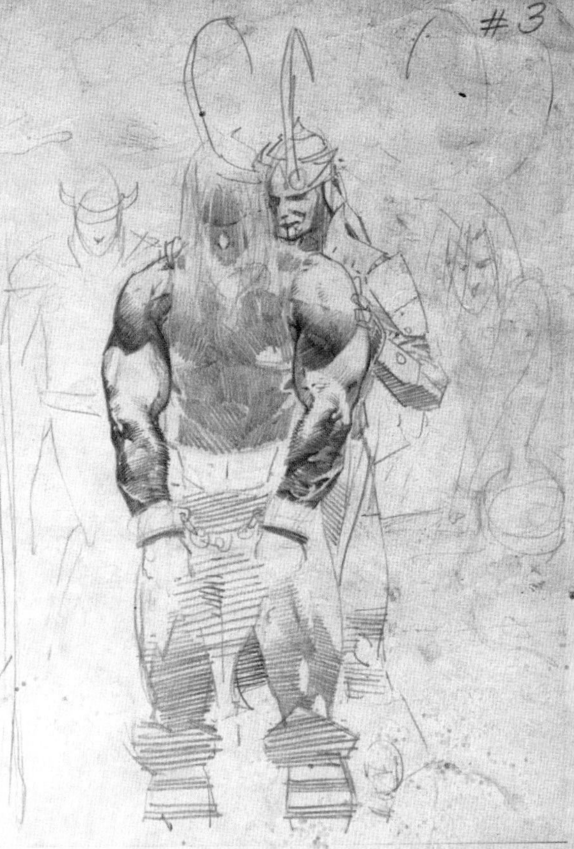
#3

# Unused Cover Sketches

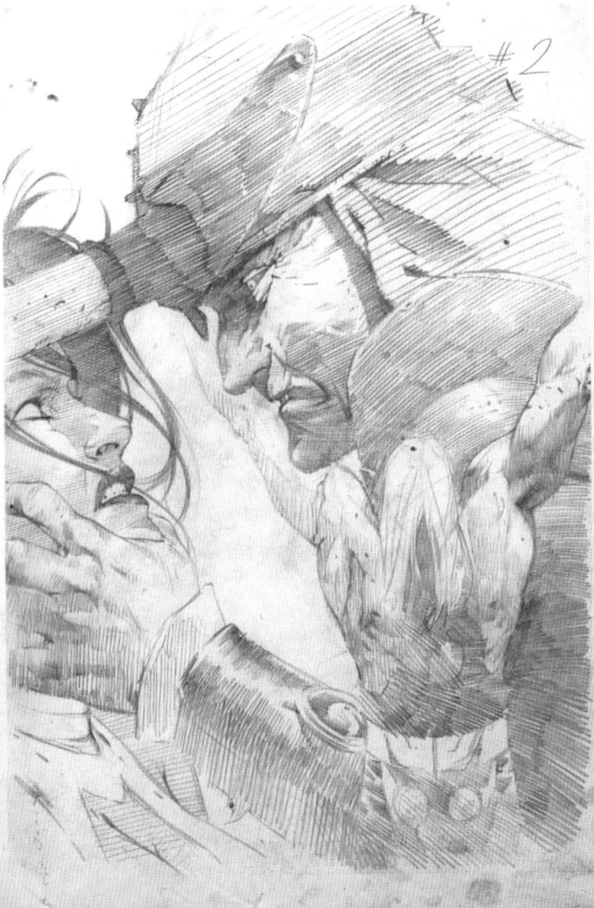
#2

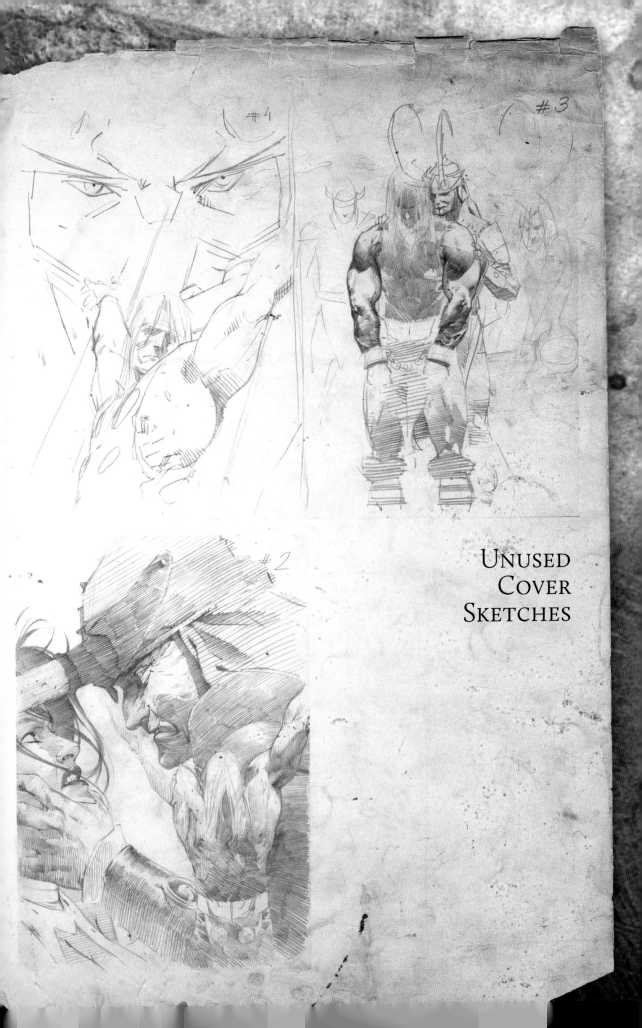

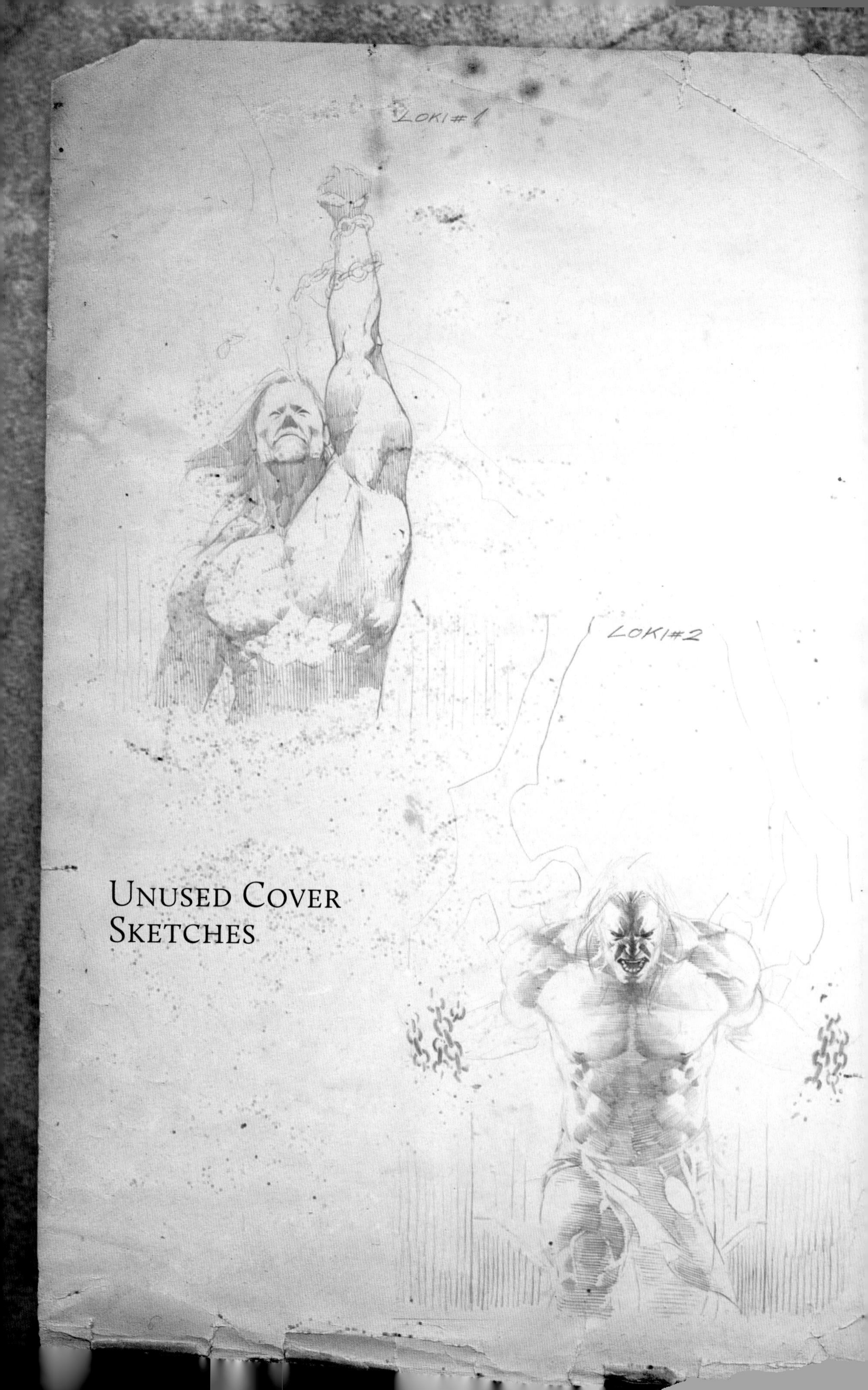
LOKI #1
LOKI #2

Unused Cover Sketches

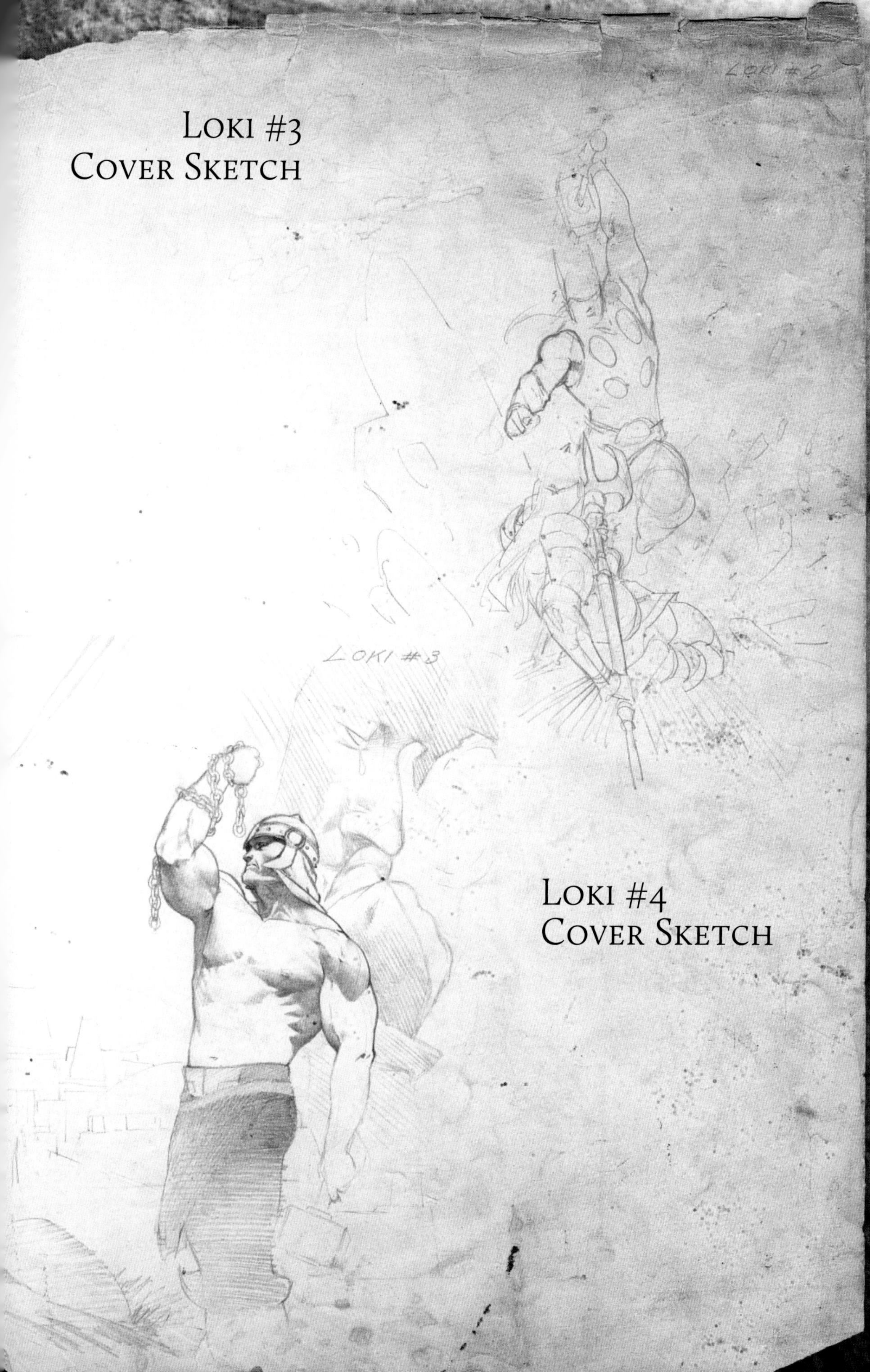
LOKI #2
LOKI #3

Loki #3
Cover Sketch

Loki #4
Cover Sketch

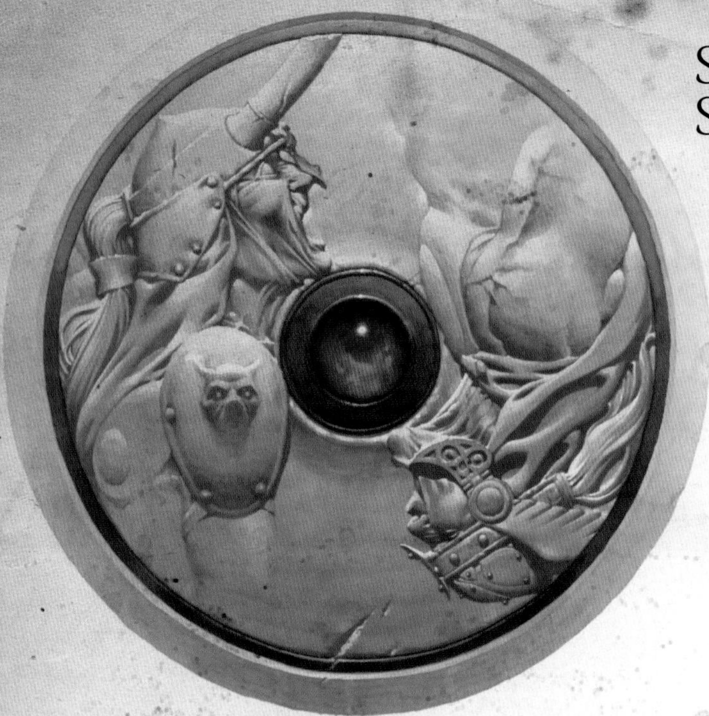

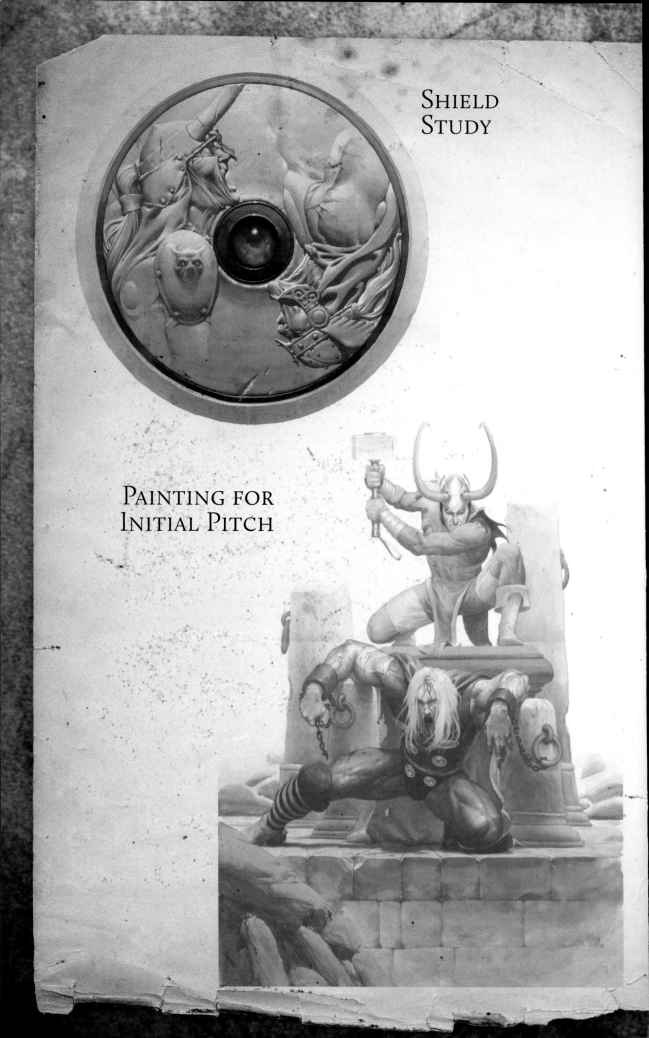

Shield Study

Painting for Initial Pitch

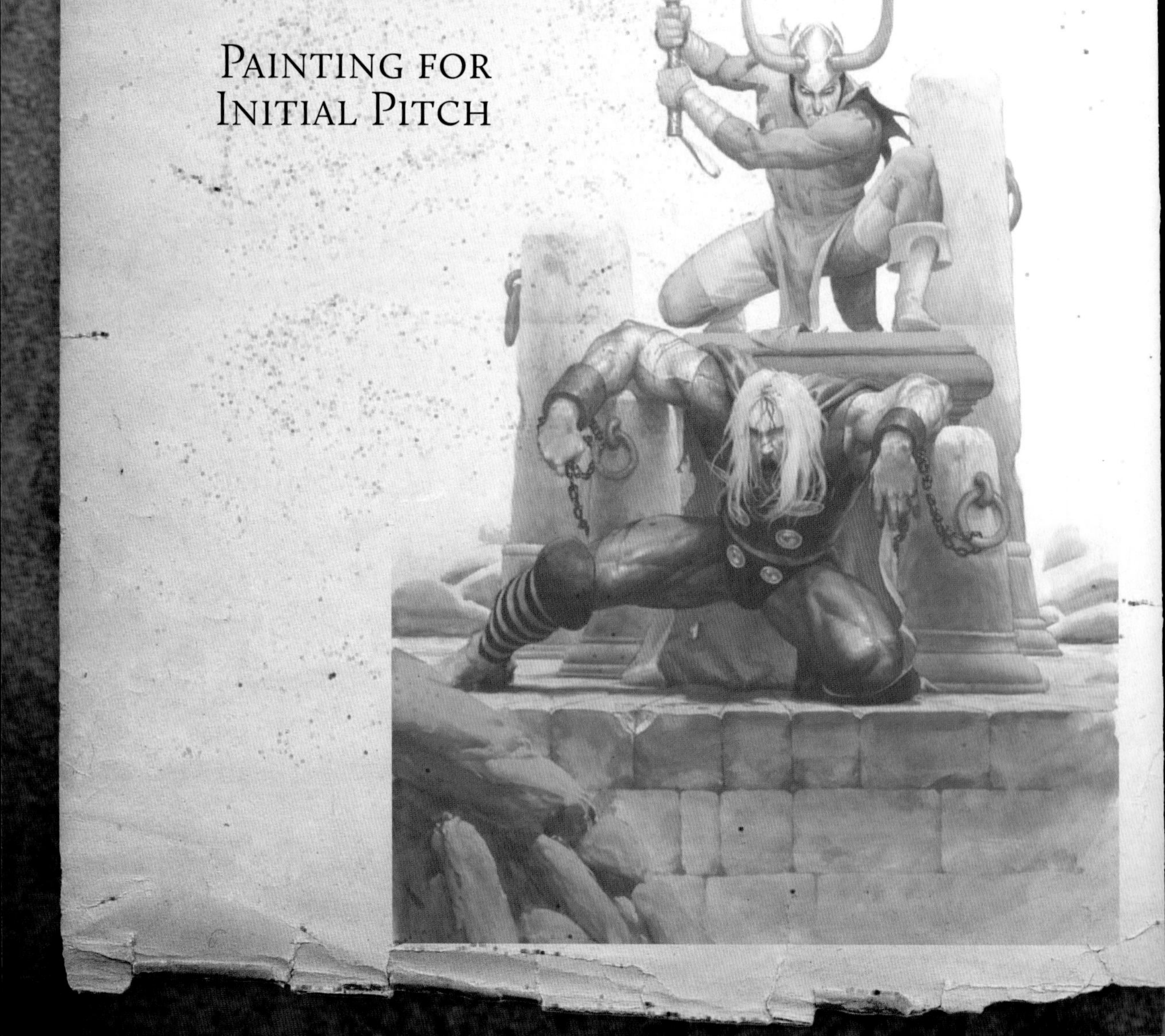

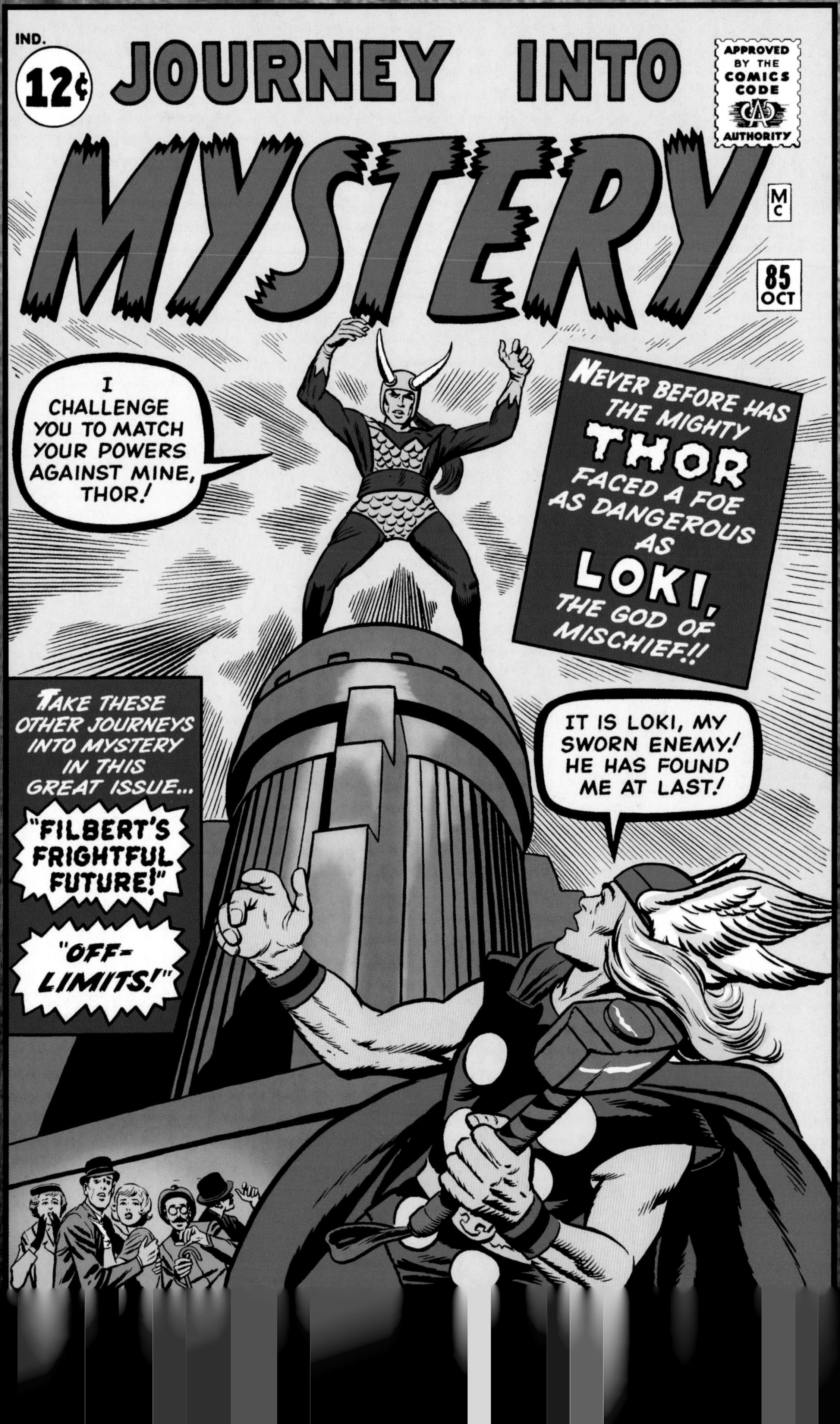
IND.
12¢
JOURNEY INTO
MYSTERY
APPROVED BY THE COMICS CODE AUTHORITY
MC
85 OCT
I CHALLENGE YOU TO MATCH YOUR POWERS AGAINST MINE, THOR!
NEVER BEFORE HAS THE MIGHTY THOR FACED A FOE AS DANGEROUS AS LOKI, THE GOD OF MISCHIEF!!
TAKE THESE OTHER JOURNEYS INTO MYSTERY IN THIS GREAT ISSUE...
"FILBERT'S FRIGHTFUL FUTURE!"
"OFF-LIMITS!"
IT IS LOKI, MY SWORN ENEMY! HE HAS FOUND ME AT LAST!

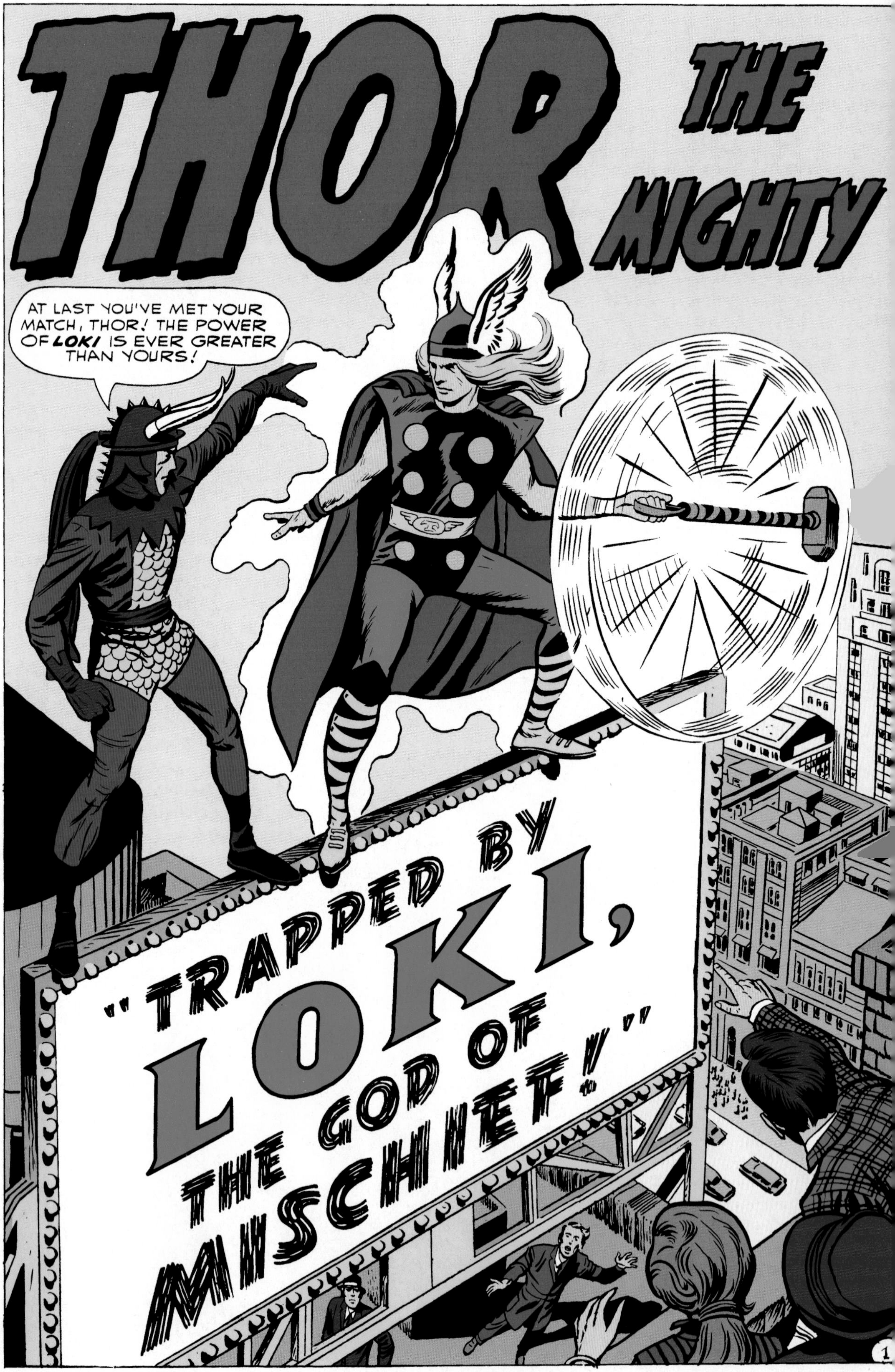
THOR THE MIGHTY
AT LAST YOU'VE MET YOUR MATCH, THOR! THE POWER OF LOKI IS EVER GREATER THAN YOURS!
"TRAPPED BY LOKI, THE GOD OF MISCHIEF!"
1

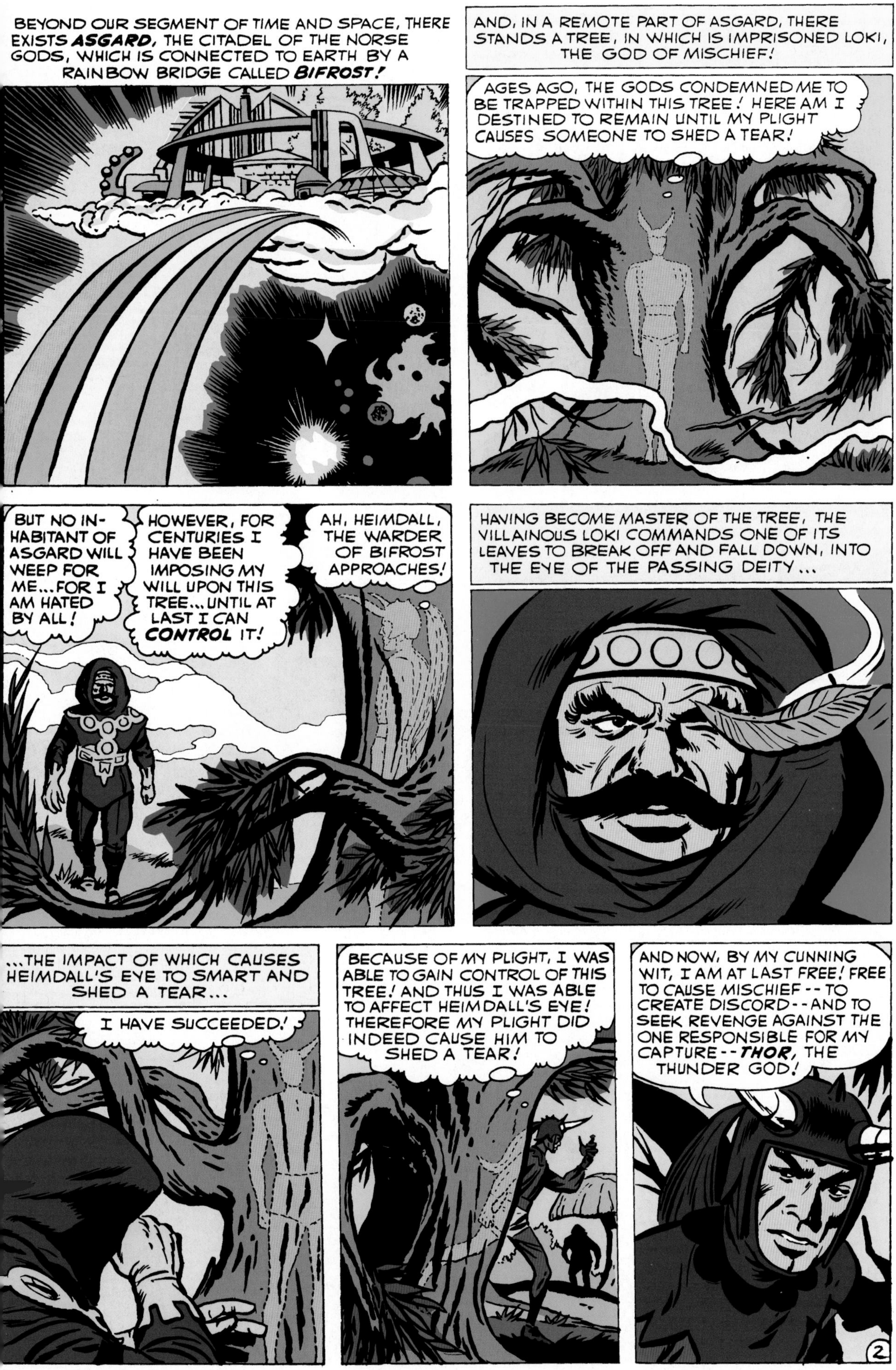
BEYOND OUR SEGMENT OF TIME AND SPACE, THERE EXISTS ASGARD, THE CITADEL OF THE NORSE GODS, WHICH IS CONNECTED TO EARTH BY A RAINBOW BRIDGE CALLED BIFROST!
AND, IN A REMOTE PART OF ASGARD, THERE STANDS A TREE, IN WHICH IS IMPRISONED LOKI, THE GOD OF MISCHIEF!
AGES AGO, THE GODS CONDEMNED ME TO BE TRAPPED WITHIN THIS TREE! HERE AM I DESTINED TO REMAIN UNTIL MY PLIGHT CAUSES SOMEONE TO SHED A TEAR!
BUT NO INHABITANT OF ASGARD WILL WEEP FOR ME...FOR I AM HATED BY ALL!
HOWEVER, FOR CENTURIES I HAVE BEEN IMPOSING MY WILL UPON THIS TREE...UNTIL AT LAST I CAN CONTROL IT!
AH, HEIMDALL, THE WARDER OF BIFROST APPROACHES!
HAVING BECOME MASTER OF THE TREE, THE VILLAINOUS LOKI COMMANDS ONE OF ITS LEAVES TO BREAK OFF AND FALL DOWN, INTO THE EYE OF THE PASSING DEITY...
...THE IMPACT OF WHICH CAUSES HEIMDALL'S EYE TO SMART AND SHED A TEAR...
I HAVE SUCCEEDED!
BECAUSE OF MY PLIGHT, I WAS ABLE TO GAIN CONTROL OF THIS TREE! AND THUS I WAS ABLE TO AFFECT HEIMDALL'S EYE! THEREFORE MY PLIGHT DID INDEED CAUSE HIM TO SHED A TEAR!
AND NOW, BY MY CUNNING WIT, I AM AT LAST FREE! FREE TO CAUSE MISCHIEF--TO CREATE DISCORD--AND TO SEEK REVENGE AGAINST THE ONE RESPONSIBLE FOR MY CAPTURE--THOR, THE THUNDER GOD!
2

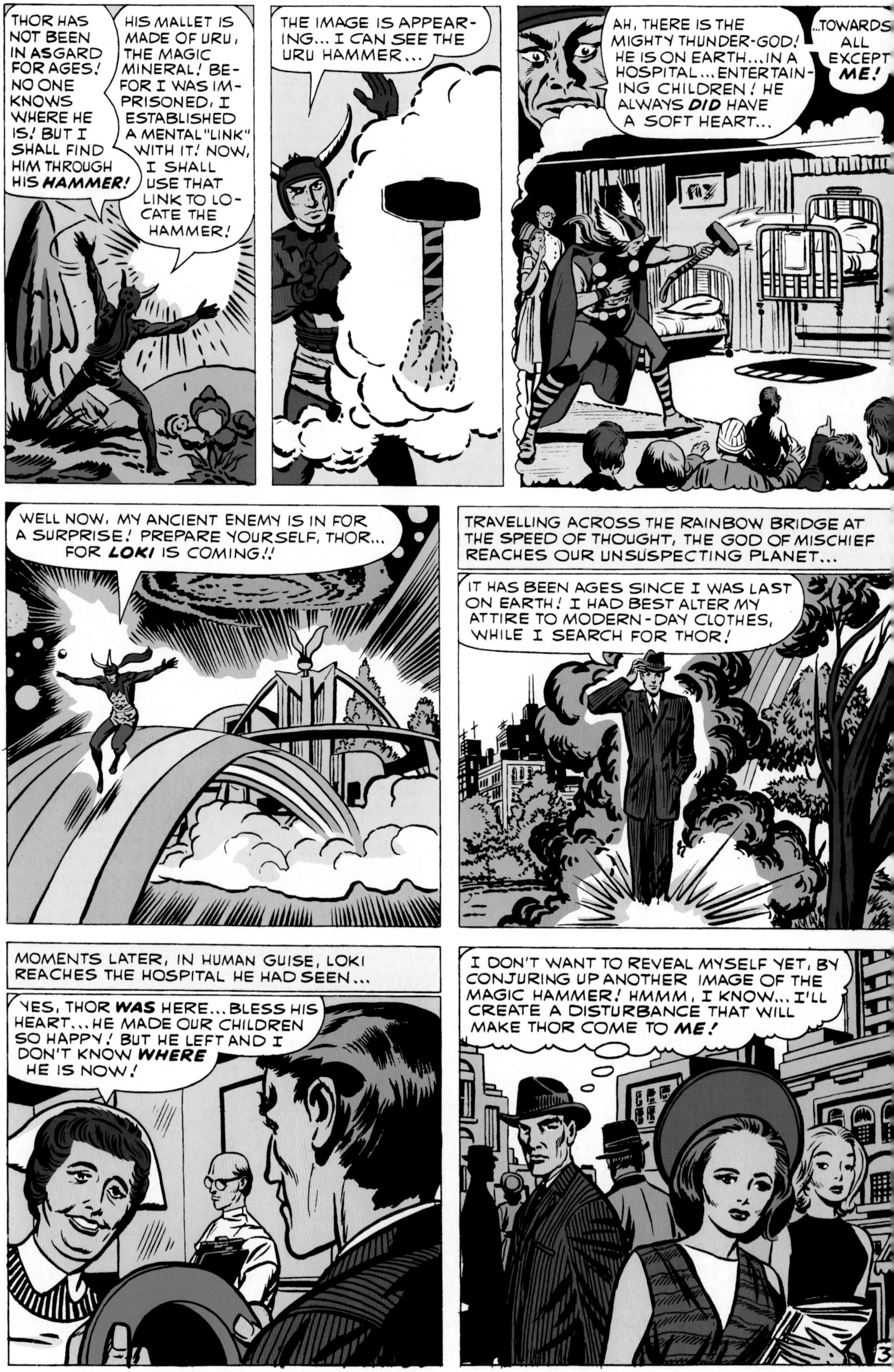
THOR HAS NOT BEEN IN ASGARD FOR AGES! NO ONE KNOWS WHERE HE IS! BUT I SHALL FIND HIM THROUGH HIS HAMMER!
HIS MALLET IS MADE OF URU, THE MAGIC MINERAL! BEFOR I WAS IMPRISONED, I ESTABLISHED A MENTAL "LINK" WITH IT! NOW, I SHALL USE THAT LINK TO LOCATE THE HAMMER!
THE IMAGE IS APPEARING... I CAN SEE THE URU HAMMER...
AH, THERE IS THE MIGHTY THUNDER-GOD! HE IS ON EARTH... IN A HOSPITAL... ENTERTAINING CHILDREN! HE ALWAYS DID HAVE A SOFT HEART...
...TOWARDS ALL EXCEPT ME!
WELL NOW, MY ANCIENT ENEMY IS IN FOR A SURPRISE! PREPARE YOURSELF, THOR... FOR LOKI IS COMING!!
TRAVELLING ACROSS THE RAINBOW BRIDGE AT THE SPEED OF THOUGHT, THE GOD OF MISCHIEF REACHES OUR UNSUSPECTING PLANET...
IT HAS BEEN AGES SINCE I WAS LAST ON EARTH! I HAD BEST ALTER MY ATTIRE TO MODERN-DAY CLOTHES, WHILE I SEARCH FOR THOR!
MOMENTS LATER, IN HUMAN GUISE, LOKI REACHES THE HOSPITAL HE HAD SEEN...
YES, THOR WAS HERE... BLESS HIS HEART... HE MADE OUR CHILDREN SO HAPPY! BUT HE LEFT AND I DON'T KNOW WHERE HE IS NOW!
I DON'T WANT TO REVEAL MYSELF YET, BY CONJURING UP ANOTHER IMAGE OF THE MAGIC HAMMER! HMMM, I KNOW... I'LL CREATE A DISTURBANCE THAT WILL MAKE THOR COME TO ME!
3

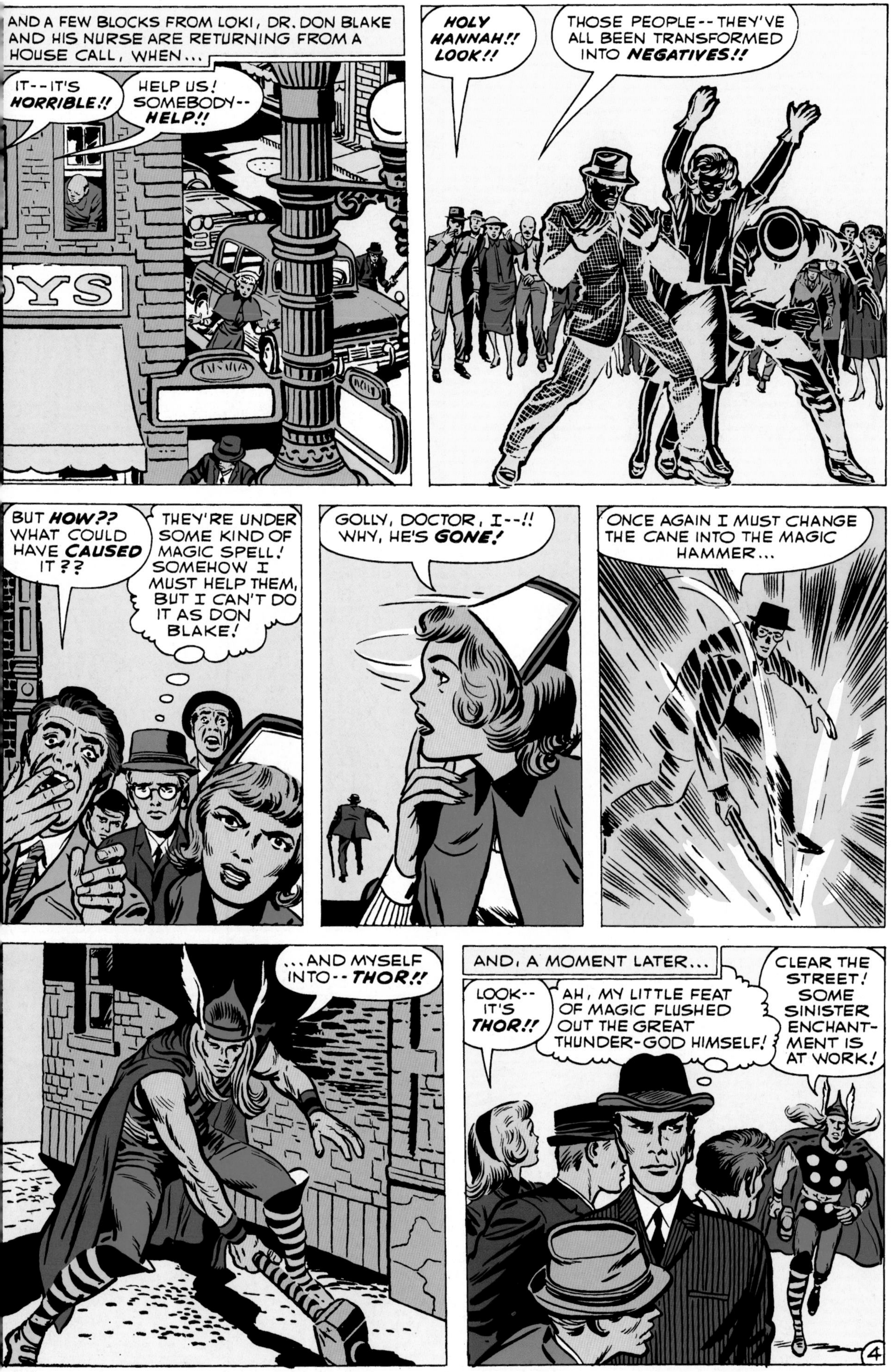
AND A FEW BLOCKS FROM LOKI, DR. DON BLAKE AND HIS NURSE ARE RETURNING FROM A HOUSE CALL, WHEN...
IT--IT'S HORRIBLE!!
HELP US! SOMEBODY--HELP!!
DYS
HOLY HANNAH!! LOOK!!
THOSE PEOPLE--THEY'VE ALL BEEN TRANSFORMED INTO NEGATIVES!!
BUT HOW?? WHAT COULD HAVE CAUSED IT??
THEY'RE UNDER SOME KIND OF MAGIC SPELL! SOMEHOW I MUST HELP THEM, BUT I CAN'T DO IT AS DON BLAKE!
GOLLY, DOCTOR, I--!! WHY, HE'S GONE!
ONCE AGAIN I MUST CHANGE THE CANE INTO THE MAGIC HAMMER...
...AND MYSELF INTO--THOR!!
AND, A MOMENT LATER...
LOOK--IT'S THOR!!
AH, MY LITTLE FEAT OF MAGIC FLUSHED OUT THE GREAT THUNDER-GOD HIMSELF!
CLEAR THE STREET! SOME SINISTER ENCHANTMENT IS AT WORK!
4

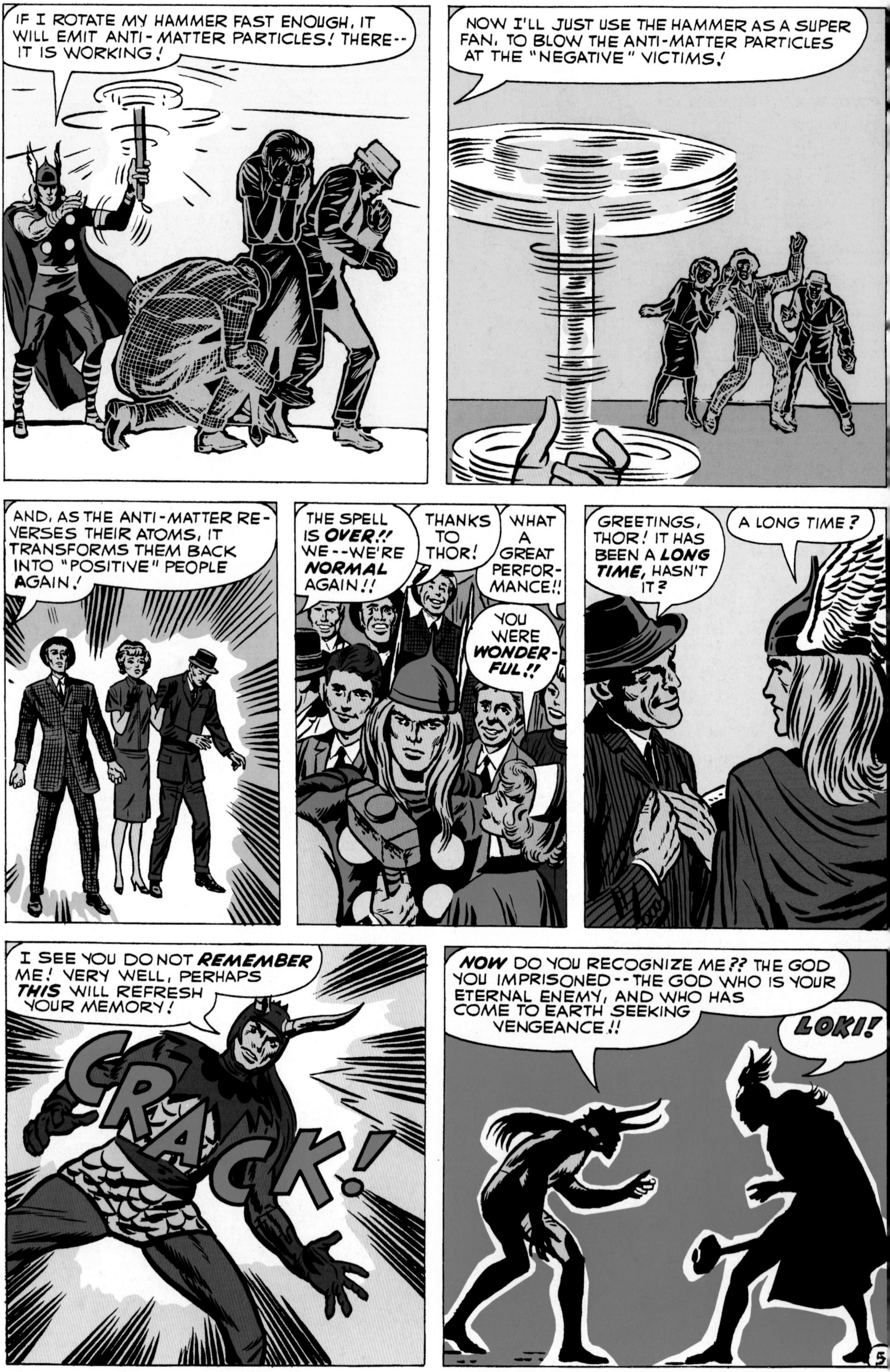
IF I ROTATE MY HAMMER FAST ENOUGH, IT WILL EMIT ANTI-MATTER PARTICLES! THERE-- IT IS WORKING!
NOW I'LL JUST USE THE HAMMER AS A SUPER FAN, TO BLOW THE ANTI-MATTER PARTICLES AT THE "NEGATIVE" VICTIMS!
AND, AS THE ANTI-MATTER REVERSES THEIR ATOMS, IT TRANSFORMS THEM BACK INTO "POSITIVE" PEOPLE AGAIN!
THE SPELL IS OVER!! WE--WE'RE NORMAL AGAIN!!
THANKS TO THOR!
WHAT A GREAT PERFORMANCE!!
YOU WERE WONDERFUL!!
GREETINGS, THOR! IT HAS BEEN A LONG TIME, HASN'T IT?
A LONG TIME?
I SEE YOU DO NOT REMEMBER ME! VERY WELL, PERHAPS THIS WILL REFRESH YOUR MEMORY!
CRACK!
NOW DO YOU RECOGNIZE ME?? THE GOD YOU IMPRISONED--THE GOD WHO IS YOUR ETERNAL ENEMY, AND WHO HAS COME TO EARTH SEEKING VENGEANCE!!
LOKI!
5

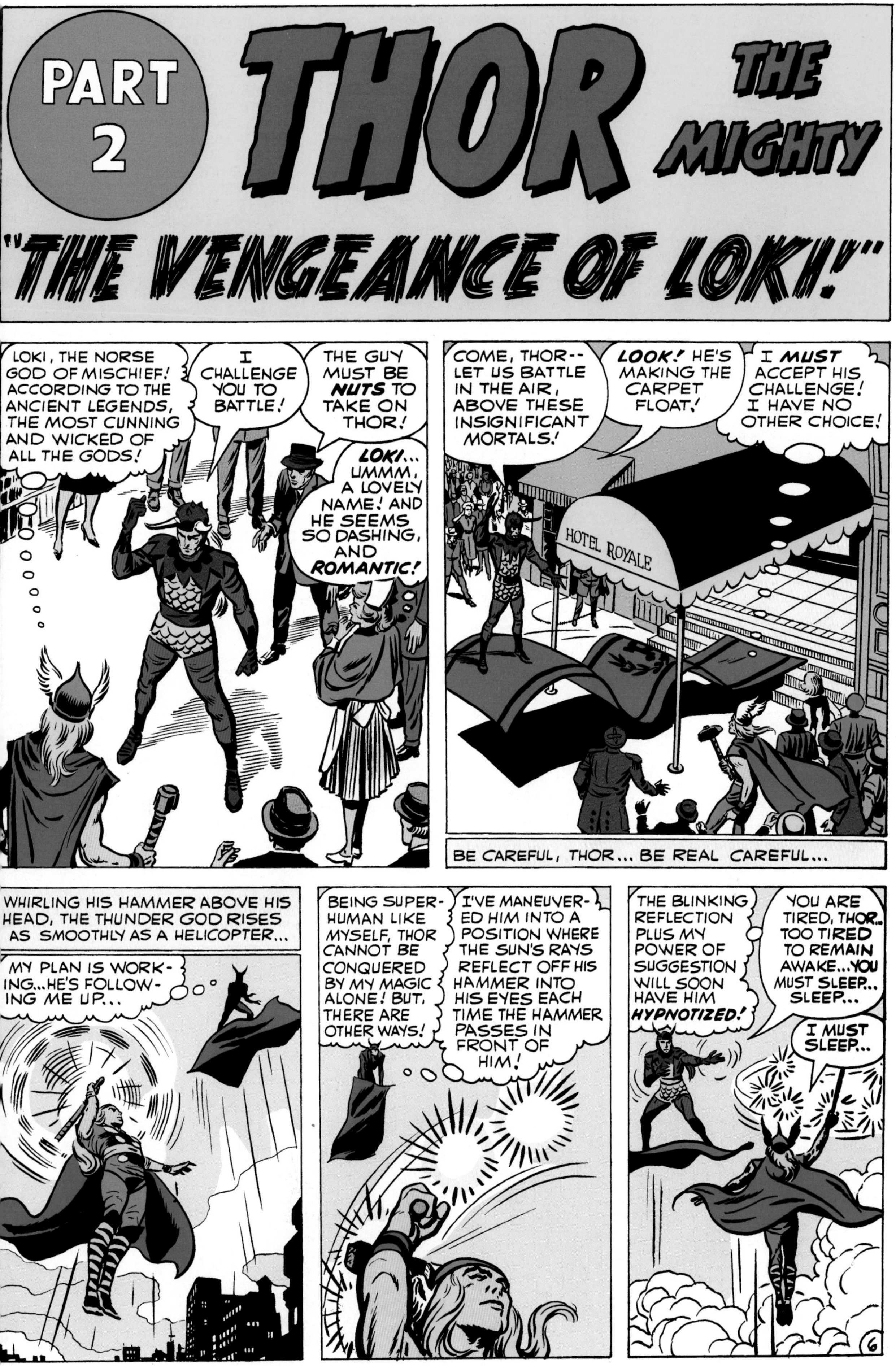
PART 2
THOR THE MIGHTY
"THE VENGEANCE OF LOKI!"
LOKI, THE NORSE GOD OF MISCHIEF! ACCORDING TO THE ANCIENT LEGENDS, THE MOST CUNNING AND WICKED OF ALL THE GODS!
I CHALLENGE YOU TO BATTLE!
THE GUY MUST BE NUTS TO TAKE ON THOR!
LOKI... UMMM, A LOVELY NAME! AND HE SEEMS SO DASHING, AND ROMANTIC!
COME, THOR-- LET US BATTLE IN THE AIR, ABOVE THESE INSIGNIFICANT MORTALS!
LOOK! HE'S MAKING THE CARPET FLOAT!
I MUST ACCEPT HIS CHALLENGE! I HAVE NO OTHER CHOICE!
HOTEL ROYALE
BE CAREFUL, THOR... BE REAL CAREFUL...
WHIRLING HIS HAMMER ABOVE HIS HEAD, THE THUNDER GOD RISES AS SMOOTHLY AS A HELICOPTER...
MY PLAN IS WORKING...HE'S FOLLOWING ME UP...
BEING SUPER-HUMAN LIKE MYSELF, THOR CANNOT BE CONQUERED BY MY MAGIC ALONE! BUT, THERE ARE OTHER WAYS!
I'VE MANEUVERED HIM INTO A POSITION WHERE THE SUN'S RAYS REFLECT OFF HIS HAMMER INTO HIS EYES EACH TIME THE HAMMER PASSES IN FRONT OF HIM!
THE BLINKING REFLECTION PLUS MY POWER OF SUGGESTION WILL SOON HAVE HIM HYPNOTIZED!
YOU ARE TIRED, THOR... TOO TIRED TO REMAIN AWAKE...YOU MUST SLEEP... SLEEP...
I MUST SLEEP...
6

YOU ARE IN MY POWER... I AM YOUR MASTER... YOU MUST OBEY ME...

I MUST... OBEY YOU...

I HAVE *TRIUMPHED!* NOW TO HAVE MY REVENGE! I SHALL USE *THOR* AS MY INSTRUMENT FOR CREATING MISCHIEF!

DESCEND TO EARTH, THOR!

YES, LOKI!

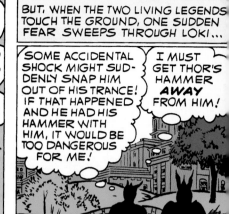

BUT, WHEN THE TWO LIVING LEGENDS TOUCH THE GROUND, ONE SUDDEN FEAR SWEEPS THROUGH LOKI...

SOME ACCIDENTAL SHOCK MIGHT SUDDENLY SNAP HIM OUT OF HIS TRANCE! IF THAT HAPPENED AND HE HAD HIS HAMMER WITH HIM, IT WOULD BE TOO DANGEROUS FOR ME!

I MUST GET THOR'S HAMMER *AWAY* FROM HIM!

I COMMAND YOU TO GIVE ME THE ENCHANTED HAMMER!

I...I CANNOT OBEY YOU, LOKI! BY THE WILL OF ODIN* THE MAGIC WEAPON MUST NEVER BE WRESTED FROM THOR!

*EDITOR'S NOTE!* ODIN IS THE RULER OF ALL NORSE GODS!

HIS ATTACHMENT TO THE HAMMER IS TOO STRONG FOR EVEN *HYPNOSIS* TO OVERCOME!

I WILL HAVE TO RESORT TO *TRICKERY!*

*LOOK*, THOR--THERE IS A *SEA BEAST* BENEATH THE SURFACE! IT IS ATTACKING THAT SMALL BOAT!

INSTINCTIVELY, THE GOD OF THUNDER HURLS HIS MIGHTY HAMMER IN THE DIRECTION INDICATED BY LOKI...

*HAH!* IT WORKED! HE BELIEVED THERE REALLY *WAS* A MENACE AND HE TRIED TO DESTROY IT!

BUT, AN INSTANT LATER...

OHH--I *FORGOT*--THE HAMMER'S GREATEST POWER---WHENEVER THOR THROWS IT, IT *RETURNS* TO HIM!

7

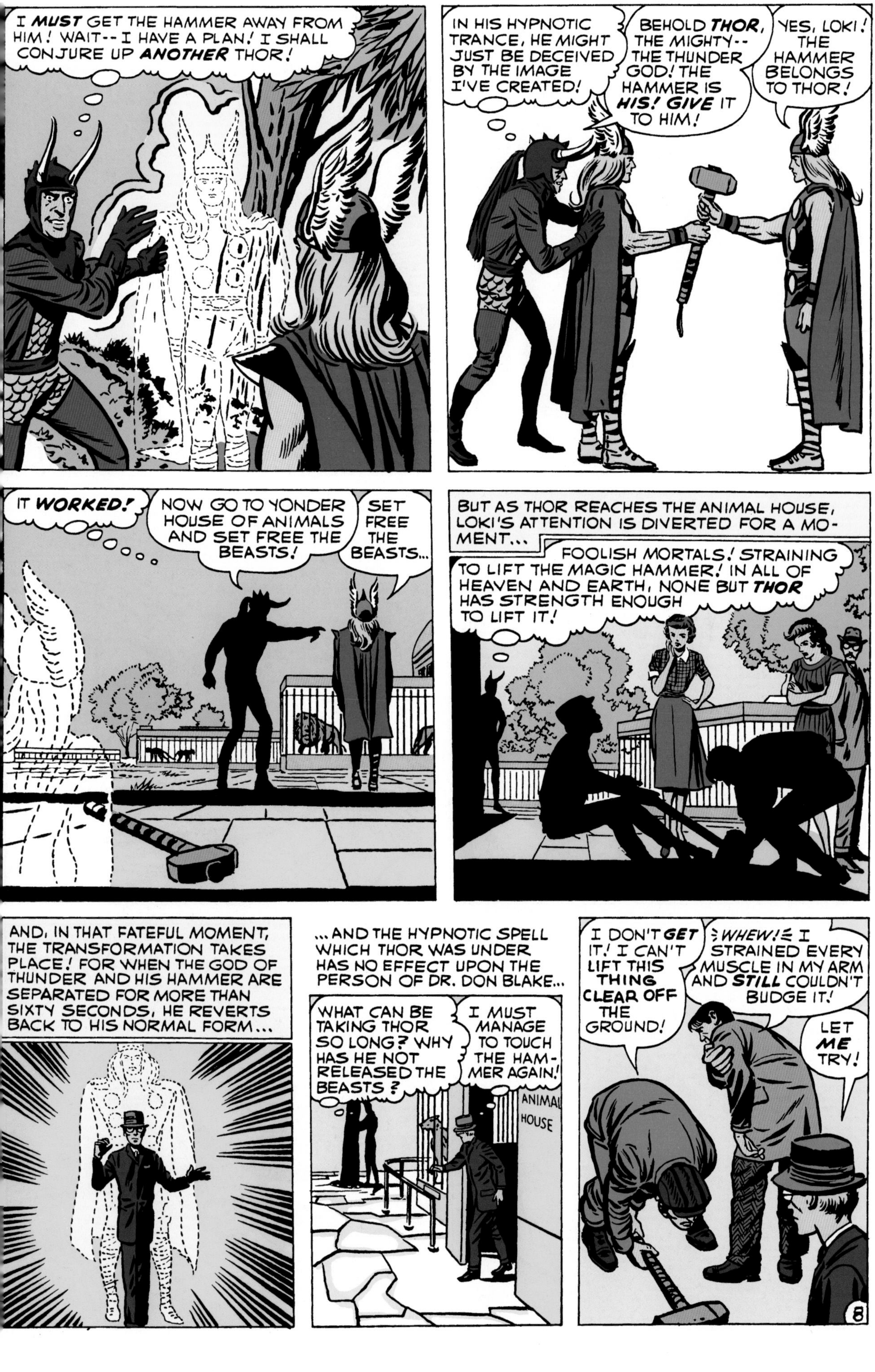

I MUST GET THE HAMMER AWAY FROM HIM! WAIT-- I HAVE A PLAN! I SHALL CONJURE UP ANOTHER THOR!
IN HIS HYPNOTIC TRANCE, HE MIGHT JUST BE DECEIVED BY THE IMAGE I'VE CREATED!
BEHOLD THOR, THE MIGHTY-- THE THUNDER GOD! THE HAMMER IS HIS! GIVE IT TO HIM!
YES, LOKI! THE HAMMER BELONGS TO THOR!
IT WORKED!
NOW GO TO YONDER HOUSE OF ANIMALS AND SET FREE THE BEASTS!
SET FREE THE BEASTS...
BUT AS THOR REACHES THE ANIMAL HOUSE, LOKI'S ATTENTION IS DIVERTED FOR A MOMENT...
FOOLISH MORTALS! STRAINING TO LIFT THE MAGIC HAMMER! IN ALL OF HEAVEN AND EARTH, NONE BUT THOR HAS STRENGTH ENOUGH TO LIFT IT!
AND, IN THAT FATEFUL MOMENT, THE TRANSFORMATION TAKES PLACE! FOR WHEN THE GOD OF THUNDER AND HIS HAMMER ARE SEPARATED FOR MORE THAN SIXTY SECONDS, HE REVERTS BACK TO HIS NORMAL FORM...
...AND THE HYPNOTIC SPELL WHICH THOR WAS UNDER HAS NO EFFECT UPON THE PERSON OF DR. DON BLAKE...
WHAT CAN BE TAKING THOR SO LONG? WHY HAS HE NOT RELEASED THE BEASTS?
I MUST MANAGE TO TOUCH THE HAMMER AGAIN!
ANIMAL HOUSE
I DON'T GET IT! I CAN'T LIFT THIS THING CLEAR OFF THE GROUND!
WHEW! I STRAINED EVERY MUSCLE IN MY ARM AND STILL COULDN'T BUDGE IT!
LET ME TRY!
8

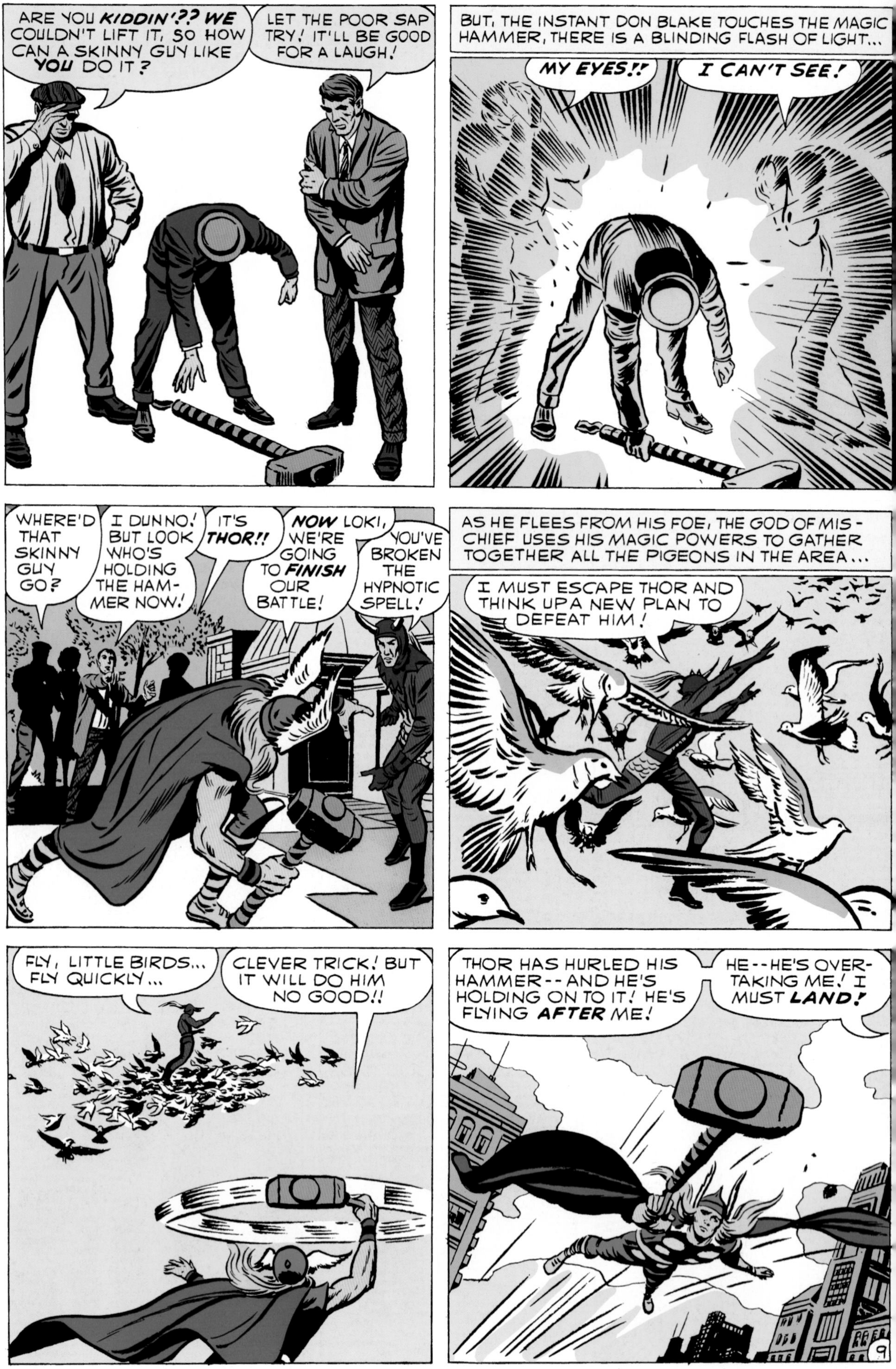
ARE YOU KIDDIN'?? WE COULDN'T LIFT IT, SO HOW CAN A SKINNY GUY LIKE YOU DO IT?
LET THE POOR SAP TRY! IT'LL BE GOOD FOR A LAUGH!
BUT, THE INSTANT DON BLAKE TOUCHES THE MAGIC HAMMER, THERE IS A BLINDING FLASH OF LIGHT...
MY EYES!!
I CAN'T SEE!
WHERE'D THAT SKINNY GUY GO?
I DUNNO! BUT LOOK WHO'S HOLDING THE HAMMER NOW!
IT'S THOR!!
NOW LOKI, WE'RE GOING TO FINISH OUR BATTLE!
YOU'VE BROKEN THE HYPNOTIC SPELL!
AS HE FLEES FROM HIS FOE, THE GOD OF MISCHIEF USES HIS MAGIC POWERS TO GATHER TOGETHER ALL THE PIGEONS IN THE AREA...
I MUST ESCAPE THOR AND THINK UP A NEW PLAN TO DEFEAT HIM!
FLY, LITTLE BIRDS... FLY QUICKLY...
CLEVER TRICK! BUT IT WILL DO HIM NO GOOD!!
THOR HAS HURLED HIS HAMMER--AND HE'S HOLDING ON TO IT! HE'S FLYING AFTER ME!
HE--HE'S OVERTAKING ME! I MUST LAND!
9

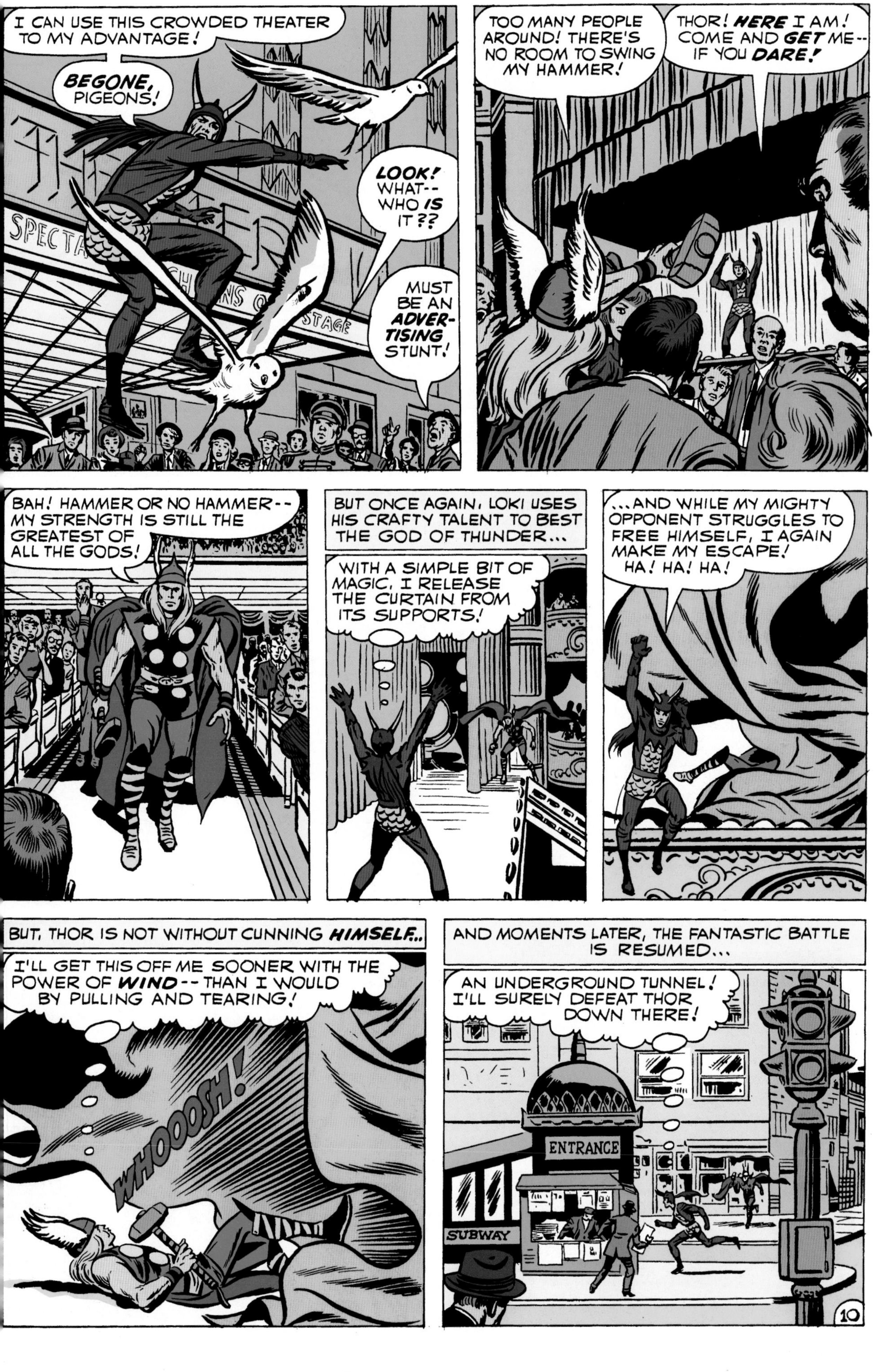

I CAN USE THIS CROWDED THEATER TO MY ADVANTAGE!
BEGONE, PIGEONS!
LOOK! WHAT-- WHO IS IT??
MUST BE AN ADVERTISING STUNT!
SPECTA
STAGE
TOO MANY PEOPLE AROUND! THERE'S NO ROOM TO SWING MY HAMMER!
THOR! HERE I AM! COME AND GET ME-- IF YOU DARE!
BAH! HAMMER OR NO HAMMER-- MY STRENGTH IS STILL THE GREATEST OF ALL THE GODS!
BUT ONCE AGAIN, LOKI USES HIS CRAFTY TALENT TO BEST THE GOD OF THUNDER...
WITH A SIMPLE BIT OF MAGIC, I RELEASE THE CURTAIN FROM ITS SUPPORTS!
...AND WHILE MY MIGHTY OPPONENT STRUGGLES TO FREE HIMSELF, I AGAIN MAKE MY ESCAPE! HA! HA! HA!
BUT, THOR IS NOT WITHOUT CUNNING HIMSELF...
I'LL GET THIS OFF ME SOONER WITH THE POWER OF WIND-- THAN I WOULD BY PULLING AND TEARING!
WHOOOSH!
AND MOMENTS LATER, THE FANTASTIC BATTLE IS RESUMED...
AN UNDERGROUND TUNNEL! I'LL SURELY DEFEAT THOR DOWN THERE!
ENTRANCE
SUBWAY
10

HE'S PUSHING THOSE PEOPLE OFF THE PLATFORM -- AND A *TRAIN'S* COMING!

*AWAY,* PUNY MORTALS!

HAH! I *KNEW* THE SOFT-HEARTED THOR WOULD STOP TO HELP THE USELESS HUMANS!

NO TIME TO LOSE! THE TRAIN WILL PASS WITHIN SECONDS!

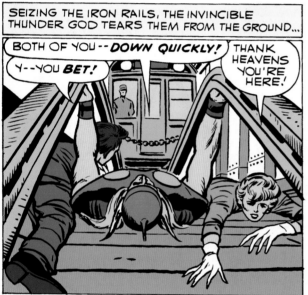

SEIZING THE IRON RAILS, THE INVINCIBLE THUNDER GOD TEARS THEM FROM THE GROUND...

BOTH OF YOU -- *DOWN QUICKLY!*

Y--YOU *BET!*

THANK HEAVENS YOU'RE HERE!

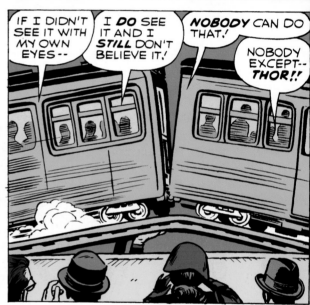

IF I DIDN'T SEE IT WITH MY OWN EYES --

I *DO* SEE IT AND I *STILL* DON'T BELIEVE IT!

*NOBODY* CAN DO THAT!

NOBODY EXCEPT-- THOR!!

WE'RE *SAVED!!*

NOW TO FIND LOKI, BEFORE HE DOES ANY *MORE* HARM!

UP *THERE!* HE'S BROUGHT THE WINGED HORSE OF A GASOLINE SIGN TO LIFE! NOW HE CAN *FLY* AGAIN!

AND IN THIS TIMES SQUARE CROWD, I CAN'T SWING MY HAMMER! I CAN'T FLY AFTER HIM!

11

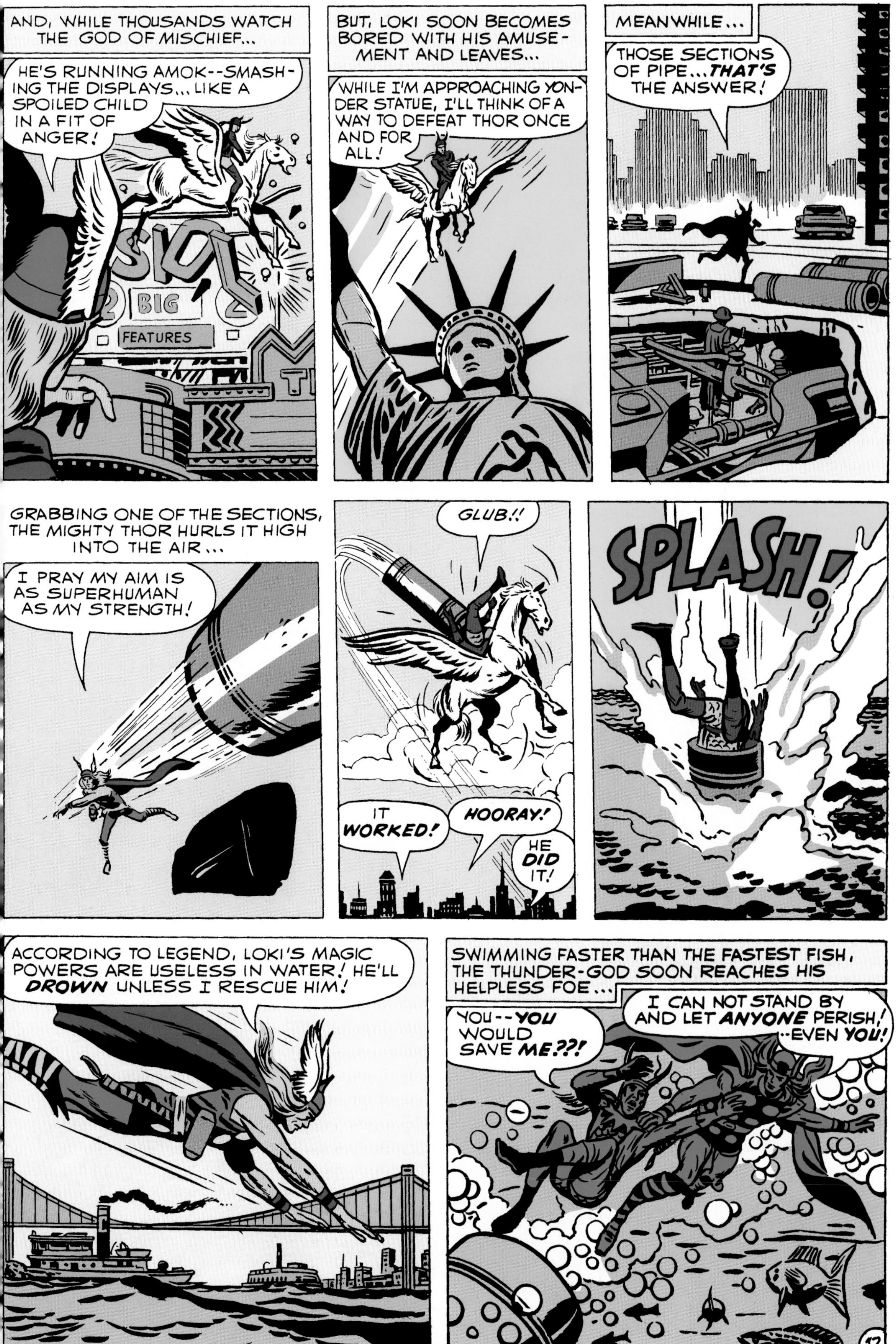
AND, WHILE THOUSANDS WATCH THE GOD OF MISCHIEF...
HE'S RUNNING AMOK--SMASHING THE DISPLAYS... LIKE A SPOILED CHILD IN A FIT OF ANGER!
2 BIG 2
FEATURES
BUT, LOKI SOON BECOMES BORED WITH HIS AMUSEMENT AND LEAVES...
WHILE I'M APPROACHING YONDER STATUE, I'LL THINK OF A WAY TO DEFEAT THOR ONCE AND FOR ALL!
MEANWHILE...
THOSE SECTIONS OF PIPE... THAT'S THE ANSWER!
GRABBING ONE OF THE SECTIONS, THE MIGHTY THOR HURLS IT HIGH INTO THE AIR...
I PRAY MY AIM IS AS SUPERHUMAN AS MY STRENGTH!
GLUB!!
IT WORKED!
HOORAY!
HE DID IT!
SPLASH!
ACCORDING TO LEGEND, LOKI'S MAGIC POWERS ARE USELESS IN WATER! HE'LL DROWN UNLESS I RESCUE HIM!
SWIMMING FASTER THAN THE FASTEST FISH, THE THUNDER-GOD SOON REACHES HIS HELPLESS FOE...
YOU--YOU WOULD SAVE ME??!
I CAN NOT STAND BY AND LET ANYONE PERISH! --EVEN YOU!
12

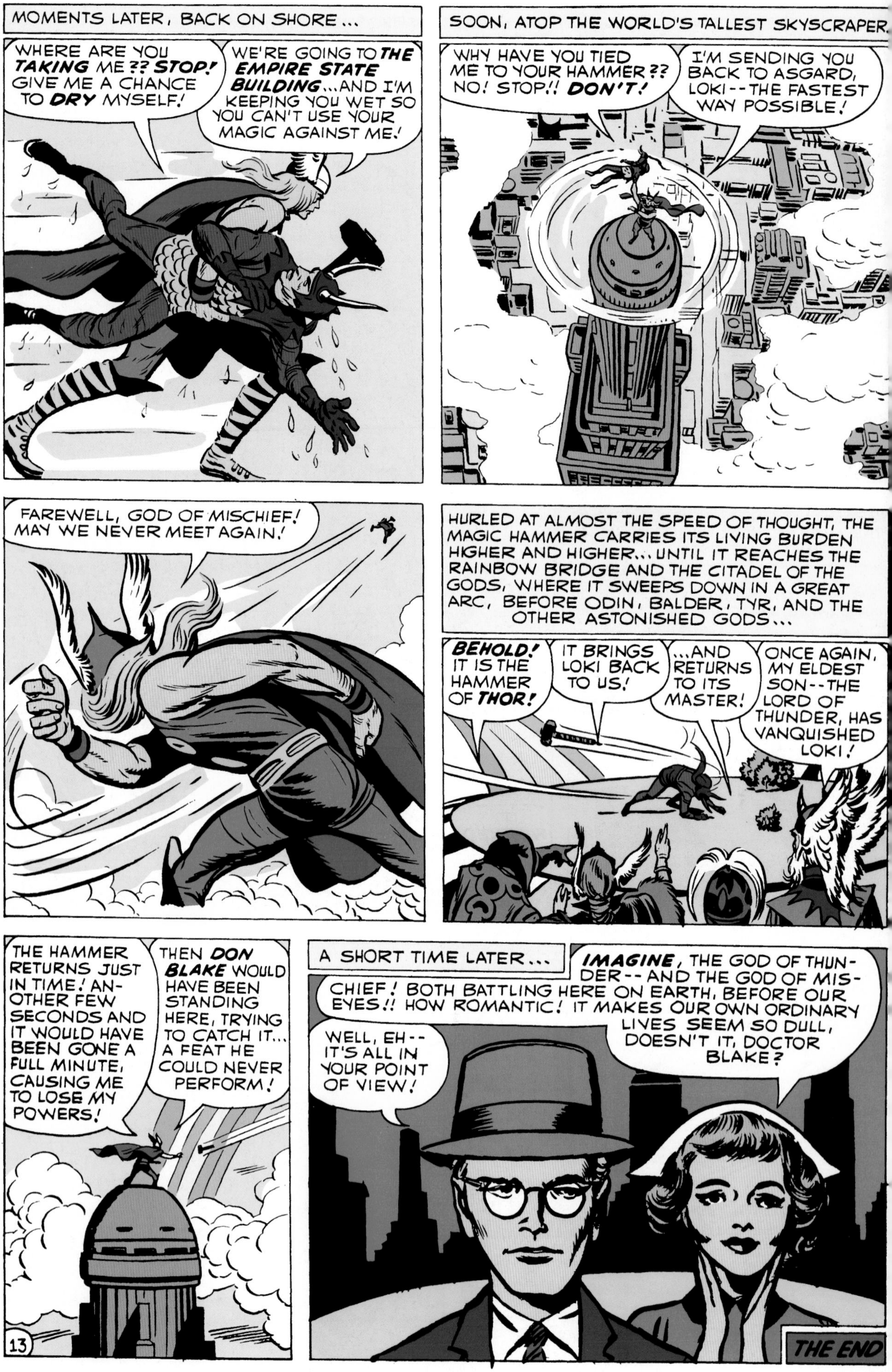
MOMENTS LATER, BACK ON SHORE...
WHERE ARE YOU TAKING ME?? STOP! GIVE ME A CHANCE TO DRY MYSELF!
WE'RE GOING TO THE EMPIRE STATE BUILDING...AND I'M KEEPING YOU WET SO YOU CAN'T USE YOUR MAGIC AGAINST ME!
SOON, ATOP THE WORLD'S TALLEST SKYSCRAPER.
WHY HAVE YOU TIED ME TO YOUR HAMMER?? NO! STOP!! DON'T!
I'M SENDING YOU BACK TO ASGARD, LOKI--THE FASTEST WAY POSSIBLE!
FAREWELL, GOD OF MISCHIEF! MAY WE NEVER MEET AGAIN!
HURLED AT ALMOST THE SPEED OF THOUGHT, THE MAGIC HAMMER CARRIES ITS LIVING BURDEN HIGHER AND HIGHER... UNTIL IT REACHES THE RAINBOW BRIDGE AND THE CITADEL OF THE GODS, WHERE IT SWEEPS DOWN IN A GREAT ARC, BEFORE ODIN, BALDER, TYR, AND THE OTHER ASTONISHED GODS...
BEHOLD! IT IS THE HAMMER OF THOR!
IT BRINGS LOKI BACK TO US!
...AND RETURNS TO ITS MASTER!
ONCE AGAIN, MY ELDEST SON--THE LORD OF THUNDER, HAS VANQUISHED LOKI!
THE HAMMER RETURNS JUST IN TIME! ANOTHER FEW SECONDS AND IT WOULD HAVE BEEN GONE A FULL MINUTE, CAUSING ME TO LOSE MY POWERS!
THEN DON BLAKE WOULD HAVE BEEN STANDING HERE, TRYING TO CATCH IT... A FEAT HE COULD NEVER PERFORM!
A SHORT TIME LATER...
IMAGINE, THE GOD OF THUNDER--AND THE GOD OF MISCHIEF! BOTH BATTLING HERE ON EARTH, BEFORE OUR EYES!! HOW ROMANTIC! IT MAKES OUR OWN ORDINARY LIVES SEEM SO DULL, DOESN'T IT, DOCTOR BLAKE?
WELL, EH--IT'S ALL IN YOUR POINT OF VIEW!
THE END

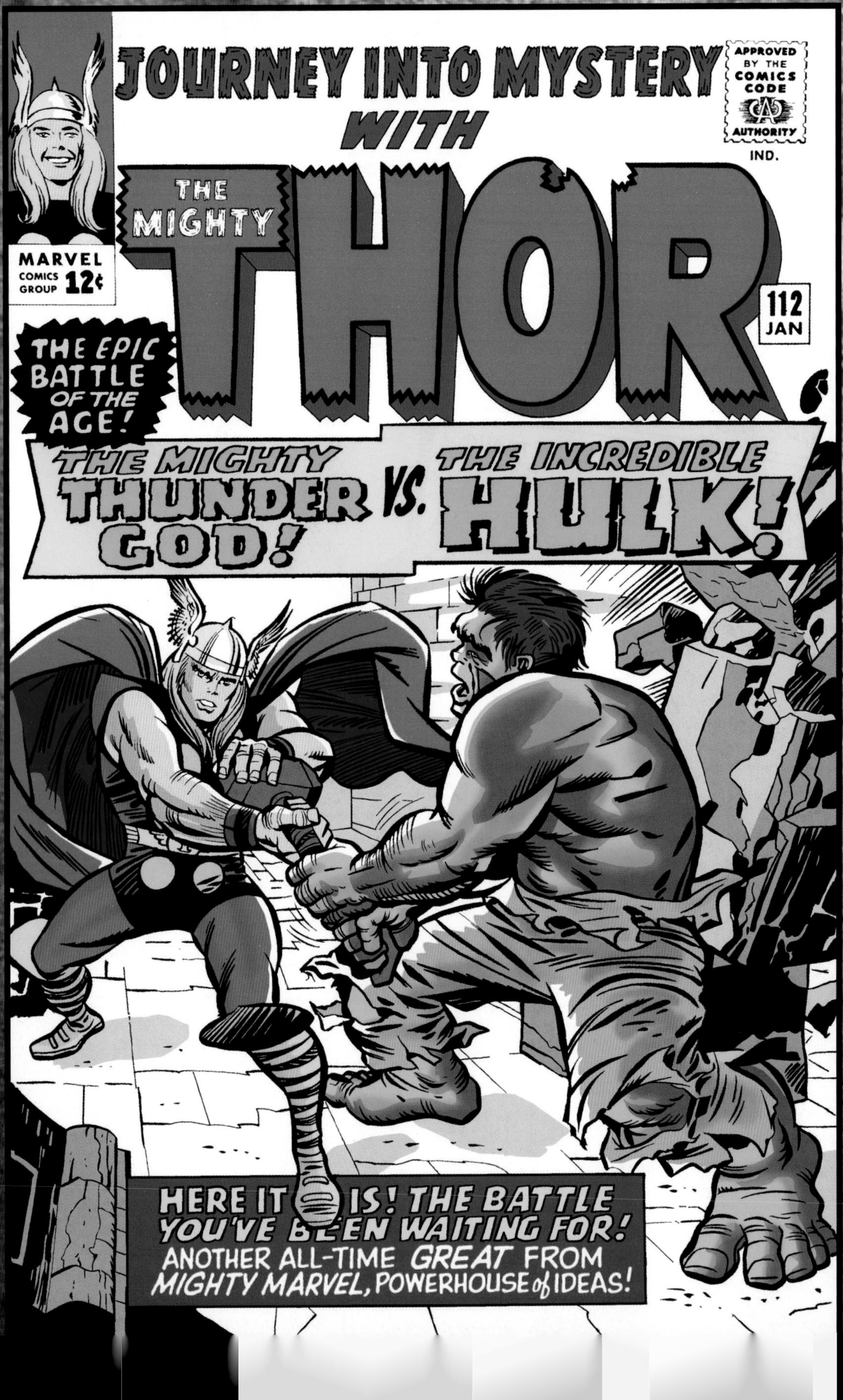

JOURNEY INTO MYSTERY
WITH
THE MIGHTY
THOR
APPROVED BY THE COMICS CODE AUTHORITY
IND.
MARVEL COMICS GROUP 12¢
112 JAN
THE EPIC BATTLE OF THE AGE!
THE MIGHTY THUNDER GOD! VS. THE INCREDIBLE HULK!
HERE IT IS! THE BATTLE YOU'VE BEEN WAITING FOR!
ANOTHER ALL-TIME GREAT FROM MIGHTY MARVEL, POWERHOUSE of IDEAS!

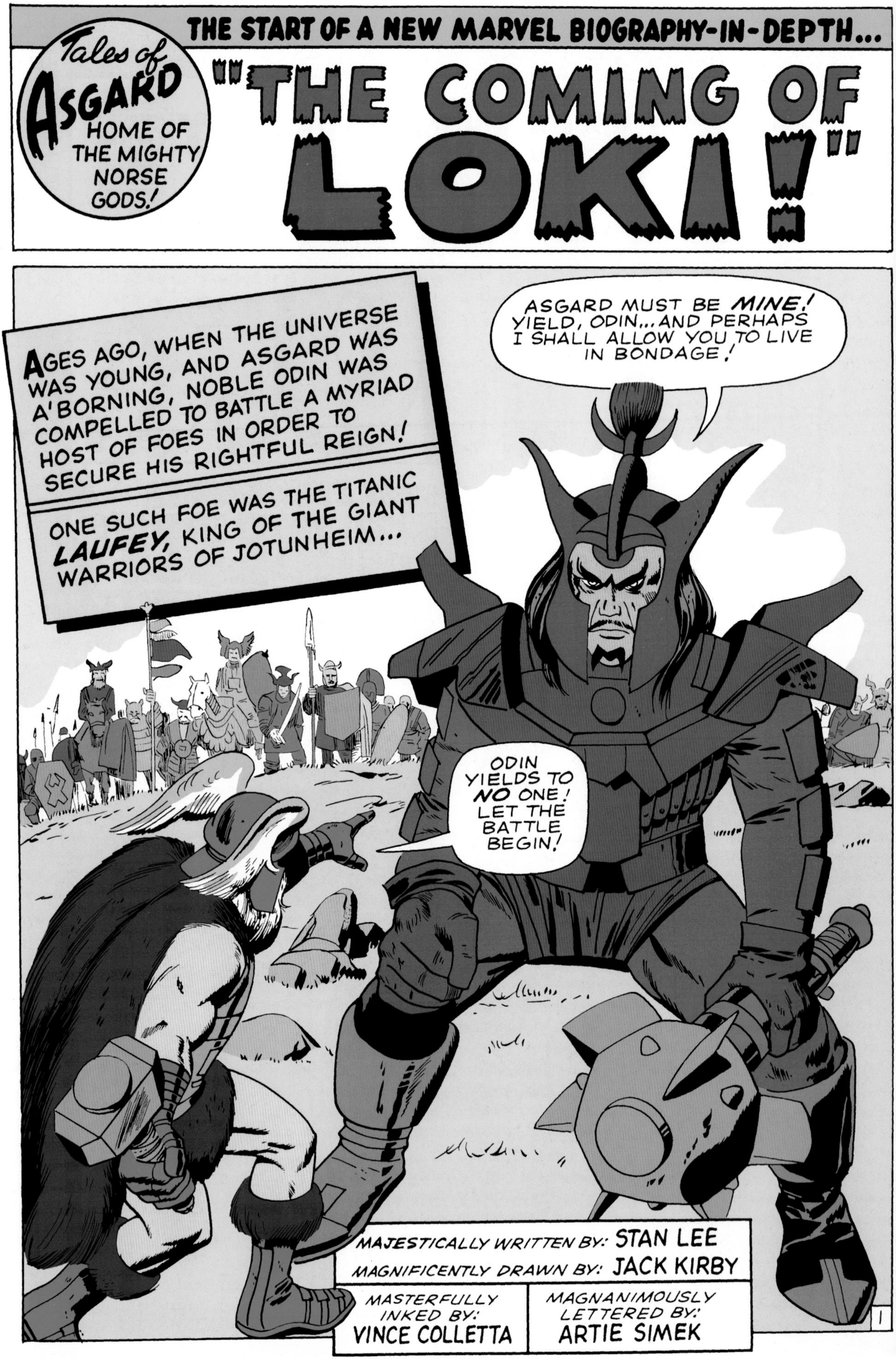
THE START OF A NEW MARVEL BIOGRAPHY-IN-DEPTH...
Tales of ASGARD HOME OF THE MIGHTY NORSE GODS!
"THE COMING OF LOKI!"
AGES AGO, WHEN THE UNIVERSE WAS YOUNG, AND ASGARD WAS A'BORNING, NOBLE ODIN WAS COMPELLED TO BATTLE A MYRIAD HOST OF FOES IN ORDER TO SECURE HIS RIGHTFUL REIGN!
ONE SUCH FOE WAS THE TITANIC LAUFEY, KING OF THE GIANT WARRIORS OF JOTUNHEIM...
ASGARD MUST BE MINE! YIELD, ODIN... AND PERHAPS I SHALL ALLOW YOU TO LIVE IN BONDAGE!
ODIN YIELDS TO NO ONE! LET THE BATTLE BEGIN!
MAJESTICALLY WRITTEN BY: STAN LEE
MAGNIFICENTLY DRAWN BY: JACK KIRBY
MASTERFULLY INKED BY: VINCE COLLETTA
MAGNANIMOUSLY LETTERED BY: ARTIE SIMEK
1

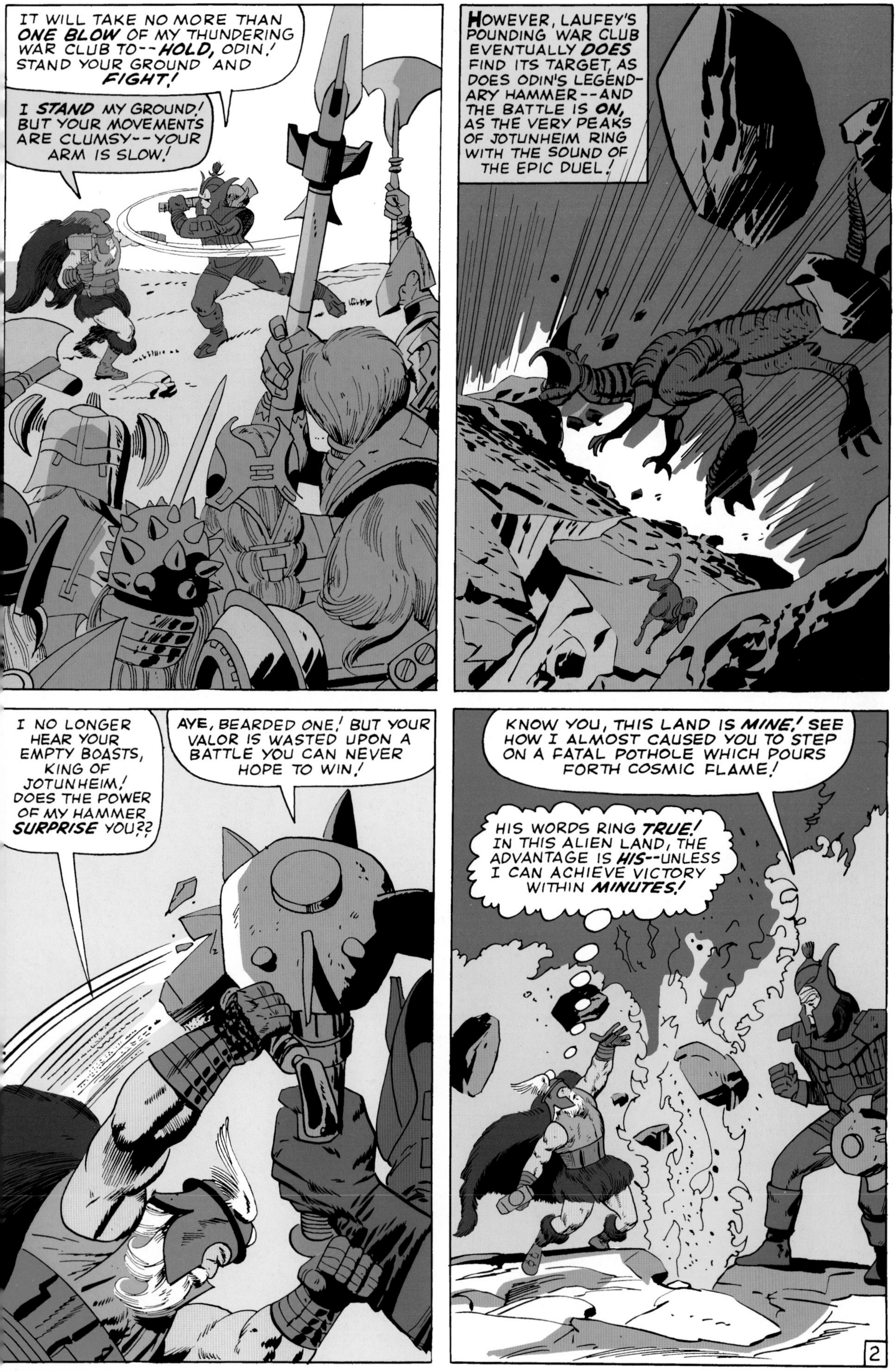
IT WILL TAKE NO MORE THAN ONE BLOW OF MY THUNDERING WAR CLUB TO--HOLD, ODIN! STAND YOUR GROUND AND FIGHT!
I STAND MY GROUND! BUT YOUR MOVEMENTS ARE CLUMSY--YOUR ARM IS SLOW!
HOWEVER, LAUFEY'S POUNDING WAR CLUB EVENTUALLY DOES FIND ITS TARGET, AS DOES ODIN'S LEGENDARY HAMMER--AND THE BATTLE IS ON, AS THE VERY PEAKS OF JOTUNHEIM RING WITH THE SOUND OF THE EPIC DUEL!
I NO LONGER HEAR YOUR EMPTY BOASTS, KING OF JOTUNHEIM! DOES THE POWER OF MY HAMMER SURPRISE YOU??
AYE, BEARDED ONE! BUT YOUR VALOR IS WASTED UPON A BATTLE YOU CAN NEVER HOPE TO WIN!
KNOW YOU, THIS LAND IS MINE! SEE HOW I ALMOST CAUSED YOU TO STEP ON A FATAL POTHOLE WHICH POURS FORTH COSMIC FLAME!
HIS WORDS RING TRUE! IN THIS ALIEN LAND, THE ADVANTAGE IS HIS--UNLESS I CAN ACHIEVE VICTORY WITHIN MINUTES!
2

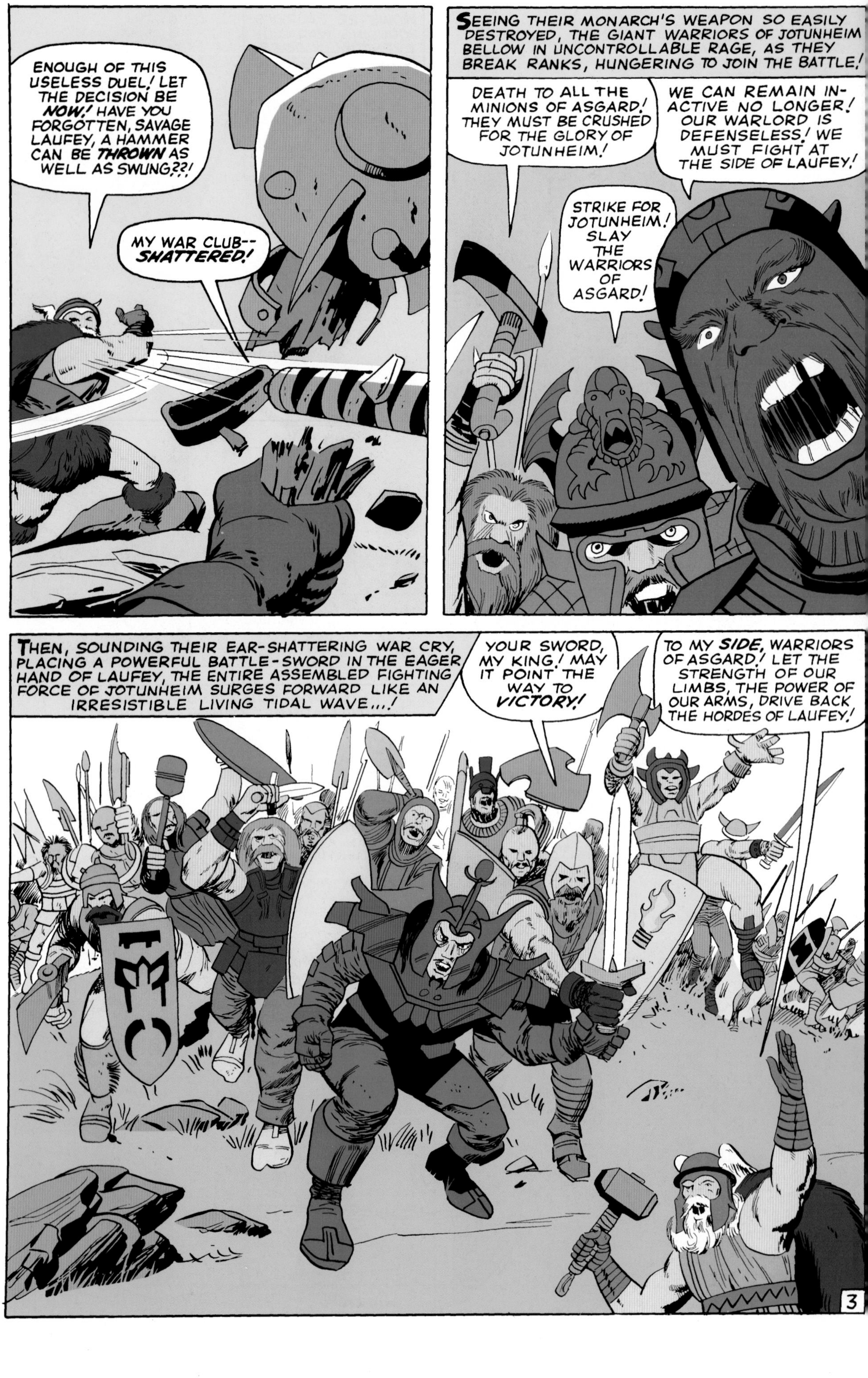
ENOUGH OF THIS USELESS DUEL! LET THE DECISION BE NOW! HAVE YOU FORGOTTEN, SAVAGE LAUFEY, A HAMMER CAN BE THROWN AS WELL AS SWUNG??!
MY WAR CLUB-- SHATTERED!
SEEING THEIR MONARCH'S WEAPON SO EASILY DESTROYED, THE GIANT WARRIORS OF JOTUNHEIM BELLOW IN UNCONTROLLABLE RAGE, AS THEY BREAK RANKS, HUNGERING TO JOIN THE BATTLE!
DEATH TO ALL THE MINIONS OF ASGARD! THEY MUST BE CRUSHED FOR THE GLORY OF JOTUNHEIM!
WE CAN REMAIN INACTIVE NO LONGER! OUR WARLORD IS DEFENSELESS! WE MUST FIGHT AT THE SIDE OF LAUFEY!
STRIKE FOR JOTUNHEIM! SLAY THE WARRIORS OF ASGARD!
THEN, SOUNDING THEIR EAR-SHATTERING WAR CRY, PLACING A POWERFUL BATTLE-SWORD IN THE EAGER HAND OF LAUFEY, THE ENTIRE ASSEMBLED FIGHTING FORCE OF JOTUNHEIM SURGES FORWARD LIKE AN IRRESISTIBLE LIVING TIDAL WAVE...!
YOUR SWORD, MY KING! MAY IT POINT THE WAY TO VICTORY!
TO MY SIDE, WARRIORS OF ASGARD! LET THE STRENGTH OF OUR LIMBS, THE POWER OF OUR ARMS, DRIVE BACK THE HORDES OF LAUFEY!
3

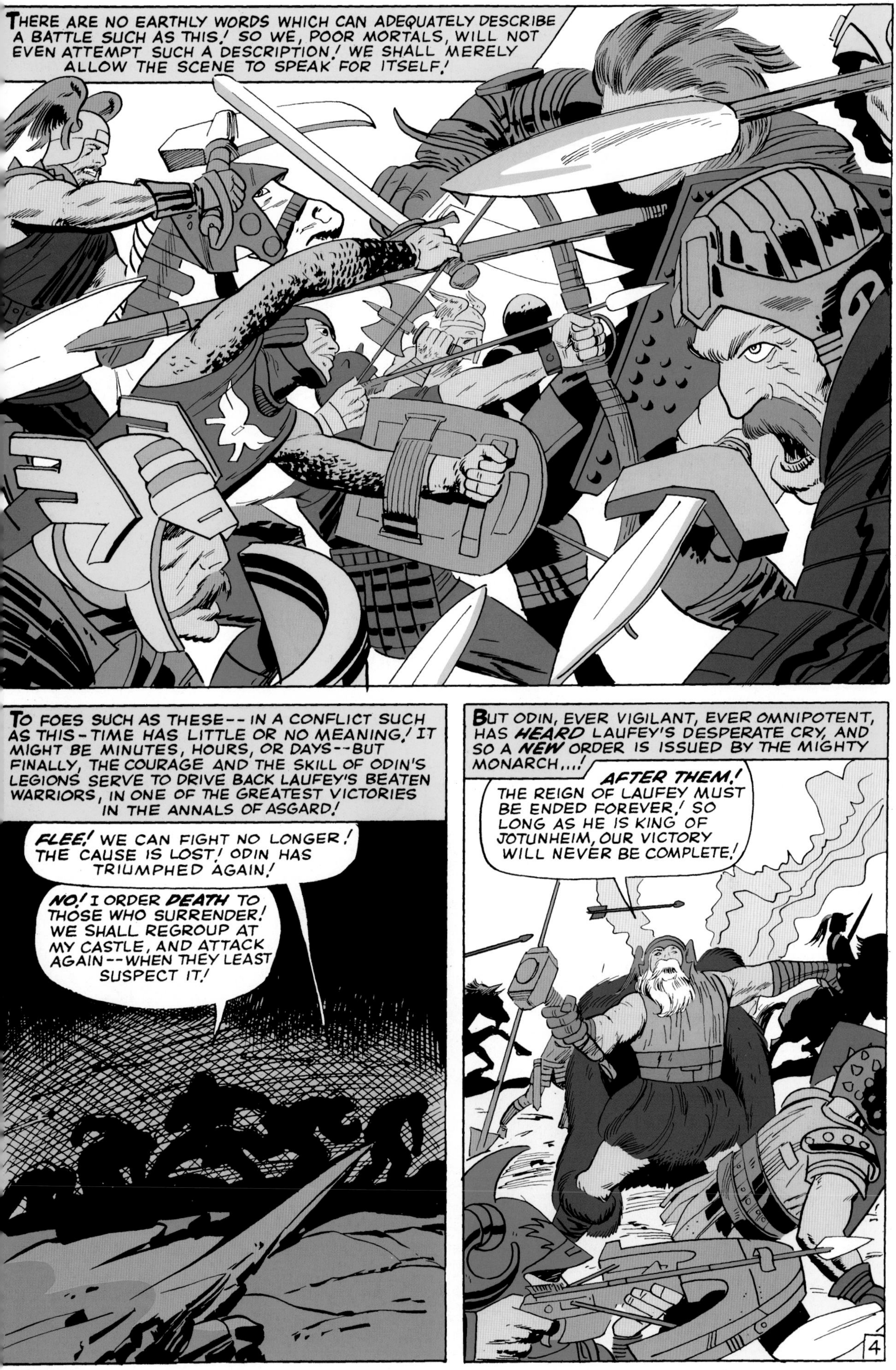
THERE ARE NO EARTHLY WORDS WHICH CAN ADEQUATELY DESCRIBE A BATTLE SUCH AS THIS! SO WE, POOR MORTALS, WILL NOT EVEN ATTEMPT SUCH A DESCRIPTION! WE SHALL MERELY ALLOW THE SCENE TO SPEAK FOR ITSELF!
TO FOES SUCH AS THESE-- IN A CONFLICT SUCH AS THIS-TIME HAS LITTLE OR NO MEANING! IT MIGHT BE MINUTES, HOURS, OR DAYS--BUT FINALLY, THE COURAGE AND THE SKILL OF ODIN'S LEGIONS SERVE TO DRIVE BACK LAUFEY'S BEATEN WARRIORS, IN ONE OF THE GREATEST VICTORIES IN THE ANNALS OF ASGARD!
FLEE! WE CAN FIGHT NO LONGER! THE CAUSE IS LOST! ODIN HAS TRIUMPHED AGAIN!
NO! I ORDER DEATH TO THOSE WHO SURRENDER! WE SHALL REGROUP AT MY CASTLE, AND ATTACK AGAIN--WHEN THEY LEAST SUSPECT IT!
BUT ODIN, EVER VIGILANT, EVER OMNIPOTENT, HAS HEARD LAUFEY'S DESPERATE CRY, AND SO A NEW ORDER IS ISSUED BY THE MIGHTY MONARCH...!
AFTER THEM! THE REIGN OF LAUFEY MUST BE ENDED FOREVER! SO LONG AS HE IS KING OF JOTUNHEIM, OUR VICTORY WILL NEVER BE COMPLETE!
4

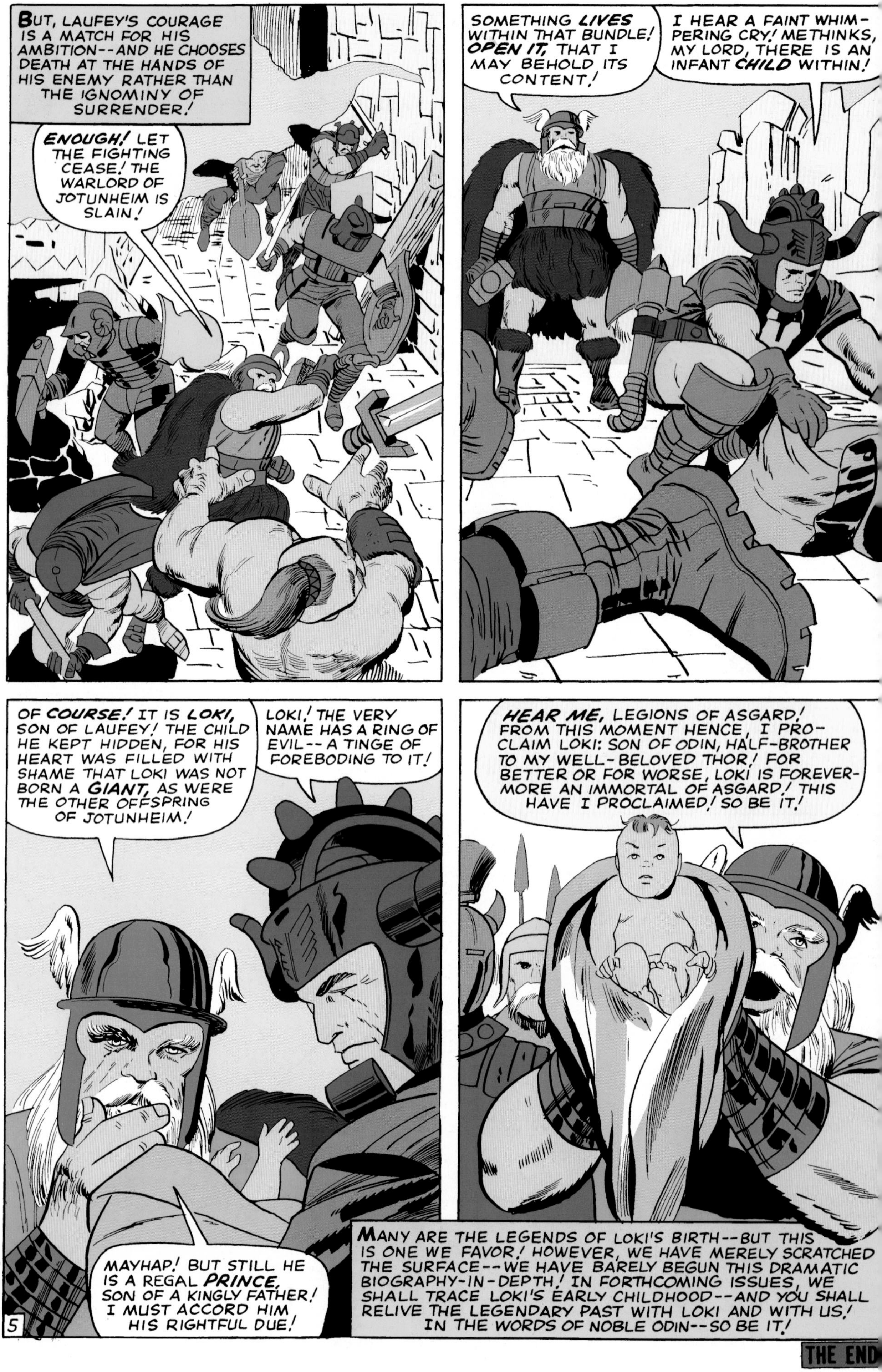
BUT, LAUFEY'S COURAGE IS A MATCH FOR HIS AMBITION--AND HE CHOOSES DEATH AT THE HANDS OF HIS ENEMY RATHER THAN THE IGNOMINY OF SURRENDER!
ENOUGH! LET THE FIGHTING CEASE! THE WARLORD OF JOTUNHEIM IS SLAIN!
SOMETHING LIVES WITHIN THAT BUNDLE! OPEN IT, THAT I MAY BEHOLD ITS CONTENT!
I HEAR A FAINT WHIMPERING CRY! METHINKS, MY LORD, THERE IS AN INFANT CHILD WITHIN!
OF COURSE! IT IS LOKI, SON OF LAUFEY! THE CHILD HE KEPT HIDDEN, FOR HIS HEART WAS FILLED WITH SHAME THAT LOKI WAS NOT BORN A GIANT, AS WERE THE OTHER OFFSPRING OF JOTUNHEIM!
LOKI! THE VERY NAME HAS A RING OF EVIL--A TINGE OF FOREBODING TO IT!
MAYHAP! BUT STILL HE IS A REGAL PRINCE, SON OF A KINGLY FATHER! I MUST ACCORD HIM HIS RIGHTFUL DUE!
HEAR ME, LEGIONS OF ASGARD! FROM THIS MOMENT HENCE, I PROCLAIM LOKI: SON OF ODIN, HALF-BROTHER TO MY WELL-BELOVED THOR! FOR BETTER OR FOR WORSE, LOKI IS FOREVERMORE AN IMMORTAL OF ASGARD! THIS HAVE I PROCLAIMED! SO BE IT!
MANY ARE THE LEGENDS OF LOKI'S BIRTH--BUT THIS IS ONE WE FAVOR! HOWEVER, WE HAVE MERELY SCRATCHED THE SURFACE--WE HAVE BARELY BEGUN THIS DRAMATIC BIOGRAPHY-IN-DEPTH! IN FORTHCOMING ISSUES, WE SHALL TRACE LOKI'S EARLY CHILDHOOD--AND YOU SHALL RELIVE THE LEGENDARY PAST WITH LOKI AND WITH US! IN THE WORDS OF NOBLE ODIN--SO BE IT!
5
THE END

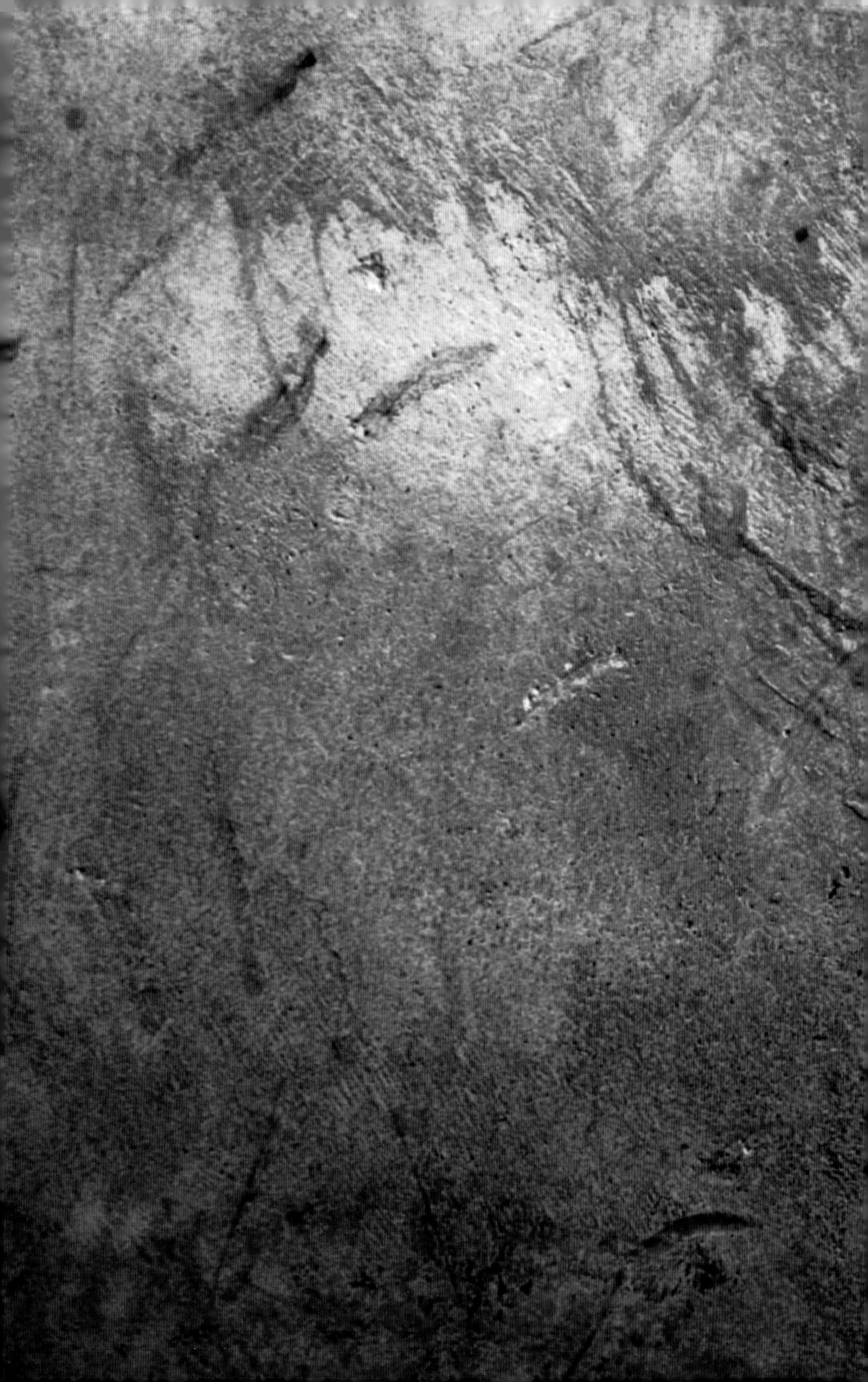

# THOR #12

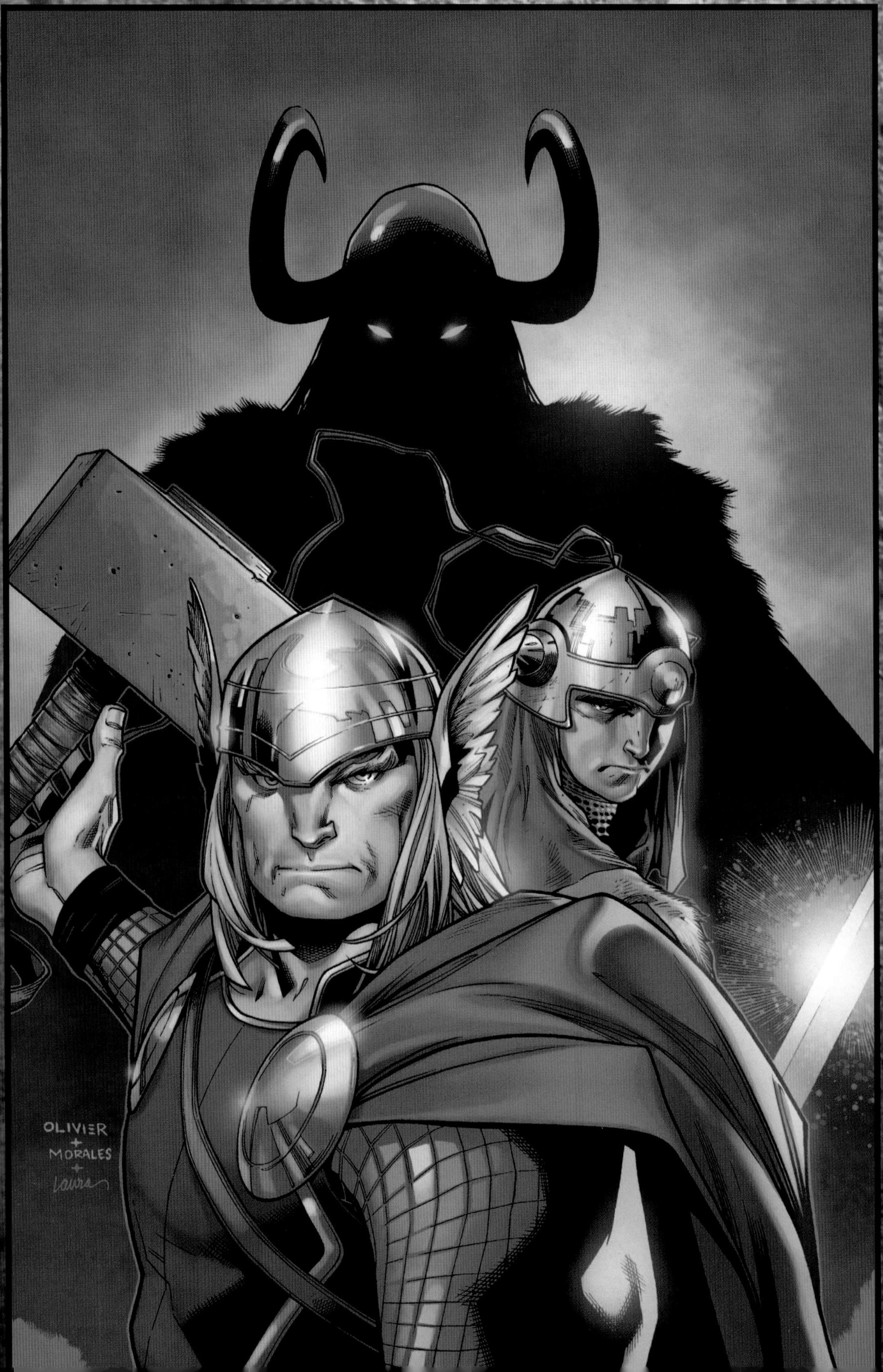
OLIVIER
+
MORALES
+
Laura

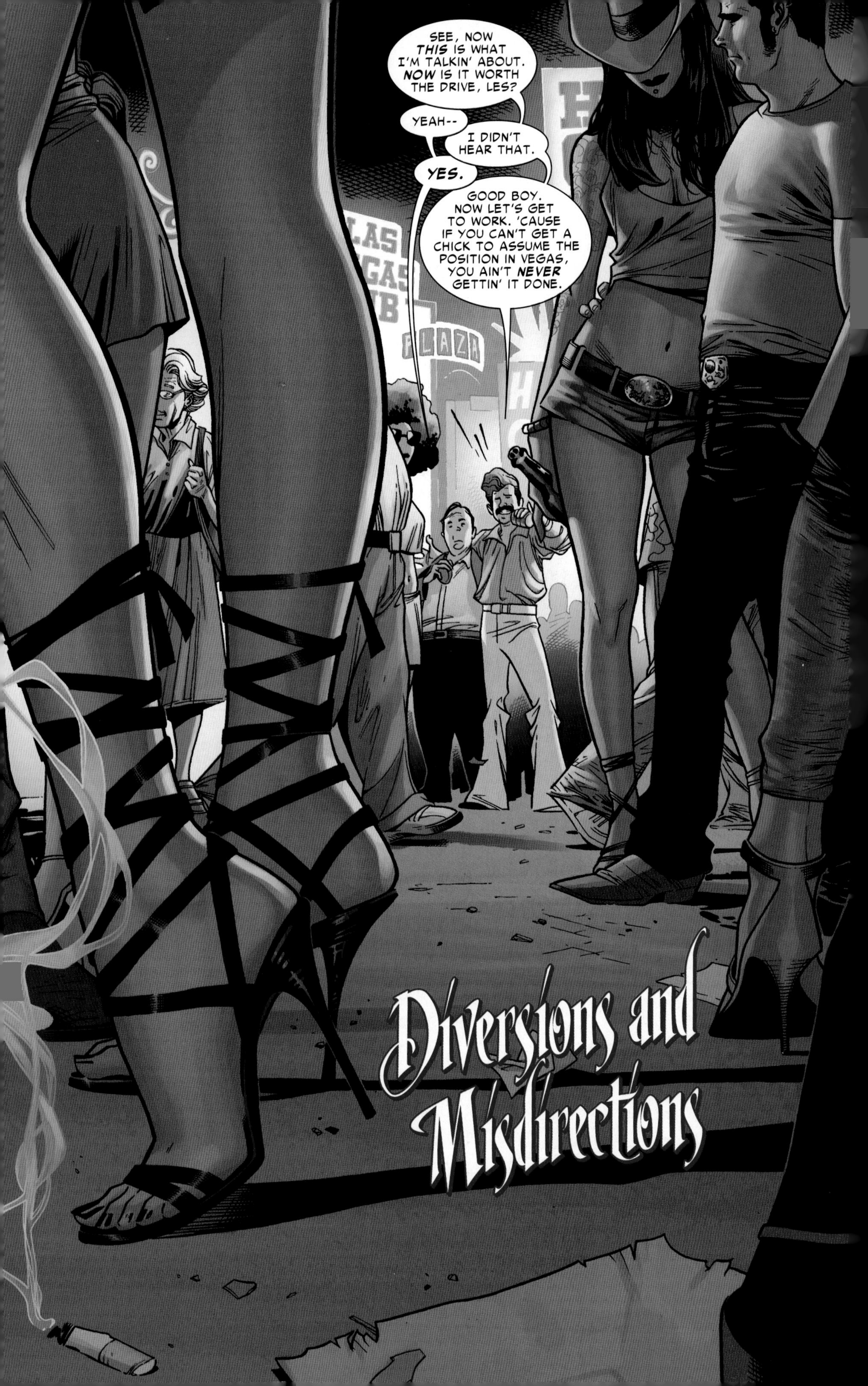
SEE, NOW *THIS* IS WHAT I'M TALKIN' ABOUT. *NOW* IS IT WORTH THE DRIVE, LES?
YEAH--
I DIDN'T HEAR THAT.
*YES.*
GOOD BOY. NOW LET'S GET TO WORK. 'CAUSE IF YOU CAN'T GET A CHICK TO ASSUME THE POSITION IN VEGAS, YOU AIN'T *NEVER* GETTIN' IT DONE.
PLAZA
Diversions and Misdirections

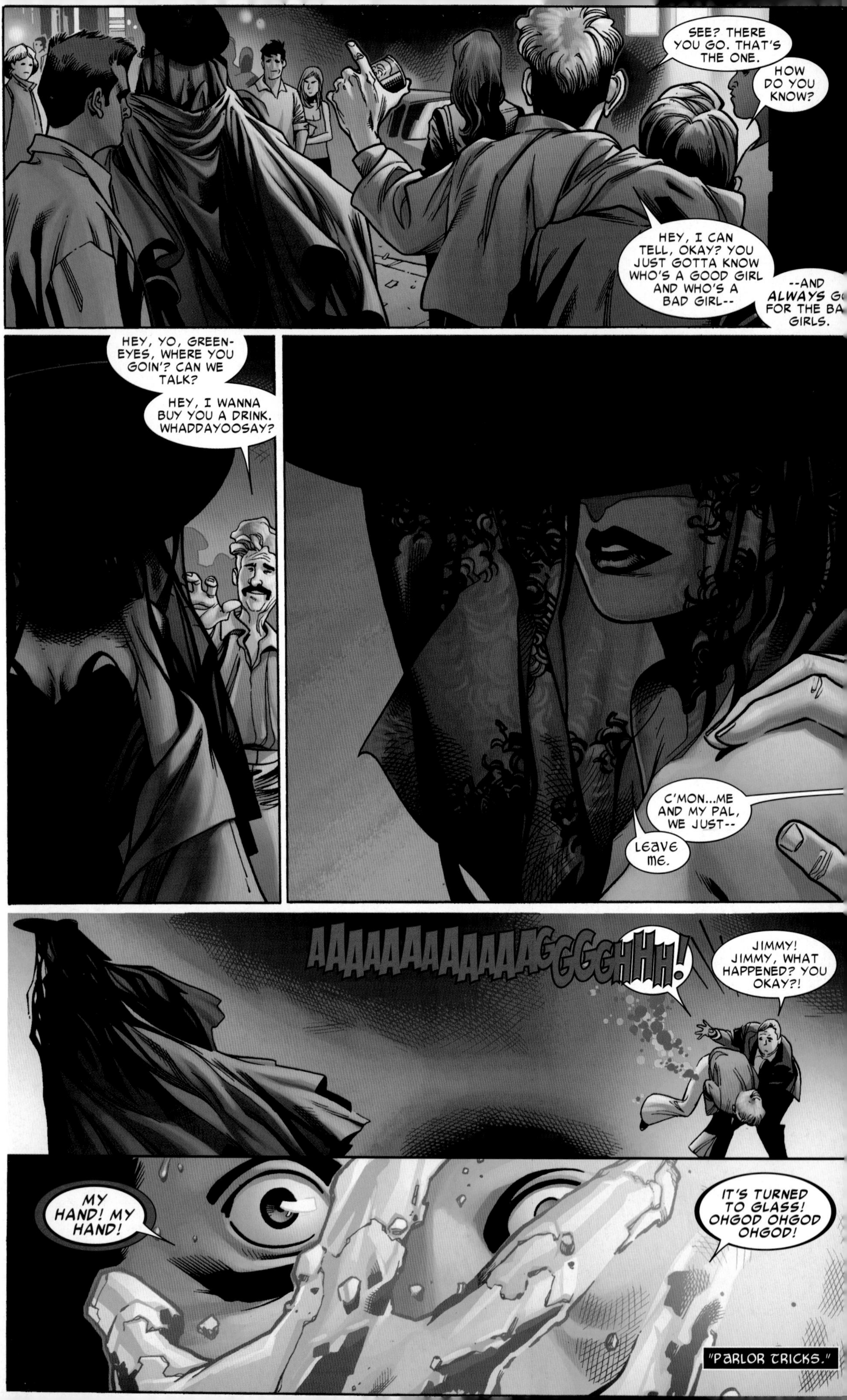
SEE? THERE YOU GO. THAT'S THE ONE.
HOW DO YOU KNOW?
HEY, I CAN TELL, OKAY? YOU JUST GOTTA KNOW WHO'S A GOOD GIRL AND WHO'S A BAD GIRL--
--AND ALWAYS GO FOR THE BAD GIRLS.
HEY, YO, GREEN-EYES, WHERE YOU GOIN'? CAN WE TALK?
HEY, I WANNA BUY YOU A DRINK. WHADDAYOOSAY?
C'MON...ME AND MY PAL, WE JUST--
LEAVE ME.
AAAAAAAAAAAAGGGHHH!
JIMMY! JIMMY, WHAT HAPPENED? YOU OKAY?!
MY HAND! MY HAND!
IT'S TURNED TO GLASS! OHGOD OHGOD OHGOD!
"PARLOR TRICKS."

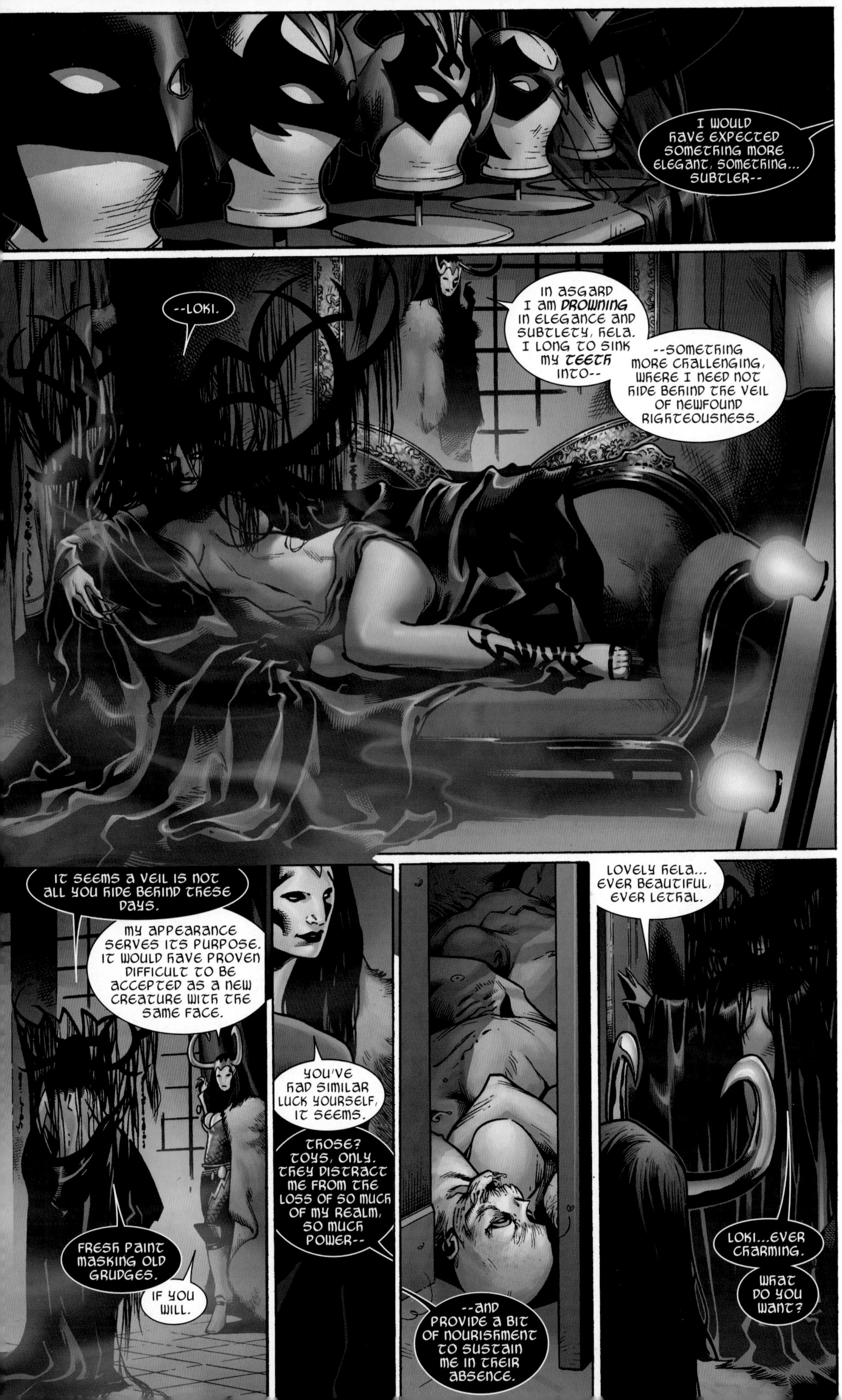
I WOULD HAVE EXPECTED SOMETHING MORE ELEGANT, SOMETHING... SUBTLER--
--LOKI.
IN ASGARD I AM DROWNING IN ELEGANCE AND SUBTLETY, HELA. I LONG TO SINK MY TEETH INTO--
--SOMETHING MORE CHALLENGING, WHERE I NEED NOT HIDE BEHIND THE VEIL OF NEWFOUND RIGHTEOUSNESS.
IT SEEMS A VEIL IS NOT ALL YOU HIDE BEHIND THESE DAYS.
MY APPEARANCE SERVES ITS PURPOSE. IT WOULD HAVE PROVEN DIFFICULT TO BE ACCEPTED AS A NEW CREATURE WITH THE SAME FACE.
FRESH PAINT MASKING OLD GRUDGES.
IF YOU WILL.
YOU'VE HAD SIMILAR LUCK YOURSELF, IT SEEMS.
THOSE? TOYS, ONLY. THEY DISTRACT ME FROM THE LOSS OF SO MUCH OF MY REALM, SO MUCH POWER--
--AND PROVIDE A BIT OF NOURISHMENT TO SUSTAIN ME IN THEIR ABSENCE.
LOVELY HELA... EVER BEAUTIFUL, EVER LETHAL.
LOKI...EVER CHARMING.
WHAT DO YOU WANT?

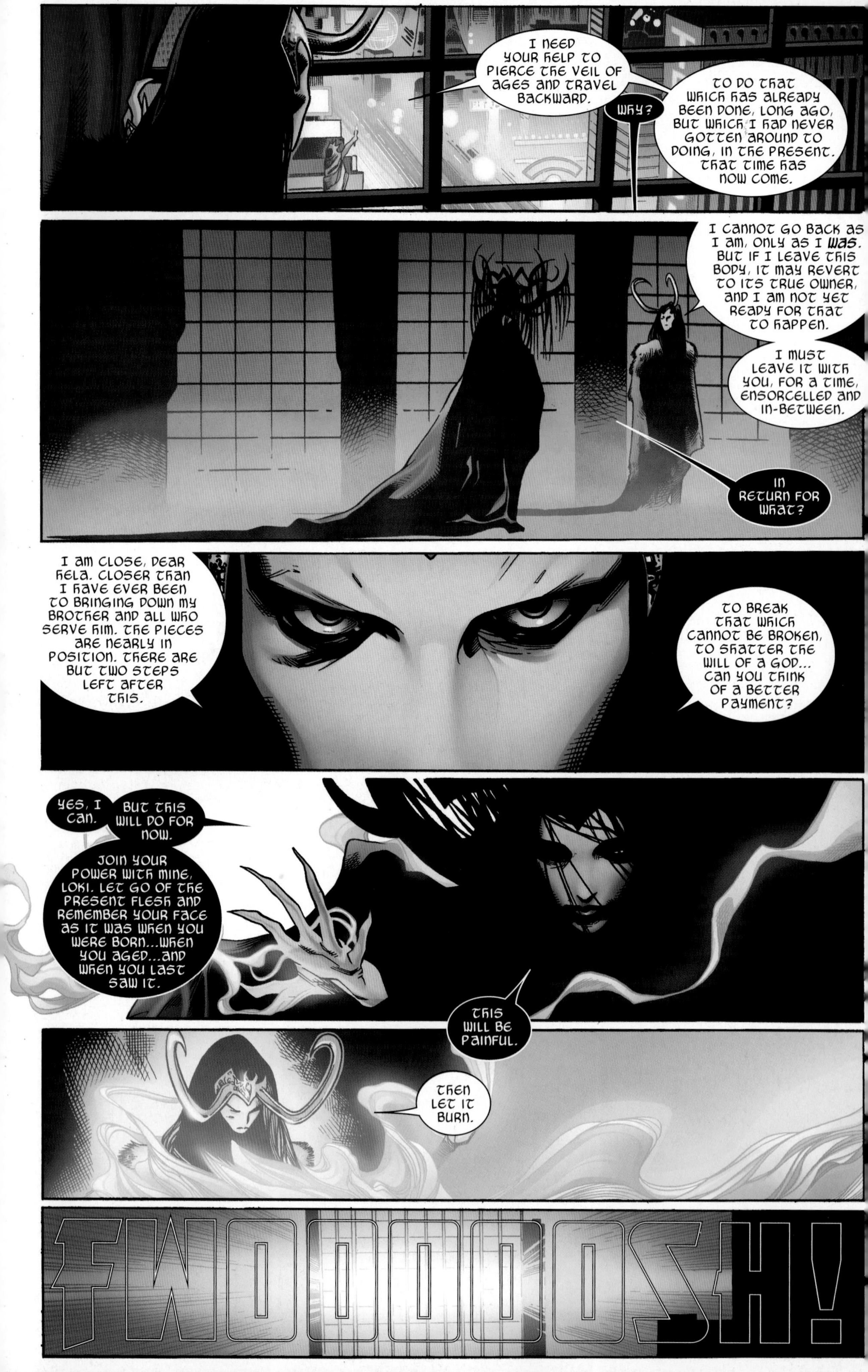
I NEED YOUR HELP TO PIERCE THE VEIL OF AGES AND TRAVEL BACKWARD.
WHY?
TO DO THAT WHICH HAS ALREADY BEEN DONE, LONG AGO, BUT WHICH I HAD NEVER GOTTEN AROUND TO DOING, IN THE PRESENT. THAT TIME HAS NOW COME.
I CANNOT GO BACK AS I AM, ONLY AS I *WAS*. BUT IF I LEAVE THIS BODY, IT MAY REVERT TO ITS TRUE OWNER, AND I AM NOT YET READY FOR THAT TO HAPPEN.
I MUST LEAVE IT WITH YOU, FOR A TIME, ENSORCELLED AND IN-BETWEEN.
IN RETURN FOR WHAT?
I AM CLOSE, DEAR HELA. CLOSER THAN I HAVE EVER BEEN TO BRINGING DOWN MY BROTHER AND ALL WHO SERVE HIM. THE PIECES ARE NEARLY IN POSITION. THERE ARE BUT TWO STEPS LEFT AFTER THIS.
TO BREAK THAT WHICH CANNOT BE BROKEN, TO SHATTER THE WILL OF A GOD... CAN YOU THINK OF A BETTER PAYMENT?
YES, I CAN.
BUT THIS WILL DO FOR NOW.
JOIN YOUR POWER WITH MINE, LOKI. LET GO OF THE PRESENT FLESH AND REMEMBER YOUR FACE AS IT WAS WHEN YOU WERE BORN...WHEN YOU AGED...AND WHEN YOU LAST SAW IT.
THIS WILL BE PAINFUL.
THEN LET IT BURN.
FWOOOOOSH!

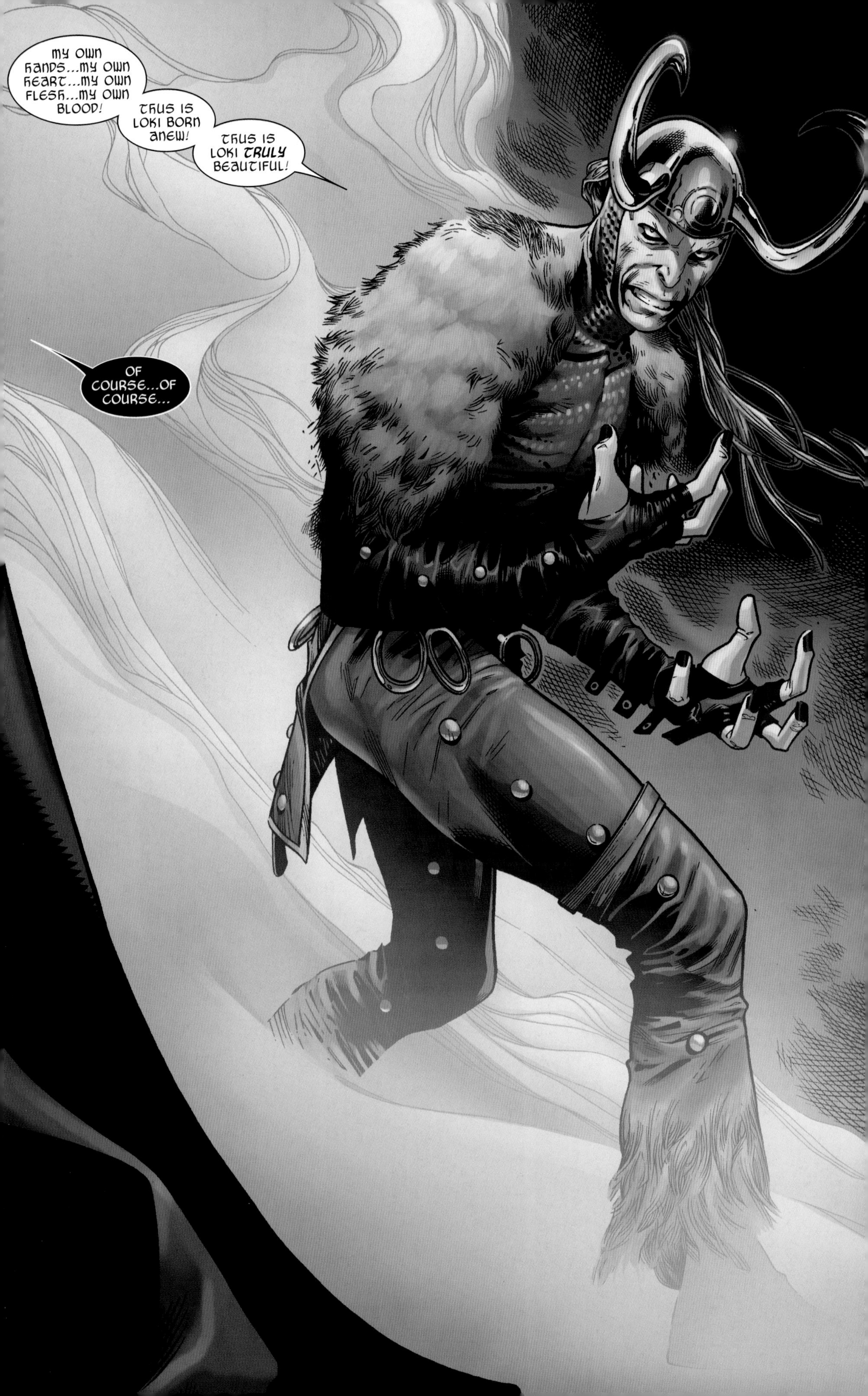
MY OWN HANDS...MY OWN HEART...MY OWN FLESH...MY OWN BLOOD!
THUS IS LOKI BORN ANEW!
THUS IS LOKI *TRULY* BEAUTIFUL!
OF COURSE...OF COURSE...

THERE IS SOMETHING ABOUT THIS BODY THAT FEELS...FAMILIAR TO ME.

I WOULD NOT BE AT ALL SURPRISED. LET'S JUST SAY FOR NOW THAT I *BORROWED* IT FROM SOMEONE WHO WILL HAVE NO USE FOR IT VERY SOON.

NOW...WE MUST MOVE QUICKLY. THE SKIN CANNOT LONG SURVIVE WITHOUT A HOST.

THEN PREPARE YOURSELF, LOKI.

MY POWER IS YOUR POWER...MY VOICE, YOUR VOICE...MY STRENGTH, YOUR STRENGTH...TO PIERCE THE VEIL OF TIME AND SPACE.

DO WHAT YOU MUST AND DO NOT TARRY, LOKI. CALL MY NAME WHEN YOU ARE READY TO RETURN.

I SHALL.

YOU SHALL BE WELL REPAID FOR THIS KINDNESS, HELA...YOU SHALL BE...

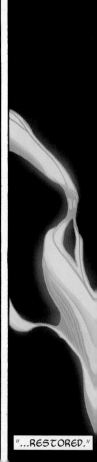

"...RESTORED."

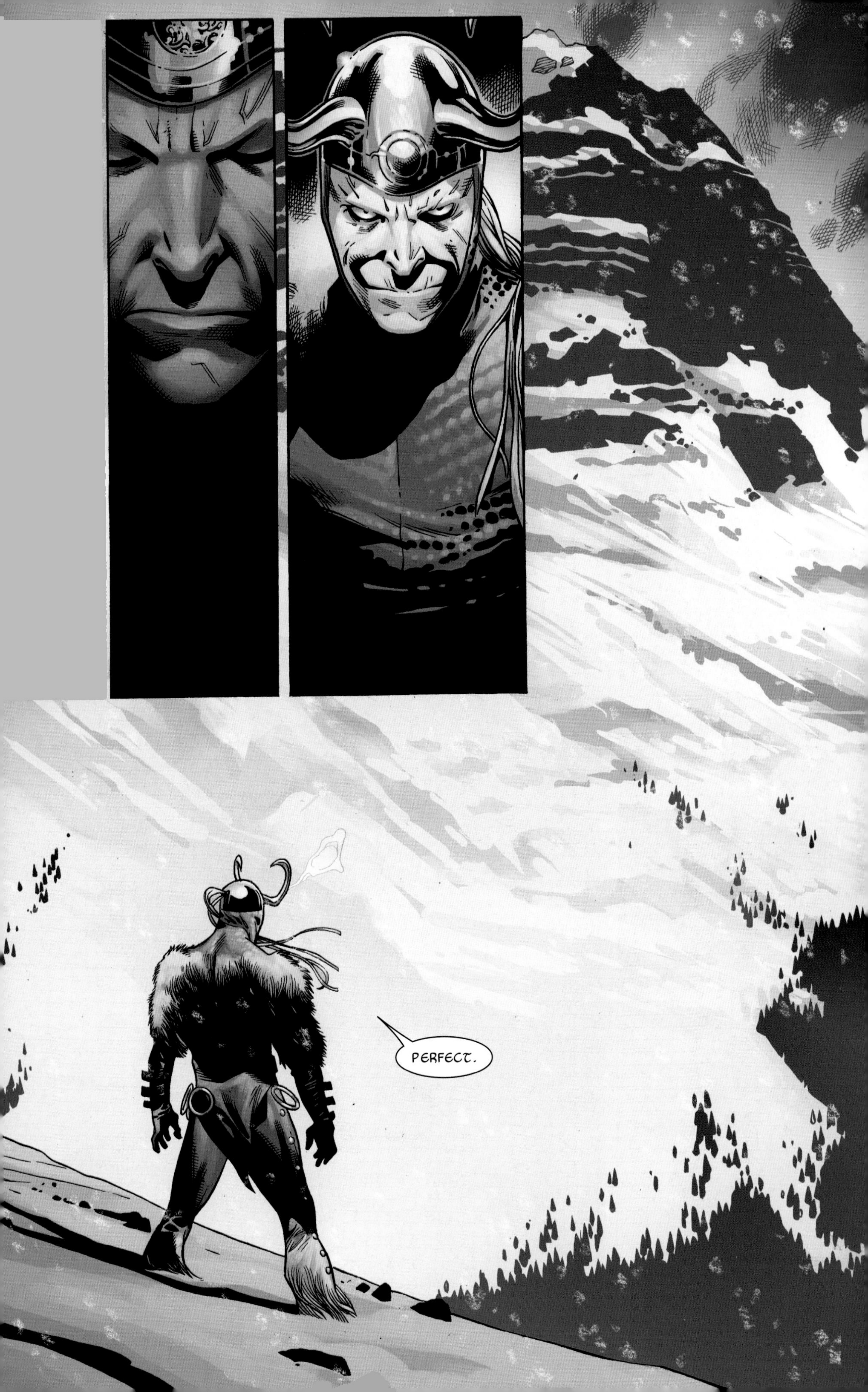
PERFECT.

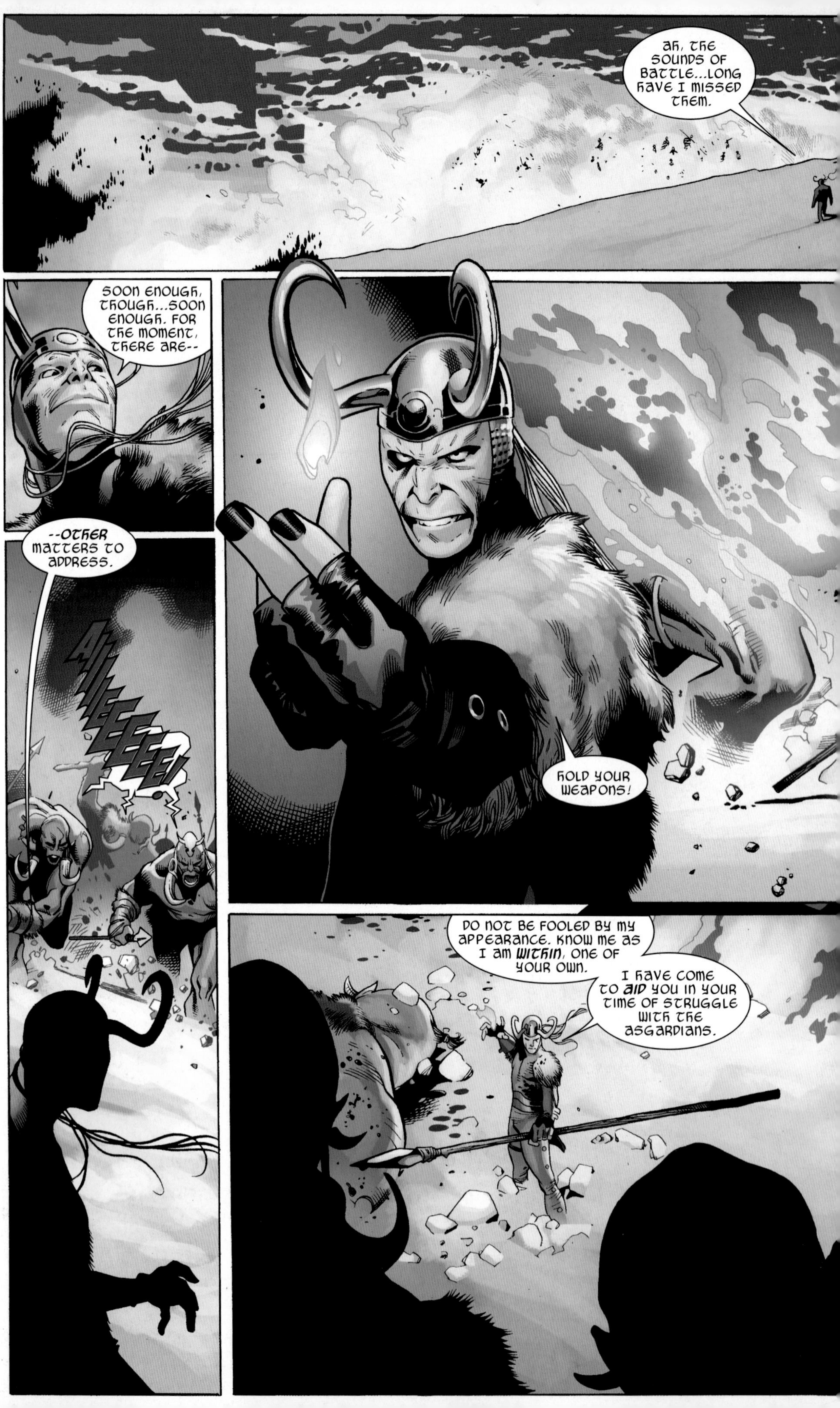
AH, THE SOUNDS OF BATTLE...LONG HAVE I MISSED THEM.
SOON ENOUGH, THOUGH...SOON ENOUGH. FOR THE MOMENT, THERE ARE--
--OTHER MATTERS TO ADDRESS.
AIIEEEEEE!
HOLD YOUR WEAPONS!
DO NOT BE FOOLED BY MY APPEARANCE. KNOW ME AS I AM WITHIN, ONE OF YOUR OWN.
I HAVE COME TO AID YOU IN YOUR TIME OF STRUGGLE WITH THE ASGARDIANS.

I SAID--

--HOLD!

I SMELL IN YOU THE BLOOD THAT RUNS THROUGH MY VEINS.

WHAT DO YOU WANT FROM US?

A MOMENT ONLY. A FLICKER OF TIME.

A CLOAK, THAT I MAY CONCEAL MY APPEARANCE.

AND YOUR FASTEST RUNNER.

"ONE WHOSE SPEED AND SKILL WILL DRAW THE ATTENTION OF THE LORD OF ASGARD--

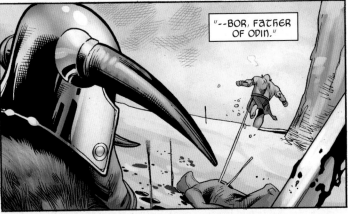

"--BOR, FATHER OF ODIN."

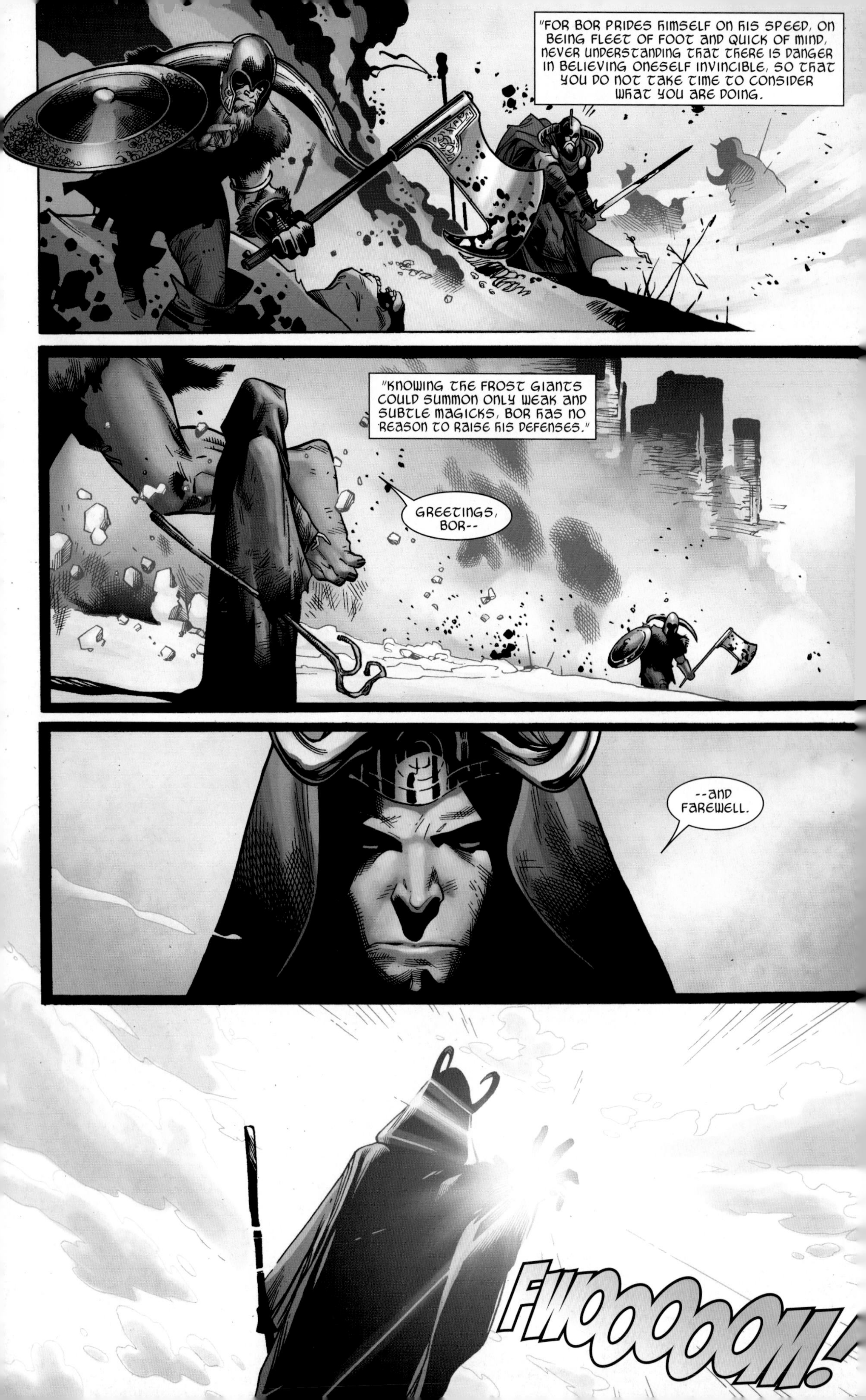
"FOR BOR PRIDES HIMSELF ON HIS SPEED, ON BEING FLEET OF FOOT AND QUICK OF MIND, NEVER UNDERSTANDING THAT THERE IS DANGER IN BELIEVING ONESELF INVINCIBLE, SO THAT YOU DO NOT TAKE TIME TO CONSIDER WHAT YOU ARE DOING.
"KNOWING THE FROST GIANTS COULD SUMMON ONLY WEAK AND SUBTLE MAGICKS, BOR HAS NO REASON TO RAISE HIS DEFENSES."
GREETINGS, BOR--
--AND FAREWELL.
FWOOOOOM!

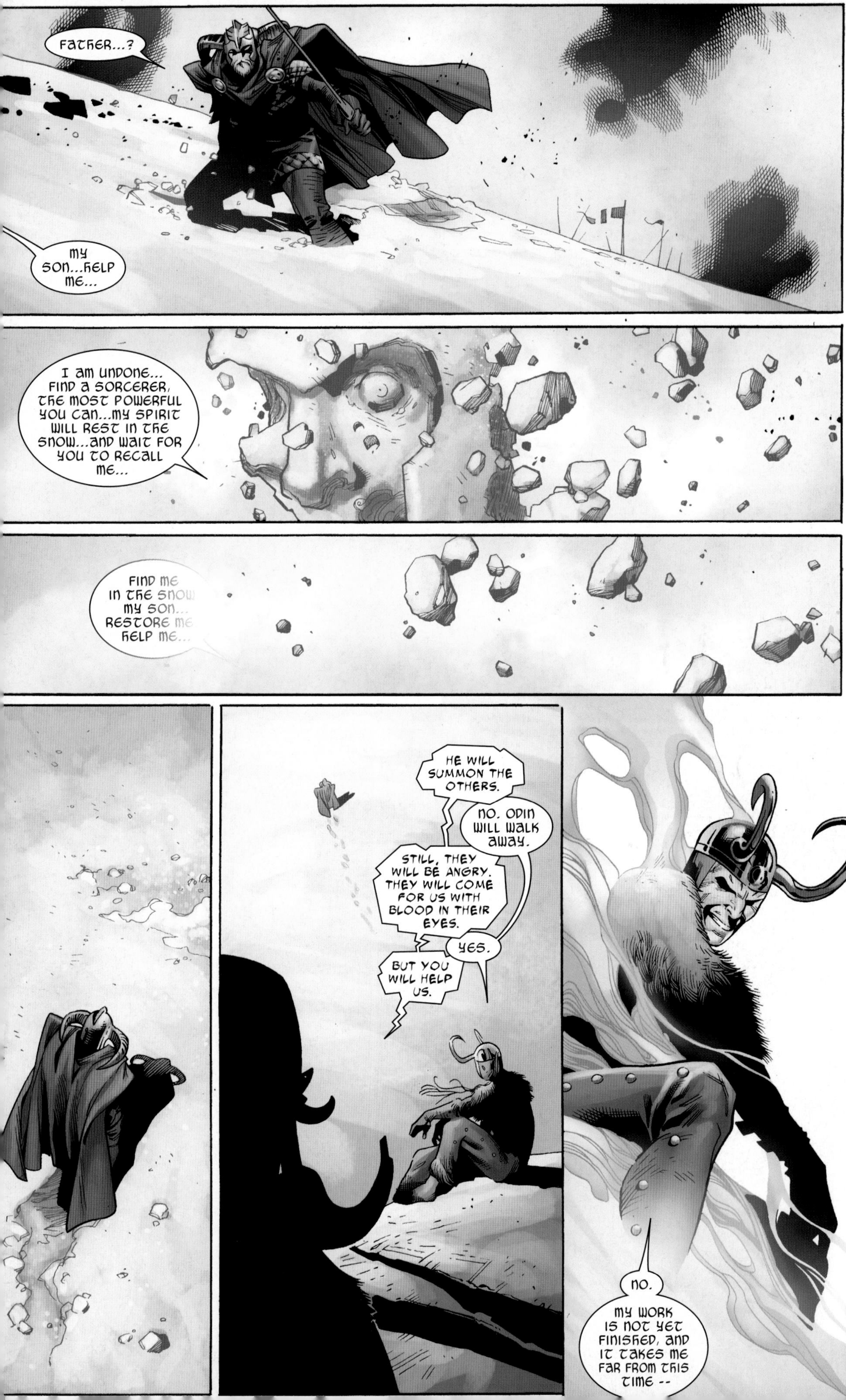
FATHER...?
MY SON...HELP ME...
I AM UNDONE... FIND A SORCERER, THE MOST POWERFUL YOU CAN...MY SPIRIT WILL REST IN THE SNOW...AND WAIT FOR YOU TO RECALL ME...
FIND ME IN THE SNOW MY SON... RESTORE ME HELP ME...
HE WILL SUMMON THE OTHERS.
NO. ODIN WILL WALK AWAY.
STILL, THEY WILL BE ANGRY. THEY WILL COME FOR US WITH BLOOD IN THEIR EYES.
YES.
BUT YOU WILL HELP US.
NO.
MY WORK IS NOT YET FINISHED, AND IT TAKES ME FAR FROM THIS TIME --

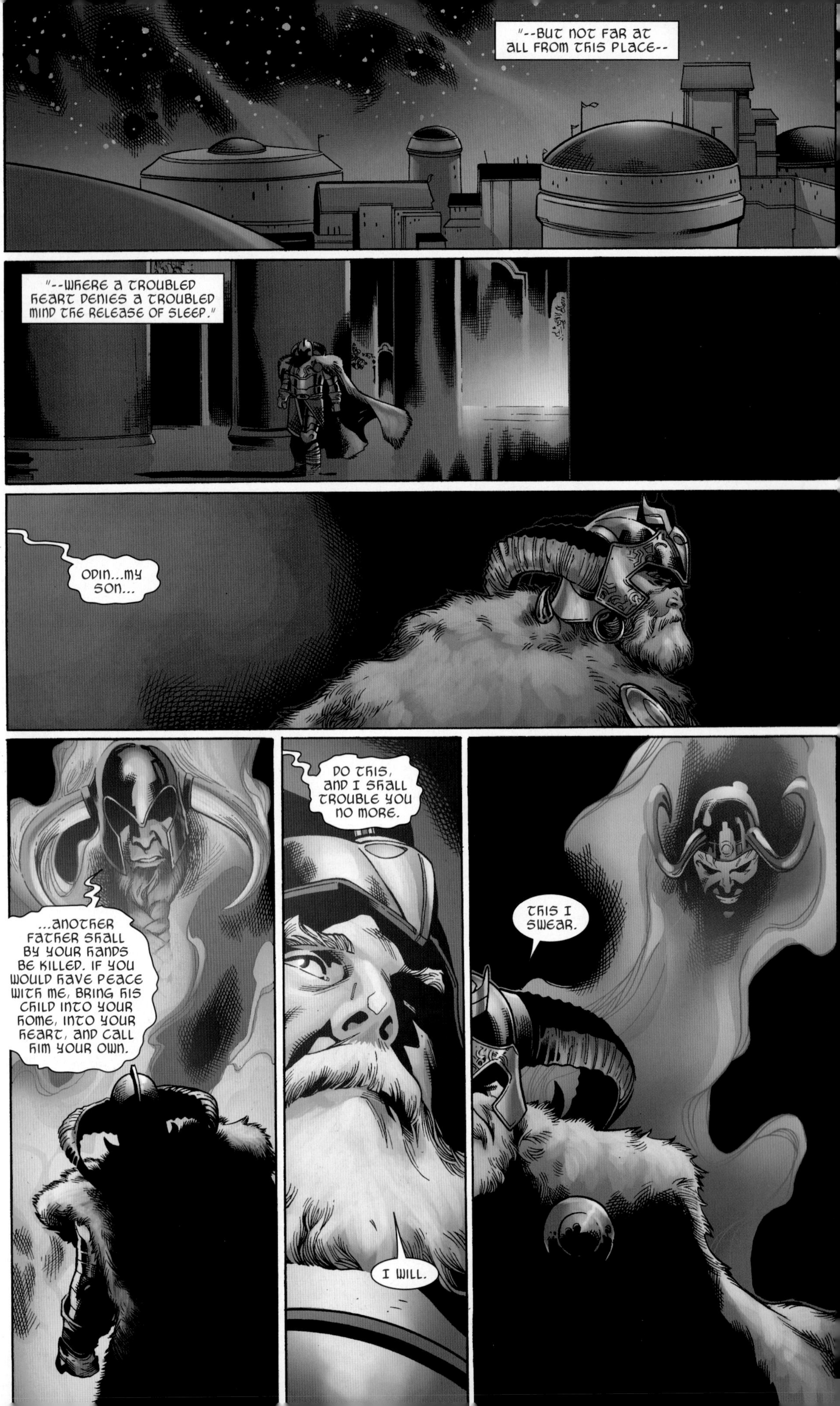
"--BUT NOT FAR AT ALL FROM THIS PLACE--
"--WHERE A TROUBLED HEART DENIES A TROUBLED MIND THE RELEASE OF SLEEP."
ODIN...MY SON...
...ANOTHER FATHER SHALL BY YOUR HANDS BE KILLED. IF YOU WOULD HAVE PEACE WITH ME, BRING HIS CHILD INTO YOUR HOME, INTO YOUR HEART, AND CALL HIM YOUR OWN.
DO THIS, AND I SHALL TROUBLE YOU NO MORE.
I WILL.
THIS I SWEAR.

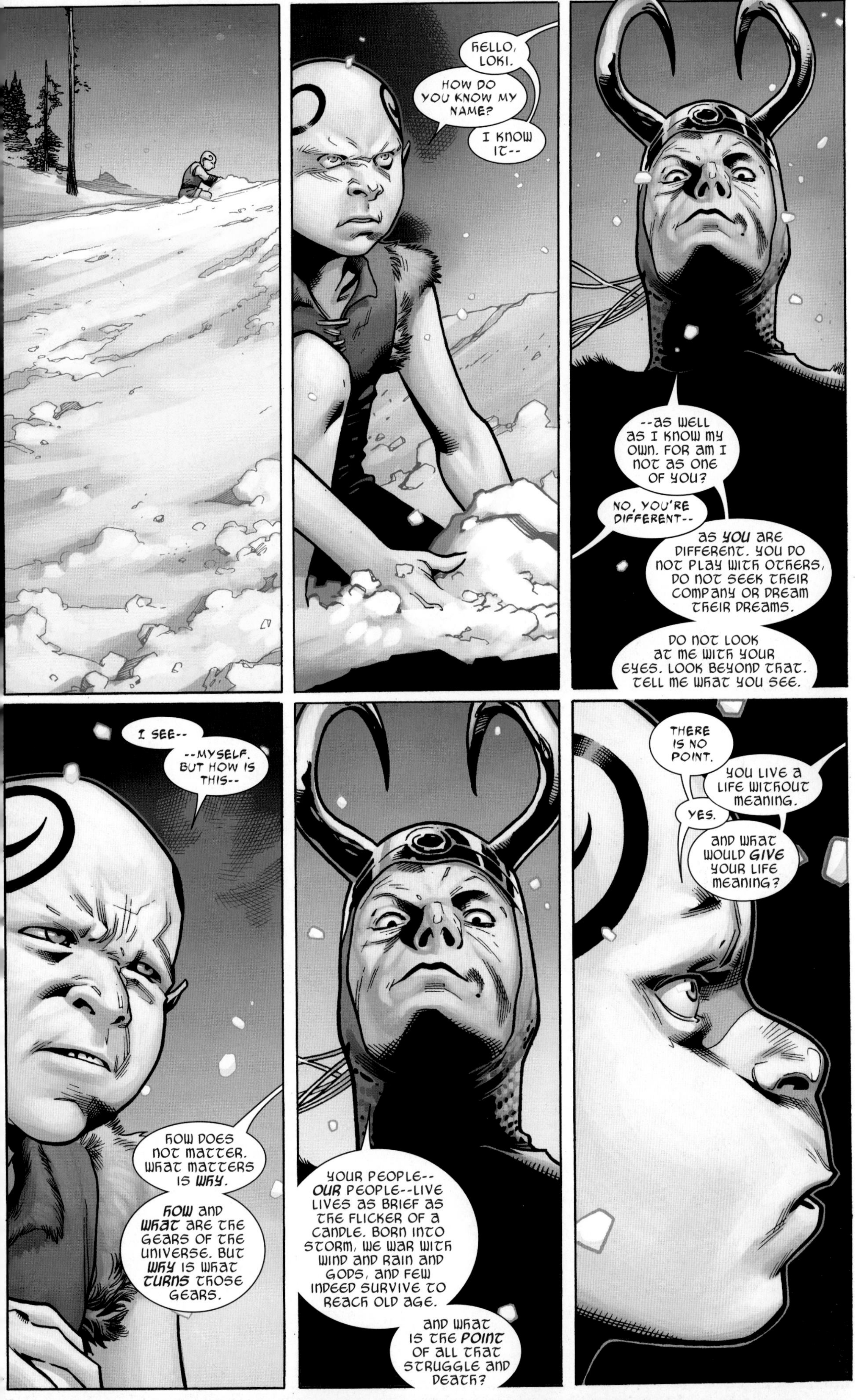
HELLO, LOKI.
HOW DO YOU KNOW MY NAME?
I KNOW IT--
--AS WELL AS I KNOW MY OWN. FOR AM I NOT AS ONE OF YOU?
NO, YOU'RE DIFFERENT--
AS YOU ARE DIFFERENT. YOU DO NOT PLAY WITH OTHERS, DO NOT SEEK THEIR COMPANY OR DREAM THEIR DREAMS.
DO NOT LOOK AT ME WITH YOUR EYES. LOOK BEYOND THAT. TELL ME WHAT YOU SEE.
I SEE--
--MYSELF. BUT HOW IS THIS--
HOW DOES NOT MATTER. WHAT MATTERS IS WHY.
HOW AND WHAT ARE THE GEARS OF THE UNIVERSE. BUT WHY IS WHAT TURNS THOSE GEARS.
YOUR PEOPLE-- OUR PEOPLE--LIVE LIVES AS BRIEF AS THE FLICKER OF A CANDLE. BORN INTO STORM, WE WAR WITH WIND AND RAIN AND GODS, AND FEW INDEED SURVIVE TO REACH OLD AGE.
AND WHAT IS THE POINT OF ALL THAT STRUGGLE AND DEATH?
THERE IS NO POINT.
YOU LIVE A LIFE WITHOUT MEANING.
YES.
AND WHAT WOULD GIVE YOUR LIFE MEANING?

TO LIVE FOREVER. TO HAVE THE POWER OF THE GODS. TO KILL WHO I WISH, AS I WISH. TO LEAVE BEHIND THE STINK OF THIS PLACE.

THEN YOU DO NOT LOVE YOUR MOTHER?

NO. SHE IS STUPID AND SLOW.

YOUR FATHER?

NO. HE IS BRUTISH AND CRUEL.

WOULD YOU SELL THEM INTO DEATH IF IT WOULD BRING YOU THOSE THINGS AND TAKE YOU FROM THIS PLACE FOREVER?

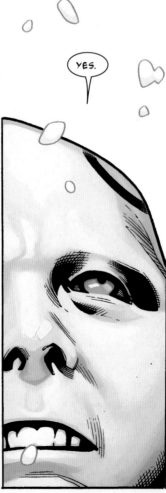

YES.

I WILL NOT EXPLAIN *HOW* I KNOW WHAT IT IS YOU SHOULD DO, FOR THERE ARE THINGS YOU SHOULD NOT YET KNOW. YOU WILL DEDUCE THEM IN TIME.

FOR NOW, JUST LISTEN CAREFULLY, AND DO EXACTLY WHAT I TELL YOU.

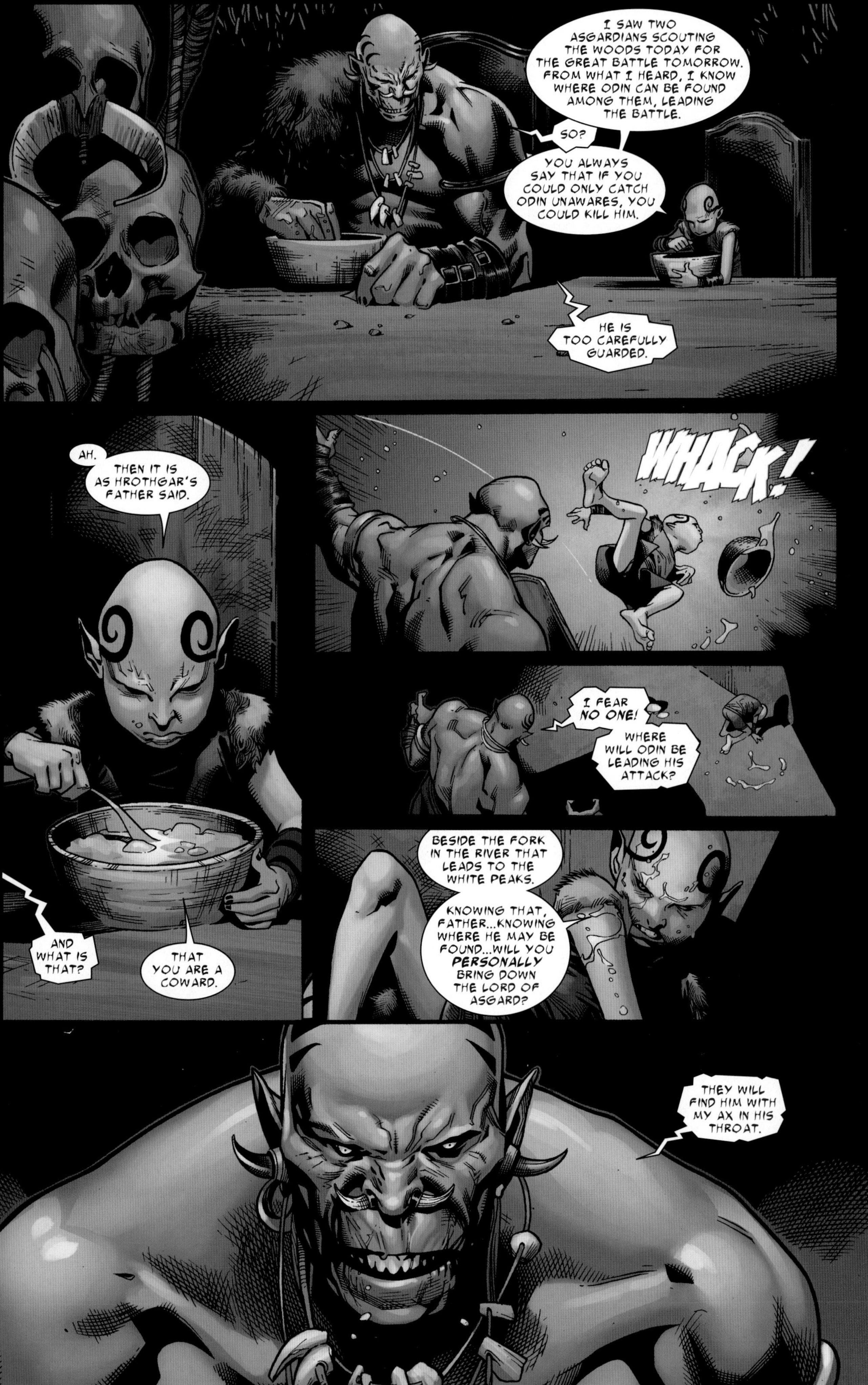

I SAW TWO ASGARDIANS SCOUTING THE WOODS TODAY FOR THE GREAT BATTLE TOMORROW. FROM WHAT I HEARD, I KNOW WHERE ODIN CAN BE FOUND AMONG THEM, LEADING THE BATTLE.
SO?
YOU ALWAYS SAY THAT IF YOU COULD ONLY CATCH ODIN UNAWARES, YOU COULD KILL HIM.
HE IS TOO CAREFULLY GUARDED.
AH.
THEN IT IS AS HROTHGAR'S FATHER SAID.
AND WHAT IS THAT?
THAT YOU ARE A COWARD.
WHACK!
I FEAR NO ONE!
WHERE WILL ODIN BE LEADING HIS ATTACK?
BESIDE THE FORK IN THE RIVER THAT LEADS TO THE WHITE PEAKS.
KNOWING THAT, FATHER...KNOWING WHERE HE MAY BE FOUND...WILL YOU PERSONALLY BRING DOWN THE LORD OF ASGARD?
THEY WILL FIND HIM WITH MY AX IN HIS THROAT.

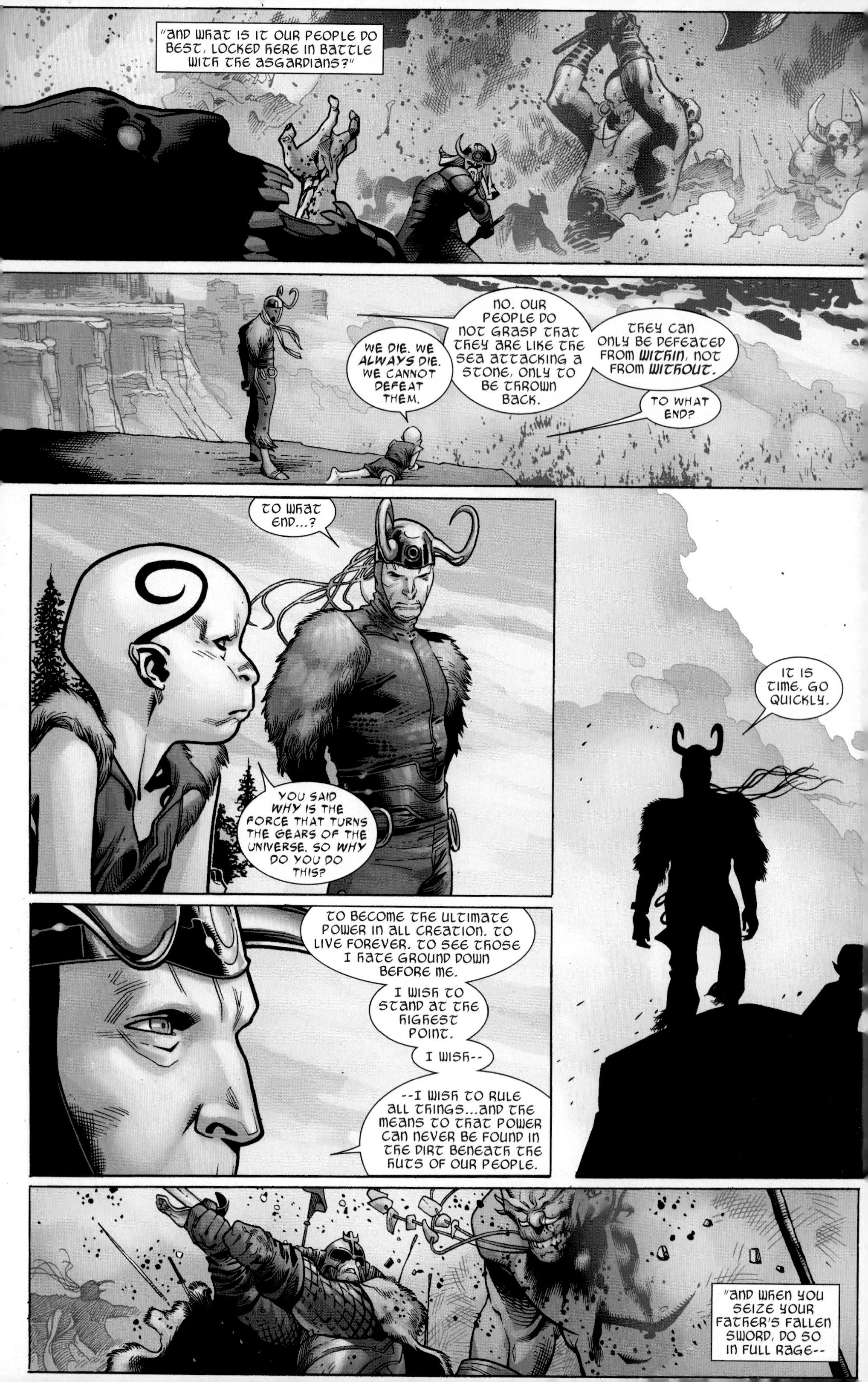
"AND WHAT IS IT OUR PEOPLE DO BEST, LOCKED HERE IN BATTLE WITH THE ASGARDIANS?"
WE DIE. WE ALWAYS DIE. WE CANNOT DEFEAT THEM.
NO. OUR PEOPLE DO NOT GRASP THAT THEY ARE LIKE THE SEA ATTACKING A STONE, ONLY TO BE THROWN BACK.
THEY CAN ONLY BE DEFEATED FROM WITHIN, NOT FROM WITHOUT.
TO WHAT END?
TO WHAT END...?
YOU SAID WHY IS THE FORCE THAT TURNS THE GEARS OF THE UNIVERSE. SO WHY DO YOU DO THIS?
TO BECOME THE ULTIMATE POWER IN ALL CREATION. TO LIVE FOREVER. TO SEE THOSE I HATE GROUND DOWN BEFORE ME.
I WISH TO STAND AT THE HIGHEST POINT.
I WISH--
--I WISH TO RULE ALL THINGS...AND THE MEANS TO THAT POWER CAN NEVER BE FOUND IN THE DIRT BENEATH THE HUTS OF OUR PEOPLE.
IT IS TIME. GO QUICKLY.
"AND WHEN YOU SEIZE YOUR FATHER'S FALLEN SWORD, DO SO IN FULL RAGE--

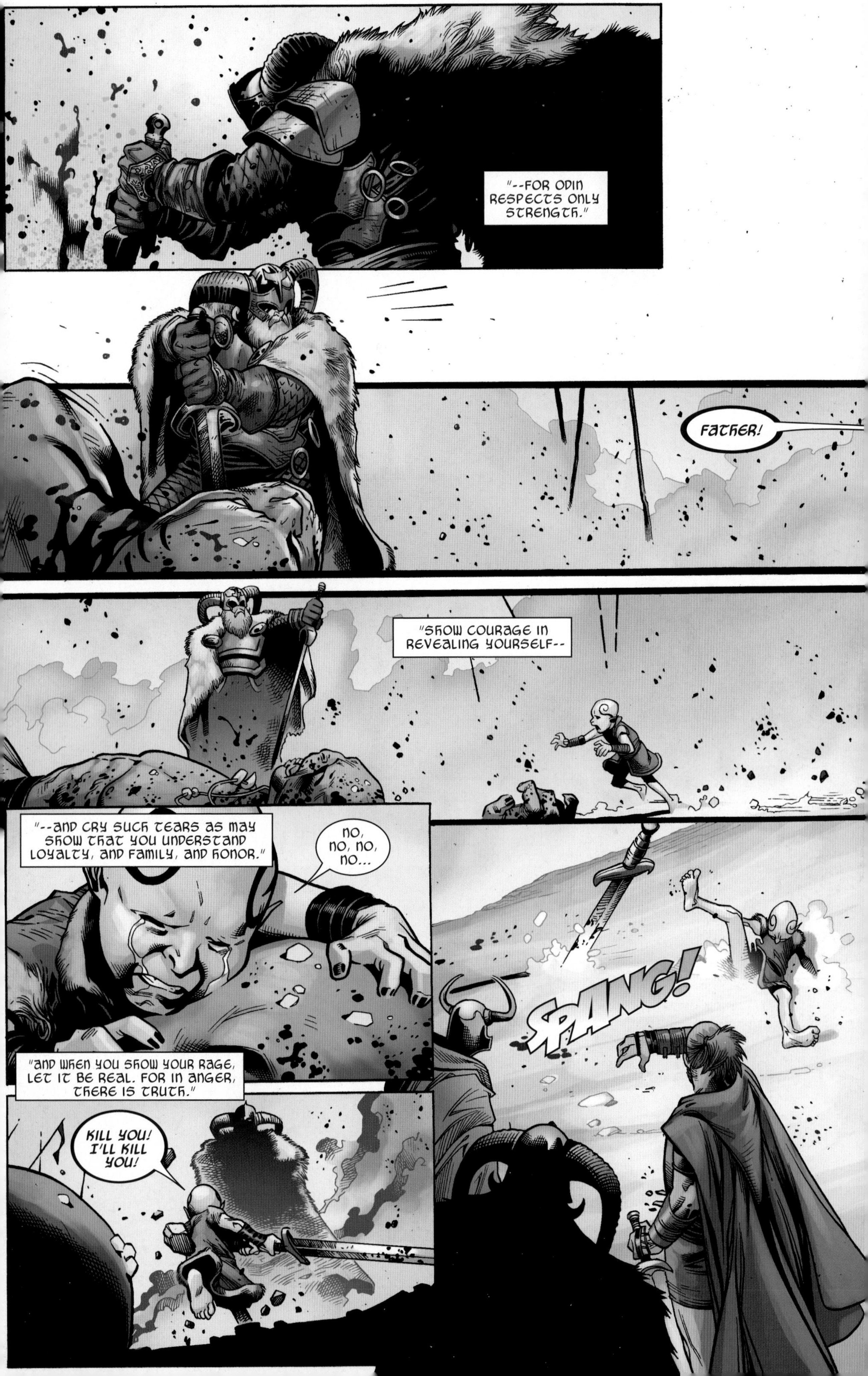
"--FOR ODIN RESPECTS ONLY STRENGTH."
FATHER!
"SHOW COURAGE IN REVEALING YOURSELF--
"--AND CRY SUCH TEARS AS MAY SHOW THAT YOU UNDERSTAND LOYALTY, AND FAMILY, AND HONOR."
NO, NO, NO, NO...
SPANG!
"AND WHEN YOU SHOW YOUR RAGE, LET IT BE REAL. FOR IN ANGER, THERE IS TRUTH."
KILL YOU! I'LL KILL YOU!

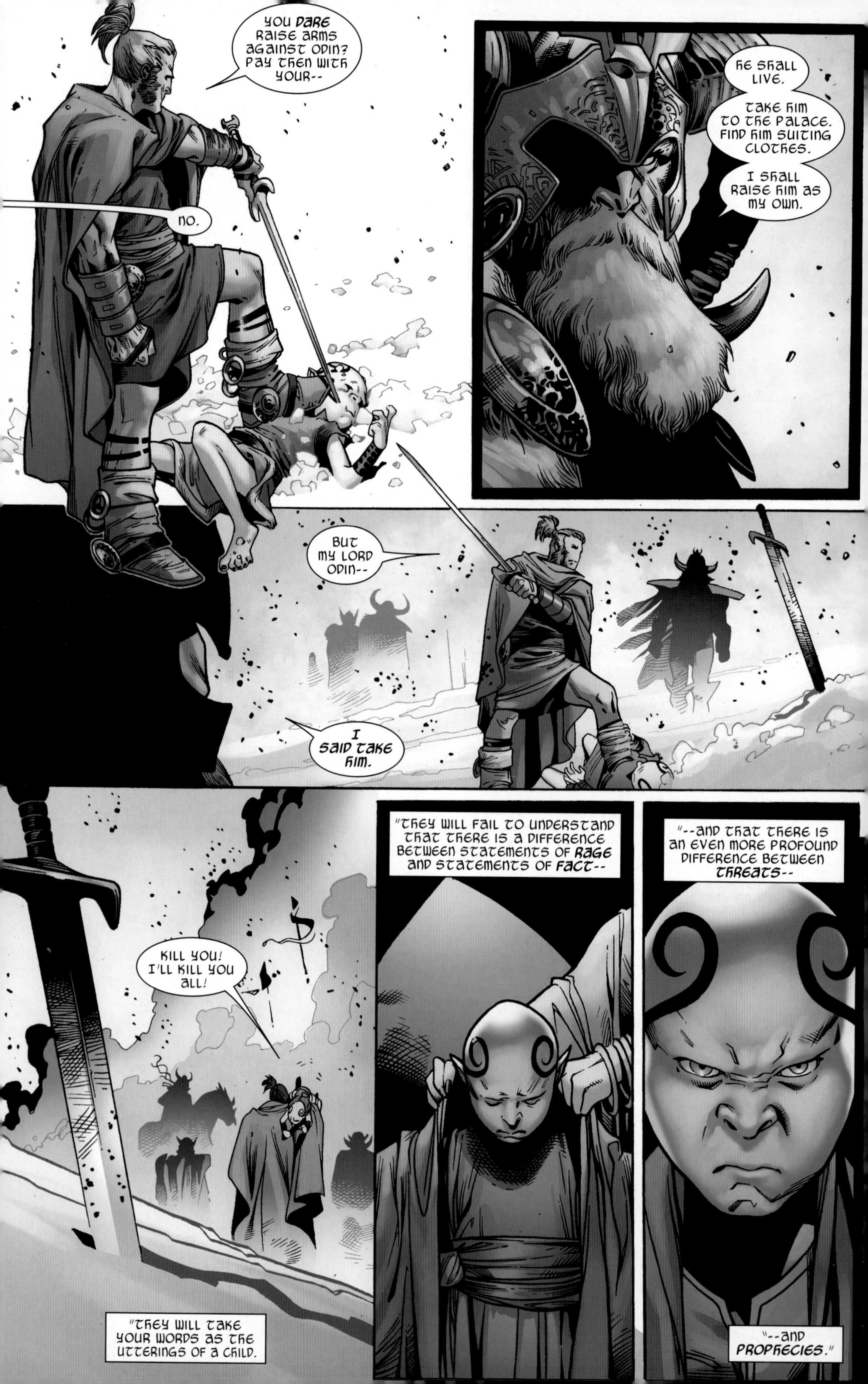
YOU DARE RAISE ARMS AGAINST ODIN? PAY THEN WITH YOUR--
NO.
HE SHALL LIVE.
TAKE HIM TO THE PALACE. FIND HIM SUITING CLOTHES.
I SHALL RAISE HIM AS MY OWN.
BUT MY LORD ODIN--
I SAID TAKE HIM.
KILL YOU! I'LL KILL YOU ALL!
"THEY WILL TAKE YOUR WORDS AS THE UTTERINGS OF A CHILD.
"THEY WILL FAIL TO UNDERSTAND THAT THERE IS A DIFFERENCE BETWEEN STATEMENTS OF RAGE AND STATEMENTS OF FACT--
"--AND THAT THERE IS AN EVEN MORE PROFOUND DIFFERENCE BETWEEN THREATS--
"--AND PROPHECIES."

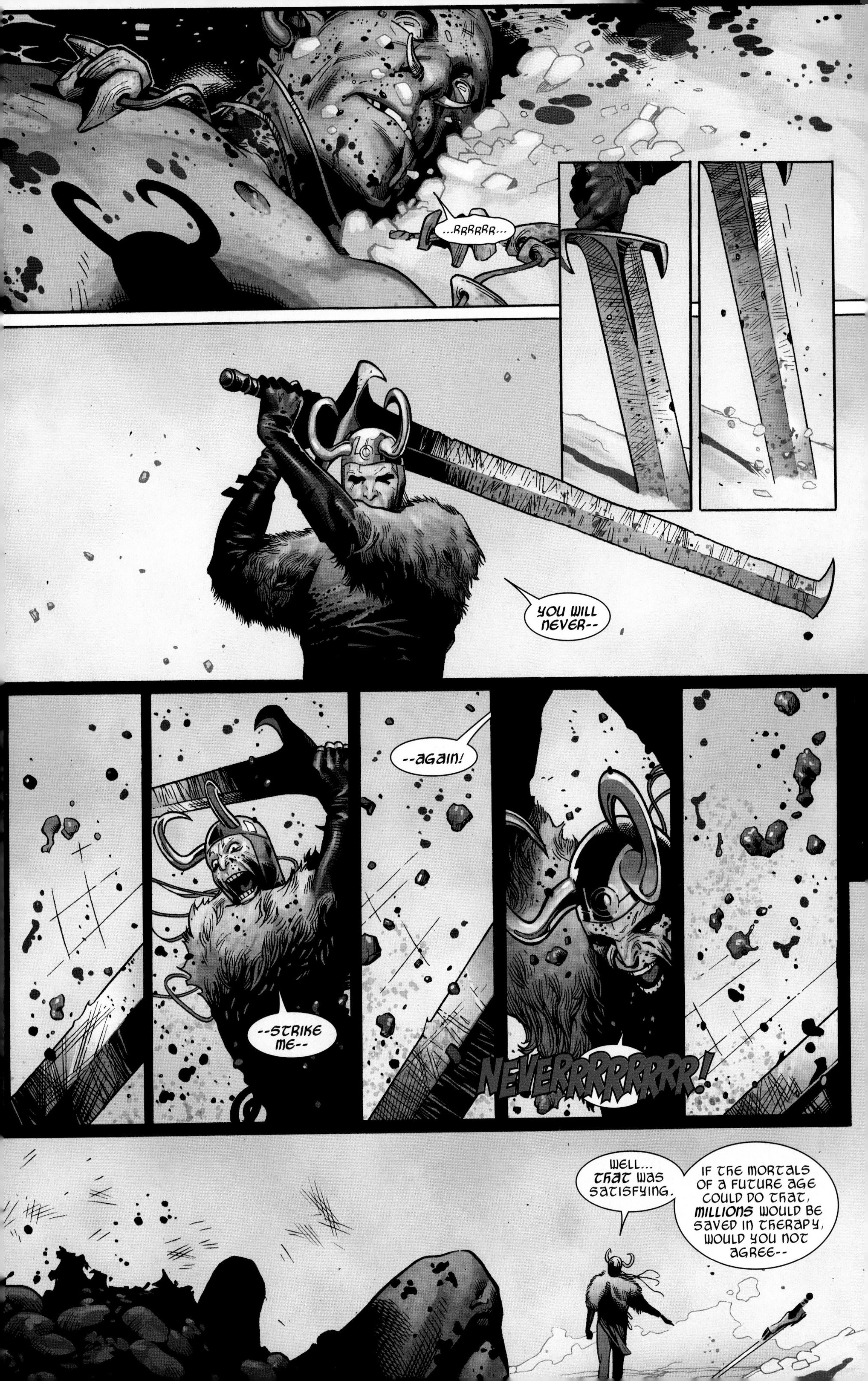
...RRRRRR...
YOU WILL NEVER--
--STRIKE ME--
--AGAIN!
NEVERRRRRRRR!
WELL... THAT WAS SATISFYING.
IF THE MORTALS OF A FUTURE AGE COULD DO THAT, MILLIONS WOULD BE SAVED IN THERAPY, WOULD YOU NOT AGREE--

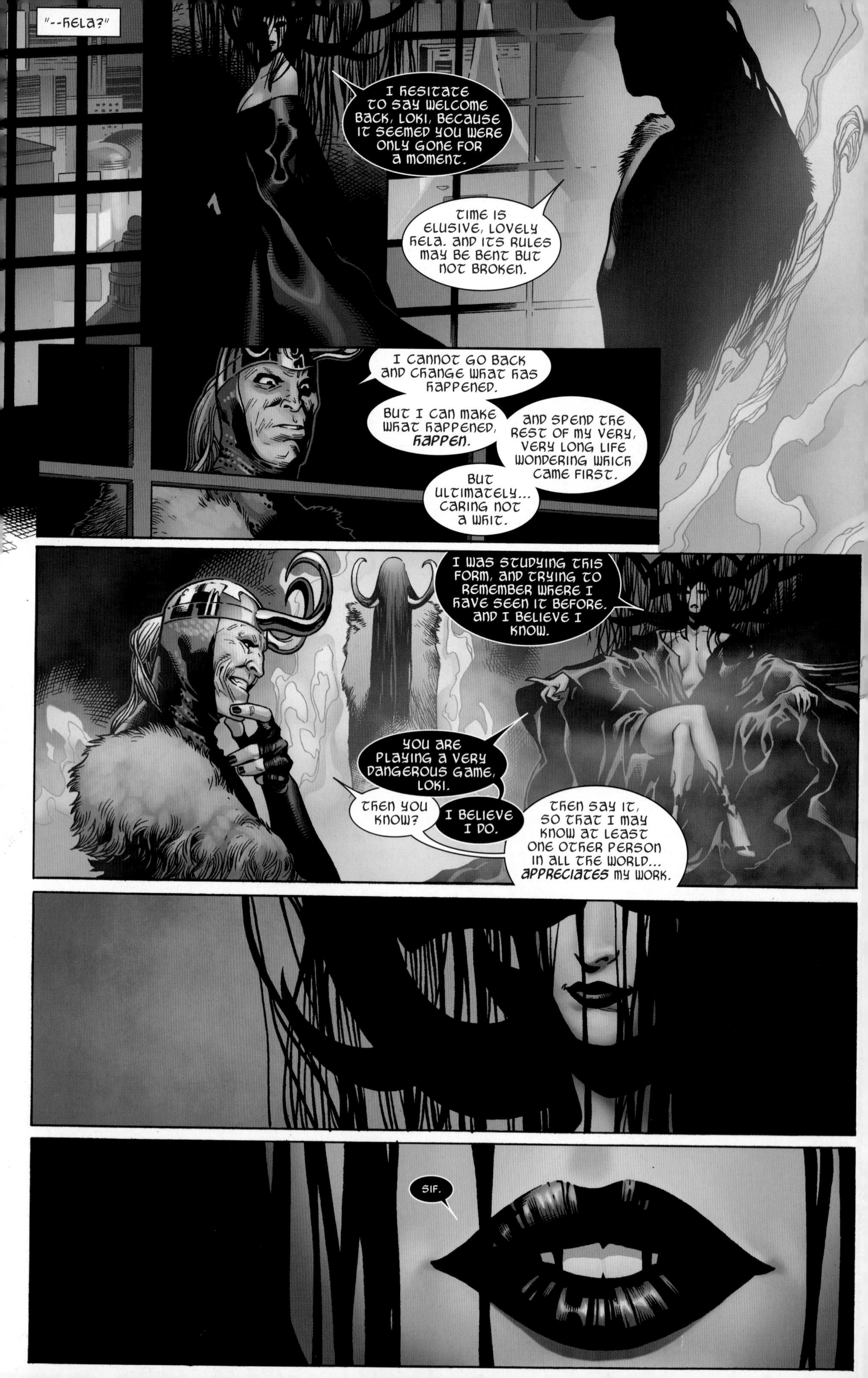
"--HELA?"
I HESITATE TO SAY WELCOME BACK, LOKI, BECAUSE IT SEEMED YOU WERE ONLY GONE FOR A MOMENT.
TIME IS ELUSIVE, LOVELY HELA. AND ITS RULES MAY BE BENT BUT NOT BROKEN.
I CANNOT GO BACK AND CHANGE WHAT HAS HAPPENED.
BUT I CAN MAKE WHAT HAPPENED, HAPPEN.
AND SPEND THE REST OF MY VERY, VERY LONG LIFE WONDERING WHICH CAME FIRST.
BUT ULTIMATELY... CARING NOT A WHIT.
I WAS STUDYING THIS FORM, AND TRYING TO REMEMBER WHERE I HAVE SEEN IT BEFORE. AND I BELIEVE I KNOW.
YOU ARE PLAYING A VERY DANGEROUS GAME, LOKI.
THEN YOU KNOW?
I BELIEVE I DO.
THEN SAY IT, SO THAT I MAY KNOW AT LEAST ONE OTHER PERSON IN ALL THE WORLD... APPRECIATES MY WORK.
SIF.

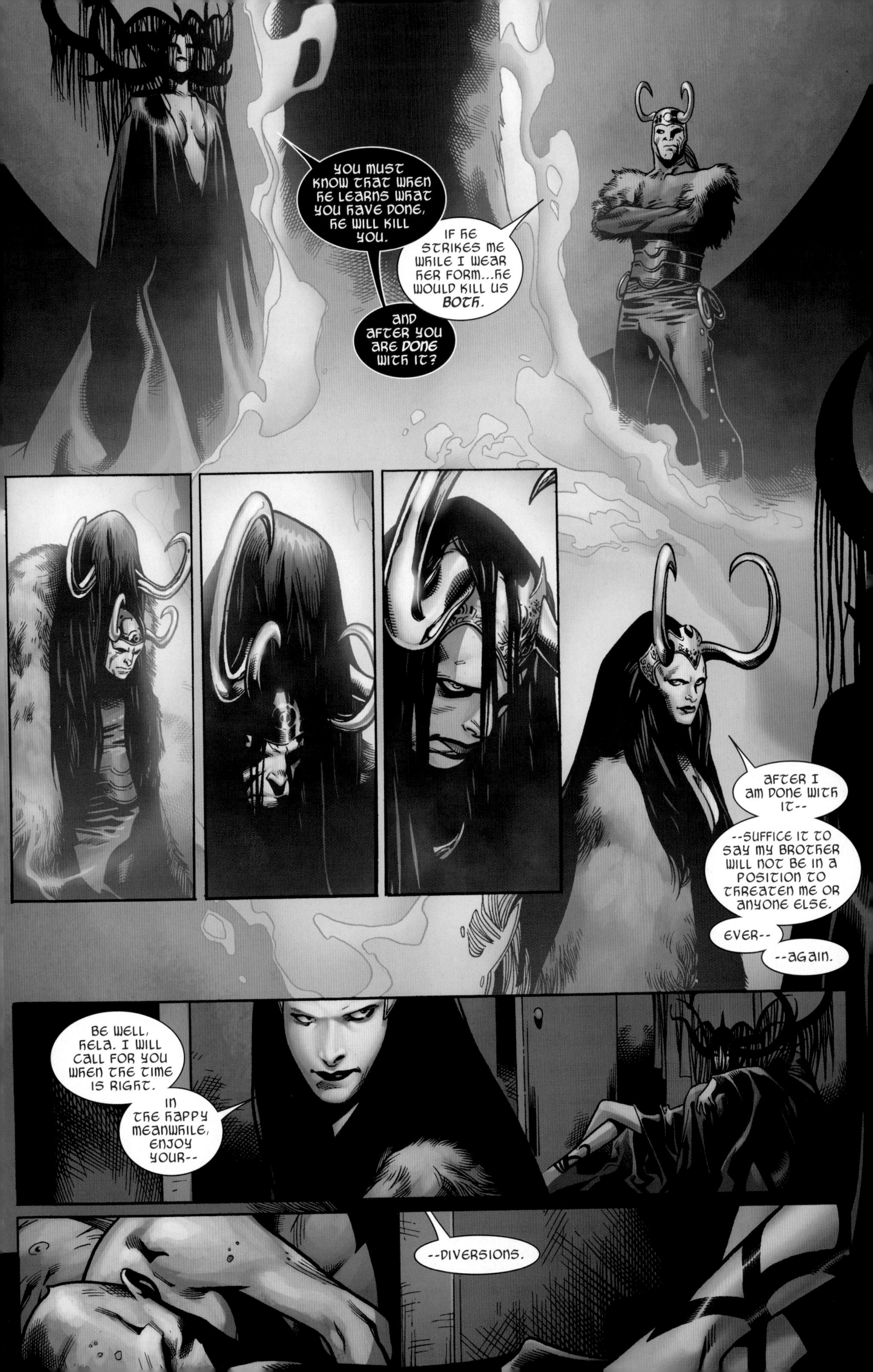
YOU MUST KNOW THAT WHEN HE LEARNS WHAT YOU HAVE DONE, HE WILL KILL YOU.
IF HE STRIKES ME WHILE I WEAR HER FORM...HE WOULD KILL US BOTH.
AND AFTER YOU ARE DONE WITH IT?
AFTER I AM DONE WITH IT--
--SUFFICE IT TO SAY MY BROTHER WILL NOT BE IN A POSITION TO THREATEN ME OR ANYONE ELSE.
EVER--
--AGAIN.
BE WELL, HELA. I WILL CALL FOR YOU WHEN THE TIME IS RIGHT.
IN THE HAPPY MEANWHILE, ENJOY YOUR--
--DIVERSIONS.

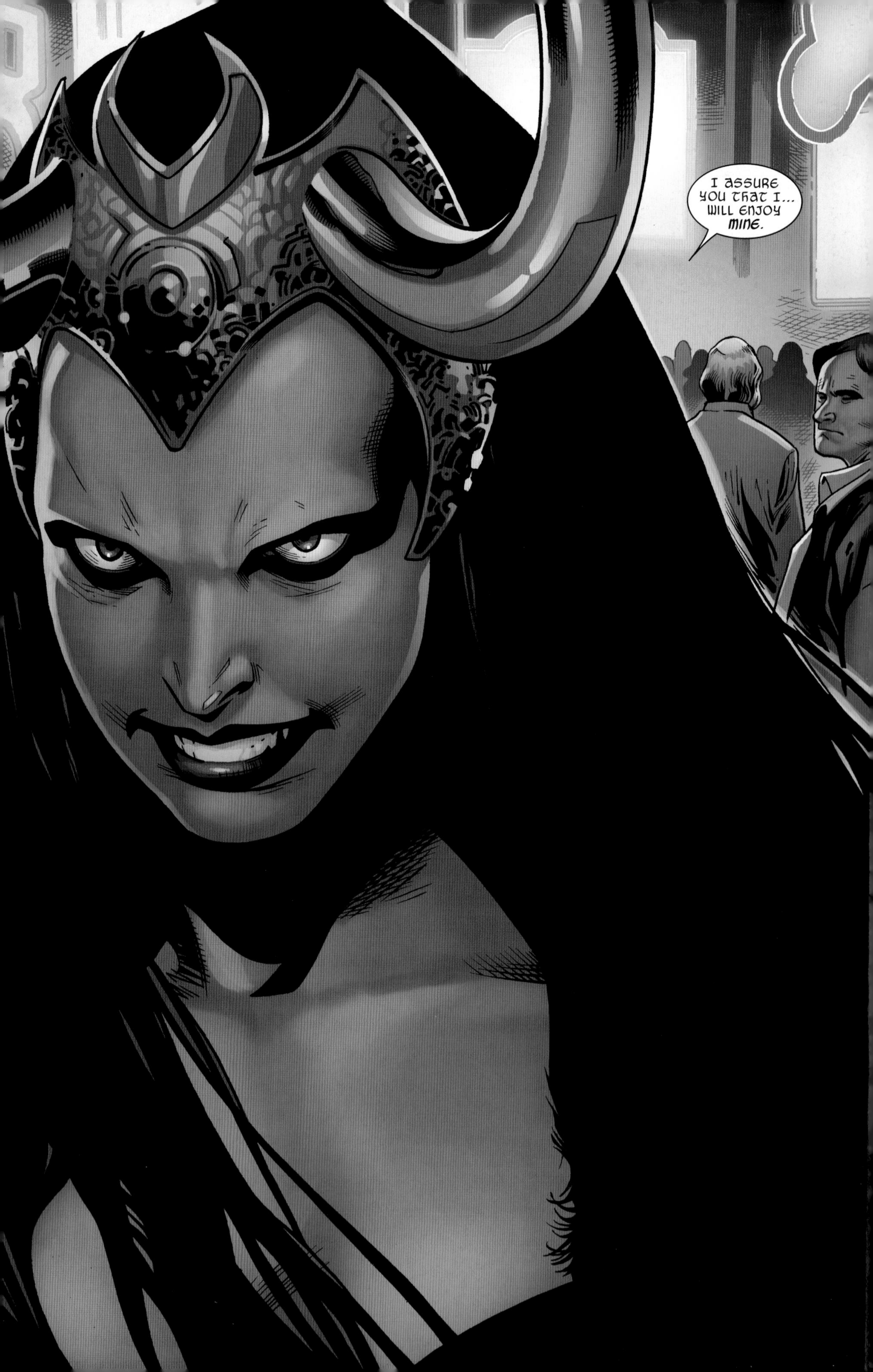
I ASSURE YOU THAT I... WILL ENJOY MINE.

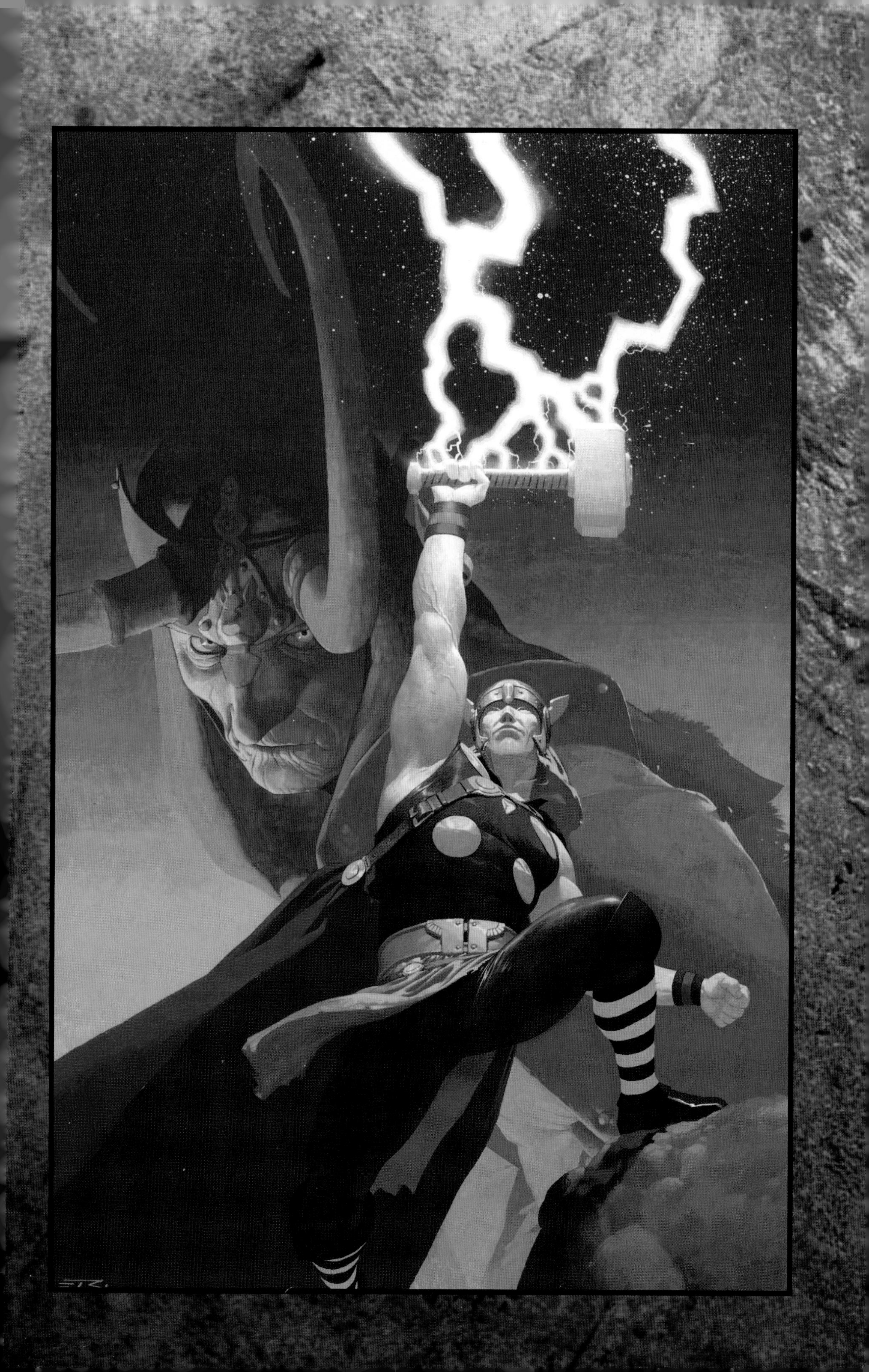

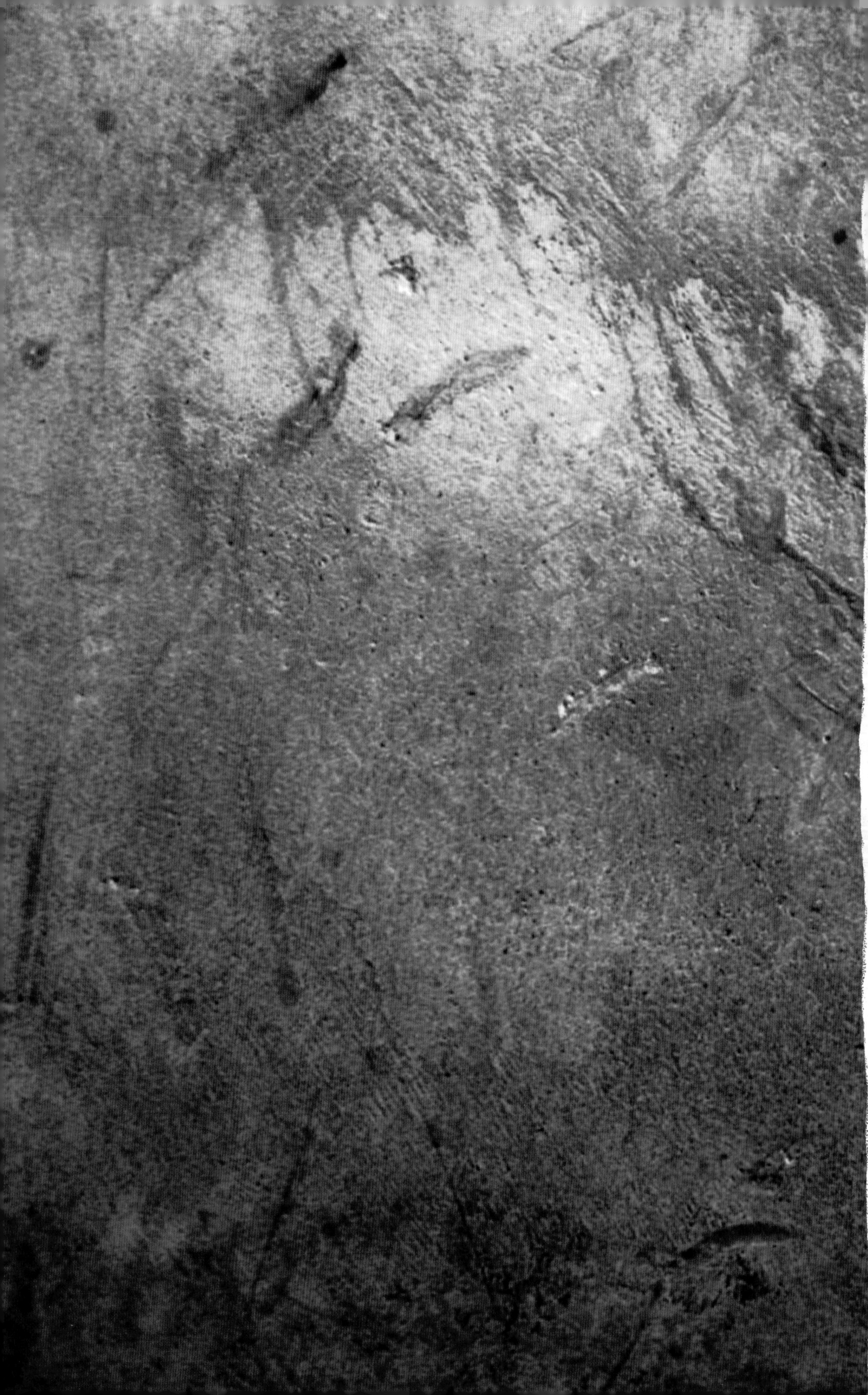